THE ANNOTATED SCREENPLAYS

Star Wars: A New Hope

The Empire Strikes Back

Return of the Jedi

STAR WARS

THE ANNOTATED SCREENPLAYS

Star Wars: A New Hope

Based on the story and screenplay by George Lucas

The Empire Strikes Back

Based on the story by George Lucas and screenplay by
Leigh Brackett and Lawrence Kasdan

Return of the Jedi

Based on the story by George Lucas and screenplay by
Lawrence Kasdan and George Lucas

LAURENT BOUZEREAU

BALLANTINE BOOKS • NEW YORK

A Del Rey® Book
Published by Ballantine Books

All rights reserved under International and Pan-American Copyright Conventions.
Published in the United States by Ballantine Books,
a division of Random House, Inc., New York, and simultaneously in Canada
by Random House of Canada Limited, Toronto.

http://www.randomhouse.com/delrey/

LIBRARY OF CONGRESS CATALOG CARD NUMBER: 97-93469

ISBN: 0-345-40981-7

Cover design by David Stevenson
Text design by BTD

Manufactured in the United States of America
First Edition: September 1997

10 9 8 7 6 5

ACKNOWLEDGMENTS

Thank you to Lucy Autrey Wilson for believing in my ideas and for making this book a reality, and to Sue Rostoni for her collaboration, her enormous contribution, and generous support.

Thank you to Howard Roffman, Lynne Hale, and Jane Bay at Lucasfilm for their help, trust and efforts.

Thank you to my editor Peter Borland for having faith in this project and for helping me realize my vision, and to Steve Saffel at Ballantine Books for his hard work.

Special thanks to my faithful and life-saver agent Kay McCauley and to my good friend Steven Asbell, who helped me a great deal in refining this book and in providing a generous amount of advice and support.

I also owe a debt of gratitude to Martin Cohen for continuing to share with me his considerable experience as well as his friendship. Many thanks also to Colleen A. Benn for contributing to the realization of my dreams; Joe Lajeunesse for giving me valuable advice on this project; my friends at Amblin/DreamWorks SKG, Industrial Light & Magic, Universal Home Video, and Universal Pictures.

This book could not have been possible without the collaboration and generosity of (in alphabetical order): Richard Chew, Duwayne Dunham, Paul Hirsch, Joe Johnston, Lawrence Kasdan, Irvin Kershner, Rick McCallum, Ralph McQuarrie, Nilo Rodis-Jamero, and Phil Tippett.

I would like to thank George Lucas for his collaboration, contribution, and inspiration. Mr. Lucas, this book is yours more than mine.

Of course, none of it would have been possible without the love and support of my parents, Daniel and Micheline; my sisters, Cécile and Géraldine; and my family back in France and England.

Finally, I dedicate this book to my niece and nephew, Maud and Guillaume: "Remember, the Force will be with you . . . always."

INTRODUCTION

All of us have experienced great moments of revelation, things that have left everlasting memories in our minds. *Star Wars* had that effect on many people, including me. I saw the film in Athens, Georgia, when I was a teenager; I was visiting from France, staying with an American family for the summer, and although I could barely speak English at the time, I remember seeing *Star Wars* and understanding everything about it. The film was so visually gripping that it spoke an international language, leaving me with the feeling that I had experienced something incredible and special. Seeing *Star Wars* that day was an extraordinary event.

Needless to say, writing this book on the history of the *Star Wars* screenplays twenty years later is not only a great honor but a dream come true. Like many fans, I thought I knew everything about *Star Wars*, yet as I began doing research for this book, I realized that most of the things I had read or heard about the different screenplays were either false assumptions or distorted versions of the truth. Luckily, since I wrote this book with direct access to all the different scripts, treatments, and story conference transcripts and with George Lucas's direct input, the information in this volume will set the record straight on how the *Star Wars* saga was conceived.

It is through a long and arduous process that stories come together. A writer will put his tale through many different phases before a plot and characters actually come alive on paper. When the camera starts rolling, the story often metamorphoses further. When the editing begins, some scenes are cut out and others are shot at the last minute and added on. The *Star Wars* movies were no exception to this rule.

George Lucas went through many different permutations of plot, subplot, and character before he was satisfied with what he had. In the case of *Star Wars: A New Hope* this process took place on the typewriter (Lucas wrote the screenplay), on the set (he directed the picture), and in the editing room over a period of about four years. It all began in 1973 when Lucas sat down and wrote a forty-page outline entitled "Journal of the Whills" about "Mace Windy, a revered Jedi Bendu of Ophuchi," as told by "C.J. Thorpe, Padawaan learner of the famed Jedi."

Following the outline was a list of characters, and among them were some names that survived the different drafts of the story: General Luke Skywalker; See-Threepio and Artoo-Detoo, two workmen, General Vader; Han Solo; Chewbacca, a Wookiee prince; and Bail Antilles, a trader. There was also a list of planets: Aquilae, a desert planet; Yavin, a jungle planet; Ophuchi, a cloud planet; and Alderaan, a city planet. In compiling this information and these background details, Lucas created a reference book he called "Journal of the Whills," which eventually became the starting point for the *Star Wars* saga.

After the enormous success of *Star Wars: A New Hope* in 1977, Lucas wrote the story and several drafts of the script and executive produced *The Empire Strikes Back* (1980), followed by *Return of the Jedi* (1983), for which Lucas wrote the story and cowrote the script and which he executive produced.

Because the *Star Wars* films have become indelible landmarks on the landscape of popular cinema, it is fascinating to go back and explore how Lucas created the stories and the characters and try to visualize what the movies might have been like if Luke Skywalker had been over sixty years old or Han Solo had been "a huge green-skinned monster with no nose and large gills."

The annotations featured in this book with the actual continuity scripts were not always easy to organize. Several drafts were so drastically different from the films as we saw them that placing the notes became a challenge. My goal was not to interpret the different stories; it was to present as much information as possible and to illustrate some of the most interesting changes, story points, and character developments with comments from Lucas himself and from some of the key people who helped him realize his vision. In alphabetical order they are as follows:

Richard Chew co-edited *Star Wars* and received an Oscar for best editing.

Duwayne Dunham was assistant editor on *The Empire Strikes Back* and co-edited *Return of the Jedi*.

Paul Hirsch co-edited *Star Wars* and edited *The Empire Strikes Back*. He received an Oscar for best editing for *Star Wars*.

Joe Johnston was art director/visual effects creator on *The Empire Strikes Back* and *Return of the Jedi*.

Lawrence Kasdan co-wrote *The Empire Strikes Back* and *Return of the Jedi*.

Irvin Kershner directed *The Empire Strikes Back*.

Rick McCallum produced the special editions of *Star Wars: A New Hope*, *The Empire Strikes Back*, and *Return of the Jedi*.

Ralph McQuarrie was production illustrator on *Star Wars*, design consultant and conceptual artist on *The Empire Strikes Back*, and conceptual artist on *Return of the Jedi*.

Nilo Rodis-Jamero was assistant art director and visual effects creator on *The Empire Strikes Back* and costume designer on *Return of the Jedi*.

Phil Tippett worked as stop motion animator on *Star Wars* and *The Empire Strikes Back* and became makeup and creature designer on *Return of the Jedi*.

Some of the quotes may seem more relevant to the production of the films than to the development of the stories but in fact, these comments are meant to convey how some elements that barely existed on paper, the creatures for instance, were created and designed. Other comments show how certain choices made during production might have affected the stories or character development. And I'll admit that some of the stories were just too good to be dismissed!

George Lucas and his collaborators were able to transcend

words, break new barriers, and put into images a believable imaginary world. This book is a tribute to their genius and a journey through the creative process. In the case of George Lucas and *Star Wars*, it had nothing to do with the Force . . . It all began with the written word . . . It all began "in a galaxy far, far away . . ."

EPISODE IV

Star Wars: A New Hope

Star Wars. Episode IV: A New Hope
Annotations and Interviews by Laurent Bouzereau

Annotations on *Star Wars: A New Hope* are based on the following materials, all written by George Lucas:

Partial handwritten outline entitled "Journal of the Whills" (no date)

Handwritten list of characters (no date)

Handwritten list of planets (no date)

The Star Wars—synopsis (no date)

The Star Wars, May 1973—treatment typed from original notes

The Star Wars, May 1974—rough draft

The Adventures of Luke Starkiller. Episode I: *The Star Wars*, May 1, 1975—story synopsis

The Star Wars, July 1974—first draft

Adventures of the Starkiller. Episode I: *The Star Wars*, January 28, 1975

Original handwritten notes, January 30, 1975

From the Adventures of Luke Starkiller as taken from the "Journal of the Whills." SAGA I: *The Star Wars*, January 1, 1976—fourth draft with George Lucas's original notes

The Adventures of Luke Starkiller as taken from the "Journal of the Whills." *Saga I: The Star Wars*, January 1, 1976—fourth draft

Fourth draft, *Battle*, retyped January 1, 1976. Copy of original retyped version with final changes and suggested scene numbers

Fourth draft, *Battle*, retyped January 1, 1976. Copy of original new pages with suggested scene numbers

Fourth draft, *Battle*, retyped January 1, 1976 (Int. Luke's starship)

Fourth draft, *Battle*, storyboard numbers, January 1, 1976. (Ext. space around fourth moon of Yavin)

The Adventures of Luke Starkiller as taken from the "Journal of the Whills." *Saga I: The Star Wars*, March 15, 1976—revised fourth draft with George Lucas's original notes

The Adventures of Luke Starkiller as taken from the "Journal of the Whills." *Saga I: The Star Wars*, March 15, 1976—revised fourth draft

Revised fourth draft, pages 55–68, April 13, 1976 (Int. Death Star—corridor)

Revised fourth draft, Greedo dialogue Add. February 5, 1977 (Greedo scene title cards)

STAR WARS

A long time ago in a galaxy far, far away . . .

A vast sea of stars serves as the backdrop for the main title. War drums echo through the heavens as a roll-up slowly crawls into infinity.

EPISODE IV
A NEW HOPE

It is a period of civil war.
Rebel spaceships, striking
from a hidden base, have won
their first victory against
the evil Galactic Empire.

During the battle, Rebel
spies managed to steal secret
plans to the Empire's
ultimate weapon, the DEATH
STAR, an armored space
station with enough power to
destroy an entire planet.

Pursued by the Empire's
sinister agents, Princess
Leia races home aboard her
starship, custodian of the
stolen plans that can save
her people and restore
freedom to the galaxy . . .

Star Wars did not always take place "a long time ago in a galaxy far, far away . . ." The treatment *(The Star Wars)* set the story in the thirty-third century, during a period of civil war in the galaxy. In fact, the famous line appeared for the first time in the fourth draft and read: "A long, long time ago in a galaxy far, far away an incredible adventure took place."

George Lucas: "I knew from the beginning that I was not doing science fiction. I was doing a space opera, a fantasy film, a mythological piece, a fairy tale. I really thought I needed to establish from the start that this was a completely made up world so that I could do anything I wanted."

The second draft as well as the third draft began with the following quote: "And in time of greatest despair there shall come a savior and he shall be known as: THE SON OF THE SUN" ("Journal of the Whills," 3:12).

George Lucas: "Originally, I was trying to have the story be told by somebody else; there was somebody watching this whole story and recording it, somebody probably wiser than the mortal players in the actual events. I eventually dropped this idea, and the concepts behind the Whills turned into the Force. But the Whills became part of this massive amount of notes, quotes, background information that I used for the scripts; the stories were actually taken from the 'Journal of the Whills.' "

Like the story itself, the roll-up went through many different permutations. Initially, the first shot of the film showed a vast sea of stars, a planet, and five moons surrounding it. In the third draft George Lucas simply used the sea of stars as the backdrop to the main titles and the roll-up. Originally, in the rough draft, the roll-up only defined the notion of a new Empire with its ferocious "Knights of Sith" (who became "Legions of Lettow" in the first draft) hunting down the legendary "Jedi Bendu" warriors (called "Dai Nogas" in the first draft). Eventually, the notion of civil wars, the Rebellion, and the Death Star were added to the text, providing the audience with more background information on the plot and the characters.

George Lucas: "The roll-up came out of the serial concept, which was that this was a series of movies and not a single movie. At the beginning, it was pretty long and unwieldy, and I kept paring it down and paring it down. Finally, I showed it to my friends Brian De Palma, Jay Cocks, Gloria Katz, and Willard Huyck, and we made it simpler and easier to read. Right before I was going to shoot the film, I did a final draft of the script, but I never felt confident with the dialogue. Dialogue has never been my strong point, and so I talked to Willard and Gloria and asked them to do a quick dialogue polish. I gave them the fourth draft of the script, and they just improved the dialogue where they felt they could make a contribution. Then I took their changes, and sometimes I rewrote some of their lines. Some of their dialogue of course changed again when we started shooting. Some of it survived; some of it didn't. They did about thirty percent of the dialogue."

The * (asterisk) symbol to the left of the character name indicates some of the most significant dialogue contributions by Gloria Katz and Willard Huyck, which they wrote for the revised fourth draft.

The awesome yellow planet of Tatooine emerges from a total eclipse, her two moons glowing against the darkness. A tiny silver spacecraft, a Rebel Blockade Runner firing lasers from the back of the ship, races through space. It is pursued by a giant Imperial starship. Hundreds of deadly laserbolts streak from the Imperial Star Destroyer, causing the main solar fin of the Rebel craft to disintegrate.

The treatment opened with a battle between "6 fighter-type spacecrafts" and a gargantuan space fortress. The rough and first drafts, however, took a completely different approach; instead of beginning the story, as in all the subsequent drafts and in the film, with a battle in space between a small Rebel fighter and an Imperial Star Destroyer, the story starts with young Annikin Starkiller spotting a spacecraft orbiting the fourth moon of Utapau, where he is hiding with Kane, his father, and Deak, his ten-year-old brother. Annikin is sixteen and is described as tall and heavyset. Annikin rushes back to the shabby hut where he lives with his father and brother. Kane is one of the last Jedi warriors and is hiding with his two sons from a rival sect, the Knights of Sith. Kane is a large, burly man "wearing the distinctive robes of a Jedi" and has been imparting his knowledge to his two boys. Deak has dusty blond hair and a large scratch on his cheek. Kane and his two sons go check out the Sith spacecraft that Annikin spotted; Kane walks toward it, leaving the boys behind. Suddenly, a Sith warrior dressed in black robes and wearing a face mask, an outfit that would later become

Darth Vader's, appears behind the two boys and kills Deak with a long lasersword. Annikin pulls out his lasersword, "which creates an eerie red glow," and fights the enemy. Kane comes to the rescue and kills the Sith warrior with his sword. After burying Deak, Kane and Annikin get aboard the Sith warrior's craft and head for their home system of Aquilae, which would later become Tatooine. They reach General Skywalker's underground fortress. Kane and Skywalker are old friends, and Kane asks him to complete his son's training. In fact, Kane is dying; except for his head and right arm, his body has been replaced by electronic components (this of course foreshadows the concept of Vader being half man and half machine). Skywalker agrees to take Annikin under his command and makes him a captain.

Annikin combined some of the qualities that would later define both Luke Skywalker and Han Solo.

George Lucas: "His character is basically a cynical loner who realizes the importance of being part of a group and helping for the common good . . . compromising and sacrificing his own welfare for those of others. I had a list of about thirty-five themes that I wanted to explore in the film, and giving up your own personal gratification for the good of others was one of them."

In the first draft, which is practically identical to the rough version of the script, Kane is Akira Valor, named after the famous director Akira Kurosawa, and his sons are Justin and Bink. Akira is a "Dai" warrior from the Townowi system. In subsequent drafts, Lucas reverted to the word "Jedi."

George Lucas: "Dai has other connotations. Dai sounded too much like death, and it was not a positive idea."

INT. REBEL BLOCKADE RUNNER—MAIN PASSAGEWAY

An explosion rocks the ship as two robots, Artoo-Detoo (R2-D2) and See-Threepio (C-3PO) struggle to make their way through the shaking, bouncing passageway. Both robots are old and battered. Artoo is a short, claw-armed tripod. His face is a mass of computer lights surrounding a radar eye. Threepio, on the other hand, is a tall, slender robot of human proportions. He has a gleaming bronzelike metallic surface of an Art Deco design.

Rebel troops rush past, and another blast shakes them as they struggle along their way.

THREEPIO: Did you hear that? They've shut down the main reactor. We'll be destroyed for sure. This is madness!

Rebel troopers continue to rush past the robots and take up positions in the main passageway. They aim their weapons toward the door.

THREEPIO: We're doomed!

The little R2 unit makes a series of electronic sounds that only another robot could understand.

THREEPIO: There'll be no escape for the princess this time.

Artoo continues making beeping sounds. Tension mounts as loud metallic latches clank and the screams of heavy equipment are heard moving around the outside hull of the ship.

THREEPIO: What's that?

A strong influence on *Star Wars* was Akira Kurosawa's epic film *The Hidden Fortress* (1958); the story is about a princess who escapes the clutches of an enemy clan with her faithful commander. They make a dangerous journey disguised as peasants, with the royal fortune in gold hidden in sticks of firewood and with help from two bumbling farmers who hope to get a share of the treasure.

The two droids did not exist in the first treatment; instead, George Lucas created two Imperial bureaucrats modeled after the two farmers from *The Hidden Fortress*, who were basically placed in the story for comic relief and who are taken prisoner by General Luke Skywalker after they escape from an Imperial space fortress during a battle.

George Lucas: "You focus on the human story first, and then you begin to create this world that everybody inhabits, and playing with the lowest person in this hierarchy, I created droids. And that is really how they came about. I was looking for the lowest person on the pecking order, basically like the farmers in *Hidden Fortress* were."

The robots made their first appearance aboard the Death Star in the rough draft during an attack on Aquilae. Quickly, Lucas decided that the story would be told from their point of view.

George Lucas: "The part that was the most interesting in *Hidden Fortress* was that it was told from the point of view of the farmers, and not from the point of view of the princess. I liked that idea. It set me off on a very interesting course because it really did frame the movie in a very interesting way and altered the point of view of all three movies."

In the rough draft, R2-D2 (Artoo-Detoo), a fusion droid, is already described as a three-foot tall claw-armed tripod with a mass of computer lights surrounding a radar eye, and C-3PO (See-Threepio) of Human Cyborg Relations is a tall, gleaming android with human proportions.

Ralph McQuarrie: "George said that Artoo-Detoo should be a kind of repair guy. At first my feeling was that See-Threepio should have very delicate lines and smooth surfaces, like an Ernst Trova sculpture. George said to make him more like a boy."

In the rough and first drafts both robots have human speech, and faithful to their nature in all subsequent scripts and in the movie, they are always arguing with each other. Fearing the destruction of the space fortress during a battle, they escape in a lifepod, and R2-D2, who was then less bold than he subsequently became, worries that they've become deserters. In the first draft the droids' names were simplified: R2-D2 became A-2, and C-3PO became C-3. In the second draft George Lucas reverted to the names he had originally created. Everyone has heard the story that Lucas had in mind the film term "Reel 2, Dialogue 2" when he called one of his robots R2-D2. In most cases, however, the names in the *Star Wars* trilogy were simply created phonetically.

George Lucas: "As I was writing, I would say the names to myself, and if I had a hard time dealing with a name phonetically, I would change it. It had to do with hearing the name a lot and whether I got used to it or not."

Lucas's notes around the time the second draft was written suggest that Artoo is a staunch, loyal servant, slightly conservative, puppylike, very naive but very bright. Threepio, by contrast, is a coward, greedy and a fast talker, almost a con man. In the second draft, all subsequent scripts, and the film Artoo does not talk but communicates via a series of electronic sounds.

George Lucas: "I remember at some point it seemed dramatically more interesting to me to have both droids talk, but it took some of the mystery, charm, and uniqueness out of the characters. The idea was to make them different, have them bounce off of each other to identify them easily as separate characters. I tried to make them as opposite as possible."

In the second draft there is no Princess Leia; instead, a character named Deak Starkiller, a twenty-five-year-old Jedi Knight, is part of the Rebel Blockade Runner and is taken prisoner by Vader. As in the movie, the droids escape in the lifepod and Artoo communicates to Threepio that he has received orders from Deak to seek someone named Lars Owen, who will lead them to "the one called Angel Blue" (Deak's brother).

The Imperial craft has easily overtaken the Rebel Blockade Runner. The smaller Rebel ship is being drawn into the underside dock of the giant Imperial starship.
INT. REBEL BLOCKADE RUNNER
The nervous Rebel troopers aim their weapons. Suddenly a tremendous blast opens up a hole in the main passageway, and a score of fearsome armored spacesuited stormtroopers make their way into the smoke-filled corridor.
In a few minutes the entire passageway is ablaze with laserfire. The deadly bolts ricochet in wild random patterns, creating huge explosions. Stormtroopers scatter and duck behind storage lockers. Laserbolts hit several Rebel soldiers, who scream and stagger through the smoke, holding shattered arms and faces.
An explosion hits near the robots.

Richard Chew: "About the first scene, George staged the stormtroopers breaking through the door only twice; that's all he had time to do, but he shot with six different cameras . . . It was six different angles. The scene was very short, but because the angles were so drastically different, we were able to overlap some of the action and extend the length of the scene. Basically, the audience didn't realize that we covered some of the action twice because we managed to go from tight angles to very wide angles."

The awesome, seven-foot-tall Dark Lord of the Sith makes his way into the blinding light of the main passageway. This is Darth Vader, right hand of the Emperor. His face is obscured by his flowing black robes and grotesque breath mask, which stands out next to the fascist white-armored suits of the Imperial stormtroopers.
Everyone instinctively backs away from the imposing warrior.

George Lucas: "Having machines, like the droids, that are reasonably compassionate and a man like Vader who becomes a machine and loses his compassion was a theme that interested me."

In the rough draft Darth Vader is introduced during a scene on Alderaan (Granicus in the first draft), the capital of the new Galactic Empire. Vader, who is a relatively minor character in this version of the story, is a tall grim-looking general. When we meet Vader, Cos Dashit (Son Hhat in the first draft), Lord of Alderaan, Consul to the Supreme Tribunal, and Ruler of the Galactic Empire, is announcing to his troops that he has decided to conquer the Aquilae system, the last refuge of the sect of the Jedi. In the second draft and all subsequent screenplays Lord Darth Vader became the character we all know from the film. In that same draft, however, Deak Starkiller, who replaces Leia in this incarnation of the story, makes a suicidal attempt to kill the troopers with his lasersword and laserpistol and suddenly is confronted by Darth Vader. The Dark Lord raises his arms, and every object that is not bolted down is picked up by an invisible force and hurled at Deak, who protects himself with an invisible shield. Vader and Starkiller have a duel, and eventually Vader drains all the Force from the Jedi warrior. With Deak under his control, Vader declares that the Rebellion has at last been crushed. A commander who doesn't share Vader's enthusiasm suggests that they send a platoon of "Tuskens" to the planet of Ogana to see if Deak has any allies or another brother still hiding. Vader gives the commander an angry look, and suddenly it appears as if the commander can't catch his breath; the man rushes out as Vader starts punching Deak violently.

INT. REBEL BLOCKADE RUNNER
A woman's hand puts a card into an opening in Artoo's dome. Artoo makes beeping sounds.

INT. REBEL BLOCKADE RUNNER

Threepio stands in a hallway, somewhat bewildered. Artoo is nowhere in sight. Fighting can be heard in the distance.

THREEPIO: Artoo-Detoo, where are you?

A familiar beeping sound attracts Threepio's attention, and he spots little Artoo at the end of the hallway in a smoke-filled alcove. A beautiful young girl (about sixteen years old) stands in front of Artoo. Surreal and out of place, dreamlike and half-hidden in the smoke, she finishes adjusting something on Artoo's computer face, then disappears as the little robot joins his companion. Stormtroopers can be heard battling in the distance.

*****THREEPIO:** At last! Where have you been? They're heading in this direction. What are we going to do? We'll be sent to the spice mines of Kessel or smashed into who knows what!

Artoo scoots past his bronze friend and races down the subhallway. Threepio chases after him.

THREEPIO: Wait a minute, where are you going?

Artoo responds with electronic beeps.
  The lovely young girl watches them go.

INT. REBEL BLOCKADE RUNNER—CORRIDOR

Captured Rebel troops are marched away. The evil Darth Vader holds a wounded Rebel officer by the neck as an Imperial officer rushes up to the Dark Lord.

IMPERIAL OFFICER: The Death Star plans are not in the main computer.

Vader squeezes the neck of the Rebel officer, who struggles in vain.

VADER: Where are those transmissions you intercepted? What have you done with those plans?

Vader lifts the Rebel off his feet by his throat.

REBEL OFFICER: We intercepted no transmissions. Aaah . . . This is a consular ship. We're on a diplomatic mission.

VADER: If this is a consular ship . . . where is the ambassador?

The Dark Lord begins to squeeze the officer's throat, creating a gruesome snapping and choking, until the soldier goes limp. Vader tosses the dead soldier against the wall and turns to his troops.

VADER: Commander, tear this ship apart until you've found those plans and bring me the passengers. I want them alive!

The stormtroopers scurry into the subhallways.

INT. REBEL BLOCKADE RUNNER—SUBHALLWAY

The lovely young girl huddles in a small alcove as the stormtroopers search through the ship. She is Princess Leia Organa, a member of the Alderaan Senate. The stormtroopers approach. One of the troopers spots her.

TROOPER: There's one! Set for stun!

Leia steps from her hiding place and blasts a trooper with her laserpistol. She starts to run but is felled by a paralyzing ray. The troopers inspect her inert body.

TROOPER: She'll be all right. Inform Lord Vader we have a prisoner.

In the treatment Princess Leia and her family are being pursued by the Empire. Her goal is to reach the friendly planet of Ophuchi, and she enrolls General Luke Skywalker to protect her. In the rough draft Leia (Zara in the first draft) is a fourteen-year-old beauty with an iron will. She lives on Aquilae and is the daughter of King Kayos and Queen Breha; she has two brothers, Biggs (Oeta in the first draft), age seven, and Windom (Puck in the first draft), age five. At the beginning of the script Leia is introduced as she is leaving for the Academy of Chatos with her two maids.

In the second draft Leia is the daughter of Owen Lars and his wife, Beru, and appears only briefly; remember, in that particular script Deak Starkiller, not the princess, is held captive by Vader. In the third draft Princess Leia Organa is described as a beautiful young girl about sixteen years old, and as in the film and all subsequent screenplays, she is introduced at the beginning of the story, aboard the Rebel ship. Finally, in the fourth draft and as in the movie, Leia, a member of the Alderaan Senate, is introduced in a subhallway, kneeling in front of Artoo.

George Lucas: "I felt that I needed to have a woman in the script. The interesting thing is she does get in jeopardy, but she is very capable of taking care of herself; she is a central character, and I wanted a woman to be at the center of the story. I knew I didn't want to have three guys. It wouldn't have been nearly as interesting. She is a leader, and even though she gets captured, the guys are the ones who are fumbling around and being in trouble . . . I mean, they can't even rescue her!"

INT. REBEL BLOCKADE RUNNER—SUBHALLWAY

Artoo stops before the small hatch of an emergency lifepod. The stubby astrorobot works his way into the cramped four-man pod.

THREEPIO: Hey, you're not permitted in there. It's restricted. You'll be deactivated for sure.

Artoo beeps something to him.

THREEPIO: Don't you call me a mindless philosopher, you overweight glob of grease! Now come out before somebody sees you.

Artoo whistles something at his reluctant friend regarding the mission he is about to perform.

THREEPIO: Secret mission? What plans? What are you talking about? I'm not getting in there!

A new explosion, this time very close, sends dust and debris through the narrow subhallway. Flames lick at Threepio, and after a flurry of electronic swearing from Artoo, the lanky robot jumps into the lifepod.

THREEPIO: I'm going to regret this.

INT. REBEL BLOCKADE RUNNER

The safety door snaps shut, and with the thunder of exploding latches the tiny lifepod ejects from the disabled ship.

INT. IMPERIAL STAR DESTROYER

On the main viewscreen, the lifepod carrying the two terrified robots speeds away from the stricken Rebel spacecraft.

CHIEF PILOT: There goes another one.

CAPTAIN: Hold your fire. There's no life-forms. It must have short-circuited.

INT. LIFEPOD

Artoo and Threepio look out at the receding Imperial starship. Stars circle as the pod rotates through the galaxy.

THREEPIO: That's funny, the damage doesn't look as bad from out here.

Artoo beeps an assuring response.

THREEPIO: Are you sure this thing is safe?

EXT. SPACE—PLANET TATOOINE

The lifepod disappears in the direction of the planet.

INT. REBEL BLOCKADE RUNNER—HALLWAY

Princess Leia is led down a low-ceilinged hallway by a squad of briskly marching armored stormtroopers. Her hands are bound. They stop in a smoky hallway as Darth Vader appears.

LEIA: Darth Vader. Only you could be so bold. The Imperial Senate will not sit still for this. When they hear you've attacked a diplomatic—

VADER: Don't act so surprised, Your Highness. You weren't on any mercy mission this time. Several transmissions were beamed to this ship by Rebel spies. I want to know what happened to the plans they sent you.

LEIA: I don't know what you're talking about. I'm a member of the Imperial Senate on a diplomatic mission to Alderaan . . .

VADER: You are a part of the Rebel Alliance . . . and a traitor. Take her away!

Leia is marched away down the hallway. An Imperial commander turns to Vader.

COMMANDER: Holding her is dangerous. If word of this gets out, it could generate sympathy for the Rebellion in the Senate.

VADER: I have traced the Rebel spies to her. Now she is my only link to finding their secret base.

COMMANDER: She'll die before she'll tell you anything.

VADER: Leave that to me. Send a distress signal and then inform the Senate that all aboard were killed!

Another Imperial commander approaches Vader and the first commander.

SECOND COMMANDER: Lord Vader, the battle station plans are not aboard this ship! And no transmissions were made. An escape pod was jettisoned during the fighting, but no life-forms were aboard.

VADER: She must have hidden the plans in the escape pod. Send a detachment down to retrieve them. See to it personally, Commander. There'll be no one to stop us this time.

SECOND COMMANDER: Yes, sir.

EXT. SPACE

The Imperial Star Destroyer comes over the surface of the planet Tatooine.

EXT. TATOOINE—DESERT

Jundland, or "No Man's Land," where the rugged desert mesas meet the foreboding Dune Sea. The two helpless astrorobots kick up clouds of sand as they leave the lifepod and clumsily work their way across the desert wasteland. The lifepod in the distance rests half-buried in the sand.

THREEPIO: How did we get into this mess? I really don't know how. We seem to be made to suffer. It's our lot in life.

Artoo answers with beeping sounds.

THREEPIO: I've got to rest before I fall apart. My joints are almost frozen.

Artoo continues to respond with beeping sounds.

THREEPIO: What a desolate place this is.

Suddenly Artoo whistles, makes a sharp right turn, and starts off in the direction of the rocky desert mesas. Threepio stops and yells at him.

THREEPIO: Where do you think you're going?

A stream of electronic noises continues to pour forth from the small robot.

THREEPIO: Well, I'm not going that way. It's much too rocky. This way is much easier.

Artoo counters with a beep.

THREEPIO: What makes you think there are settlements over there?

Artoo continues to make beeping sounds.

THREEPIO: Don't get technical with me.

Artoo continues to make beeping sounds.

THREEPIO: What mission? What are you talking about? I've just about had enough of you! Go that way! You'll be malfunctioning within a day, you near-sighted scrap pile!

Threepio gives the little robot a kick and starts in the direction of the vast dune sea.

THREEPIO: And don't let me catch you following me begging for help, because you won't get it.

Artoo's reply is a rather rude sound. He turns in the direction of the towering mesas.

THREEPIO: No more adventures. I'm not going that way.

Artoo beeps to himself as he makes his way toward the distant mountains.

EXT. TATOOINE—DUNE SEA

Threepio, hot and tired, struggles up over the ridge of a dune, only to find more dunes, which seem to go on for endless miles. He looks back in the direction of the now distant rock mesas.

THREEPIO: That malfunctioning little twerp. This is all his fault! He tricked me into going this way, but he'll do no better.

His plight seems hopeless, when a glint of reflected light in the distance reveals an object moving toward him.

THREEPIO: Wait, what's that? A transport! I'm saved!

The bronze droid waves frantically and yells at the approaching transport.

THREEPIO: Over here! Hey! Hey! Help! Please, help!

EXT. TATOOINE—ROCK CANYON—SUNSET

The gargantuan rock formations are shrouded in a strange foreboding mist, and the ominous sounds of unearthly creatures fill the air. Artoo moves cautiously through the creepy rock canyon, inadvertently making a loud whirring noise as he goes.

A little farther up the canyon a slight flicker of lights reveals a pair of eyes in the dark recesses only a few feet from the narrow path.

The unsuspecting robot waddles along the rugged trail until suddenly, out of nowhere, a powerful magnetic ray shoots out of the rocks and engulfs him in an eerie glow.

He manages a few electronic squeaks before he topples over, his bright computer lights extinguished. Out of the rocks scurry several Jawas, no taller than Artoo. They holster strange and complex weapons as they cautiously approach the robot. They wear grubby cloaks, and their faces are shrouded so that only their glowing yellow eyes can be seen. They hiss and make odd guttural sounds as they heave the heavy robot onto their shoulders and carry him off down the trail.

EXT. TATOOINE—ROCK CANYON—SANDCRAWLER—SUNSET

The Jawas carry Artoo out of the canyon to a huge tanklike vehicle the size of a four-story house. They weld a small disk on the side of Artoo and then put him under a large tube on the side of the vehicle, and the little robot is sucked into the giant machine.

The filthy little Jawas scurry like rats up a ladder and enter the main cabin of the behemoth transport.

INT. SANDCRAWLER—HOLD AREA

It is dim inside the hold area of the sandcrawler. Artoo switches on a small floodlight on his forehead and stumbles around the scrap heap. The narrow beam swings across rusty metal rocket parts and an array of grotesquely twisted and maimed astrorobots. He lets out a pathetic electronic whimper and stumbles off toward what appears to be a door at the end of the chamber.

INT. SANDCRAWLER—PRISON AREA

Artoo enters a wide room with a low ceiling. In the middle of the scrap heap sit a dozen or so robots of various shapes and sizes. Some are engaged in electronic conversation, while others simply mill about. A voice calls out from the gloom.

THREEPIO: Artoo? Artoo-Detoo! It is you! It is you!

A battered Threepio scrambles up to Artoo and embraces him.

In the rough draft R2-D2 and C-3PO land at the edge of the Dune Sea on Aquilae (Townowi in the first draft), in a place called Kuroland or "No Man's Land," after they've escaped from the Death Star during a battle. The two robots argue and go their separate ways. In this version the robots are reunited by young Annikin, who has been ordered to rescue Princess Leia. During an unexpected Imperial attack he picks them up in his landspeeder and brings them back to General Skywalker's underground fortress.

In the second draft the droids land at Jundland, the edge of the Dune Sea on the planet of Utapau, and after they separate, Artoo is captured by the Jawas. In this early draft their description is identical to the way they ended up looking in the film. In that same draft, after Artoo and Threepio have been reunited aboard the sandcrawler, the Jawas try to drive their tank down a trail but get stuck. During the commotion the droids manage to escape; they reach the Anchorhead settlement and ask an old mechanic where to find Owen Lars.

"The bleached bones of a dinosaurlike beast" lying in the dunes first appeared in the fourth draft.

EXT. TATOOINE—ROCK CANYON—SANDCRAWLER—SUNSET

The enormous sandcrawler lumbers off.
EXT. TATOOINE—DESERT—DAY
Imperial stormtroopers mill about in front of the half-buried lifepod that brought Artoo and Threepio to Tatooine. A trooper radios to an officer some distance away.
FIRST TROOPER: Somone was in the pod. The tracks go off in this direction.
A second trooper picks up a small bit of metal out of the sand and gives it to the first trooper.
SECOND TROOPER: Look, sir— droids.

From the Special Edition:
EXT. TATOOINE—DESERT—DAY
Imperial stormtroopers mill about in front of the half-buried lifepod that brought Artoo and Threepio to Tatooine, searching for the droids on foot and mounted on dewbacks. An Imperial heavy shuttle transport lifts off in the background, wings unfolding as it flies off. A trooper yells to an officer some distance away.
FIRST TROOPER: Someone was in the pod. The tracks go off in this direction.
A second trooper picks a small bit of metal out of the sand and holds it up.
SECOND TROOPER: Look, sir— droids.

When George Lucas decided to restore *Star Wars: A New Hope,* a number of sequences and shots were selected to be added, altered, or cleaned up. The scene with the stormtroopers in the desert, for example, is now quite different from the way it was presented in the original version of the film. One additional shot was filmed in 1995 with stormtroopers riding dewbacks and, via computer animation, an Imperial shuttle taking off in the background was added later. The scene with the troopers was shot in Yuma, Arizona, in one day, with five actors, under the supervision of the producer, Rick McCallum, with the director of photography, Joe Murray, and was designed by George Lucas, using computerized storyboards.

Rick McCallum: "That way, there's no interpretation; we know exactly what we have to shoot. Setting up the shot in Yuma had to be extremely precise since the dewbacks and the Imperial shuttle were added later on."

One challenge was to match the new footage to the original film. The sequence in the desert, for instance, was shot on location in Tunisia in 1975 with a filter on a very cloudy day. The shot in Yuma was done on the hottest day on record in the United States (132 degrees). There was not a cloud in the sky, and painstaking efforts had to be made to match the two skies.

The shot with the stormtrooper finding the small bit of metal was also altered. In the original film, the dewbacks were in the background, barely moving, but now, thanks to computer graphic animation, they are moving through the desert.

EXT. TATOOINE—DUNES
The sandcrawler moves slowly down a great sand dune.

From the Special Edition:
EXT. TATOOINE—DUNES
The sandcrawler moves slowly over the rocky terrain.

The shot of the sandcrawler lumbering off in the rock canyon was completely redone and replaced during the restoration of *Star Wars*.

Rick McCallum: "The original shot wasn't dynamic enough. So we made the camera angle lower, the sandcrawler bigger, and replaced the original shot."

Ralph McQuarrie: "The sandcrawler was just said to be an enormous iron-tracked vehicle, and I put a big trapdoor on the front because it's collecting junk, and I made it huge and put a little driver's compartment at the top and designed this peak that comes off the front. I added engines, exhaust pipes, and plenty of tracks. In fact, there are four different tanklike tracks on the crawler. I wanted it to look like an old warehouse on tracks."

INT. SANDCRAWLER

Threepio and Artoo travel along inside the cramped prison chamber. Artoo appears to be shut off.

THREEPIO: Wake up! Wake up!

As the sandcrawler stops, Threepio's fist bangs the head of Artoo, whose computer lights pop on as he begins beeping. At the far end of the long chamber a hatch opens, filling the chamber with blinding white light. A dozen or so Jawas make their way through the odd assortment of robots.

THREEPIO: We're doomed.

A Jawa starts moving toward them.

THREEPIO: Do you think they'll melt us down?

Artoo responds, making beeping sounds.

THREEPIO: Don't shoot! Don't shoot! Will this never end?

EXT. TATOOINE—DESERT—LARS HOMESTEAD—AFTERNOON

The Jawas mutter gibberish as they busily line up their battered captives, including Artoo and Threepio, in front of the enormous sandcrawler, which is parked beside a small homestead consisting of three large holes in the ground surrounded by several tall moisture vaporators and one small adobe blockhouse.

The Jawas scurry around fussing over the robots, straightening them up or brushing some dust from a dented metallic elbow.

Out of the shadows of a dingy side building limps Owen Lars, a large burly man in his mid-fifties. His reddish eyes are sunken in a dust-covered face.

In the second draft the droids have been sent to Owen Lars by Deak Starkiller, now prisoner of the Empire, to seek the one called "Angel Blue." The droids are greeted by Biggs and Windy Starkiller, who are Deak's seven-year-old twin brothers. Owen Lars is a bearded, sturdy, burly man in his early fifties married to his "plump-jolly" wife, Beru. It is interesting to note that in the rough draft Owen Lars (Huu Tho in the first draft) was an old and scruffy anthropologist who lived with his wife, Beru, in a tree house on the Wookiee planet of Yavin.

As the farmer carefully inspects each of the robots, he is closely followed by his slump-shouldered nephew, Luke Skywalker. One of the vile little Jawas walks ahead of the farmer, spouting an animated sales pitch in a queer, unintelligible language.

OWEN: Yeah, all right, fine. Let's go.

A voice calls out from one of the huge holes that form the homestead.

BERU: Luke! Luke!

Luke goes over to the edge and sees his aunt Beru standing in the main courtyard.

BERU: Luke, tell Uncle, if he gets a translator, be sure it speaks Bocce.

LUKE: Doesn't look like we have much of a choice, but I'll remind him.

Luke returns to his uncle as they look over the equipment for sale with the Jawa leader.

OWEN: No, not that one . . . (addressing Threepio) You, I suppose you're programmed for etiquette and protocol?

THREEPIO: Protocol? Why, it's my primary function, sir. I am well versed in all the customs—

OWEN: I have no need for a protocol droid.

THREEPIO: (quickly) Of course you haven't, sir—not in an environment such as this—that's why I have been programmed—

OWEN: What I really need is a droid who understands the binary language of moisture vaporators.

THREEPIO: Vaporators! Sir—my first job was programming binary load lifters . . . very similar to your vaporators in most respects . . .

OWEN: Can you speak Bocce?

THREEPIO: Of course I can, sir. It's like a second language to me . . . I'm as fluent in—

OWEN: All right; shut up! (turning to Jawa) I'll take this one.

THREEPIO: Shutting up, sir.

OWEN: Luke! Take these two over to the garage, will you? I want them cleaned up before dinner.

LUKE: But I was going into Toshi Station to pick up some power converters . . .

OWEN: You can waste time with your friends when your chores are done. Now, come on, get to it!

LUKE: All right, come on. And the red one, come on. Well, come on, Red, let's go.

As the Jawas start to lead the remaining robots back into the sandcrawler, Artoo lets out a pathetic little beep and starts after his old friend Threepio. He is restrained by a slimy Jawa, who zaps him with a control box.

Owen is negotiating with the head Jawa. Luke and the two robots start for the garage when a plate pops off the head of the red astrodroid, throwing parts all over the ground.

LUKE: Uncle Owen . . .

OWEN: Yeah?

LUKE: This R2 unit has a bad motivator. Look!

OWEN: *(to the head Jawa)* Hey, what're you trying to push on us?

The Jawa goes into a loud spiel. Meanwhile, Artoo is moving up and down, trying to attract attention. He lets out a low whistle. Threepio taps Luke on the shoulder.

THREEPIO: *(pointing to Artoo)* Excuse me, sir, but that R2 unit is in prime condition. A real bargain.

LUKE: Uncle Owen . . .

OWEN: Yeah?

LUKE: What about that one?

OWEN: *(to Jawa)* What about that blue one? We'll take that one.

With a little reluctance the scruffy dwarf trades the damaged astrorobot for Artoo.

LUKE: Yeah, take this away.

THREEPIO: I'm quite sure you'll be very pleased with that one, sir. He really is in first-class condition. I've worked with him before. Here he comes.

The two robots trudge off toward a grimy homestead entry.

LUKE: Okay, let's go.

THREEPIO: *(to Artoo)* Now, don't you forget this! Why I should stick my neck out for you is quite beyond my capacity!

In the rough and first drafts we meet General Luke Skywalker on Aquilae as he walks into the middle of a meeting that King Kayos is having with the High Senate. Skywalker is described as a large man, "apparently in his early sixties but actually much older." In a sense his description and function in this version of the story foreshadow the character of Obi-Wan Kenobi. Skywalker is very much a leader who speaks his mind; the king appreciates him, but the members of the Senate, especially the corrupt Count Sandage, do not. In the second draft Luke is Deak Starkiller's brother and is known as "Angel Blue, the Skywalker." He is a short and chubby boy of about eighteen. The first time we see him, he is training with his lasersword and a chrome baseball that fires laserbolts. In the third draft Luke Starkiller is introduced at the beginning of the story in the desert of Utapau, a planet with two suns, intercut with scenes of Vader invading the Rebel spaceship. Luke is a farm boy who looks younger than his twenty-two years, and "his short hair and baggy tunic give him the air of a simpleminded but lovable lout with a prize-winning smile." George Lucas's notes indicate that he saw Luke as an ugly duckling, sort of like Cinderella; he is made fun of and wants to become a starpilot, but when he is confronted with reality, he still thinks like a farm boy. He is honest, simple, and good-hearted.

Ralph McQuarrie: "I had a lot more equipment on him at first, very tailored-looking piping, tubing, and little gadgets sewn into his costume. But I got the impression that George wanted all the costumes to be a lot more simple. He didn't want the costumes to be the center of attention."

In this third draft Luke is introduced working on a large pipe, some kind of oil rig. A sparkle in the sky catches his eye; he grabs his binoculars and spots the Imperial starship. As he hurriedly climbs in his landspeeder, his robot breaks down. Luke then arrives at a power station at the Anchorhead Settlement; there we meet the Fixer (a rugged-looking man in his thirties); his girlfriend, Camie, eighteen; Deak and Windy, two tough boys the same age as Luke; and Biggs, a tall and handsome but somewhat blasé startrooper cadet who just graduated from the Academy. Luke tries to convince his friends that there's a battle going on in space, but none of them believe him. Biggs, like the others, seems to ignore what Luke is saying and complains that nothing ever happens and that his life is boring. Yet Luke envies him and looks upon him as a role model. In the fourth draft we're still introduced to Luke on page two of the script, just as Vader is invading the Rebel spaceship. The sequence is similar to the previous draft, but here the scene with Biggs is completely different; Biggs explains that he didn't graduate. Instead, he signed up with the Alliance; the Rebels were looking for good pilots and found him. He tries to convince Luke to come with him instead of going to the Academy, but Luke explains that his uncle needs him. In the revised fourth draft Luke is now twenty (not twenty-two) and has shaggy hair (not curly). The scene with Biggs has once again changed; here he explains that he has made some friends at the Academy and that they intend to jump ship to join the Alliance. Biggs tells Luke that soon his uncle will be nothing more than a slave to the Emperor. Luke says he will be joining the Academy next season. Biggs is leaving the next morning; the two young men say good-bye, and Luke takes off.

When George Lucas shared his ideas early on with his friends and colleagues, they kept telling him that it was a bad idea to start the film with only the droids, that it was too much like his first film, *THX 1138* (1971), and that he should introduce Luke, his leading character, at the beginning of the story:

"So I did it. I wrote it, and I shot it, and I looked at it. It worked okay, but it wasn't great. I could not get out of my mind that poetically speaking I really wanted to have this clean line of the robots taking you to Luke, Luke taking you to Ben, Ben taking you to Han, Han taking you to Princess Leia. I wanted each character to take you to the next person. I finally said, 'I don't care what people say, that they don't like this movie about robots.' I thought they were charming, interesting, and entertaining. They weren't cold like the robots in my first film, *THX 1138*. So I just decided to trust my heart, and I structured the story that way because of the way I felt about it, not because it was logical."

INT. LARS HOMESTEAD—GARAGE AREA—LATE AFTERNOON

The garage is cluttered and worn, but a friendly peaceful atmosphere permeates the low gray chamber. Threepio lowers himself into a large tub filled with warm oil. Near the battered landspeeder little Artoo rests on a large battery with a cord attached to his face.

THREEPIO: Thank the maker! This oil bath is going to feel so good. I've got such a bad case of dust contamination, I can barely move!

Luke seems to be lost in thought as he plays with the damaged fin of a small two-man skyhopper spaceship. Finally Luke's frustrations get the better of him.

LUKE: It just isn't fair. Oh, Biggs is right. I'm never gonna get out of here!

THREEPIO: Is there anything I might do to help?

Luke glances at the battered robot. A bit of his anger drains.

*LUKE: Well, not unless you can alter time, speed up the harvest, or teleport me off this rock!

*THREEPIO: I don't think so, sir. I'm only a droid and not very knowledgeable about such things. Not on this planet, anyway. As a matter of fact, I'm not even sure which planet I'm on.

*LUKE: Well, if there's a bright center to the universe, you're on the planet that it's farthest from.

*THREEPIO: I see, sir.

*LUKE: Uh, you can call me Luke.

*THREEPIO: I see, Sir Luke.

*LUKE: *[laughing]* Just Luke.

*THREEPIO: *[climbing out of the oil tub]* Oh! And I am See-Threepio, Human Cyborg Relations, and this is my counterpart, Artoo-Detoo.

LUKE: Hello.

Artoo beeps in response. Luke unplugs Artoo and begins to scrape several connectors on the robot's head with a chrome pick.

LUKE: You got a lot of carbon scoring here. It looks like you boys have seen a lot of action.

THREEPIO: With all we've been through, sometimes I'm amazed we're in as good condition as we are, what with the Rebellion and all.

Luke sparks to life at the mention of the Rebellion.

LUKE: You know of the Rebellion against the Empire?

THREEPIO: That's how we came to be in your service, if you take my meaning, sir.

LUKE: Have you been in many battles?

THREEPIO: Several, I think. Actually, there's not much to tell. I'm not much more than an interpreter, and not very good at telling stories. Well, not at making them interesting, anyway.

Luke struggles to remove a small metal fragment from Artoo's neck joint. He uses a larger pick.

LUKE: Well, my little friend, you've got something jammed in here real good. Were you on a starcruiser or . . .

The fragment breaks loose with a snap, sending Luke tumbling head over heels. He sits up and sees a twelve-inch three-dimensional hologram of Leia Organa, the Rebel Senator, being projected from the face of little Artoo. The image is a rainbow of colors as it flickers and jiggles in the dimly lit garage. Luke's mouth hangs open in awe.

LEIA: Help me, Obi-Wan Kenobi. You're my only hope.

LUKE: What's this?

Artoo looks around and sheepishly beeps an answer for Threepio to translate.

THREEPIO: What is what?!? He asked you a question . . . What is that?

Leia continues to repeat the sentence fragment over and over.

LEIA: Help me, Obi-Wan Kenobi. You're my only hope. Help me, Obi-Wan Kenobi. You're my only hope.

Artoo whistles his surprise as he pretends to just notice the hologram. He looks around and sheepishly beeps an answer for Threepio to translate.

THREEPIO: Oh, he says it's nothing, sir. Merely a malfunction. Old data. Pay it no mind.

Luke becomes intrigued by the beautiful young girl.

LUKE: Who is she? She's beautiful.

THREEPIO: I'm afraid I'm not quite sure, sir.

LEIA: Help me, Obi-Wan Kenobi. You're my only hope . . .

THREEPIO: I think she was a passenger on our last voyage. A person of some importance, sir—I believe. Our captain was attached to . . .

LUKE: Is there more to this recording?

Artoo lets out several squeaks.

THREEPIO: Behave yourself, Artoo. You're going to get us into trouble. It's all right, you can trust him. He's our new master.

Artoo whistles and beeps a long message to Threepio.

THREEPIO: He says that he's the property of Obi-Wan Kenobi, a resident of these parts. And it's a private message for him. Quite frankly, sir, I don't know what he's talking about. Our last master was Captain Antilles, but with all we've been through, this little R2 unit has become a bit eccentric.

LUKE: Obi-Wan Kenobi? I wonder if he means old Ben Kenobi?

THREEPIO: I beg your pardon, sir, but do you know what he's talking about?

LUKE: Well, I don't know anyone named Obi-Wan, but old Ben lives out beyond the Dune Sea. He's kind of a strange old hermit.

Luke gazes at the beautiful young princess for a few moments.

LUKE: I wonder who she is. It sounds like she's in trouble. I'd better play back the whole thing.

Artoo beeps something to Threepio.

THREEPIO: He says the restraining bolt has short-circuited his recording system. He suggests that if you remove the bolt, he might be able to play back the entire recording.

Luke has been looking longingly at the lovely little princess and hasn't really heard what Threepio has been saying.

LUKE: H'm? Oh, yeah, well, I guess you're too small to run away on me if I take this off. Okay.

Luke takes a wedged bolt and pops the restraining bolt off Artoo's side.

LUKE: There you go.

The princess immediately disappears.

LUKE: Hey, wait a minute. Where'd she go? Bring her back! Play back the entire message.

Artoo beeps an innocent reply as Threepio sits up in embarrassment.

THREEPIO: What message? The one you've just been playing. The one you're carrying inside your rusty innards!

A woman's voice calls out from the other room.

AUNT BERU: Luke? Luke!

LUKE: All right, I'll be right there, Aunt Beru.

THREEPIO: I'm sorry, sir, but he appears to have picked up a slight flutter.

Luke gives Artoo's restraining bolt to Threepio.

LUKE: Here, see what you can do with him. I'll be right back.

Luke hurries out of the room.

THREEPIO: *(to Artoo)* Just you reconsider playing that message for him.

Artoo beeps in response.

THREEPIO: No, I don't think he likes you at all.

Artoo beeps.

THREEPIO: No. I don't like you either.

The idea of the three-dimensional hologram message first appeared in the second draft; the message is from Deak Starkiller to his brother, Luke: "Whippersnapper, I didn't make it . . . I'm sorry. The forces of the Bogan [the dark side] have become strong and deadly . . . I am lost. Father is in grave danger. He needs you and he needs the Kiber Crystal [which intensifies the Force]. You must find a way to get to Ogana Major on your own. He is waiting for you there. Be careful, though, Ogana Major is under siege by the Imperial Legions of Alderaan. You must hurry, for the force of the Ashla [the good side] grows weak, and I don't know how much longer Father can hold out. The enemy has constructed a powerful weapon to use against him. Warn Uncle."

George Lucas: "I had a longtime interest in fairy tales and mythology, that sort of thing. I had decided that there was no modern mythology. The western was the last American mythological genre, and there had not been anything since then. I wanted to take all the old myths and put them into a new format that young people could relate to. Mythology always exists in unusual, unknown environments, so I chose space. I liked *Flash Gordon* as a kid, the Republic serials. It was the only sort of action-adventure thing I came across as a kid that I could remember. So I got interested in that. I went and actually talked to the people that owned the rights to it. They said they weren't interested. And I thought, I really don't need *Flash Gordon* to do what I want to do. I can create my own situation. So I just started from scratch. I went around a lot of different ways before I wound my way to where I finally ended up."

Ralph McQuarrie: "I met George while he was finishing *THX 1138*, and he talked about this *Star Wars* idea at that time. He just said it was going to be a vast galactic battle between factions of interplanetary war, and I said that sounded interesting, but I didn't expect to ever hear from him again. He didn't talk to me at that time about doing any work, but he wanted to see some of the drawings I had done. So when he finished *American Graffiti* [1973], *Star Wars* was apparently turned down by Universal with the idea that it was too much money to put into a film that had a limited audience like science fiction. He decided that he needed to have some illustrations when he went in to talk to Twentieth Century-Fox. He gave me the script to read, and I would do sketches of various key scenes like the one with the robots coming across the desert, which is the first one I did."

INT. LARS HOMESTEAD—DINING AREA

Luke's Aunt Beru, a warm, motherly woman, fills a pitcher with blue fluid from a refrigerated container in the well-used kitchen. She puts the pitcher on a tray with some bowls of food in the dining area.

    Luke sits with his Uncle Owen and Aunt Beru before a table covered with bowls of food.

LUKE: You know, I think that R2 unit we bought might have been stolen.

OWEN: What makes you think that?

LUKE: Well, I stumbled across a recording while I was cleaning him. He says he belongs to someone called Obi-Wan Kenobi.

Owen is greatly alarmed at the mention of this name but manages to control himself.

LUKE: I thought he might have meant old Ben. Do you know what he's talking about? Well, I wonder if he's related to Ben.

Owen breaks loose with a fit of uncontrolled anger.

OWEN: That wizard's just a crazy old man. Tomorrow I want you to take that R2 unit into Anchorhead and have its memory erased. That'll be the end of it. It belongs to us now.

LUKE: But what if this Obi-Wan comes looking for him?

OWEN: He won't. I don't think he exists anymore. He died about the same time as your father.

LUKE: He knew my father?

OWEN: I told you to forget it. Your only concern is to prepare those two new droids for tomorrow. In the morning I want them up there on the south ridge working on those condensers.

LUKE: Yes, sir. I think those new droids are going to work out fine. In fact, I, uh, was also thinking about our agreement, about me staying on another season. And if these new droids do work out, I want to transmit my application to the Academy this year.

Owen's face becomes a scowl, although he tries to suppress it.

OWEN: You mean the next semester before harvest?

LUKE: Sure. There's more than enough droids.

OWEN: Harvest is when I need you the most. It's only one season more. This year we'll make enough on the harvest that I'll be able to hire some more hands. And then you can go to the Academy next year. You must understand I need you here, Luke.

LUKE: But it's a whole 'nother year.

OWEN: Look, it's only one more season.

Luke pushes his half-eaten plate of food aside and stands.

LUKE: Yeah, that's what you said last year when Biggs and Tank left.

AUNT BERU: Where are you going?

LUKE: It looks like I'm going nowhere. I have to go finish cleaning those droids.

Resigned to his fate, Luke paddles out of the room.

AUNT BERU: Owen, he can't stay here forever. Most of his friends have gone. It means so much to him.

OWEN: I'll make it up to him next year. I promise.

AUNT BERU: Luke's just not a farmer, Owen. He has too much of his father in him.

OWEN: That's what I'm afraid of.

EXT. TATOOINE—LARS HOMESTEAD

The giant twin suns of Tatooine slowly disappear behind a distant dune range. Luke stands watching them for a few moments, then reluctantly enters the domed entrance to the homestead.

INT. LARS HOMESTEAD—GARAGE

Luke enters the garage to discover the robots nowhere in sight. He takes a small control box from his utility belt similar to the one the Jawas were carrying. He activates the box, which creates a low buzz, and Threepio, letting out a short cry, pops up from behind the family landspeeder.

LUKE: What are you doing hiding back there?

Threepio stumbles forward, but Artoo is still nowhere in sight.

THREEPIO: It wasn't my fault, sir. Please don't deactivate me. I told him not to go, but he's faulty, malfunctioning; kept babbling on about his mission.

LUKE: Oh, no!

Luke races out of the garage, followed by Threepio.

EXT. TATOOINE—LARS HOMESTEAD

Luke rushes out of the small domed entry to the homestead and searches the darkening horizon for the small tripod astrorobot. Threepio struggles out of the homestead and onto the salt flat as Luke scans the landscape with his electrobinoculars.

THREEPIO: That R2 unit has always been a problem. These astrodroids are getting quite out of hand. Even I can't understand their logic at times.

LUKE: How could I be so stupid? He's nowhere in sight. Blast it!

THREEPIO: Pardon me, sir, but couldn't we go after him?

LUKE: It's too dangerous with all the Sand People around. We'll have to wait until morning.

Owen yells up from the homestead plaza.

OWEN: Luke, I'm shutting the power down.

LUKE: All right, I'll be there in a few minutes. Boy, am I gonna get it!

He takes one final look across the dim horizon.

LUKE: You know that little droid is going to cause me a lot of trouble.

THREEPIO: Oh, he excels at that, sir.

INT. LARS HOMESTEAD—PLAZA

Morning slowly creeps into the sparse but sparkling oasis of the open courtyard. The idyll is broken by the yelling of Uncle Owen, his voice echoing throughout the homestead.

OWEN: Luke? Luke? Luke?

INT. LARS HOMESTEAD—KITCHEN

The interior of the kitchen is a warm glow as Aunt Beru prepares the morning breakfast. Owen enters in a huff.

OWEN: Have you seen Luke this morning?

AUNT BERU: He said he had some things to do before he started today, so he left early.

OWEN: Uh? Did he take those two new droids with him?

AUNT BERU: I think so.

OWEN: Well, he better have those units in the south range repaired by midday or there'll be hell to pay!

INT./EXT. LUKE'S SPEEDER—DESERT WASTELAND—TRAVELING—DAY

The rock and sand of the desert floor are a blur as Threepio pilots the sleek landspeeder gracefully across the vast wasteland.

LUKE: Look, there's a droid on the scanner. Dead ahead. Might be our little R2 unit. Hit the accelerator.

Ralph McQuarrie: "George told me to make sure that everything in my sketches, especially all the different vehicles, should look like they had been used. My original drawings for the speeder were a lot more ornate, but a lot of the things were not incorporated in the actual vehicle you see in the film."

EXT. TATOOINE—ROCK MESA—DUNE SEA—COASTLINE—DAY

From high on a rock mesa, the tiny landspeeder can be seen gliding across the desert floor. Suddenly, in the foreground two weather-beaten Sand People shrouded in their grimy desert cloaks peer over the edge of the rock mesa. One of the marginally human creatures raises a long ominous laser rifle and points it at the speeder, but the second creature grabs the gun before it can be fired.

The Sand People, or Tusken Raiders, as they're sometimes called, speak in a coarse barbaric language as they get into an animated argument. The second Tusken Raider seems to get in the final word, and the nomads scurry over the rocky terrain.

EXT. TATOOINE—ROCK MESA—CANYON

The Tusken Raiders approach two large banthas standing tied to a rock. The monstrous, bearlike creatures are as large as elephants, with huge red eyes, tremendous looped horns, and long, furry, dinosaurlike tails. The Tusken Raiders mount saddles strapped to the huge creatures' shaggy backs and ride off down the rugged bluff.

The Sand People, or Tusken Raiders, first appeared in the third draft, and as in the film, Luke is attacked by one of them. The difference in this draft is that after he's been taken prisoner, Luke is left hanging ten feet in the air. Large gold bracelets with small antennas are attached to his wrists and ankles. He is spread-eagle and slowly rotating. Artoo tries to free him with a wire he gets from the speeder's engine compartment.

Ralph McQuarrie: "George described the Tusken Raiders to me as nomads in the desert, Bedouin type of people. I could have created some alien-type creatures, but I simply decided to give them this mask instead. I knew they were going to have to live in dust storms, and I decided that they were aliens that required an adaptive sort of breathing device to make their life on Tatooine possible."

EXT. TATOOINE—ROCK CANYON—FLOOR.
The speeder is parked on the floor of a massive canyon. Luke runs up to stand before little Artoo.
LUKE: Hey, whoa, just where do you think you're going?
The little droid whistles a feeble reply as Threepio poses menacingly behind the little runaway.
THREEPIO: Master Luke is your rightful owner now. We'll have no more of this Obi-Wan Kenobi gibberish . . . and don't talk to me of your mission, either. You're fortunate he doesn't blast you into a million pieces right here.
LUKE: No, it's all right, but I think we better go.
Suddenly the little robot jumps to life with a mass of frantic whistles and screams.
*LUKE: What's wrong with him now?
*THREEPIO: There are several creatures approaching from the southeast.
Luke looks to the south and fetches his long laser rifle from the landspeeder.
LUKE: Sand People! Or worse! Come on, let's go have a look. Come on.
EXT. TATOOINE—ROCK CANYON—RIDGE—DAY
Luke carefully makes his way to the top of a rock ridge and scans the canyon with his electrobinoculars.
He spots the two riderless banthas. Threepio struggles up behind the young adventurer.
LUKE: Well, there are two banthas down there, but I don't see any . . . wait a second, they're Sand People all right. I can see one of them now.
Luke watches the distant Tusken Raiders through his electrobinoculars. Suddenly something huge moves in front of his field of view. Before Luke or Threepio can react, a large gruesome Tusken Raider looms over them. Threepio is startled and backs away, right off the side of the cliff. He can be heard for several moments as he clangs, bangs, and rattles down the side of the mountain.
The towering creature brings down his curved, double-pointed gaderffii—the dreaded ax blade that has struck terror in the heart of the local settlers. But Luke manages to block the blow with his laser rifle, which is smashed to pieces. The ter-

rified farm boy scrambles backward until he is forced to the edge of a deep crevice. The sinister Raider stands over him with his weapon raised and lets out a horrible shrieking laugh.

EXT. TATOOINE—ROCK CANYON FLOOR—DAY

Artoo forces himself into the shadows of a small alcove in the rocks as the vicious Sand People walk past carrying the inert Luke Skywalker, who is dropped in a heap before the speeder. The Sand People ransack the speeder, throwing parts and supplies in all directions. Suddenly they stop. Then everything is quiet for a few moments. A great howling moan is heard echoing through the canyon which sends the Sand People fleeing in terror.

Artoo moves even tighter into the shadows as the slight swishing sound that frightened off the Sand People grows even closer, until a shabby old desert rat of a man appears and leans over Luke. His ancient leathery face, cracked and weathered by exotic climates, is set off by dark, penetrating eyes and a scraggly white beard. Ben Kenobi squints his eyes as he scrutinizes the unconscious farm boy. Artoo makes a slight sound, and Ben turns and looks right at him.

BEN: Hello there! Come here, my little friend. Don't be afraid.

Artoo begins to whistle and beep his concern about Luke. Luke begins to come around.

BEN: Oh, don't worry, he'll be all right. Rest easy, son, you've had a busy day. You're fortunate to be all in one piece.

LUKE: Ben? Ben Kenobi? Boy am I glad to see you!

BEN: The Jundland Wastes are not to be traveled lightly. Tell me, young Luke, what brings you out this far?

LUKE: Oh, this little droid! I think he's searching for his former master, but I've never seen such devotion in a droid before . . . Ah, he claims to be the property of an Obi-Wan Kenobi. Is he a relative of yours? Do you know who he's talking about?

Ben ponders this for a moment.

BEN: Obi-Wan Kenobi . . . Obi-Wan? Now that's a name I've not heard in a long time . . . a long time.

LUKE: I think my uncle knows him. He said he was dead . . .

BEN: Oh, he's not dead, or . . . not yet.

LUKE: You know him?

BEN: Well, of course I know him. He's me! I haven't gone by the name Obi-Wan since, oh, before you were born.

LUKE: Well, then, the droid does belong to you.

BEN: Don't seem to remember ever owning a droid. Very interesting . . .

He suddenly looks up at the overhanging cliffs.

BEN: I think we better get indoors. The Sand People are easily startled, but they will soon be back. And in greater numbers.

Luke gets up. Artoo lets out a pathetic beep, causing Luke to remember something. He looks around.

LUKE: . . . Threepio!

EXT. TATOOINE—SAND PIT—ROCK MESA—DAY

Luke and Ben stand over a very dented and tangled Threepio lying half-buried in the sand. One of his arms has broken off.

THREEPIO: Where am I? I must have taken a bad step . . .

LUKE: Well, can you stand? We've got to get out of here before the Sand People return.

THREEPIO: I don't think I can make it. You go on, Master Luke. There's no sense in you risking yourself on my account. I'm done for.

Artoo makes a beeping sound.

LUKE: No, you're not. What kind of talk is that?

BEN: Quickly . . . They're on the move.

Luke and Ben help the battered robot to his feet.

In the third draft Artoo is desperately trying to save Luke, who has been taken prisoner by the Tusken Raiders and is hanging in the air. Suddenly a "shabby old desert rat of a man who appears to be at least seventy years old" shows up; he has an ancient, leathery, cracked and weathered face, dark penetrating eyes, and a scraggly white beard.

In his early notes George Lucas described Ben as an eccentric but kindly old man trying to make a comeback. "He has the James Bond–like quality of always being in control; he is very sure of himself and always comes out ahead, regardless of the danger."

In the third draft the encounter between Ben and Luke is quite different from the way it is presented in all subsequent drafts and in the film and is somewhat reminiscent of the first interaction Luke and Yoda have in *The Empire Strikes Back*. Ben laughs when he sees Luke hanging in the air; he then takes out a laser pistol and frees the young man. Luke has no idea that Ben is the man he is looking for, and in order to maintain an air of credibility, he lies and says he is "Officer" Luke Starkiller. Finally Ben introduces himself as Ben Kenobi, former Commander of the White Legions. Luke is of course shocked; he apologizes and tells Ben that he knows his *Diary of the Clone Wars* by heart and that he is the son of Annikin Starkiller. In fact, Ben knew all along who Luke was. "You saw through me?" Luke asks, and Ben replies: "You could put it that way," giving a hint that he has unusual powers. One of Lucas's early concepts had Jedi warriors letting out a shrieking scream each time they attacked; all that survived of this idea is encapsulated in the great howling noise Ben makes to scare the Sand People.

George Lucas: "I wanted the father to be Darth Vader, but I also wanted a father figure. So I created Ben as the other half. You have one who is the light half and one who is the dark half . . . the positive and the negative. This sort of gave a twist to the whole story."

INT. KENOBI'S DWELLING

The small, spartan hovel is cluttered with desert junk but still manages to radiate an air of timeworn comfort and security. Luke is in one corner, repairing Threepio's arm, as old Ben sits thinking.

LUKE: No, my father didn't fight in the wars. He was a navigator on a spice freighter.

BEN: That's what your uncle told you. He didn't hold with your father's ideals. Thought he should have stayed here and not gotten involved.

LUKE: You fought in the Clone Wars?

BEN: Yes. I was once a Jedi Knight, the same as your father.

LUKE: I wish I'd known him.

BEN: He was the best starpilot in the galaxy and a cunning warrior. I understand you've become quite a good pilot yourself. And he was a good friend. Which reminds me . . .

Ben gets up and goes to a chest, where he rummages around as Luke finishes repairing Threepio.

BEN: I have something here for you. Your father wanted you to have this when you were old enough, but your uncle wouldn't allow it. He feared you might follow old Obi-Wan on some damned-fool idealistic crusade like your father did.

THREEPIO: Sir, if you'll not be needing me, I'll close down for a while.

LUKE: Sure, go ahead.

Ben shuffles up and presents Luke with a short handle with several electronic gadgets attached to it.

LUKE: What is it?

BEN: Your father's lightsaber. This is the weapon of a Jedi Knight. Not as clumsy or random as a blaster.

Luke pushes a button on the handle. A long beam shoots out about four feet and flickers there. The light plays across the ceiling.

BEN: An elegant weapon for a more civilized day. For over a thousand generations the Jedi Knights were the guardians of peace and justice in the Old Republic. Before the dark times, before the Empire.

In the early drafts the lasersword was a generic weapon, but eventually the sword became a unique weapon characteristic of a Jedi warrior.

George Lucas: "What I wanted to do was give the Jedi some kind of individuality. Their weapons, their way of thinking, what they did had to be different from everybody else. So I came up with the laser-sword and a lot of different powers."

Ralph McQuarrie: "George said it was a lasersword, and I know that when you project a laser beam, it doesn't just end after three feet, it continues to project out. But because it had to be used in fights, I gave it about the length of a medieval broadsword. I tried to make the laser beam as bright as possible, and I changed the colors for the various swords: a color for the good guys and a color for the bad guys. The lightsaber was just a cylinder thing that you could grip in your hands, a little longer than a cavalry saber and more like a two-handed sword."

Luke hasn't really been listening.
LUKE: How did my father die?
BEN: A young Jedi named Darth Vader, who was a pupil of mine until he turned to evil, helped the Empire hunt down and destroy the Jedi Knights. He betrayed and murdered your father. Now the Jedi are all but extinct. Vader was seduced by the dark side of the Force.
LUKE: The Force?
BEN: The Force is what gives the Jedi his power. It's an energy field created by all living things. It surrounds us and penetrates us. It binds the galaxy together.

The notion of the Force appeared in the rough draft when the king sends a delegation to deal with the New Galactic Empire and says, "May the force of others be with you," an obvious variation on the Christian phrase "May the Lord be with you and with your spirit." But the definition of the powers of the Force was developed in the second draft.

George Lucas: "I read a lot of books about mythology and theories behind mythology; one of the books was *The Hero with a Thousand Faces* by Joseph Campbell, but there were many others, maybe as many as fifty books. I basically worked out a general theory for the Force, and then I played with it. The more detail I went into, the more it detracted from the concept I was trying to put forward. I wanted to take all religions, major religions and primitive religions, and come up with something they might have in common. It worked better as I got less specific . . . So the real essence was to try to deal with the Force but not to be too specific about it."

In the second draft, after he has listened to the message from his brother Deak to find their father, Luke Starkiller visits his mother's grave. Before he leaves, he tells his twin brothers about their family history and heritage: Long before the Empire, a holy man called "the Skywalker" became aware of a powerful energy field that he believed influenced the destiny of all living creatures: the Force of Others. The Force has two halves: Ashla, the good, and Bogan, the paraforce of evil. He entrusted his secret to his twelve children, who passed on the knowledge to their children; they became known as "The Jedi Bendu of the Ashla." But as the Republic spread throughout the galaxy, the Great Senate became corrupt and the Jedi warriors tried to purge it. They were denounced as traitors and executed: The Empire was born. During one of his lessons a young "Padawan-Jedi" named Darklighter came to know the Bogan. He joined Sith pirates, and together they became the Emperor's bodyguards. They hunted the remaining Jedi warriors; with each death, the Bogan grew stronger. Luke tells his brothers that their father is one of the only Jedi survivors, and he must bring to him a small diamond called "the Kiber Crystal," the only thing that can intensify the Ashla, although in the hands of the "Sith" warriors it could intensify the Bogan as well.

George Lucas: "I felt the Kiber Crystal was a way of articulating what was going on, but I decided that I didn't need it. It was better to make the Force more ethereal than to have it solidified in a thing like the crystal.

"The idea of positive and negative, that there are two sides to an entity, a push and a pull, a yin and a yang, and the struggle between the two sides are issues of nature that I wanted to include in the film. Obviously, in terms of moral issues, you always have what's considered moral and what's considered immoral. At the same time, if you are dealing with possible influences beyond what we can see, it's traditionally been the good and the bad."

In the third draft Ben explains the Force to Luke: "It is an energy field in oneself, a power that controls one's acts yet obeys one's commands. It is nothing, yet it makes marvels appear before your very eyes. All living things generate this Force field . . ." Ben says that the Force can be collected and amplified through the use of a "Kiber Crystal." In this draft the crystal was stolen by the Sith Lords of Alderaan during the Battle of Condawn, the same battle that killed Luke's father, and they must recover it. As Ben is explaining the two sides of the Force, there is a brief sequence in the "Crystal Chamber" with Vader and two other Sith warriors. The bright light of the crystal suddenly fades, blinks, and then regains its natural brilliance. The three warriors feel the disturbance, and Vader says, "Something old has been awakened."

Artoo makes beeping sounds.
BEN: Now, let's see if we can't figure out what you are, my little friend. And where you come from.
LUKE: I saw part of the message he was . . .
Luke is cut short as the recorded image of the beautiful young Rebel princess is projected from Artoo's face.
BEN: I seem to have found it.
The lovely girl's image flickers.
LEIA: General Kenobi, years ago you served my father in the Clone Wars. Now he begs you to help him in his struggle against the Empire. I regret that I am unable to present my father's request to you in person, but my ship has fallen under attack, and I'm afraid my mission to bring you to Alderaan has failed. I have placed information vital to the survival of the Rebellion into the memory systems of this R2 unit. My father will know how to retrieve it. You must see this droid safely delivered to him on Alderaan. This is our most desperate hour. Help me, Obi-Wan Kenobi, you're my only hope.
There is a little static, and the transmission is cut short. Old Ben leans back and scratches his beard. Luke has stars in his eyes.

Paul Hirsch: "We called the scene 'Interior—Ben's Cave,' even though it didn't really look like a cave. In the original cut of the film Ben and Luke heard the whole message first, and then they talked about Luke's father and the sword. I looked at the scene, and I said,

'George, there's something wrong here; Leia's message basically says that the whole universe is about to blow out, and we have this long dialogue between Ben and Luke about something else right after it.' So I suggested that they have the talk first and then listen to the message, and we restructured the scene that way."

BEN: You must learn the ways of the Force if you're to come with me to Alderaan.

LUKE: Alderaan? *(laughing)* I'm not going to Alderaan. I've got to get home. It's late; I'm in for it as it is.

BEN: I need your help, Luke. She needs your help. I'm getting too old for this sort of thing.

LUKE: I can't get involved! I've got work to do! It's not that I like the Empire! I hate it! But there's nothing I can do about it right now. It's such a long way from here.

BEN: That's your uncle talking.

LUKE: *(sighing)* Oh, boy, my uncle. How am I ever going to explain this?

BEN: Learn about the Force, Luke.

LUKE: Look, I can take you as far as Anchorhead. You can get a transport there to Mos Eisley or wherever you're going.

BEN: You must do what you feel is right, of course.

EXT. SPACE

An Imperial Star Destroyer heads towards the evil planetlike battle station: the Death Star!

INT. DEATH STAR—CONFERENCE ROOM

Imperial senators and generals sit around a black conference table. Imperial stormtroopers stand guard around the room. Commander Tagge, a young, slimy-looking general, is speaking.

TAGGE: Until this battle station is fully operational we are vulnerable. The Rebel Alliance is too well equipped. They're more dangerous than you realize.

The bitter Admiral Motti replies.

MOTTI: Dangerous to your starfleet, Commander, not to this battle station!

TAGGE: The Rebellion will continue to gain a support in the Imperial Senate as long as . . .

Suddenly all heads turn as Commander Tagge's speech is cut short and the Grand Moff Tarkin, governor of the Imperial outland regions, enters. He is followed by his powerful ally, the Sith Lord, Darth Vader. The thin, evil-looking governor takes his place at the head of the table. The Dark Lord stands behind him.

TARKIN: The Imperial Senate will no longer be of any concern to us. I have just received word that the Emperor has dissolved the council permanently. The last remnants of the Old Republic have been swept away.

TAGGE: That's impossible. How will the Emperor maintain control without the bureaucracy?

TARKIN: The regional governors now have direct control over their territories. Fear will keep the local systems in line. Fear of this battle station.

TAGGE: And what of the Rebellion? If the Rebels have obtained a complete technical readout of this station, it is possible, however unlikely, that they might find a weakness and exploit it.

VADER: The plans you refer to will soon be back in our hands.

MOTTI: Any attack made by the Rebels against this station would be a useless gesture, no matter what technical data they've obtained. This station is now the ultimate power in the universe. I suggest we use it!

VADER: Don't be too proud of this technological terror you've constructed. The ability to destroy a planet is insignificant next to the power of the Force.

MOTTI: Don't try to frighten us with your sorcerer's ways, Lord Vader. Your sad devotion to that ancient religion has not helped you conjure up the stolen data tapes or given you clairvoyance enough to find the Rebels' hidden fort . . .

Suddenly Motti chokes and starts to turn blue under Vader's spell.

VADER: I find your lack of faith disturbing.

TARKIN: Enough of this! Vader, release him!

VADER: As you wish.

TARKIN: This bickering is pointless. Lord Vader will provide us with the location of the Rebel fortress by the time this station is operational. We will then crush the Rebellion with one swift stroke.

The scene in the conference room of the Death Star that introduces Grand Moff Tarkin, Commander Tagge, and Admiral Motti first appeared in the fourth draft. The exchange between Motti and Vader is different from the scene in the film; during the meeting, Vader stirs slightly and a metal cup mysteriously floats into his hands. Vader tries to strangle Motti without touching him, and after he releases him, he crumples the metal cup with the Force. In the rough and first drafts Tarkin was a priest who opposed General Skywalker when he tried to begin an offensive against the New Galactic Empire. In the second draft Tarkin was a commander with the Rebellion and appeared at the Massassi Outpost toward the end of the story.

EXT. TATOOINE—WASTELAND

Threepio, Artoo, Luke, and Ben walk among the scattered bodies and rubble of what remains of the huge Jawa sandcrawler.

LUKE: It looks like the Sand People did this, all right. Look, there's gaffi sticks, bantha tracks. It's just . . . I never heard of them hitting anything this big before.

BEN: They didn't. But we are meant to think they did. These tracks are side by side. Sand People always ride single file to hide their numbers.

LUKE: These are the same Jawas that sold us Artoo and Threepio.

BEN: And these blast points, too accurate for Sand People. Only Imperial stormtroopers are so precise.

LUKE: But why would Imperial troops want to slaughter Jawas?

Luke looks back at the speeder where Artoo and Threepio are inspecting the dead Jawas and puts two and two together.

LUKE: If they traced the robots here, they may have learned who they sold them to, and that would lead them back home!

BEN: Wait, Luke! It's too dangerous!

Luke races off, leaving Ben and the two robots alone with the burning sandcrawler.

EXT. TATOOINE—WASTELAND

Luke races across the flat landscape in his battered landspeeder.

EXT. TATOOINE—LARS HOMESTEAD

The speeder roars up the homestead.

Luke jumps out and runs to the smoking holes that were once his home. Debris is scattered everywhere, and it looks as if a great battle has taken place.

LUKE: Uncle Owen! Aunt Beru! Uncle Owen!

Luke stumbles around in a daze looking for his aunt and uncle. Suddenly he comes upon their smoldering remains. He is stunned and cannot speak. Hate replaces fear, and a new resolve comes over him.

EXT. SPACE

Imperial TIE fighters race toward the Death Star.

INT. DEATH STAR—DETENTION CORRIDOR

Two stormtroopers open an electronic cell door and allow Darth Vader to enter. Princess Leia's face is filled with defiance.

VADER: And now, Your Highness, we will discuss the location of your hidden Rebel base.

A black torture robot enters, giving off a steady beeping sound as it approaches Princess Leia and extends one of its mechanical arms bearing a large hypodermic needle. The door slides shut.

In the rough draft Vader tortures Princess Leia with powerful electroshocks. In the third draft Vader steps into the cell, and the door slams shut; "her screams can barely be heard." The giant black torture robot first appeared in the fourth draft.

Ralph McQuarrie: "I was working with a friend on an idea we had for an animated film, and we had this black sphere floating around through these hallways with this scanner going around it. And I thought, This might make a pretty good idea for the torture robot."

EXT. TATOOINE—WASTELAND

There is a large bonfire of Jawa bodies blazing in front of the sandcrawler as Ben and the robots finish burning the dead. Luke drives up in the speeder and walks over to Ben.

BEN: There's nothing you could have done, Luke, had you been there. You'd have been killed, too, and the droids would now be in the hands of the Empire.

LUKE: I want to come with you to Alderaan. There's nothing for me here now. I want to learn the ways of the Force and become a Jedi like my father.

EXT. TATOOINE—WASTELAND

The landspeeder with Luke, Artoo, Threepio, and Ben in it zooms across the desert. The speeder stops on a bluff overlooking the spaceport at Mos Eisley. It is a haphazard array of low, gray concrete structures and semidomes. A harsh gale blows across the stark canyon floor. The four stand on the edge of the craggy bluff.

BEN: Mos Eisley spaceport. You will never find a more wretched hive of scum and villainy. We must be cautious.

From the Special Edition:

EXT. TATOOINE—MOS EISLEY— APPROACH TO SPACEPORT

The landspeeder zooms into the spaceport of Mos Eisley, scattering small scurriers, who jump to get out of the way.

EXT. TATOOINE—MOS EISLEY— MAIN STREET

The landspeeder heads toward the cantina, passing domed structures, circular landing bays, and an Asp droid who gets into an argument with a passing probe droid.

EXT. TATOOINE—MOS EISLEY— STREET

Two Jawas ride a large ronto, an unusual beast of burden, who rears up as a speeder bike veers in front of it, tossing one Jawa off its back onto the ground as the second Jawa swings forward under the ronto's head, holding on to the reins.

The entrance to Mos Eisley has gone through a major transformation for the special edition of *Star Wars*. Because of time and budget restrictions, George Lucas could never show Mos Eisley as he had really imagined it. Now, with new technologies, he was able to realize his vision.

Rick McCallum: "We added some more buildings; we added more of a sense that it's a real community where pilots come and go. Now it's a real trader port. It needed to have size; it needed to have a little bit more menace. When the stormtroopers are interrogating Luke, you'll also notice a little gizmo flying about; that's a probe droid. It works for the stormtroopers; it goes out and scouts locations and goes around corners. There's another shot of it when Artoo and Threepio are hiding. As the stormtrooper tells Luke to drive on, there's a ronto behind them and another one walks in front of the speeder; we wanted to give a feeling that they were all over the place. You know, they're like big camels that take people and goods around from one part of the city to the other. They're like transport vehicles. Also, thanks to computer graphic animation, the dewback outside the cantina is now moving."

EXT. TATOOINE—MOS EISLEY—STREET

The speeder is stopped on a crowded street by several combat-hardened stormtroopers, who look over the two robots. An Imperial trooper questions Luke.

From the Special Edition:
Luke pilots his landspeeder carrying Ben and the two droids into the center of the spaceport, past a large crashed vehicle, winding his way among various rontos taking up much of the street. A starship, the Outrider, takes off overhead.

TROOPER: How long have you had these droids?

LUKE: About three or four seasons.

BEN: They're up for sale if you want them.

TROOPER: Let me see your identification.

Ben speaks to the trooper in a very controlled voice.

BEN: You don't need to see his identification.

TROOPER: We don't need to see his identification.

BEN: These aren't the droids you're looking for.

TROOPER: These aren't the droids we're looking for.

BEN: He can go about his business.

TROOPER: You can go about your business.

BEN: *(to Luke)* Move along.

TROOPER: Move along. Move along.

EXT. TATOOINE—MOS EISLEY—STREET

THREEPIO: I can't abide those Jawas. Disgusting creatures.

The speeder pulls up in front of a run-down blockhouse cantina on the outskirts of the spaceport. A Jawa runs up and begins to fondle the speeder. As Luke gets out of the speeder, he tries to shoo the Jawa away.

LUKE: Go on, go on. I can't understand how we got by those troops. I thought we were dead.

BEN: The Force can have a strong influence on the weak-minded.

LUKE: Do you really think we're going to find a pilot here that'll take us to Alderaan?

BEN: Well, most of the best freighter pilots can be found here. Only watch your step. This place can be a little rough.

LUKE: I'm ready for anything.

THREEPIO: Come along, Artoo.

INT. TATOOINE—MOS EISLEY—CANTINA

The young adventurer and his two mechanical servants follow Ben Kenobi into the smoke-filled cantina. The murky, moldy den is filled with a startling array of weird and exotic alien creatures and monsters at the long metallic bar. At first the sight is horrifying. One-eyed, thousand-eyed, slimy, furry, scaly, tentacled, and clawed creatures huddle over drinks. Ben moves to an empty spot at the bar. A huge, rough-looking bartender calls out to Luke and points at the robots.

BARTENDER: Hey, we don't serve their kind here!

Luke, still recovering from the shock of seeing so many outlandish creatures, doesn't quite catch the bartender's drift.

LUKE: What?

BARTENDER: Your droids. They'll have to wait outside. We don't want them here.

LUKE: Listen, why don't you wait out by the speeder. We don't want any trouble.

Luke pats Threepio on the shoulder.

THREEPIO: I heartily agree with you, sir.

Threepio and his stubby partner go outside, and most of the creatures at the bar go back to their drinks.

Luke is terrified but tries not to show it. He quietly sips his drink, looking over the crowd for a more sympathetic ear or whatever.

Ben is standing next to Chewbacca, an eight-foot-tall savage-looking creature resembling a huge gray bushbaby monkey with fierce baboonlike fangs. His large blue eyes dominate a fur-covered face and soften his otherwise awesome appearance. Over his matted, furred body he wears two chrome bandoliers and little else. He is a two-hundred-year-old Wookiee and a sight to behold.

Chewbacca wasn't always introduced in the cantina. In fact, he made his first appearance in the rough draft on Yavin, then a Wookiee (spelled Wookee) planet, and in the first draft Wookiees were actually known as Jawas. In the second draft and in the film Chewbacca is introduced in the cantina. His description is a bit different from the way he ended up looking in the film; here, in addition to the two chrome bandoliers, the two-hundred-year-old Chewbacca "wears a flak jacket painted in a bizarre camouflage pattern, brown cloth shorts, and little else."

George Lucas: "My dog Indiana used to ride on the front seat of my car. He was a big dog, and when he sat there, he was bigger than a person, so I had this image in my mind of this huge furry animal riding with me. That's where the inspiration for Chewbacca came from."

Ralph McQuarrie: "George thought of him as looking like a lemur with fur over his whole body and a big huge apelike figure. I took another track, added an ammunition bandolier, and put a rifle in his hands. I had shorts on him and a flak jacket and all kinds of gear, but that was edited out. Actually, the man who made the costume had done the apes for Kubrick's *2001* and I think he based Chewbacca on the apes he had designed for that movie. In my drawings he had more of a longer jaw; he looked more like a wolf."

A large-eyed creature gives Luke a rough shove.

CREATURE: Negola dewaghi wooldugger?!?

The hideous freak is obviously drunk. Luke tries to ignore the creature and turns back to his drink. A disfigured belligerent monstrosity.

HUMAN: He doesn't like you.

LUKE: I'm sorry.

The big creature is getting agitated and yells some unintelligible gibberish at the now rather nervous young adventurer.

HUMAN: I don't like you either.

HUMAN: *(continuing)* You just watch yourself. We're wanted men. I have the death sentence on twelve systems.

LUKE: I'll be careful.

HUMAN: You'll be dead.

Old Ben moves in behind Luke.

BEN: This little one's not worth the effort. Come, let me get you something.

A powerful throw from the unpleasant human sends the young would-be Jedi sailing across the room, crashing through tables. With a bloodcurdling shriek the human draws a wicked chrome laser pistol from his belt and levels it at old Ben. The bartender panics.

BARTENDER: No blasters! No blasters!

With astounding agility old Ben's lasersword sparks to life, and in a flash an arm lies on the floor. Ben carefully and precisely turns off his lasersword. Luke is totally amazed at the old man's abilities. The entire fight has lasted only a matter of seconds. The cantina goes back to normal as Ben helps Luke to his feet.

LUKE: I'm all right.

Ben nods to the Wookiee.

BEN: Chewbacca here is first mate on a ship that might suit us.

In the treatment General Skywalker hooks up with a Rebel band of ten teenage boys. With one of the bureaucrats and one of the boys, Skywalker goes to a shabby cantina, looking for a Rebel contact who will help them get a spaceship. The place is filled with aliens, and the boy is ridiculed by a group of bullies. Skywalker pulls out his lasersword, and suddenly an arm is on the floor while one of the bullies lies doubled over, slashed from chin to groin. In the rough draft General Skywalker goes to the cantina with Clieg Whitsun (Clieg Oxus in the first draft); Whitsun is actually introduced early in the story as a spy who finds out that the Empire is planning an attack and warns Skywalker. In the cantina Skywalker and Whitsun look for their friend Han Solo. Skywalker has an altercation with two aliens (one is a large multiple-eyed monster, and the other is a small rodentlike creature) and a grubby-looking human; in the blink of an eye he pulls out his lasersword and slices up the two aliens. Later, in the third draft and as in the film, Ben does the fighting to defend Luke, establishing the fact that Ben is indeed more powerful than he seems.

Paul Hirsch: "Well, the cantina scene was hopeless. The original shoot of that was giant mice and things that looked like Peter Rabbit. It didn't look at all like what it became. Then one day I remember George brought drawings of creatures to the editing room, and he asked us which ones we liked. We made a selection, and next thing I knew, all the creatures had been built. George had a two- or three-day shoot in LA on a soundstage where he had built these alcoves and filmed the creatures."

EXT. TATOOINE—MOS EISLEY—STREET
Threepio paces in front of the cantina as Artoo carries on an electronic conversation with another little red astrodroid. Someone last seen in the cantina approaches two stormtroopers in the street.
THREEPIO: I don't like the look of this.
INT. TATOOINE—MOS EISLEY—CANTINA
Strange creatures play exotic big band music on odd-looking instruments. Luke has followed Ben and Chewbacca to a booth, where they are joined by Han Solo. Han is a tough, roguish starpilot about thirty years old. A mercenary on a starship, he is simple, sentimental, and cocksure.

HAN: Han Solo. I'm captain of the *Millennium Falcon*. Chewie here tells me you're looking for passage to the Alderaan system.

BEN: Yes, indeed. If it's a fast ship.

HAN: Fast ship? You've never heard of the *Millennium Falcon*?

BEN: Should I have?

HAN: It's the ship that made the Kessel run in less than twelve parsecs!

Ben reacts to Solo's stupid attempt to impress them with obvious misinformation.

HAN: *(continuing)* I've outrun Imperial starships, not the local bulk cruisers, mind you. I'm talking about the big Corellian ships now. She's fast enough for you, old man. What's the cargo?

BEN: Only passengers. Myself, the boy, two droids, and no questions asked.

HAN: What is it? Some kind of local trouble?

BEN: Let's just say we'd like to avoid any Imperial entanglements.

HAN: Well, that's the real trick, isn't it? And it's going to cost you something extra. Ten thousand, all in advance.

LUKE: Ten thousand? We could almost buy our own ship for that!

HAN: But who's going to fly it, kid? You?

LUKE: You bet I could. I'm not such a bad pilot myself! We don't have to sit here and listen . . .

BEN: We can pay you two thousand now, plus fifteen when we reach Alderaan.

HAN: Seventeen, huh!

Han ponders this for a few moments.

HAN: Okay. You guys got yourselves a ship. We'll leave as soon as you're ready. Docking Bay Ninety-four.

BEN: Ninety-four.

HAN: Looks like somebody's beginning to take an interest in your handiwork.

Ben and Luke turn around to see four Imperial stormtroopers looking at the dead bodies and asking the bartender some questions. The bartender points to the booth.

TROOPER: All right, we'll check it out.

The stormtroopers look over at the booth, but Luke and Ben are gone.

HAN: Seventeen thousand! Those guys must really be desperate. This could really save my neck. Get back to the ship and get her ready.

George Lucas: "The idea was that Han Solo was an orphan. He was raised by Wookiees, befriended Chewbacca, and they went off."

Han Solo appeared originally in the rough and first drafts as a "huge green-skinned monster with no nose and large gills." In the early version of the story Solo is a Jedi warrior and an old friend of General Skywalker. He's been hiding and protecting Kane Star-killer, Annikin's father. Solo takes Skywalker to meet three underground leaders named Datos, Occo, and Quist, who have arranged for the group to travel undercover aboard a "Baltarian freighter." It's interesting to note that in the first and rough drafts the personality of Annikin is close to what Han Solo would become in later drafts, especially in his behavior with Leia and in the development of their love-hate relationship. In the second draft Han Solo is a young Corellian pirate only a few years older than Luke. He is burly, bearded, ruggedly handsome, and dressed in gaudy, flamboyant apparel. George Lucas's notes describe Solo as a pirate and thug with a heart of gold; he is amoral and a lady-killer, and his goal is to buy a new ship. In this draft Han takes Luke to his home, a seedy slum dwelling where he lives with a female "Boma" named Oeeta, who is described as a fur-covered creature about five feet high, a "cross between a brown bear and a guinea pig" who speaks in a strange baboonlike call. In the third draft we're introduced to Han Solo in the docking area. This time he is described as a tough James Dean–style starpilot, about twenty-five, who is simple, sentimental, and sure of himself. A very interesting change occurred in the hand-written version of the fourth draft, in which Solo's character is called "Jabba the Hutt." But then Lucas reverted to the name "Solo."

The revised fourth draft introduces Solo in the cantina in the arms of a lovely young alien girl, and for the first time we hear the name of his ship, "the *Millennium Falcon*."

George Lucas: "I was looking for a 'foil' for Luke. Luke is the young, idealistic, naive, clean kid about to be initiated into the rites of man-hood. So to make that really work, I needed something to contrast him against. Obviously, Ben is the wise teacher; he is really good and conservative, but there was no fun in that. Just like I had Vader to contrast with Ben, I created Solo as a cynical world-weary pessimist to play opposite Luke. I tried to establish this kind of contrast with all the characters, even with the robots. You always try to set up a char-acter, and then you create an opposite, another character who has a different point of view on everything so that they can argue. If you have two guys that are the same, talk the same, think the same, and feel the same, then there is nothing for them to talk about, ever."

Ralph McQuarrie: "In my early sketches I had Solo looking very dapper. He had a lasersword and some sort of Flash Gordon headpiece that went over his forehead. But George wanted him to be simpler, and he told me to just give him a vest, a shirt, trousers, and boots."

EXT. TATOOINE—MOS EISLEY—STREET

BEN: You'll have to sell your speeder.

LUKE: That's okay. I'm never coming back to this planet again.

INT. MOS EISLEY—CANTINA

As Han is about to leave, Greedo, a slimy green-faced alien with a short trunk nose, pokes a gun in his chest. The creature speaks in a foreign tongue translated into English subtitles.

GREEDO: Going somewhere, Solo?

HAN: Yes, Greedo. As a matter of fact, I was just going to see your boss. Tell Jabba that I've got his money.

Han sits down, and the alien sits across from him, holding the gun on him.

GREEDO: It's too late. You should have paid him when you had the chance. Jabba's put a price on your head so large, every bounty hunter in the galaxy will be looking for you. I'm lucky I found you first.

HAN: Yeah, but this time I've got the money.

GREEDO: If you give it to me, I might forget I found you.

HAN: I don't have it with me. Tell Jabba . . .

GREEDO: Jabba's through with you. He has no time for smugglers who drop their shipments at the first sign of an Imperial cruiser.

HAN: Even I get boarded sometimes. Do you think I had a choice?

Han Solo reaches for his gun under the table.

GREEDO: You can tell that to Jabba. He may only take your ship.

HAN: Over my dead body.

GREEDO: That's the idea. I've been looking forward to this for a long time.

HAN: Yes, I'll bet you have.

Han had his encounter with Greedo for the first time in the revised fourth draft. In the script Greedo speaks English with an electronically translated voice, but for the movie George Lucas decided that he should speak a foreign language.

George Lucas: "Someone said to me, 'Why don't you have the creatures just speak English?' Well, it is the same thing in World War II films where you have Germans speaking English; it would be much better if they spoke their native tongue. And I didn't want to assume that everyone in the universe spoke the same language. I wanted to give that exotic feel to things, but I didn't want to have someone translating all the time. And the studio said to me, 'What about children who can't read the subtitles?' I said, 'It will encourage them to learn how to read or it will bond them with their parents as they are reading the subtitles to them.'"

Paul Hirsch: "Ben Burtt came up with the language for Greedo. But one of the words he had was actually Spanish slang. He didn't know, and so he changed the word. Actually, all the words had to be checked to make sure they were okay."

Suddenly, the slimy alien disappears in a blinding flash of light. Han pulls his smoking gun from beneath the table as the other patrons look on in bemused amazement. Han gets up and starts out of the cantina, flipping the bartender some coins as he leaves.

From the Special Edition:
Suddenly the slimy alien fires his blaster at Han, hitting the wall just to the right of Han's head. In a blinding flash of light and smoke Greedo disappears as Han pulls his gun from beneath the table while the other patrons look on in bemused amazement. Han gets up and starts out of the cantina, flipping the bartender some coins as he leaves.

HAN: Sorry about the mess.
EXT. SPACE
Two TIE fighters approach the Death Star.
INT. DEATH STAR—CONTROL ROOM
VADER: Her resistance to the mind probe is considerable. It will be some time before we can extract any information from her.
An Imperial Officer interrupts the meeting.
IMPERIAL OFFICER: The final checkout is completed. All systems are operational. What course shall we set?
TARKIN: Perhaps she would respond to an alternative form of persuasion.
VADER: What do you mean?
TARKIN: I think it is time we demonstrated the full power of this station. *(to soldier)* Set your course for Alderaan.
IMPERIAL OFFICER: With pleasure.

EXT. TATOOINE—MOS EISLEY—STREET

Threepio is standing in a doorway.

THREEPIO: Lock the door, Artoo.

Heavily armed stormtroopers move menacingly along a narrow slum alleyway.

TROOPER: All right, check this side of the street. *[One of the troopers checks a tightly locked door.]* The door's locked? Move on to the next one.

The door opens. Threepio moves into the doorway.

THREEPIO: I would much rather have gone with Master Luke than stay here with you. I don't know what all this trouble is about, but I'm sure it must be your fault.

Artoo makes beeping sounds.

THREEPIO: You watch your language!

EXT. TATOOINE—MOS EISLEY—STREET—ALLEYWAY—USED SPEEDER LOT

Ben and Luke are standing in a sleazy used speeder lot, talking with a tall, grotesque insectlike used speeder dealer. Strange exotic bodies and spindly-legged beasts pass by as the insect concludes the sale by giving Luke some coins.

LUKE: All right, give it to me, I'll take it. Look at this. Ever since the XP-Thirty-eight came out, they just aren't in demand.

BEN: It will be enough.

Ben and Luke leave the speeder lot and walk down the dusty alleyway. A darkly clad creature moves out of the shadows as they pass and watches them as they disappear down another alley.

From the Special Edition:

INT. DOCKING BAY 94—DAY

Jabba the Hutt and various grisly alien pirates stand in the middle of the docking bay. Jabba is the grossest of the slavering hulks, and his scarred face is a grim testimonial to his prowess as a vicious killer. He is a fat sluglike creature with yellow eyes and a huge ugly mouth.

JABBA: Solo, come out of there, Solo!

A voice from directly behind the pirates startles them, and they turn around to see Han Solo and the giant Wookiee, Chewbacca, standing behind them with no weapons in sight.

HAN: Right here, Jabba. I've been waiting for you.

JABBA: Have you now?

HAN: You didn't think I was gonna run, did you?

Han leaves Chewbacca's side and walks toward Jabba as Jabba's sluglike body oozes forward.

JABBA: Han, my boy, you disappoint me. Why haven't you paid me . . . Why did you fry poor Greedo?

HAN: Look, Jabba, next time you want to talk to me, come see me yourself. Don't send one of these twerps.

Jabba puts his arm around Han, and the two walk together.

JABBA: Han, I can't make exceptions. What if everyone who smuggled for me dropped their cargo at the first sign of an Imperial starship? It's not good for business.

HAN: Look, Jabba. Even I get boarded sometimes.

Han walks around behind Jabba, stepping on his tail—which causes Jabba's eyes to bug out momentarily.

HAN: You think I had a choice? I got a nice easy charter now. Pay you back plus a little extra. I just need a little more time.

JABBA: Han, my boy, you're the best. So, for an extra twenty percent . . .

HAN: Fifteen, Jabba. Don't push it.

JABBA: Okay, fifteen percent. But if you fail me again, I'll put a price on your head so big, you won't be able to go near a civilized system.

Han turns and walks away from Jabba toward the Falcon's boarding ramp. He stops for a moment at the foot of the ramp and turns back toward Jabba.

HAN: Jabba, you're a wonderful human being.

As Chewbacca follows Han up the boarding ramp, Boba Fett walks into view, casing the area. Jabba yells out as he and his thugs depart.

JABBA: Come on!

When George Lucas directed *Star Wars*, there was a scene with Han Solo and Jabba, only Jabba was played by a human standing in for a specialty creature. The scene was ultimately cut, and with the new version of *Star Wars*, Lucas finally got a chance to restore it and to recreate Jabba. In order to incorporate this new computer image of Jabba (which was animated by Steve Williams) within the old footage, Han Solo had to be matted around the digital creature. For the bit where Han steps over Jabba's tail, his image had to be moved up step by step, since in the original footage he just walked around the actor playing Jabba.

What makes this shot even more compelling is Jabba's subtle reaction as Han steps on his tail. Boba Fett was also added in this sequence as a way to tie him into the whole story. An ILM employee was filmed in the Boba Fett costume, and his image was then added into the shot. The other aliens present in the scene, which include another creature of the same race as Greedo, were already in the original footage. Jabba's dialogue is in Huttese.

George Lucas: "Even when I first shot the scene with an actor, I had planned to replace him later with some kind of stop motion animated character. I imagined Jabba would be furry, but we just never had the time or the money to do that shot, and I had to eliminate the scene. But I always wanted it in there."

EXT. DOCKING PORT ENTRY—ALLEYWAY
Luke, Ben, and the droids continue down the alleyway toward the docking bay entrance, where Chewbacca waits restlessly.
BEN: If the ship's as fast as he's boasting, we ought to do well.
EXT. DOCKING PORT ENTRY—ALLEYWAY
Chewbacca waits restlessly at the entrance to Docking Bay 94. Ben, Luke, and the robots make their way up the street. The darkly clad creature has followed them from the speeder lot. He stops in a nearby doorway and speaks into a small transmitter.
INT. MOS EISLEY SPACEPORT—DOCKING BAY 94
Chewbacca leads the group into the giant dirt pit that is Docking Bay 94. Resting in the middle of the huge hole is a large, round, beat-up, pieced-together hunk of junk that could only loosely be called a starship.
LUKE: What a piece of junk.
The tall figure of Han Solo comes down the boarding ramp.
HAN: She'll make point five past lightspeed. She may not look like much, but she's got it where it counts, kid. I've made a lot of special modifications myself. But we're a little rushed, so if you'll just get on board, we'll get out of here.

Joe Johnston: "The *Millennium Falcon* was originally the Rebel blockade vessel you see in the opening scene. The long ship with the engine in the back was the *Falcon*. The model had been designed based on one of Ralph McQuarrie's designs, and George had signed off on it. Then, during production, this show came out on TV called *Space 1999*, and one of the ships they had was similar to the *Falcon*. It was a long ship with a pointed front end and a bunch of rockets in the back; in a way, it was your basic spaceship design: long and thin, cockpit in the front, engine in the back, cargo in the middle. And the two designs looked similar enough that George said, 'We don't want to look like we're copying anybody, so let's change the design.'

The truth is, we designed our ship first, but the TV show got into production before we did. At this point we had something like four weeks to design and build a new *Millennium Falcon*. We did two things: We took the old *Falcon*, and we changed the cockpit and put in that sort of hammerhead cockpit, and what was the

Falcon became the Blockade Runner. Then we started from scratch on Solo's ship, and the only input I remember from George was, 'Think of a flying saucer.' I didn't want a basic flying saucer, so I added the cockpit off to the side and these weird freight-loading arms at the front, and instead of a series of round engines in the back, we just made one big opening slot. It was the kind of design that was simple enough that it could be built and engineered in about four weeks. I had painted the first *Falcon*, so I painted this one as well. The new *Falcon* was probably one of the most intense projects we had."

INT. *MILLENNIUM FALCON*
Chewbacca settles into the pilot's chair and starts the mighty engines of the starship.
INT. MOS EISLEY SPACEPORT—DOCKING BAY 94
Luke, Ben, Threepio, and Artoo move toward the Millennium Falcon, *passing Solo.*
THREEPIO: Hello, sir.
EXT. TATOOINE—MOS EISLEY—STREET
Seven Imperial stormtroopers rush up to the darkly clad creature.
TROOPER: Which way?
The darkly clad creature points to the door of the docking bay.
TROOPER: All right, men. Load your weapons!
INT. MOS EISLEY SPACEPORT—DOCKING BAY 94
The troops hold their guns at the ready and charge down the docking bay entrance.
TROOPER: Stop that ship!
Han Solo looks up and sees the Imperial stormtroopers rushing into the docking bay. Several of the troopers fire at Han as he ducks into the spaceship.
TROOPER: Blast 'em!
Han draws his laser pistol and pops off a couple of shots which force the stormtroopers to dive for safety. The pirate ship's engines whine as Han hits the release button that slams the overhead entry shut.
INT. *MILLENNIUM FALCON*
HAN: Chewie, get us out of here!
The group straps in for takeoff.
THREEPIO: Oh, my, I'd forgotten how much I hate space travel.

From the Special Edition:
INT. MOS EISLEY SPACEPORT—DOCKING BAY 94
The Falcon *lifts off out of the docking bay and into the sky.*

In the treatment Skywalker, the princess, and their party (which includes the Rebel band of boys and the two bureaucrats) make contact with the Rebel underground, but they've been followed by an Imperial spy who reports them to the city governor. The Rebels are about to board "the trader ship of a captain friendly to their cause," only to realize that they've fallen into a trap. They escape on a stolen spaceship and lose themselves among the Imperial fleet, but they blow their cover when they refuse to let a patrol come aboard. The group is attacked, and Skywalker manages to hide on an asteroid. The ship has been damaged, and they have to abandon it; they land on the forbidden planet of Yavin, using "rocket packs" (which later became known as "lifepods"). In the rough and first drafts Solo (who in those two scripts is an alien) has arranged for the group to travel undercover as the crew of a "Baltarian Freighter." But there is a problem: They're missing a "powerpack" for one of the princess's brothers. Kane Starkiller, whose entire body except for his head and right arm is made of electronics, sacrifices himself by pulling a miniature power unit from his body. But General Skywalker and Solo are arrested by Prince Valorum, Black Knight of Sith (Dodonna in the first draft). On their way to jail they manage to free themselves and retreat back aboard the starship with Annikin, the princess, her brothers, the robots, and Whitsun, General Skywalker's right-hand man. In space, they're attacked by starfighters and Justin's gunport is hit; he hangs in space until R2-D2 succeeds in pulling him back into the ship. They reach an asteroid field and escape in lifepods, except for Whitsun, who dies in the explosion of the spaceship. The survivors land on a Wookiee planet in the forbidden system of Yavin.

In the second draft, while Luke is trying to sell his speeder, Han tries to enroll his friend Montross Holdaak (who, like Kane Starkiller in the rough and first drafts, is part man, part machine). In the main lounge of the docking bay a pirate named Jabba the Hutt, described as a large hulk, is playing dice with Chewbacca. Han's boss is Captain Oxus, "a man of the grossest dimensions with a scarred face." In order to steal one of the pirate spaceships (described as "a long complex spacecraft"), Han and Montross set off an alarm and rig the ship to appear as though it were going to explode. Chewbacca receives a message on his belt comlink and signals to Luke and the two robots to come in. Oxus and Jabba stand dumbfounded as Han Solo takes off in the stolen ship. In the third draft we meet Han at the docking area; his ship is described as "a long Rube Goldberg pieced-together contraption." After Ben and Luke make a deal with Solo, they go off to try to sell the landspeeder to an insectlike dealer, with Threepio acting as their translator. Meanwhile, Han is surrounded by "a gross slavering hulk" named Jabba the Hutt and a dozen of his fellow pirates; Jabba wants Solo to reroute a shipment for him. As in the previous draft, Solo rigs something on the ship, and it erupts into a cacophony of alarms and flashing lights. Eventually Ben, Luke, the droids, Chewbacca, and Han take off, leaving Jabba and his pirates furious.

This whole sequence went through yet another permutation in the fourth draft: While Ben and Luke are selling the landspeeder, Han is confronted by Montross, an Imperial bureaucrat, and two local policemen. Vader has ordered that no ship leave Mos Eisley, and Montross, who doesn't trust Solo, has decided to stay aboard Han's ship until the spaceport reopens. As was done previously, Solo creates a diversion and forces Montross off the ship as Chewbacca brings in Luke, Ben, and the droids. Troopers arrive just as the pirate ship takes off. In this draft, for the first time Han calls the Wookiee "Chewie." In the revised fourth draft Jabba the Hutt shows up with a half dozen grisly pirates and purple aliens. Jabba is "the grossest of the slavering hulks, and his scarred face is a grim testimonial to his prowess as a vicious killer." Solo dumped a shipment when he was boarded by an Imperial starship, and Jabba has come to collect his money. Han promises to pay him back soon, although he realizes that if he makes one more mistake, there will be a price on his head throughout the galaxy. The notion of the ship jumping to hyperspace appeared for the first time in the fourth draft.

EXT. TATOOINE—MOS EISLEY—STREETS
The half dozen stormtroopers at a checkpoint hear the general alarm and look to the sky as the huge starship rises above the dingy slum dwellings and quickly disappears into the morning sky.

INT. *MILLENNIUM FALCON*

Han sits in the pilot's chair, typing information into the ship's computer.

EXT. SPACE—PLANET TATOOINE

The starship climbs away from the planet.

INT. *MILLENNIUM FALCON*—CABIN

Chewbacca points out something on the radar scope.

HAN: Looks like an Imperial cruiser. Our passengers must be hotter than I thought. Try and hold them off. Angle the deflector shield while I make the calculations for the jump to lightspeed.

EXT. SPACE—PLANET TATOOINE

The Millennium Falcon pirate ship races away from the yellow planet. It is followed by two huge Imperial Star Destroyers.

INT. *MILLENNIUM FALCON*—COCKPIT

Over the shoulders of Chewbacca and Han, we can see the galaxy spread before them. Luke and Ben make their way into the cramped cockpit, where Han continues his calculation.

HAN: Stay sharp! There are two more coming in; they're going to try to cut us off.

LUKE: Why don't you outrun them? I thought you said this thing was fast.

HAN: Watch your mouth, kid, or you're going to find yourself floating home. We'll be safe enough once we make the jump to hyperspace. Besides, I know a few maneuvers. We'll lose them!

EXT. SPACE—PLANET TATOOINE

Imperial cruisers fire at the pirate ship.

INT. *MILLENNIUM FALCON*—COCKPIT

The ship shudders as an explosion flashes outside the window.

HAN: Here's where the fun begins!

BEN: How long before you can make the jump to lightspeed?

HAN: It'll take a few moments to get the coordinates from the nav computer.

The ship begins to rock violently as lasers hit it.

LUKE: Are you kidding? At the rate they're gaining . . .

HAN: Traveling through hyperspace isn't like dusting crops, boy! Without precise calculations we could fly right through a star or bounce too close to a supernova and that'd end your trip real quick, wouldn't it?

The ship is now constantly battered with laserfire as a red warning light begins to flash.

LUKE: What's that flashing?

HAN: We're losing our deflector shield. Go strap yourselves in. I'm going to make the jump to lightspeed.

The galaxy brightens, and they move faster, almost as if crashing a barrier. Stars become streaks as the pirate ship makes the jump to hyperspace.

EXT. SPACE

The Millennium Falcon zooms into infinity in less than a second.

EXT. DEATH STAR

Alderaan looms behind the Death Star battle station.

INT. DEATH STAR—CONTROL ROOM—CORRIDOR

Governor Tarkin stands before the huge wall screen displaying a small green planet.

  Vader and two stormtroopers march Princess Leia toward the control room.
  Admiral Motti reports to Governor Tarkin.

MOTTI: We've entered the Alderaan system.

Vader and two stormtroopers enter with Princess Leia. Her hands are bound.

LEIA: Governor Tarkin. I should have expected to find you holding Vader's leash. I recognized your foul stench when I was brought on board.

TARKIN: Charming to the last. You don't know how hard I found it signing the order to terminate your life!

LEIA: I'm surprised you had the courage to take the responsibility yourself!

TARKIN: Princess Leia, before your execution I would like you to be my guest at a ceremony that will make this battle station operational. No star system will dare oppose the Emperor now.

LEIA: The more you tighten your grip, Tarkin, the more star systems will slip through your fingers.

TARKIN: Not after we demonstrate the power of this station. In a way, you have determined the choice of the planet that'll be destroyed first. Since you are reluctant to provide us with the location of the Rebel base, I have chosen to test this station's destructive power . . . on your home planet of Alderaan.

LEIA: No! Alderaan is peaceful. We have no weapons. You can't possibly . . .

TARKIN: You would prefer another target? A military target? Then name the system!

Tarkin looks menacingly at Leia.

TARKIN: I grow tired of asking this. So it'll be the last time. Where is the Rebel base?

Leia sees Alderaan on the huge wall screen.

LEIA: *(softly)* Dantooine.

Leia lowers her head.

LEIA: They're on Dantooine.

TARKIN: There. You see, Lord Vader, she can be reasonable. *(addressing Motti)* Continue with the operation. You may fire when ready.

LEIA: What?

TARKIN: You're far too trusting. Dantooine is too remote to make an effective demonstration. But don't worry. We will deal with your Rebel friends soon enough.

LEIA: No!

INT. DEATH STAR—BLAST CHAMBER

DEATH STAR INTERCOM VOICE: Commence primary ignition.

A button is pressed which switches on a panel of lights. A hooded Imperial soldier reaches overhead and pulls a lever. Another lever is pulled, and a bank of lights on a panel and wall lights up. A huge beam of light emanates from within a cone-shaped area and converges into a single laser beam out toward Alderaan. The small green planet of Alderaan is blown into space dust.

INT. *MILLENNIUM FALCON*—CENTRAL HOLD AREA

Ben watches as Luke practices the lightsaber with a small "seeker" robot. Ben suddenly turns away and sits down. He falters, seems almost faint.

LUKE: Are you all right? What's wrong?

BEN: I felt a great disturbance in the Force . . . as if millions of voices suddenly cried out in terror and were suddenly silenced. I fear something terrible has happened.

Ben rubs his forehead. He seems to drift into a trance. Then he fixes his gaze on Luke.

The idea of the Death Star destroying Organa Major (which would later become Alderaan) did not appear until the third draft, and George Lucas did not intend to show the planet being blown up until the revised fourth draft. In the third draft, aboard Han's spaceship and after the planet has been destroyed, Ben suddenly lapses into unconsciousness; he shudders all over, regains consciousness, and says that something horrible has happened. His reaction in subsequent drafts and in the movie was toned down and made less operatic.

BEN: You'd better get on with your exercises.

Han Solo enters the room.

HAN: Well, you can forget your troubles with those Imperial slugs. I told you I'd outrun 'em.

Luke is once again practicing with the lightsaber.

HAN: Don't everybody thank me at once.

Threepio watches Chewbacca and Artoo, who are engrossed in a game in which three-dimensional holographic figures move along a chess-type board.

HAN: Anyway, we should be at Alderaan at about oh two hundred hours.

Chewbacca and the two robots sit around the lighted table covered with small holographic monsters. Each side of the table has a small computer monitor embedded in it. Chewbacca seems very pleased with himself.

THREEPIO: Now be careful, Artoo.

Artoo immediately reaches up and taps the computer with his stubby claw hand, causing one of the holographic creatures to walk to the new square. A sudden frown crosses Chewbacca's face, and he begins yelling at the tiny robot. Threepio intercedes on behalf of his small companion and begins to argue with the huge Wookiee.

THREEPIO: He made a fair move. Screaming about it can't help you.

HAN: *(interrupting)* Let him have it. It's not wise to upset a Wookiee.

THREEPIO: But sir, nobody worries about upsetting a droid.

*****HAN:** That's because a droid don't pull people's arms out of their sockets when they lose. Wookiees are known to do that.

*****THREEPIO:** I see your point, sir. I suggest a new strategy, Artoo. Let the Wookiee win.

Luke stands in the middle of the small hold area: he seems frozen in place. A humming lightsaber is held out in front of him. Ben watches him from the corner, studying his movements.

BEN: Remember, a Jedi can feel the Force flowing through him.

LUKE: You mean it controls your actions?

BEN: Partially. But it also obeys your commands.

Suspended at eye level, about ten feet in front of Luke, a "seeker," a chrome baseball-like robot covered with antennae, hovers slowly in a wide arc. The ball floats to one side of the youth, then to the other. Suddenly it makes a lightning-swift lunge, emitting a bloodred laser beam as it attacks. It hits Luke in the leg. Han lets loose with a burst of laughter.

HAN: *(laughing)* Hokey religions and ancient weapons are no match for a good blaster at your side, kid.

LUKE: You don't believe in the Force, do you?

HAN: Kid, I've flown from one side of this galaxy to the other. I've seen a lot of strange stuff, but I've never seen anything to make me believe there's one all-powerful force controlling everything. There's no mystical energy field that controls my destiny.

Ben smiles quietly.

HAN: It's all a lot of simple tricks and nonsense.

BEN: I suggest you try it again, Luke. This time, let go your conscious self and act on instinct.

Ben places a large helmet on Luke's head which covers his eyes.

LUKE: *(laughing)* With the blast shield down, I can't even see. How am I supposed to fight?

BEN: Your eyes can deceive you. Don't trust them.

The ball shoots straight up in the air. Luke swings the lightsaber around blindly, missing the seeker, which fires off a laserbolt which hits Luke.

BEN: Stretch out with your feelings.

Luke stands in one place, seemingly frozen. The seeker fires at Luke, and incredibly, he manages to deflect the bolts. The ball ceases firing and moves back to its original position.

BEN: You see, you can do it.

HAN: I call it luck.

BEN: In my experience, there is no such thing as luck.

HAN: Look, good against remotes is one thing. Good against the living? That's something else.

Solo notes a small light flashing on the far side of the control panel.
HAN: Looks like we're coming up on Alderaan.
Han and Chewbacca head back to the cockpit.
LUKE: You know, I did feel something. I could almost see the remote.
BEN: That's good. You have taken your first step into a larger world.

The scene with the droids playing a holographic game with Chewbacca, Luke training aboard the *Falcon* with the seeker ball, and the bit with Han joking about the Force first appeared in the third draft. In the fourth draft, however, to teach Han a lesson, Ben makes a slight gesture toward him, and suddenly his laser pistol goes off in his holster, causing a small explosion at his feet. Han, of course, jumps to attention.

INT. DEATH STAR—CONFERENCE ROOM
Imperial Officer Cass enters to stand before Governor Tarkin and the evil Dark Lord Darth Vader.
TARKIN: Yes.
OFFICER CASS: Our scout ships have reached Dantooine. They found the remains of a Rebel base, but they estimate that it has been deserted for some time. They are now conducting an extensive search of the surrounding systems.
TARKIN: She lied! She lied to us!
VADER: I told you she would never consciously betray the Rebellion.
TARKIN: Terminate her . . . immediately!
EXT. HYPERSPACE
The pirate ship is just coming out of hyperspace: a strange surreal light show surrounds the ship.
INT. *MILLENNIUM FALCON*—COCKPIT
HAN: Stand by, Chewie, here we go. Cut in the sublight engines.
Han pulls back on a control lever. Outside the cockpit window stars begin streaking past, seem to decrease in speed, then stop. Suddenly the starship begins to shudder and violently shake about. Asteroids begin to race toward them, battering the sides of the ship.
HAN: What the . . . ? Aw, we've come out of hyperspace into a meteor shower. Some kind of asteroid collision. It's not on any of the charts.
The giant Wookiee flips off several controls and seems very cool in the emergency. Luke makes his way into the bouncing cockpit, followed by Ben.
LUKE: What's going on?
HAN: Our position is correct, except . . . no Alderaan!
LUKE: What do you mean? Where is it?

HAN: That's what I'm trying to tell you, kid. It ain't there. It's been totally blown away.

LUKE: What? How?

The ship begins to settle down.

BEN: Destroyed . . . by the Empire!

HAN: The entire starfleet couldn't destroy the whole planet. It'd take a thousand ships with more firepower than I've . . .

A muffled alarm starts sounding on the control panel.

HAN: There's another ship coming in.

LUKE: Maybe they know what happened.

BEN: It's an Imperial fighter.

A huge explosion bursts outside the cockpit window, shaking the ship violently. A tiny, finned Imperial TIE fighter races past the cockpit window.

LUKE: It followed us!

BEN: No. It's a short-range fighter.

HAN: There aren't any bases around here. Where did it come from?

EXT. SPACE

The fighter races past the Corellian pirate ship.

INT. *MILLENNIUM FALCON*—COCKPIT

LUKE: It sure is leaving in a big hurry. If they identify us, we're in big trouble.

HAN: Not if I can help it. Chewie . . . jam its transmissions.

BEN: It'd be as well to let it go. It's too far out of range.

HAN: Not for long . . .

EXT. SPACE

The pirate ship zooms over the camera and away into the vastness of space after the Imperial TIE fighter.

INT. *MILLENNIUM FALCON*—COCKPIT

The tension mounts as the pirate ship gains on the tiny fighter. Ben stands behind Han.

BEN: A fighter that size couldn't get this deep into space on its own.

LUKE: Then he must have gotten lost, been part of a convoy, or something . . .

HAN: Well, he ain't going to be around long enough to tell anybody about us.

EXT. SPACE

The TIE fighter is losing ground to the larger pirate ship as they race toward camera and disappear overhead.

INT. *MILLENNIUM FALCON*—COCKPIT

A distant star can now be distinguished as a small moon or planet.

LUKE: Look at him. He's heading for that small moon.

HAN: I think I can get him before he gets there . . . he's almost in range.

BEN: That's no moon! It's a space station.

HAN: It's too big to be a space station.

LUKE: I have a very bad feeling about this.

George Lucas: "I used the line 'I have a bad feeling about this' in all three films. It was just a funny understatement, and I liked using it whenever something really bad was going to happen, something outrageously bad. At the same time I was doing *Star Wars*, I was working on *Raiders of the Lost Ark* [1981], and it was a line that I was really going to use in *Raiders of the Lost Ark*, but I realized that Indiana Jones, most of the time, is by himself when he is in those desperate situations. But I had so many characters in *Star Wars* that no matter what, I figured that there would always be someone there to say the line and someone else to hear it. So the line became a joke that floated through not only in *Star Wars* but in all my movies."

BEN: Turn the ship around!

HAN: Yeah. I think you're right. Full reverse! Chewie, lock in the auxiliary power.

The pirate ship shudders, and the TIE fighter accelerates away toward the gargantuan battle station.

HAN: Chewie, lock in the auxiliary power.

LUKE: Why are we still moving toward it?

HAN: We're caught in a tractor beam! It's pulling us in.

LUKE: There's gotta be something you can do!

HAN: There's nothin' I can do about it, kid. I'm in full power. I'm going to have to shut down. But they're not going to get me without a fight!

BEN: You can't win. But there are alternatives to fighting.

INT. *MILLENNIUM FALCON*—DEATH STAR

As the battered starship is towed closer to the awesome metal moon, the immense size of the massive battle station becomes staggering. Running along the equator of the gigantic sphere is a mile-high band of huge docking ports into which the helpless pirate ship is dragged.

INT. DEATH STAR—HUGE PORT DOORS

The helpless Millennium Falcon *is pulled past a docking port control room and huge laser turret cannons.*

VOICE OVER DEATH STAR INTERCOM: Clear Bay Three-two-oh-seven. We are opening the magnetic field.

INT. DEATH STAR—DOCKING BAY 3207

As the pirate ship is pulled in through port doors of the Death Star, stormtroopers stand at attention in a central assembly area.

OFFICER: To your stations!

OFFICER: *(to another officer)* Come with me.

INT. DEATH STAR—HALLWAY

Stormtroopers run to their posts.

INT. DEATH STAR—HANGAR 3207

A line of stormtroopers marches toward the pirate ship, which has come to rest in a huge hangar, in readiness to board it, while other troopers stand with weapons ready to fire.

OFFICER: Close all outboard shields! Close all outboard shields!

INT. DEATH STAR—CONFERENCE ROOM

Tarkin responds to intercom buzz and pushes a button.

TARKIN: Yes.

VOICE: *(over intercom)* We've captured a freighter entering the remains of the Alderaan system. Its markings match those of a ship that blasted its way out of Mos Eisley.

VADER: They must be trying to return the stolen plans to the princess. She may yet be of some use to us.

INT. DEATH STAR—DOCKING BAY 3207

Vader and a commander approach the troops as an officer and several heavily armed troops exit the spacecraft.

VOICE: *(over intercom)* Unlock one, five, seven, and nine. Release charges.

OFFICER: *(to Vader)* There's no one on board, sir. According to the log, the crew abandoned ship right after takeoff. It must be a decoy, sir. Several of the escape pods have been jettisoned.

VADER: Did you find any droids?

*****OFFICER:** No, sir. If there were any on board, they must also have been jettisoned.

*****VADER:** Send a scanning crew aboard. I want every part of the ship checked.

*****OFFICER:** Yes, sir.

*****VADER:** I sense something . . . a presence I've not felt since . . .

Vader turns quickly and exits the hangar.

OFFICER: Get me a scanning crew in here on the double. I want every part of this ship checked!

INT. *MILLENNIUM FALCON*—HALLWAY

A trooper strides through the hallway, heading for the exit. In a few moments all is quiet. The muffled sounds of a distant officer giving orders finally fade. Two floor panels suddenly pop up, revealing Han Solo and Luke. Ben Kenobi sticks his head out of a third locker.

Paul Hirsch: "We had a fabulous temp score before we got John Williams's music. We used a lot of classical pieces, like 'Mars' from *The Planets* and *Le Sacre du Printemps*. In any case, I had worked with the composer Bernard Herrmann on Brian De Palma's *Sisters* [1972] and *Obsession* [1975]. There's a point in *Star Wars* where Harrison Ford pops out from the floor of the *Falcon*, and I put in that very famous cue from *Psycho* [1961] composed by Herrmann as temp music. John Williams, who is very fond of Herrmann's music, quoted it when he did the final score."

LUKE: Boy, it's lucky you had these compartments.

HAN: I use them for smuggling. I never thought I'd be smuggling myself in them. This is ridiculous. Even if I could take off, I'd never get past the tractor beam.

BEN: Leave that to me!

HAN: Damn fool. I knew that you were going to say that!

BEN: Who's the more foolish . . . the fool or the fool who follows him?

Han sighs. Chewbacca agrees.

INT. DEATH STAR—MAIN FORWARD BAY

Two crewmen bring a heavy box toward the ship.

TROOPER: The ship's all yours. If the scanners pick up anything, report it immediately. All right, let's go.

The crewmen enter the pirate ship, and a loud crashing sound is followed by a voice calling to the guard below.

HAN'S VOICE: Hey down there! Could you give us a hand with this?

The two stormtroopers guarding either side of the ramp enter the ship, and a quick round of gunfire is heard.

INT. DEATH STAR—FORWARD BAY—COMMAND OFFICE

In a very small command office near the entrance to the pirate ship, a gantry officer looks out his window and notices the guards are missing. He speaks into the comlink.

GANTRY OFFICER: TK-four-two-one. Why aren't you at your post? TK-four-two-one, do you copy?

A stormtrooper comes down the ramp of the pirate ship and waves to the gantry officer, pointing to his ear, indicating his comlink is not working. The gantry officer heads for the door, giving his aide instructions.

GANTRY OFFICER: Take over. We've got a bad transmitter. I'll see what I can do.

As the officer approaches the door, it slides open, revealing the towering Chewbacca. The gantry officer, in a momentary state of shock, fails to react. With a bone-chilling howl, the giant Wookiee flattens the officer with one blow. The aide immediately reaches for his pistol but is blasted by Han, dressed as an Imperial stormtrooper.

  Ben and the robots enter the room quickly, followed by Luke, also dressed as a stormtrooper. Luke quickly removes his helmet.

LUKE: You know, between his howling and your blasting everything in sight, it's a wonder the whole station doesn't know we're here.

HAN: Bring them on! I prefer a straight fight to all this sneaking around.

THREEPIO: We found the computer outlet, sir.

BEN: Plug in. He should be able to interpret the entire Imperial network.

Artoo punches his claw arm into the computer socket, and the vast Imperial brain network comes to life, feeding information to the little robot. After a few moments, he beeps something.

THREEPIO: He says he's found the main controls to the power beam that's holding the ship here. He'll try to make the precise location appear on the monitor.

The computer monitor flashes readouts.

THREEPIO: The tractor beam is coupled to the main reactor in seven locations. A power loss at one of the terminals will allow the ship to leave.

Ben studies the data on the monitor readout.

BEN: I don't think you boys can help. I must go alone.

HAN: Whatever you say. I've done more than I bargained for on this trip already.

LUKE: I want to go with you.

BEN: Be patient, Luke. Stay and watch over the droids.

LUKE: But he can—

BEN: They must be delivered safely or other star systems will suffer the same fate as Alderaan. Your destiny lies along a different path from mine. The Force will be with you . . . always!

Ben steps out of the command office, then disappears down a long gray hallway. Chewbacca barks a comment, and Han agrees.

HAN: Boy, you said it, Chewie.

Han looks at Luke.

HAN: Where did you dig up that old fossil?

LUKE: Ben is a great man.

HAN: Yeah, great at getting us into trouble.

LUKE: I didn't hear you give any ideas . . .

HAN: Well, anything's better than just hanging around waiting for them to pick us up . . .

LUKE: Who do you think . . .

Suddenly Artoo begins to whistle and beep a blue streak. Luke goes over to him.

LUKE: What is it?

THREEPIO: I'm afraid I'm not quite sure, sir. He says 'I found her' and keeps repeating 'She's here.'

LUKE: Well, who . . . who has he found?

THREEPIO: Princess Leia.

LUKE: The princess? She's here?

HAN: Princess?

LUKE: Where . . . where is she?

HAN: Princess? What's going on?

THREEPIO: Level five, Detention block AA-twenty-three. I'm afraid she's scheduled to be terminated.

LUKE: Oh, no! We've got to do something.

HAN: What are you talking about?

LUKE: The droids belonged to her. She's the one in the message. We've got to help her.

HAN: Now, look, don't get any funny ideas. The old man wants us to wait right here.

LUKE: But he didn't know she was here. Look, will you just find a way back into that detention block?

HAN: I'm not going anywhere.

LUKE: They're going to execute her. Look, a few minutes ago you said you didn't want to just wait here to be captured. Now all you want to do is stay.

HAN: Marching into the detention area is not what I had in mind.

*****LUKE:** But they're going to kill her!

*****HAN:** Better her than me.

*****LUKE:** She's rich.

Chewbacca growls.

*****HAN:** Rich?

*****LUKE:** Rich, powerful! Listen, if you were to rescue her, the reward would be . . .

*****HAN:** What?

*****LUKE:** Well, more wealth than you can imagine.

*****HAN:** I don't know, I can imagine quite a bit!

*****LUKE:** You'll get it!

HAN: I'd better!

LUKE: You will . . .

HAN: All right, kid. But you'd better be right about this!

LUKE: All right.

HAN: What's your plan?

LUKE: Uh . . . Threepio, hand me those binders there, will you? Okay.

Luke moves toward Chewbacca with electronic cuffs.

LUKE: Now, I'm going to put these on you.

Chewie lets out a hideous growl. Luke sheepishly hands the binders to Han.

LUKE: Okay, Han, you, you put those on.

HAN: Don't worry, Chewie. I think I know what he has in mind.

Han binds the Wookiee with electronic cuffs.

THREEPIO: Er, Master Luke, sir! Pardon me for asking . . . but . . . what should Artoo and I do if we're discovered here?

LUKE: Lock the door!

HAN: And hope they don't have blasters.

THREEPIO: That isn't very reassuring.

In the first treatment, what leads to the actual capture and rescue of the princess is quite different from the way the story unfolds in the film. Remember, in the treatment Skywalker and the princess are traveling with the two bureaucrats and a group of boys, and after a battle in space against Imperial ships, they land on Yavin. They realize that one of the boys is missing, decide to look for him, and are chased by aliens riding large birdlike creatures. The bureaucrats and the princess are captured, and General Skywalker is thrown over a crevasse into a boiling lake. Unknown to everyone, Skywalker grabs an overhanging vine and swings to safety. On his way to rescue his friends he is helped by one of the aliens, who has turned against his own people.

Meanwhile, the aliens have brought the princess and the bureaucrats to Imperial troopers, and the captives are taken in a speed tank. The good alien takes Skywalker to a small farm where the boys are waiting for him, and with the help of a farmer who hates the Empire, they reach an Imperial outpost where they hope to find the princess. They attack the outpost and discover that the princess has been taken to Alderaan, the capital of the Empire. Skywalker and the boys plan the rescue of the princess and, disguised as Imperial rangers, reach the prison complex on Alderaan and save Leia.

The rough and first drafts are also quite different from the film: General Skywalker, Annikin Starkiller, Princess Leia, and the droids have escaped in lifepods after a battle in space against Imperial fighters. They land on Yavin, a Wookiee planet with huge trees and a forest known as "the forest of Gargantuans." Leia is captured by scruffy alien trappers (described as slightly human, slimy, deformed, hideous creatures who travel in two large tanklike jungle crawlers) and taken prisoner along with five Wookiees. Annikin comes to her rescue but is knocked unconscious during the fight with the trappers. The Wookiees free themselves, and one of the trappers escapes with the princess still captive aboard a crawler. Annikin is brought back to the Wookiee camp and has to prove his courage in a fight.

The Wookiees come to respect him, and when he leaves to look for his friends, Chewbacca (Boma in the first draft), the son of the chief of the tribe, follows him. This whole subplot evidently is what later inspired the concept of the Ewoks in Return of the Jedi.

Meanwhile, Princess Leia has been taken aboard the Death

Star, and Annikin comes to rescue her with R2-D2, pretending that he's been called to check vent ports on the space fortress. R2-D2 plugs himself into a computer socket and finds the detention area, but Annikin is caught and taken prisoner. He manages to escape; his freedom, however, is short-lived as he gets trapped in some kind of gas chamber. He is put on trial and sentenced to death. Luckily, Annikin is saved by Prince Valorum, who was demoted—and has switched sides—after he let Skywalker and Solo escape from Aquilae in an earlier part of the story.

In the second draft Luke Starkiller and Han Solo look for Deak, who is imprisoned on Alderaan, "an island city suspended in a sea of Cirrus Methane," obviously an early version of Cloud City, which appeared in *The Empire Strikes Back*. When the group reaches the planet, several Imperial fighters head toward its ship. The Imperial troopers don't receive answers to their signals and assume that the ship is a "Corellian Gypsy vessel" drifting; they tow it to Alderaan. Aboard the ship they find Threepio, who says that his masters have abandoned the ship (in the third draft Threepio says that his masters abandoned the ship after they passed through a "solar plague zone"). The group (which includes Montross, Han Solo's friend) has in fact been hiding in the low cabinets of the ship. As in the movie, they knock out several troopers, put on their uniforms, and break into the main gantry.

Ben saying "May the Force be with you" first appeared in the third draft.

INT. DEATH STAR—DETENTION AREA

Luke and Han start off into the giant Imperial Death Star in their armored stormtrooper helmets. They try to look inconspicuous in their armored suits as they wait for a vacuum elevator to arrive. Troops, bureaucrats, and robots bustle about, ignoring the trio completely. Only a few give the giant Wookiee a curious glance.

Finally a small elevator arrives, and the trio enters.

LUKE: I can't see a thing in this helmet.

A bureaucrat races to get aboard also but is signaled away by Han. The door to the podlike vehicle slides closed, and the elevator car takes off through a vacuum tube.

INT. DEATH STAR—MAIN HALLWAY

Several stormtroopers walk through the wide main passageway. At the far end of the hallway, a passing flash of Ben Kenobi appears, then disappears down a small hallway. Darth Vader appears menacingly in the hallway, but Ben seems to have escaped notice.

INT. DEATH STAR—INT. ELEVATOR—DETENTION SECURITY AREA

Han whispers to Luke under his breath.

HAN: This is not going to work.

LUKE: Why didn't you say so before?

HAN: I did say so before!

INT. DETENTION AREA

Elevator doors open. A tall, grim-looking officer approaches the trio.

OFFICER: Where are you taking this . . . thing?

Chewie growls a bit at the remark, but Han nudges him to shut up.

LUKE: Prisoner transfer from Cell Block one-one-three-eight.

*__OFFICER:__ I wasn't notified. I'll have to clear it.

The officer waves two troopers forward and goes back to his console to punch in the information. Han has unfastened one of Chewbacca's electronic cuffs.

Suddenly Chewbacca knocks one of the troopers aside and lets out with one of his ear-piercing howls. He grabs Han's laser rifle.

*__HAN:__ Look out! He's loose!

*__LUKE:__ He's going to pull us apart!

HAN: Go get him!

The startled guards are momentarily dumbfounded. Luke and Han have already pulled out their laser pistols and are blasting away at the camera eyes, laser gate controls, and the Imperial guards. Han rushes to the comlink system. He quickly checks the computer readout.

*__HAN:__ We've got to find out which cell this princess of yours is in. Here it is . . . twenty-one-eighty-seven. You go and get her. I'll hold them here.

Luke races down one of the cell corridors. Han speaks into the beeping comlink.

*__HAN:__ *(sounding official)* Everything's under control. Situation normal.

*__INTERCOM VOICE:__ What happened?

*__HAN:__ *(getting nervous)* Uh . . . had a slight weapons malfunction. But, uh, everything's perfectly all right now. We're fine. We're all fine here now, thank you. How are you?

*__INTERCOM VOICE:__ We're sending a squad up.

*__HAN:__ Uh, uh, negative, negative. We have a reactor leak here now. Give us a few minutes to lock it down. Large leak . . . very dangerous.

*__INTERCOM VOICE:__ Who is this? What's your operating number?

Han blasts the comlink, and it explodes.

*__HAN:__ Boring conversation anyway. *(yelling down the hallway)* Luke! We're going to have company.

INT. DEATH STAR—CELL ROW

Luke stops in front of one of the cells and opens the door. Inside, Luke sees the *dazzling young princess-senator. She had been sleeping and is now looking at him with an uncomprehending look on her face. Luke is stunned by her incredible beauty and stands staring at her.*

LEIA: *(finally)* Aren't you a little short for a stormtrooper?

LUKE: Huh? Oh . . . the uniform. *(taking off his helmet)* I'm Luke Skywalker. I'm here to rescue you.

LEIA: You're who?

LUKE: I'm here to rescue you. I've got your R2 unit. I'm here with Ben Kenobi.

LEIA: Ben Kenobi! Where is he?

LUKE: Come on!

The scheme with Chewbacca impersonating a prisoner being taken to the detention area by Han and Luke disguised as stormtroopers first appeared in the second draft. After they attack the prison guards, Luke calls security, pretending that the situation is under control, while Han and Chewbacca find Deak inside his cell. He is suspended upside down by invisible rays, and there is a strange yellow glow in his eyes. In the third draft Leia is the one hanging upside down, suspended by invisible rays. In the fourth draft, as in the film, it is Luke, not Han, who finds Leia in her cell.

INT. DEATH STAR—CONFERENCE ROOM
Darth Vader stands addressing Governor Tarkin, who sits at the far end of the conference table.

VADER: He is here . . .

TARKIN: Obi-Wan Kenobi! What makes you think so?

VADER: A tremor in the Force. The last time I felt it was in the presence of my old master.

TARKIN: Surely he must be dead by now.

VADER: Don't underestimate the Force.

TARKIN: The Jedi are extinct; their fire has gone out of the universe. You, my friend, are all that's left of their religion.

There has been a quiet buzz on the comlink.

TARKIN: Yes.

INTERCOM VOICE: We have an emergency alert in detention block AA-twenty-three.

TARKIN: The princess! Put all sections on alert!

VADER: Obi-Wan is here. The Force is with him.

TARKIN: If you're right, he must not be allowed to escape.

VADER: Escape is not his plan. I must face him alone.

INT. DEATH STAR—MAIN HALLWAY

Ben Kenobi continues to evade detection.

INT. DEATH STAR—DETENTION AREA HALLWAY

An ominous buzzing sound is heard on the other side of the elevator door. Chewbacca responds with a growling noise.

HAN: Get behind me! Get behind me!

An explosion knocks a hole in the elevator door, through which several Imperial troops begin to emerge.

Han and Chewie fire their laser pistols at them through the smoke and flames. They turn and run down the cell hallway.

TROOPER: Off to your left. They went down in the cell bay.

Han and Chewie meet up with Luke and Leia.

HAN: Can't get out that way.

LEIA: Looks like you managed to cut off our only escape route.

HAN: *(sarcastically)* Maybe you'd like it back in your cell, Your Highness.

Luke takes a small comlink transmitter from his belt as they continue to exchange fire with stormtroopers making their way down the corridor.

LUKE: See-Threepio! See-Threepio!

THREEPIO: *(over comlink)* Yes, sir?

LUKE: Are there any other ways out of the cell bay? . . . We've been cut off! What was that? I didn't copy!

INT. DEATH STAR—MAIN BAY GANTRY—CONTROL TOWER

Threepio paces the control center in the company of little Artoo. Threepio talks into the small comlink transmitter.

THREEPIO: I said all systems have been alerted to your presence, sir. The main entrance seems to be the only way in or out; all other information on your level is restricted.

Someone begins banging on the door.

TROOPER VOICE: Open up in there! Open up in there!

THREEPIO: Oh, no!

INT. DEATH STAR—DETENTION CORRIDOR

Luke and Leia crouch together in an alcove for protection as they continue to exchange fire with troops. Han and Chewbacca are barely able to keep the stormtroopers at bay at the far end of the hallway. The laserfire is very intense, and smoke fills the narrow cell corridor.

LUKE: There isn't any other way out.

HAN: I can't hold them off forever! Now what?

LEIA: This is some rescue. When you came in here, didn't you have a plan for getting out?

HAN: *(indicating Luke)* He's the brains, sweetheart.

Luke looks sheepish and shrugs.

LUKE: Well, I didn't . . .

The princess grabs Luke's gun and fires at a small grate in the wall next to Han, almost frying him.

HAN: What the hell are you doing?

LEIA: Somebody has to save our skins. Into the garbage chute, flyboy.

She tosses Luke's gun back to him and jumps through the narrow opening as Han and Chewbacca look on in amazement. Chewbacca sniffs the garbage chute and says something.

HAN: Get in there! Get in there, you big furry oaf! I don't care what you smell! Get in there and don't worry about it.

Han gives him a big kick, and the Wookiee disappears into the tiny opening. Luke and Han continue firing as they work their way toward the opening.

HAN: Wonderful girl! Either I'm going to kill her or I'm beginning to like her. Get in there!

Luke ducks laserfire as he jumps into the darkness. Han fires off a couple of quick blasts, creating a smoky cover, then dives into the chute himself and is gone.

INT. DEATH STAR—GARBAGE ROOM

Han tumbles into a large room filled with garbage and muck. Chewbacca finds a small hatchway and struggles to get it open. It won't budge.

HAN: *(sarcastically)* The garbage chute was a really wonderful idea. What an incredible smell you've discovered! Let's get out of here! Get away from there . . .

LUKE: No! Wait!

Han draws his laser pistol and fires at the hatch. The laserbolt ricochets wildly around the small metal room. Everyone dives for cover in the garbage as the bolt explodes almost on top of them. Leia climbs out of the garbage with a rather grim look on her face.

LUKE: Will you forget it? I already tried it. It's magnetically sealed.

*LEIA: Put that thing away! You're going to get us all killed.

*HAN: Absolutely, Your Worship. Look, I had everything under control until you led us down here. You know, it's not going to take them long to figure out what happened to us.

*LEIA: It could be worse.

A loud, horrible, inhuman moan works its way up from the murky depths. Chewbacca begins to back away. Han and Luke stand fast with their laser pistols drawn. The Wookiee is cowering near one of the walls.

HAN: It's worse.

LUKE: There's something alive in here!

HAN: That's your imagination.

LUKE: Something just moved past my leg! Look! Did you see that?

HAN: What?

Suddenly Luke is yanked under the garbage.

HAN: Kid! Luke! Luke! Luke!

Solo tries to get to Luke. Luke surfaces with a gasp of air and thrashing of limbs. A membraned tentacle is wrapped around his throat.

LEIA: Luke!

Leia extends a long pipe toward him.

LEIA: Luke, Luke, grab hold of this.

LUKE: Blast it, will you! My gun's jammed.

HAN: Where?

LUKE: Anywhere! Oh!!

Solo fires his gun downward. Luke is pulled back into the muck by the slimy tentacle.

HAN: Luke! Luke!

Suddenly the walls of the garbage receptacle shudder. Then everything is deathly quiet. Han and Leia give each other a worried look. With a rush of bubbles and muck Luke suddenly bobs to the surface.

LEIA: Help him!

Luke seems to be released by the thing.

LEIA: What happened?

LUKE: I don't know, it let go of me and disappeared . . .

HAN: I got a bad feeling about this.

Before anyone can say anything the walls begin to rumble and edge toward the Rebels.

LUKE: The walls are moving!

LEIA: Don't just stand there. Try and brace it with something. Help me!

They place poles and long metal beams between the closing walls, but they are simply snapped and bent as the giant trashmasher rumbles on. The situation doesn't look too good.

LUKE: Wait a minute!

Luke pulls out his comlink.

LUKE: Threepio. Come in, Threepio! Threepio! Where could he be?

INT. DEATH STAR—MAIN GANTRY—COMMAND OFFICE

The muted voice of Luke calling out to See-Threepio can be heard on Threepio's hand comlink, which is sitting on the deserted computer console. Artoo and Threepio are nowhere in sight. Suddenly there is a great explosion, and the door of the control tower opens. Armed stormtroopers enter the chamber.

FIRST TROOPER: Take over! *(indicating a dead officer)* See to him! Look, there!

A trooper pushes a button, and the supply cabinet slides open. See-Threepio and Artoo are inside. See-Threepio comes out into the office.

THREEPIO: They're madmen! They're heading for the prison level. If you hurry, you might catch them.

FIRST OFFICER: *(to his troops)* Follow me! You stand guard.

The troops hustle off down the hallway, leaving a guard to watch over the command office.

THREEPIO: *(to Artoo)* Come on!

The guard aims a blaster at them.

THREEPIO: Oh! All this excitement has overrun the circuits in my counterpart here. If you don't mind, I'd like to take him down to maintenance.

TROOPER: All right.

The guard nods, and Threepio, with little Artoo in tow, hurries out the door.

INT. DEATH STAR—GARBAGE ROOM

As the walls rumble closer, the room gets smaller and smaller. Chewie is whining and trying to hold a wall back with his giant paws. Han and Leia are trying to brace the contracting walls with a pole. Leia begins to sink into the trash. Garbage is snapping and popping. Luke is trying to reach Threepio.

LUKE: Threepio! Come in, Threepio! Threepio!

HAN: Get to the top!

LEIA: I can't.

LUKE: Where could he be? Threepio! Threepio, will you come in?

INT. DEATH STAR—MAIN FORWARD BAY—SERVICE PANEL

THREEPIO: They aren't here! Something must have happened to them. See if they've been captured.

Little Artoo carefully plugs his claw arm into a new wall socket, and a complex array of electronic sounds spew from the tiny robot.

THREEPIO: Hurry!

INT. DEATH STAR—GARBAGE ROOM

The walls are only feet apart.

HAN: One thing's for sure. We're all going to be a lot thinner! *(to Leia)* Get on top of it!

LEIA: I'm trying!

INT. DEATH STAR—MAIN FORWARD BAY—SERVICE PANEL

THREEPIO: *(to Artoo)* Thank goodness they haven't found them! Where could they be?

Artoo frantically beeps something to See-Threepio.

THREEPIO: Use the comlink? Oh, my! I forgot . . . I turned it off!

Meanwhile, Luke is lying on his side, trying to keep his head above the rising ooze.

INT. DEATH STAR—MAIN FORWARD BAY—SERVICE PANEL

THREEPIO: Are you there, sir?

INT. DEATH STAR—GARBAGE ROOM

LUKE: Threepio!

INT. DEATH STAR—MAIN FORWARD BAY

THREEPIO: We've had some problems . . .

LUKE: *(over comlink)* Will you shut up and listen to me. Shut down all the garbage mashers on the detention level, will you? Do you copy? Shut down all the garbage mashers on the detention level.

INT. DEATH STAR—MAIN FORWARD BAY—SERVICE PANEL

LUKE: *(over comlink)* Shut down all the garbage mashers on the detention level.

THREEPIO: *(to Artoo)* No. Shut them all down! Hurry!

Threepio hears the incredible screaming and hollering from Luke's comlink.

THREEPIO: Listen to them! They're dying, Artoo! Curse my metal body! I wasn't fast enough. It's all my fault! My poor master!

LUKE: *(over comlink, faintly)* Threepio, we're all right!

The idea of the heroes getting trapped in the garbage room appeared as early as the rough draft; in this version Vader finds out that Annikin, Valorum, and the princess are trapped in the garbage room and operates the far wall to close in on them. Luckily, the attack on the space fortress has begun, and all the power is knocked out. The closing wall stops, and the group makes an escape. In the second draft the group's retreat back to the ship is divided into two parts. First, after running from the detention center, they reach a wide, dark, and dank low-ceilinged corridor and encounter a creature called "Dai Noga," some kind of giant jellyfishlike monster that became a "one-eyed creature with tentacles" in the fourth draft and in the film. Chewbacca is terrified and has to be blindfolded in order to move on. Then, after escaping from the Dai Noga, the group lands in the garbage room. In the third draft Leia is unconscious for the whole episode with the Dai Noga and takes command after she regains consciousness.

INT. DEATH STAR—GARBAGE ROOM

The screaming and hollering are the sounds of joyous relief. The walls have stopped moving. Han and Leia embrace in the background.

LUKE: We're all right. You did great.

Luke moves to the pressure-sensitive hatch, looking for a number.

LUKE: Hey . . . hey, open the pressure maintenance hatch on unit number . . . where are we?

INT. DEATH STAR—MAIN FORWARD BAY—SERVICE PANEL

Threepio looks at the computer panel as Han reads the number.

HAN: *(over comlink)* Three-two-six-three-eight-two-seven.

INT. DEATH STAR—TRACTOR BEAM—POWER GENERATOR TRENCH

Ben enters a humming service trench that powers the huge tractor beam. The trench seems to be a hundred miles deep. The old Jedi edges his way along a narrow ledge leading to a control panel. He carefully makes several adjustments.

INT. DEATH STAR—UNUSED HALLWAY

The group exits the garbage room into a dusty unused hallway. Han and Luke have removed the trooper suits and strapped on the blaster belts.

HAN: If we can just avoid any more female advice, we ought to be able to get out of here.

Luke smiles and scratches his head as he takes a blaster from Solo.

LUKE: Well, let's get moving!

Chewie begins growling and runs away from the hatch to the garbage room, where the dianoga evidently still lurks.

HAN: *(to Chewie)* Where are you going?

Han aims his pistol at the doorway.

LEIA: No, wait. They'll hear!

Han fires at the doorway. The noise of the blast echoes relentlessly throughout the empty passageway. Luke simply shakes his head in disgust.

HAN: *(to Chewie)* Come here, you big coward!

Chewie shakes his head no.

HAN: Chewie! Come here!

*LEIA: Listen. I don't know who you are or where you came from, but from now on, you do as I tell you. Okay?

Han is stunned at the command of the petite young girl.

*HAN: Look, Your Worshipfulness, let's get one thing straight! I take orders from just one person! Me!

*LEIA: It's a wonder you're still alive. *(looking at Chewie)* Will somebody get this big walking carpet out of my way?

Han watches her start away.

HAN: No reward is worth this.

They follow her, moving swiftly down the deserted corridor.

INT. DEATH STAR—POWER TRENCH

Suddenly, behind Ben a detachment of stormtroopers marches to the power trench. Ben remains in the shadows as they move to within a few feet of him.

OFFICER: Give me regular reports, please.

FIRST TROOPER: Right.

All but two of the stormtroopers leave.

FIRST TROOPER: Do you know what's going on?

SECOND TROOPER: Maybe it's another drill.

Ben moves around the tractor beam, watching the stormtroopers as they turn their backs to him and chat. Ben gestures with his hand toward them as the troops think they hear something in the other hallway. With the help of the Force, Ben deftly slips past the troopers and into the main hallway.

FIRST TROOPER: Have you seen that new BT-sixteen?

SECOND TROOPER: Yeah, some of the other guys were telling me about it. They say it's, it's quite a thing to . . . What was that?

FIRST TROOPER: That's nothing. Top gassing. Don't worry about it.

An interesting scene in the third draft shows Ben Kenobi walking around the Death Star, seeking the "Kiber Crystal." He finds himself in a conference room filled with about twelve bureaucrats "listening to an instructor explaining a type of technical philosophy." Ben raises his hands, and suddenly all the bureaucrats and the instructor begin coughing and grabbing their throats. Soon they're unable to breathe and collapse. Two Sith Lords are walking near the crystal chamber, and one of them says he feels a disturbance. Eventually Ben reaches the chamber and finds the "Kiber Crystal" on a pedestal in the middle of the room. He sidesteps a series of invisible beams, his eyes light up, and he suddenly appears renewed with inner strength. He lifts his arms, and the crystal rises. It moves toward the old Jedi, but before it reaches him, it passes through a blue beam and sets off an alarm.

INT. DEATH STAR—HALLWAY

Luke, Han, Chewbacca, and Leia hurry down an empty hallway and stop before a bay window overlooking the pirate ship. Troopers are milling around the ship. Luke takes out his pocket comlink.

HAN: *(looking at his ship)* There she is.

LUKE: See-Threepio, do you copy?

THREEPIO: *(voice)* Yes, sir.

LUKE: Are you safe?

THREEPIO: *(voice)* For the moment.

INT. DEATH STAR—MAIN FORWARD BAY

THREEPIO: We're in the main hangar across from the ship.

INT. DEATH STAR—HALLWAY

LUKE: We're right above you. Stand by.

Han has been watching the troops around the pirate ship. Leia moves toward Han, touches his arm, and points out the window to the ship.

*LEIA: You came in that thing? You're braver than I thought.

HAN: *(giving her a dirty look)* Nice! Come on!

They start off down the hallway. They round a corner and run right into Imperial stormtroopers heading toward them. Both groups are taken by surprise and stop in their tracks.

FIRST TROOPER: It's them! Blast them!

Before even thinking, Han fires his laser pistol. His blast knocks one of the stormtroopers into the air. Chewie follows his captain down the corridor, stepping past the fallen trooper on the floor.

HAN: *(to Luke and Leia)* Get back to the ship!

LUKE: Where are you going? Come back!

Han has already rounded a corner and does not hear.

LEIA: He certainly has courage.

LUKE: What good will it do us if he gets himself killed? Come on!

Luke is furious but doesn't have time to think about it. Luke and Leia start off toward the starship hangar.

INT. DEATH STAR—SUBHALLWAY

Han chases the stormtroopers down a long subhallway. He is yelling and brandishing his laser pistol. The troops reach a dead end and are forced to turn and fight. Han stops a few feet from them and assumes a defensive position. The troops begin to raise their laser guns. Soon the troopers are moving into an attack position in front of the lone starpirate. Han's determined look begins to fade as the troops begin to advance. Solo jumps back as they fire at him.

INT. DEATH STAR—SUBHALLWAY

Chewbacca runs down the subhallway in a last-ditch attempt to save his bold captain. Suddenly he hears the firing of laser guns and yelling. Around the corner shoots Han, pirate extraordinaire, running for his life, followed by a host of furious stormtroopers. Chewbacca turns and starts running the other way also.

INT. DEATH STAR—HALLWAY

Luke fires his laser pistol wildly as he and Leia rush down a narrow subhallway, chased by several stormtroopers. They quickly reach the end of the subhallway and race through an open hatchway.

INT. DEATH STAR—CENTRAL CORE SHAFT

Luke and Leia race through the hatch onto a narrow bridge that spans a huge, deep shaft that seems to go into infinity. The bridge has been retracted into the wall of the shaft, and Luke almost rushes into the abyss. He loses his balance off the end of the bridge as Leia, behind him, takes hold of his arm and pulls him back.

LUKE: *(gasping)* I think we took a wrong turn.

Blasts from the stormtroopers' laser guns explode nearby, reminding them of the oncoming danger. Luke fires back at the advancing troops. Leia reaches over and hits a switch that pops the hatch door shut with a resounding boom, leaving them precariously perched on a short piece of bridge overhang.

LEIA: There's no lock!

Luke blasts the controls with his laser pistol.

LUKE: That oughta hold them for a while.

LEIA: Quick, we've got to get across. Find the controls that extend the bridge.

LUKE: Oh, I think I just blasted it.

Luke looks at the blasted bridge control.

LEIA: They're coming through!

Luke notices something on his stormtrooper belt, when laserfire hits the wall behind him. Luke aims his laser pistol at a stormtrooper perched on a higher bridge overhang across the abyss from them. They exchange fire. Three more troopers appear on another overhang, also firing. A trooper is hit by Luke's laserfire, grabs at his chest, and plummets down the shaft. Troopers move back off the bridge; Luke hands his gun to Leia.

LUKE: Here, hold this.

Luke pulls a thin nylon cable from his trooper utility belt. It has a grappler hook on it.

A trooper appears on a bridge overhang and fires at Luke and Leia. As Luke works with the rope, Leia returns the laser volley. Suddenly, the hatch door begins to open, revealing the feet of more troops.

LEIA: Here they come!

Leia hits one of the stormtroopers on the bridge above, and he falls. Luke tosses the rope across the gorge, and it wraps itself around an outcropping pipe. He tugs on the rope to make sure it is secure, then grabs the princess in his arms. Leia looks at Luke, then kisses him quickly on the cheek. Luke is very surprised.

LEIA: For luck!

Luke pushes off, and they swing across the treacherous abyss to the corresponding hatchway on the opposite side. Just as Luke and Leia reach the far side of the canyon, the stormtroopers break through the hatch and begin to fire at the escaping duo. Luke returns the fire before ducking into the tiny subhallway.

INT. DEATH STAR—NARROW PASSAGEWAY

Ben hides in the shadows of a narrow passageway as several stormtroopers rush past him in the main hallway. He checks to make sure they're gone, then moves down the hallway in the opposite direction.

TROOPER: We think they may be splitting up. They may be on levels five and six now, sir.

INT. DEATH STAR—MAIN FORWARD BAY

Threepio looks around at the troops milling about the pirate ship's entry ramp.

THREEPIO: Where could they be?

Artoo, plugged into the computer socket, swivels his dome, beeping a response.

Han and Chewbacca run down a long corridor, exchanging fire with several troopers hot on their trail.

At the end of the hallway, blast doors begin to close in front of them. The young starpilot and his furry companion race through the huge doors as they are closing.

TROOPER: Open the blast doors! Open the blast doors!

INT. DEATH STAR—HALLWAY LEADING TO MAIN FORWARD BAY

Ben moves along one of the tunnels leading to the hangar where the pirate ship waits. Just before he reaches the hangar, Darth Vader comes into view at the end of the tunnel, his saber lit. Ben also ignites his and steps slowly forward.

VADER: I've been waiting for you, Obi-Wan. We meet again, at last. The circle is now complete.

Ben Kenobi moves with elegant ease into a classical offensive position.

VADER: When I left you, I was but the learner; now I am the master.

BEN: Only a master of evil, Darth.

Ben makes a sudden lunge at the huge warrior but is checked by a lightning movement of the Sith. A masterful slash stroke by Vader is blocked by the old Jedi. Another of the Jedi's blows is blocked, then countered. Ben moves around the Dark Lord and starts backing into the massive starship hangar. The two powerful warriors stand motionless for a few moments with laserswords crossed in midair, creating a low buzzing sound.

VADER: Your powers are weak, old man.

BEN: You can't win, Darth. If you strike me down, I shall become more powerful than you can possibly imagine.

Their lightsabers continue to meet in combat.

VADER: You should not have come back.

INT. DEATH STAR—MAIN FORWARD BAY

Han Solo and Chewbacca, their weapons in hand, lean back against the wall, surveying the forward bay, watching the Imperial stormtroopers make their rounds in the hangar.

HAN: Didn't we just leave this party?

Chewbacca growls a reply, as Luke and the princess join them.

HAN: What kept you?

LEIA: We ran into some old friends.

LUKE: Is the ship all right?

HAN: Seems okay, if we can get to it. Just hope the old man got the tractor beam out of commission.

INT. DEATH STAR—HALLWAY

Vader and Ben Kenobi continue their powerful duel.

As they hit their lightsabers together, lightning flashes on impact. Troopers look on with interest as the old Jedi and the Dark Lord of the Sith fight. Suddenly Luke spots the battle from his group's vantage point.

LUKE: Look!

Leia, Han, and Chewie look up and see Ben and Vader on the far side of the docking bay.

INT. DEATH STAR—DOCKING BAY

Threepio and Artoo are in the center of the Death Star's Imperial docking bay.

As the five stormtroopers who were guarding the starship rush past them, heading toward Ben and the Sith Knight, Threepio beckons Artoo.

THREEPIO: Come on, Artoo, we're going!

INT. DEATH STAR—HALLWAY

Solo, Chewie, Luke, and Leia tensely watch the duel. The troops have rushed toward the battling knights.

HAN: Now's our chance! Go!

They start for the Millennium Falcon.

Ben has seen the troops charging toward him and realizes that he is trapped.

The old Jedi Knight looks over his shoulder at Luke, lifts his sword from Vader's, then watches his opponent with a serene look on his face.

LUKE: Ben?

Vader sweeps his sword around, cutting old Ben in half. Ben's cloak falls to the floor in two parts, but Ben is not in it. While the guards have been distracted, the adventurers and the robots have reached the starship.

Luke sees Ben cut in two. Aghast, he yells out.

LUKE: No!

The stormtroopers turn toward Luke and begin firing at him. The robots are already moving up the ramp into the Millennium Falcon *while Luke, transfixed by anger and awe, returns their fire. Solo joins in the laserfire. Vader, who, puzzled at Ben's disappearance, has been poking at the empty cloak, looks up and advances toward them as one of his troopers is struck down.*

HAN: *(to Luke)* Come on!

LEIA: Come on! Come on! Luke, it's too late!

HAN: Blast the door! Kid!

Luke fires his laser pistol at the door control panel, and it explodes. The doors begin to slide shut. Three troopers charge forward, firing laserbolts as the door slides to a close behind them . . . shutting Vader and the other troops out of the docking bay. A stormtrooper lies dead at the feet of his onrushing compatriots. Luke starts for the advancing troops as Solo and Leia move up the ramp into the pirate ship. He fires, hitting a stormtrooper, who crumples to the floor.

BEN'S VOICE: Run, Luke! Run!

Luke looks around to see where the voice came from. He turns toward the pirate ship, ducking Imperial gunfire from the troopers, and races into the ship.

In the second draft, using two Imperial officers as hostages, Solo, Luke, Chewbacca, the two droids, and the unconscious Deak retreat to the ship and take off. In the third draft, after setting off the alarm and stealing the "Kiber Crystal," Ben Kenobi has to fight a group of troopers and ultimately faces his former student, Darth Vader. They fight with their laserswords, and at one point Ben deflects a blow that cuts a safety lock; a heavy door slams down and traps Vader in a tunnel. Ben joins Luke, who is fighting his way back to the ship. While attempting to deflect a bolt fired by a trooper, Ben is wounded, but ultimately the entire group makes it back to the ship safely and takes off.

The scene with Luke and Leia trapped on the narrow bridge overlooking the deep shaft first appeared in the fourth draft. In this version Ben still escapes from Vader but is not hurt. The idea of killing Ben came later, in the revised fourth draft, as did the idea of having Ben's voice guide Luke.

George Lucas: "As I was writing the third draft of *Star Wars*, I realized that after they escape from the Death Star, there isn't anything for Ben to do, and I struggled with finding things for him to do and finally gave up. I figured I'd just write that part later on. When I came to the next draft, it became obvious that he was just standing around, and that was not good, especially for a character of his importance. So it was really in the last draft, the one I wrote before I shot the movie, that I finally came to the decision that I had to do what I had to do. In a way, I knew I would have to do it from the beginning, but I went back and forth about it. The difficult part of that decision was that I had already hired Alec Guinness, and I had to tell him that his character was going to die halfway through the script. He didn't like it very much; he was upset about it until I convinced him that it was best for the movie, nothing personal. I knew that I would have to bring him back somehow if I made the other movies, and at the time of *Star Wars* I didn't know how I was going to accomplish that. At that point I had to make *Star Wars* work, and killing Ben was a logical decision."

INT. *MILLENNIUM FALCON*— COCKPIT
Han pulls back on the controls, and the ship begins to move as Chewie adjusts his controls.
HAN: I hope the old man got that tractor beam out of commission, or this is going to be a real short trip. Okay, hit it!
Chewbacca growls in agreement.
EXT. *MILLENNIUM FALCON*
The Millennium Falcon *powers away from the Death Star docking bay, makes a spectacular turn, and disappears into the vastness of space.*
INT. *MILLENNIUM FALCON*
Chewbacca congratulates Han on their escape.
EXT. *MILLENNIUM FALCON*
The Death Star recedes in the background.

Richard Chew: "The first scene that George asked me to work on was what he called the gunport sequence. This is when Han Solo, Chewbacca, Luke, and Leia escape from the Death Star after Ben has been killed. George showed me a short compilation of dogfight footage from documentaries from World War II; it was American, German, Japanese planes, and they were doing all kinds of spins and turns, and this footage was intercut with shots of the actors against blue screens or sets. So he showed this to me and said, 'Just cut on the moves.' And George used that as a grid to tell the special effects people how long the shots should be."

INT. *MILLENNIUM FALCON*—CENTRAL HOLD AREA

Luke, saddened by the loss of Obi-Wan Kenobi, stares off blankly as the robots look on. Leia puts a blanket around him protectively, and Luke turns and looks at her. She sits down beside him.

INT. *MILLENNIUM FALCON*—COCKPIT

Solo spots approaching enemy ships.

HAN: *(to Chewie)* We're coming up on their sentry ships. Hold 'em off! Angle the deflector shields while I charge up the main guns!

EXT. *MILLENNIUM FALCON*

The pirate ship speeds through space.

INT. *MILLENNIUM FALCON*—CENTRAL HOLD AREA

Luke looks downward sadly, shaking his head back and forth, as the princess smiles comfortingly at him.

LUKE: I can't believe he's gone.

Artoo-Detoo beeps a reply.

LEIA: There wasn't anything you could have done.

Han rushes into the hold area, where Luke is sitting with the princess.

HAN: *(to Luke)* Come on, buddy, we're not out of this yet!

INT. *MILLENNIUM FALCON*—GUNPORTS—COCKPIT

Solo climbs into his attack position in the topside gunport.

INT. *MILLENNIUM FALCON*—HOLD AREA

Luke gets up and moves out toward the gunports as Leia heads for the cockpit.

INT. *MILLENNIUM FALCON*—GUNPORTS—COCKPIT

Luke climbs down the ladder into the gunport cockpit, settling into one of the two main laser cannons mounted in large rotating turrets on either side of the ship.

INT. *MILLENNIUM FALCON*—SOLO'S GUNPORT

Han adjusts his headset as he sits before the controls of his laser cannon, then speaks into the attached microphone.

HAN: *(to Luke)* You in, kid? Okay, stay sharp!

INT. *MILLENNIUM FALCON*—GUNPORTS—COCKPIT

Chewbacca and Princess Leia search the heavens for the attacking TIE fighters. The Wookiee adjusts the controls as the ship bounces slightly.

INT. *MILLENNIUM FALCON*—SOLO'S GUNPORT—COCKPIT

Computer graphic readouts form on Solo's target screen as Han reaches for controls.

INT. *MILLENNIUM FALCON*—GUNPORT—COCKPIT

Luke sits in readiness for the attack, his hands on the laser cannon's control button.

INT. *MILLENNIUM FALCON*—COCKPIT

Chewbacca spots the enemy ships and barks.

LEIA: *(into intercom)* Here they come!

INT. COCKPIT POV SPACE

The Imperial TIE fighters move toward the Millennium Falcon, one each veering off to the left and right of the pirate ship.

INT. TIE FIGHTER—COCKPIT

The stars whip past behind the Imperial pilot as he adjusts his maneuvering joystick.

EXT. *MILLENNIUM FALCON*—IN SPACE

The TIE fighter races past the Falcon, firing laser beams as it passes.

INT. *MILLENNIUM FALCON*—HOLD AREA

Threepio is seated in the hold area, next to Artoo-Detoo. The pirate ship bounces and vibrates as the power goes out in the room and then comes back on.

INT. *MILLENNIUM FALCON*—COCKPIT—GUNPORTS

A TIE fighter maneuvers in front of Han, who follows it and fires at it with the laser cannon. Luke does likewise as the fighter streaks into view. The ship has suffered a minor hit and bounces slightly.

EXT. SPACE

Two TIE fighters dive down toward the pirate ship.

INT. *MILLENNIUM FALCON*—GUNPORTS

Luke fires at an unseen fighter.

EXT. SPACE

The TIE fighter streaks past.

INT. *MILLENNIUM FALCON*—GUNPORTS

LUKE: They're coming in too fast!

INT. *MILLENNIUM FALCON*—MAIN PASSAGEWAY

A laserbolt streaks into the side of the pirate ship. The ship lurches violently, throwing poor Threepio into a cabinet full of small computer chips.

THREEPIO: Oh!

INT. *MILLENNIUM FALCON*—COCKPIT GUNPORTS

Leia watches the computer readouts as Chewbacca manipulates the ship's controls.

LEIA: We've lost lateral controls.

HAN: Don't worry, she'll hold together.

An enemy laserbolt hits the pirate ship's control panel, causing it to blow out in a shower of sparks.

HAN: *[to ship]* You hear me, baby? Hold together!

Artoo-Detoo advances toward the smoking, sparking control panel, beeping and dousing the inferno by spraying it with fire retardant.

INT. *MILLENNIUM FALCON*—GUNPORT

Luke swivels in his gun mount, following the TIE fighter with his laser cannon.

INT. *MILLENNIUM FALCON*—GUNPORT

Solo aims his laser cannon at the enemy fighters.

EXT. SPACE

A TIE fighter streaks in front of the starship.

INT. *MILLENNIUM FALCON*—COCKPIT

Leia watches the TIE ship fly over.

EXT. SPACE

A TIE fighter heads right for the pirate ship, then zooms overhead.

INT. *MILLENNIUM FALCON*—GUNPORTS

Luke follows the TIE fighter across his field of view, firing laser beams from his cannon.

EXT. TIE FIGHTER

A TIE fighter dives past the pirate ship.

INT. *MILLENNIUM FALCON*—COCKPIT—GUNPORTS

Chewbacca and Leia watch anxiously as Luke fires at a TIE fighter. At his port, Han follows a fighter in his sights, releasing a blast of laserfire. He connects, and the fighter explodes into fiery dust. Han laughs victoriously.

EXT. SPACE

Two TIE fighters move toward and over the Millennium Falcon, *unleashing a barrage of laserbolts at the ship.*

INT. *MILLENNIUM FALCON*—GUNPORTS

Another TIE fighter moves in on the pirate ship, and Luke, smiling, fires the laser cannon at it, scoring a spectacular direct hit.

LUKE: Got him! I got him!

Han turns and gives Luke a victory wave, which Luke gleefully returns.

HAN: Great, kid! Don't get cocky.

Han turns back to his laser cannon.

EXT. SPACE

Two more TIE fighters cross in front of the pirate ship.

INT. *MILLENNIUM FALCON*—COCKPIT

While Chewbacca manipulates the controls, Leia turns, looking over her shoulder out the ports.

LEIA: There are still two more of them out there!

EXT. SPACE

A TIE fighter moves up over the pirate ship, firing laserblasts at it.

INT. *MILLENNIUM FALCON*—GUNPORTS

Luke and Han look into their respective projected target screens. An Imperial fighter crosses Solo's port, and Han swivels in his chair, following it with blasts from his laser cannon. Another fighter crosses Luke's port, and he reacts in a like manner.

EXT. SPACE

The TIE fighter zooms toward the pirate ship, firing destructive blasts at it.

INT. *MILLENNIUM FALCON*—GUNPORTS—COCKPIT

Luke fires a laserblast at the approaching enemy fighter, and it bursts into spectacular explosion. Luke's projected screen gives a readout of the hit. The pirate ship bounces slightly as it is struck by enemy fire.

EXT. SPACE—TIE FIGHTER

The last of the attacking Imperial TIE fighters looms in, firing upon the Falcon.

INT. *MILLENNIUM FALCON*—GUNPORT

Solo swivels behind his laser cannon, his aim describing the arc of the TIE fighter. The fighter comes closer, firing at the pirate ship, but a well-aimed blast from Solo's laser cannon hits the attacker, which blows up in a small atomic shower of burning fragments.

LUKE: *(laughing)* That's it! We did it!

LEIA: We did it!

The princess jumps up and gives Chewie a congratulatory hug.

In the second draft, as Solo gets ready to jump into hyperspace, Luke is attending to his brother, Deak, who is still very weak. Remember, in this draft Luke carries with him the "Kiber Crystal" that was given to him by Owen, and he puts it in Deak's hands. Suddenly Deak transmits a thought to Luke, revealing that their father is on the fourth moon of Yavin.

INT. *MILLENNIUM FALCON*—PASSAGEWAY

Threepio lies on the floor of the ship, completely tangled in the smoking, sparking wires.

THREEPIO: Help! I think I'm melting! *(to Artoo)* This is all your fault.

Artoo turns his dome from side to side, beeping in response.

EXT. SPACE—*MILLENNIUM FALCON*

The victorious Millennium Falcon *moves off majestically through space.*

INT. DEATH STAR—CONTROL ROOM

Darth Vader strides into the control room, where Tarkin is watching the huge viewscreen.

TARKIN: Are they away?

VADER: They have just made the jump into hyperspace.

TARKIN: You're sure the homing beacon is secure aboard their ship? I'm taking an awful risk, Vader. This had better work.

INT. *MILLENNIUM FALCON*—COCKPIT

Han, removing his gloves and smiling, is at the controls of the ship. Chewie moves into the aft section to check the damage. Leia is seated near Han.

HAN: Not a bad bit of rescuing, huh! You know, sometimes I amaze even myself.

LEIA: That doesn't sound too hard. They let us go. It's the only explanation for the ease of our escape.

HAN: Easy . . . You call that easy?

LEIA: They're tracking us!

HAN: Not this ship, sister.

Frustrated, Leia shakes her head.

LEIA: At least the information in Artoo is still intact.

HAN: What's so important? What's he carrying?

LEIA: The technical readouts of that battle station. I only hope that when the data is analyzed, a weakness can be found. It's not over yet!

Alfred Hitchcock said: "The McGuffin is the thing that the spies are after but the audience doesn't care." In the treatment Skywalker and Leia are carrying with them "the Aura Spice" (the McGuffin!), and the two bureaucrats join them in their journey with the intention of stealing it along with one of their speeders. The spice was eventually replaced by the plans of the Death Star that Artoo carries in his unit.

George Lucas: "You always have to have something that everybody is after, something that's not necessarily tied directly to the plot. The nice thing about the plan is that it pays off at the end of the film. You always want the McGuffin to be the thing that clicks the final climax . . . You reveal it, and it culminates or perpetuates the climax."

HAN: It is for me, sister! Look, I ain't in this for your revolution, and I'm not in it for you, Princess. I expect to be well paid. I'm in it for the money!

*LEIA: You needn't worry about your reward. If money is all that you love, then that's what you'll receive.

She angrily turns and, as she starts out of the cockpit, passes Luke coming in.

*LEIA: Your friend is quite a mercenary. I wonder if he really cares about anything . . . or anybody.

*LUKE: I care!

Luke, shaking his head, sits in the copilot seat. Han stares out at the vast blackness of space.

*LUKE: So . . . what do you think of her, Han?

*HAN: I'm trying not to, kid!

*LUKE: *(under his breath)* Good . . .

HAN: Still, she's got a lot of spirit. I don't know, what do you think? Do you think a princess and a guy like me . . .

LUKE: No!

Luke says it with finality and looks away. Han smiles at young Luke's jealousy.

EXT. SPACE AROUND FOURTH MOON OF YAVIN

The battered pirate ship drifts into orbit around the planet Yavin and proceeds to one of its tiny green moons.

EXT. FOURTH MOON OF YAVIN

The pirate ship soars over the dense jungle.

EXT. MASSASSI OUTPOST

An alert guard, his laser gun in hand, scans the countryside. He sets the gun down and looks toward the temple, barely visible in the foliage.

EXT. MASSASSI OUTPOST—JUNGLE TEMPLE

In a forest of gargantuan trees lies an ancient temple. The air is heavy with the fantastic cries of unimaginable creatures. Han, Luke, and the others are greeted by the Rebel troops.

INT. MASSASSI—MAIN HANGAR DECK

A military speeder stops in a huge spaceship hangar set up in the interior of the crumbling temple.

Willard, the commander of the Rebel forces, hurries up to the group and gives Leia a big hug.

*WILLARD: *(holding Leia)* You're safe! When we heard about Alderaan, we feared the worst.

*LEIA: We have no time for sorrows, Commander. You must use the information in this R2 unit to help plan the attack. It's our only hope.

Artoo is debriefed.

EXT. SPACE

The surface of the Death Star ominously approaches the red planet Yavin.

INT. DEATH STAR—CONTROL ROOM

Grand Moff Tarkin and Lord Darth Vader are interrupted in their discussion by the buzz of the comlink. Tarkin moves to answer the call.

TARKIN: Yes.

DEATH STAR INTERCOM VOICE: We are approaching the planet Yavin. The Rebel base is on a moon on the far side. We are preparing to orbit the planet.

EXT. YAVIN—JUNGLE

A lone guard stands in a tower high above the Yavin landscape, surveying the countryside. A mist hangs over the jungle of twisted green.

INT. MASSASSI—WAR ROOM BRIEFING AREA

Dodonna stands before a large electronic wall display. Leia and several other Senators are to one side of the giant readout. The low-ceilinged room is filled with starpilots, navigators, and a sprinkling of R2-type robots. Everyone is listening intently to what Dodonna is saying. Han and Chewbacca are standing near the back.

DODONNA: The battle station is heavily shielded and carries a firepower greater than half the starfleet. Its defenses are designed around a direct large-scale assault. A small one-man fighter should be able to penetrate the outer defense.

Gold Leader, a rough-looking man in his early thirties, stands and addresses Dodonna.

GOLD LEADER: Pardon me for asking, sir, but what good are snubfighters going to be against that?

DODONNA: Well, the Empire doesn't consider a small one-man fighter to be any threat, or they'd have a tighter defense. An analysis of the plans provided by Princess Leia has demonstrated a weakness in the battle station.

Artoo-Detoo makes beeping sounds and turns his head.

DODONNA: The approach will not be easy. You are required to maneuver straight down this trench and skim the surface to this point. The target area is only two meters wide. It's a small thermal exhaust port, right below the main port. The shaft leads directly to the reactor system. A precise hit will start a chain reaction which should destroy the station. Only a precise hit will set up a chain reaction. The shaft is ray-shielded, so you'll have to use proton torpedoes.

Luke is sitting next to Wedge Antilles, a hotshot pilot about sixteen years old.

WEDGE: That's impossible, even for a computer.

LUKE: It's not impossible. I used to bull's-eye womp rats in my T-sixteen back home. They're not much bigger than two meters.

DODONNA: Then man your ships! And may the Force be with you!

The group rises and begins to leave.

In the second draft Han, Luke, the droids, and Chewbacca land on Yavin in lifepods while Montross (Solo's friend) stays behind aboard the ship. Deak is in a glass-enclosed mummy case. After landing, Luke is attacked by a two-foot-high insectlike creature and kills it by knocking it against the lifepod (this scene was actually created in the rough and first drafts but involved Annikin Starkiller).

In the second draft Luke, Han, Chewbacca, and the droids find the Rebel outpost of Massassi and are greeted by Bail Antilles, "an agent of the Starkiller." They find out that the Death Star has tracked them down. After the briefing in the war room with General Dodonna we meet the Starkiller, Deak and Luke's father, a wizened old man with long silver hair and beard and gray-blue eyes. "He is a large man shriveled by an incalculable number of years." The Grand Moff Tarkin, a Rebel commander, and a general named Aay Zavor blame Luke for their trouble; because of him the Empire was able to follow them to Yavin. Antilles takes up Luke's defense and says that Luke risked his life to bring them back the "Kiber Crystal." The Starkiller explains to Luke that Deak has the Bogan (the dark side) in him; it will be a while before he can become himself again. The Starkiller also tells his son that because his training is not complete; he is going to have to fight the Death Star as a warrior, not as a Jedi.

The concept of Han constantly asking for his reward was added in the third draft, and during the briefing in the war room a hotshot pilot of sixteen named Chewie Antilles is introduced. In the rough draft there was a galactic trader named Bail Antilles, and in the revised fourth draft Bail Antilles was the name of Leia's father and "Viceroy and Chairman of the Alderaan System." In the fourth draft the scene in which the Rebels find the group in the jungle has been omitted. Instead, the heroes arrive directly in the hangar of the Massassi Outpost and are greeted by Zan Dodonna, commander of the Rebel Forces. He tells Ben Kenobi what a great honor it is to meet him and says he thought he was dead. Ben replies, "Maybe I was." In the briefing room the hotshot pilot is now named Wedge Antilles.

EXT. SPACE

The Death Star begins to move around the planet toward the tiny green moon.

INT. DEATH STAR

Circles of light intertwine around one another on the computer-projected screen showing the position of the Death Star in relation to Yavin and the fourth moon.

DEATH STAR INTERCOM VOICE: Orbiting the planet at maximum velocity. The moon with the Rebel base will be in range in thirty minutes.

Tarkin and Vader have been watching the screen with interest.

VADER: This will be a day long remembered. It has seen the end of Kenobi. It will soon see the end of the Rebellion.

INT. MASSASSI OUTPOST—MAIN HANGAR DECK

Luke and Threepio enter the huge spaceship hangar. Flight crews rush around loading last-minute armaments and unlocking power couplings. In an area isolated from this activity, Luke sees Han and Chewbacca loading small boxes onto an armored speeder.

MAN'S VOICE: *(over loudspeaker)* All flight troops, man your stations. All flight troops, man your stations.

Han is deliberately ignoring the activity of the fighter pilots' preparations. Luke is quite saddened at the sight of his friend's departure.

LUKE: So . . . you got your reward and you're just leaving, then?

HAN: That's right, yeah! I got some old debts I got to pay off with this stuff. Even if I didn't, you don't think I'd be fool enough to stick around here, do you? Why don't you come with us? You're pretty good in a fight. I could use you.

*LUKE: *(getting angry)* Come on! Why don't you take a look around? You know what's about to happen, what they're up against. They could use a good pilot like you. You're turning your back on them.

*HAN: What good's a reward if you ain't around to use it? Besides, attacking the battle station ain't my idea of courage. It's more like suicide.

*LUKE: All right. Well, take care of yourself, Han . . . I guess that's what you're best at, isn't it?

Luke goes off, and Han hesitates, then calls to him.
HAN: Hey, Luke . . . may the Force be with you!

George Lucas: "Moving in the area of the Force and then trying to describe it, trying to come up with a name for it, trying to describe this other existence, I didn't want to use God or any of those kinds of connotations. Even though I called it the Force of this and the Force of that in the beginning, I eventually shorthanded it just to the Force."

Chewie growls at his captain. Han turns to him.
HAN: What're you lookin' at? I know what I'm doing.
INT. MAIN HANGAR DECK—LUKE'S SHIP
MAN'S VOICE: *(over loudspeaker)* All pilots to your stations. All pilots to your stations.
Luke, Leia, and Dodonna meet under a huge spacefighter.
LEIA: What's wrong?
LUKE: Oh, it's Han! I don't know, I really thought he'd change his mind.
LEIA: He's got to follow his own path. No one can choose it for him.
LUKE: I only wish Ben were here.
Leia gives Luke a little kiss, turns, and goes off.

In the second draft Han receives eight million for his trouble and brags to his friend Montross that for once they have earned their reward legally (in the fourth draft Solo is paid with boxes of spice). Luke tells Threepio and Artoo that "they can retire," but they ask if they can stay in his service. Finally, Luke leaves for the battle with Bail Antilles and Threepio in the gunpod. In the third draft, before Luke takes off with Artoo, Ben, who was wounded during the escape from the Death Star and is resting in a medical chamber, gives him the "Kiber Crystal." In the fourth draft Luke is reunited with his friend Biggs; this scene actually was shot but was deleted when the sequence at the beginning that introduced Biggs was cut out. The scene was restored in the *Special Edition.*

From the Special Edition:
INT. MAIN HANGAR DECK
As Luke heads for his ship, another pilot rushes up to him and grabs his arm.

BIGGS: Luke! I don't believe it! How'd you get here . . . are you going out with us?!

LUKE: Biggs! Of course, I'll be up there with you! Listen, have I got some stories to tell you . . .

Red Leader, a rugged handsome man in his forties, comes up behind Luke and Biggs. He has the confident smile of a born leader.

RED LEADER: Are you . . . Luke Skywalker? Have you been checked out on the Incom T-sixty-five?

BIGGS: Sir, Luke is the best bushpilot in the outer rim territories.

Pilot Leader pats Luke on the back as they stop in front of his fighter.

PILOT LEADER: I met your father once when I was just a boy. He was a great pilot. You'll do all right. If you've got half of your father's skill, you'll do better than all right.

LUKE: Thank you,sir. I'll try.

Red Leader hurries to his own ship.

BIGGS: I've got to get aboard. Listen, you'll tell me your stories when we come back. All right?

LUKE: I told you I'd make it someday, Biggs.

BIGGS: *(going off)* You did, all right. It's going to be like old times, Luke. We're a couple of shooting stars that'll never be stopped!

Luke laughs and shakes his head in agreement. He heads for his ship.

As Luke begins to climb up the ladder into his sleek, deadly spaceship, the crew chief, who is working on the craft, points to little Artoo, who is being hoisted into a socket on the back of the fighter.

CHIEF: This R2 unit of yours seems a bit beat-up. Do you want a new one?

LUKE: Not on your life! That little droid and I have been through a lot together. *(to Artoo)* You okay, Artoo?

The crewmen lower Artoo-Detoo into the craft. Now a part of the exterior shell of the starship, the little droid beeps that he is fine.

Luke climbs up into the cockpit of his fighter and puts on his helmet. Threepio looks on from the floor of the massive hangar as the crewmen secure his little electronic partner into Luke's X-wing. It's an emotion-filled moment as Artoo beeps goodbye.

CHIEF: Okay, easy she goes!

THREEPIO: Hang on tight, Artoo, you've got to come back.

Artoo beeps in agreement.

THREEPIO: You wouldn't want my life to get boring, would you?

Artoo whistles his reply.

All final preparations are made for the approaching battle. The hangar is buzzing with the last minute activity as the pilots and crewmen alike make their final adjustments.

In the second draft the battle sequence is about ten pages long. Quickly, most of the Rebel fleet is destroyed and Luke is on his own, with Vader and his two wingmen on his tail. As in the movie, Han shows up and fires at one of the wingmen. Vader's ship is hit and dives into Han's spaceship, exploding on impact, but luckily, Montross, Han, and Chewbacca have escaped in lifepods. Threepio and Antilles—who are both in Luke's ship—shoot down the exhaust port, and the Death Star explodes. In the third draft, although the script doesn't describe the action in great detail, the battle is similar to the way it ended up in the film, with a pilot leader and Blue and Red Rebel fighter squadrons. There are a few differences, however; in this version of the story, Chewie Antilles dies in the battle and when Luke is about to aim at the target, he holds the "Kiber Crystal," which suddenly begins to glow and lights up the entire cabin. In this draft and as in the film, Vader's ship, with a bent solar fin, limps into the vast darkness of space. In the fourth draft Ben Kenobi is present during the battle and gives advice to Luke, telling him to trust his feelings. In this draft, as in the film, Biggs dies during the battle and Luke switches to manual commands. After the battle, when Luke gets back to the base, Ben congratulates him and says that like his father, he has become a powerful Jedi.

EXT. MASSASSI OUTPOST—JUNGLE

All that can be seen of the fortress is a lone guard standing on a small pedestal jutting out above the dense jungle. The muted gruesome crying sounds that naturally permeate this eerie purgatory are overwhelmed by the thundering din of ion rockets as a series of silver starships catapult from the foliage into a tight formation and disappear into the morning cloud cover.

INT. MASSASSI OUTPOST—WAR ROOM

The princess, Threepio, and a field commander stand quietly before a display showing the planet Yavin and its four moons.

MASSASSI INTERCOM VOICE: Standby alert. Death Star approaching. Estimated time to firing range, fifteen minutes.

EXT. SPACE

The Death Star slowly moves behind the massive yellow surface of Yavin in the foreground as many X-wing fighters flying in formation zoom toward us and out of the frame.

INT. RED LEADER STARSHIP—COCKPIT

Red Leader to each side at his wingmen.

RED LEADER: All wings report in.

INT. ANOTHER COCKPIT

One of the Rebel fighters checks in through his mike.

RED TEN: Red Ten standing by.

INT. BIGGS'S COCKPIT

Biggs checks his fighter's controls, alert and ready for combat.

RED SEVEN: *(over Biggs's headset)* Red Seven standing by.

BIGGS: Red Three standing by.

INT. PORKINS'S COCKPIT

PORKINS: Red Six standing by.

RED NINE: *(over headset)* Red Nine standing by.

INT. WEDGE'S FIGHTER—COCKPIT

WEDGE: Red Two standing by.

INT. LUKE'S X-WING FIGHTER—COCKPIT

RED ELEVEN: *(over headset)* Red Eleven standing by.

LUKE: Red Five standing by.

EXT. LUKE'S X-WING FIGHTER

Artoo-Detoo, in position outside of the fighter, swivels his head and makes beeping sounds.

INT. RED LEADER'S FIGHTER—COCKPIT

RED LEADER: Lock S-foils in attack position.

EXT. SPACE

The group of X-wing fighters moves in formation toward the Death Star, unfolding the wings and locking them into the "X" position.

Ralph McQuarrie: "The Death Star became a sphere of enormous proportions when the guys at ILM thought that it had to have a flat surface in order to run their camera above it and we calculated the size of a sphere that would have a flat horizon when you were standing on the surface."

INT. PORKINS'S COCKPIT

RED LEADER: *(over headset)* We're passing through their magnetic field.

INT. RED LEADER'S COCKPIT

RED LEADER: Hold tight!

INT. LUKE'S X-WING FIGHTER—COCKPIT

Luke adjusts his controls as he concentrates on the approaching Death Star. The ships begin to be buffeted slightly.

RED LEADER: *(over headset)* Switch your deflectors on.

INT. ANOTHER COCKPIT

RED LEADER: *(over headset)* Double front!

EXT. SPACE

The fighters, now X-shaped darts, move in formation. The Death Star now appears to be a small moon growing rapidly in size as the Rebel fighters approach. Complex patterns on the metallic surface begin to become visible.

INT. WEDGE'S COCKPIT

Wedge is amazed and slightly frightened at the awesome spectacle.

WEDGE: Look at the size of that thing!

INT. LUKE'S COCKPIT

RED LEADER: *[over headset]* Cut the chatter, Red Two.

INT. RED LEADER'S COCKPIT

RED LEADER: Accelerate to attack speed.

EXT. SPACE

As the fighters move closer to the Death Star, the awesome size of the gargantuan Imperial fortress is revealed. Half of the deadly space station is in shadow, and this area sparkles with thousands of small lights running in thin lines and occasionally grouped in large clusters, somewhat like a city at night as seen from a weather satellite.

Joe Johnston: "The challenge in creating the surface of the Death Star was that we had to design panels that we could build the prototype of and then mass-produce in foam. But we were limited to six panels because that's all we could afford to build. And my input on the Death Star was to come up with six panels that were then divided into several sections, and for each section we had to keep the design both varied enough and generic enough so that you wouldn't see the same piece of landscape popping up several times. To enhance that, we had two scales of tower built that we could place around to sort of break the design, but the idea was to create texture that the audience couldn't recognize. We had different-size gun towers and also areas that we left undetailed so that from a distance it would look like there were parts that were not finished yet."

INT. RED LEADER'S COCKPIT

RED LEADER: This is it, boys!

INT. GOLD LEADER'S COCKPIT

GOLD LEADER: Red Leader, this is Gold Leader.

INT. LUKE'S COCKPIT

RED LEADER: *[over headset]* I copy, Gold Leader.

INT. GOLD LEADER'S COCKPIT

GOLD LEADER: We're starting for the target shaft now.

RED LEADER: We're in position. I'm going to cut across the axis and try and draw their fire.

EXT. SPACE

Two squads of Rebel fighters peel off. The X-wings dive toward the Death Star sur-
face. A thousand lights glow across the dark gray expanse of the huge station.

INT. DEATH STAR

In large turbopowered laser gun emplacements, the huge guns rotate into position
and begin firing.

EXT. SPACE AROUND THE DEATH STAR

Laserbolts streak through the star-filled night. The Rebel X-wing fighters move in
toward the Imperial base as the Death Star aims its massive laser guns at the
Rebel forces and fires.

Joe Johnston: "The X-wing was based on an idea that George had
where he wanted to see these wings unfold as the ships are getting
ready to go on to battle. He wanted to start out with the wings folded
and see them expand as they're heading toward the Death Star. This
idea dictated the design of the ship, and Colin Cantwell had
designed an early X-wing prototype that was similar, but it was much
sleeker and looked more like a racing craft. At the time reflections
were a huge problem in visual effects, and you couldn't have any
kind of rounded canopy on a ship. You couldn't take a chance on reflected blue screens or reflecting light or anything like that. So virtu-
ally all the ships except for Luke's landspeeder had flat glass panels."

INT. MASSASSI OUTPOST—WAR ROOM

Princess Leia listens to the battle over the intercom. Threepio is at her side.

WEDGE: *(over war room speaker system)* Heavy fire, boss! Twenty-three
degrees.

RED LEADER: *(over speaker)* I see it. Stay low.

EXT. SPACE

An X-wing zooms across the surface of the Death Star.

INT. DEATH STAR

A laser gun fires at the Rebel forces.

INT. WEDGE'S COCKPIT

Wedge maneuvers his fighter toward the menacing Death Star.

EXT. SPACE

X-wings continue in their attack course on the Death Star.

INT. LUKE'S X-WING FIGHTER—COCKPIT

Luke nosedives radically, starting his attack on the monstrous fortress.

LUKE: This is Red Five! I'm going in!

EXT. SPACE

Luke's X-wing races toward the Death Star. Laserbolts streak from Luke's weapons, creating a huge fireball explosion on the dim surface.

INT. LUKE'S X-WING FIGHTER—COCKPIT

Terror crosses Luke's face as he realizes he won't be able to pull out in time to avoid the fireball.

BIGGS: *(over headset)* Luke, pull out!

EXT. SURFACE OF DEATH STAR

Luke's ship emerges from the fireball with the leading edges of his wings slightly scorched.

INT. BIGGS'S COCKPIT

BIGGS: Are you all right?

INT. LUKE'S X-WING FIGHTER—COCKPIT

Luke adjusts his controls and breathes a sigh of relief. Flak bursts outside the cockpit window.

LUKE: I got a little cooked, but I'm okay.

EXT. SURFACE OF THE DEATH STAR

Rebel fighters continue to strafe the Death Star's surface with laserbolts.

Joe Johnston: "A lot of the battle sequence was cut using World War II film footage and excerpts from movies such as *The Dam Busters* [1954], *The Bridges of Toko-Ri* [1954], and *Twelve O'Clock High* [1949], and George basically got dupes of these old movies and cut a space battle using these World War II planes before he had the special effects shots. My job was to interpret and storyboard that sequence; I basically ran through his cut back and forth on the Moviola, and where there was a fighter plane attacking a bomber, I had to turn it into a TIE fighter attacking the *Millennium Falcon*. There was quite a bit of interpretation involved, but there was a blueprint to work from; the broad strokes had been determined by George and his cut, so it was just a matter of transposing the World War II planes to a set of spacecraft."

INT. DEATH STAR

The corridors are alive with activity. Alarms sound. Stormtroopers run in all directions. Walking in the middle of the chaos, a vision of calm and foreboding, is Darth Vader. One of his astro-officers rushes up to him.

ASTRO-OFFICER: We count thirty Rebel ships, Lord Vader. But they're so small, they're evading our turbolasers!

VADER: We'll have to destroy them ship to ship. Get the crews to their fighters.

EXT. SPACE

Red Leader flies through a heavy hail of flak.

INT. RED LEADER'S X-WING—COCKPIT—TRAVELING

RED LEADER: Watch yourself! There's a lot of fire coming from the right side of that deflection tower.

INT. LUKE'S X-WING FIGHTER—COCKPIT—TRAVELING

LUKE: I'm on it.

INT. BIGGS'S COCKPIT

BIGGS: I'm going in. Cover me, Porkins!

INT. PORKINS'S COCKPIT

PORKINS: I'm right with you, Red Three.

EXT. SURFACE OF THE DEATH STAR

Rebel fighters, firing laserbolts, streak toward the onrushing Death Star surface, causing a protruding tower to erupt in flames.

INT. DEATH STAR

Explosions reverberate through the massive structure. Many soldiers rush about in the chaos, silhouetted by the almost continual flash of explosions.

EXT. SPACE

A dense barrage of laserfire streaks by on all sides.

INT. PORKINS'S COCKPIT

PORKINS: I've got a problem, here.

EXT. SPACE

Laserfire continues to streak by on all sides.

INT. BIGGS'S COCKPIT

BIGGS: Eject!

INT. PORKINS'S COCKPIT

PORKINS: I can hold it.

INT. BIGGS'S COCKPIT

BIGGS: Pull out!

INT. PORKINS'S COCKPIT

PORKINS: No, I'm all right.

An explosion hits Porkins's ship, and the cabin fills with smoke.

EXT. PORKINS'S X-WING

Porkins's ship explodes.

INT. DEATH STAR

Tarkin stands in front of the computer-projected screen.

DEATH STAR INTERCOM VOICE: The Rebel base will be in firing range in seven minutes.

EXT. SPACE—LUKE'S X-WING

INT. LUKE'S COCKPIT

BEN'S VOICE: Luke, trust your feelings.

EXT. SURFACE OF THE DEATH STAR

Luke attacks the surface of the Death Star with laserfire.
DEATH STAR
Luke's attack wreaks its explosive effect inside the Death Star.
INT. LUKE'S COCKPIT
Luke peers out of his cockpit at the surface of the Death Star.
EXT. SPACE
Luke's X-wing streaks past.
INT. MASSASSI—OUTPOST—WAR ROOM
On all sides technicians work in front of many lighted glass walls. Dodonna watches quietly from one corner. One of the officers speaks into his handset.
CONTROL OFFICER: Squad leaders, we've picked up a new group of signals. Enemy fighters coming your way.
INT. LUKE'S X-WING FIGHTER—COCKPIT—TRAVELING
Luke looks around to see if he can spot the approaching Imperial fighter.
LUKE: My scope's negative. I don't see anything.
INT. RED LEADER'S X-WING—COCKPIT—TRAVELING
RED LEADER: Pick up your visual scanning.
INT. BIGGS'S COCKPIT—TRAVELING
RED LEADER: *(over headset)* Here they come.
EXT. SPACE
Five ferocious Imperial TIE ships dive on the Rebel fighters.

Joe Johnston: "The design Colin Cantwell did for the TIE fighters was extremely simple. It was basically two big panels with a straight stick in between and a spherical cockpit, and there was almost no detail on it at all. George liked the shape, liked the basic idea of what they were calling at the time 'silver panels' with basically a ball as a cockpit in between two flat panels, but beyond that it wasn't very interesting because it didn't have any detail. So the way the ball was attached and mounted and the way the glass cockpit window was incorporated in the design of the ball, all that stuff was part of the redesign that I did.

"We didn't need all the ships ready at the same time; we could shoot one set of elements and then add on the others. The X-wings were done first, and then we added the TIE fighters."

INT. RED LEADER'S COCKPIT
RED LEADER: Watch it! You've got one on your tail.
EXT. SPACE

Imperial TIE fighter fires at the Rebel X-wing.

INT. X-WING COCKPIT

Rebel pilot looks over his shoulder in panic.

INT. TIE FIGHTER'S COCKPIT

The TIE fighter pilot follows the X-wing, firing remorselessly.

EXT. SPACE *(TIE FIGHTER'S POV)*

Laserfire follows the X-wing.

INT. X-WING COCKPIT

The X-wing pilot is hit.

EXT. SPACE

The X-wing blows up.

INT. LUKE'S COCKPIT

RED LEADER: Biggs! You've picked one up . . . Watch it!

INT. BIGGS'S COCKPIT

BIGGS: I can't see it!

EXT. SPACE AROUND THE DEATH STAR

Biggs zooms off the surface and into space, closely followed by an Imperial TIE fighter.

INT. BIGGS'S COCKPIT—TRAVELING

Biggs sees the TIE ship behind him and swings around, trying to avoid him. The TIE ship fires several laserbolts at Biggs but misses.

BIGGS: They're on me tight. I can't shake him . . .

INT. LUKE'S COCKPIT

LUKE: I'll be right there.

EXT. SPACE

Luke pursues the TIE fighter which is pursuing Biggs.

INT. LUKE'S COCKPIT

Luke scans his computer.

EXT. SPACE

Luke continues to pursue the TIE ship.

INT. LUKE'S COCKPIT

Luke locks his target into his computer and fires.

EXT. SPACE

The TIE fighter explodes in a mass of flames.

INT. DEATH STAR

Darth Vader strides purposefully down a Death Star corridor and addresses two Imperial TIE fighter pilots.

VADER: Several fighters have broken off from the main group. Come with me!

INT. MASSASSI OUTPOST—WAR ROOM

A concerned Princess Leia, Threepio, Dodonna, and other officers of the Rebel-

lion stand around the huge round readout screen, listening to the ship-to-ship communication on the room's loudspeaker.

BIGGS: *(over speaker)* Pull in! Luke . . . pull in!

WEDGE: *(over speaker)* Watch your back, Luke!

INT. LUKE'S X-WING FIGHTER—COCKPIT

WEDGE: *(over headset)* Watch your back! Fighters above you, coming in!

EXT. SPACE

Luke's ship soars away from the Death Star's surface as he spots the tailing TIE fighter.

INT. TIE FIGHTER'S COCKPIT

The TIE pilot takes aim at Luke's X-wing.

EXT. SPACE

The Imperial TIE fighter pilot scores a hit on Luke's ship. Fire breaks out on the right side of the X-wing.

INT. LUKE'S X-WING FIGHTER—COCKPIT

Luke looks out of his cockpit at the flames on his ship.

LUKE: I'm hit, but not bad.

EXT. LUKE'S X-WING FIGHTER

Smoke pours out from behind Artoo-Detoo.

LUKE'S VOICE: Artoo, see what you can do with it. Hang on back there.

Green laserfire moves past the beeping little robot as his head turns.

INT. LUKE'S X-WING FIGHTER—COCKPIT

Luke nervously works his controls.

RED LEADER: *(over headset)* Red Six . . .

INT. MASSASSI OUTPOST—WAR ROOM

In the war room, Leia stands frozen as she listens and worries about Luke.

RED LEADER: *(over speaker)* Can you see Red Five?

RED TEN: *(over speaker)* There's a heavy fire zone on this side. Red Five, where are you?

INT. LUKE'S X-WING FIGHTER—COCKPIT

Luke spots the TIE fighters behind him and soars away from the Death Star surface.

LUKE: I can't shake him!

EXT. SURFACE OF THE DEATH STAR

Luke's ship soars closer to the surface of the Death Star, an Imperial TIE fighter closing in on him in hot pursuit.

INT. WEDGE'S COCKPIT

The Death Star whips below Wedge.

WEDGE: I'm on him, Luke!

INT. LUKE'S X-WING FIGHTER—COCKPIT

WEDGE: *(over headset)* Hold on!

EXT. SURFACE OF THE DEATH STAR

Wedge dives across the horizon toward Luke and the TIE fighter.

INT. WEDGE'S COCKPIT

Wedge moves his X-wing in rapidly.

INT. MASSASSI OUTPOST—WAR ROOM

Leia and Threepio follow the battle with concern.

INT. LUKE'S X-WING FIGHTER—COCKPIT

Luke reacts frantically.

LUKE: Blast it! Biggs, where are you?

INT. TIE FIGHTER—COCKPIT

The fighter pilot watches Wedge's X-wing approach. Another X-wing joins him, and both unleash a volley of laserfire on the Imperial fighter.

EXT. SPACE

The TIE fighter explodes, filling the screen with white light. Luke's ship can be seen far in the distance.

INT. LUKE'S X-WING FIGHTER—COCKPIT

Luke looks about in relief.

LUKE: Thanks, Wedge.

INT. MASSASSI OUTPOST—WAR ROOM

Leia, Threepio, Dodonna, and other Rebel officers are listening to the Rebel fighters' radio transmissions over the war room intercom.

BIGGS: *(over speaker)* Good shooting, Wedge!

GOLD LEADER: *(over speaker)* Red Leader . . .

INT. GOLD LEADER'S Y-WING—COCKPIT

Gold Leader peels off and starts toward the long trenches at the Death Star surface pole.

Joe Johnston: "The Y-wing and most of the ships originally had a bubble canopy like one sees on jet fighters. They were also delicate; they had very thin support and weaponry that would have completely disappeared in front of a blue screen. The other thing was that we wanted to make the ships look like they had been maintained with spare parts; you know, damage had been patched with big panels of a different color. George kept emphasizing that he wanted the ships to look like hot rods; they needed to look used, greasy, maintained with spare parts, sort of held together with wires and chewing gum."

GOLD LEADER: . . . This is Gold Leader. We're starting our attack run.

EXT. SPACE AROUND THE DEATH STAR

Three Y-wing fighters of the Gold group dive out of the stars toward the Death Star surface.

INT. MASSASSI OUTPOST—WAR ROOM

Leia and the others are grouped around the screen as technicians move about attending to their duties.

RED LEADER: *(over speaker)* I copy, Gold Leader. Move into position.

EXT. SPACE AROUND THE DEATH STAR

Three Imperial TIE ships in precise formation dive toward the Death Star surface.

INT. DARTH VADER'S COCKPIT

Darth Vader calmly adjusts his control stick as the surface of the Death Star whips past in the window above his head.

VADER: Stay in attack formation!

INT. MASSASSI OUTPOST—WAR ROOM

Technicians are seated at the computer readout table.

GOLD LEADER: *(over speaker)* The exhaust port is . . .

INT. GOLD LEADER'S Y-WING—COCKPIT

GOLD LEADER: . . . marked and locked in!

EXT. SPACE AROUND THE DEATH STAR

Gold Leader approaches the surface and pulls out to skim the surface of the huge station. The ship moves into a deep trench, firing laserbolts. The surface streaks past as laserfire is returned by the Death Star.

INT. GOLD FIVE'S Y-WING—COCKPIT—TRAVELING

Gold Five is a pilot in his early fifties with a very battered helmet that looks like it's been through many battles. His fighter is buffeted by Imperial flak.

GOLD LEADER: *(over headset)* Switch all power to front deflector screens.

INT. GOLD LEADER'S Y-WING—COCKPIT

Gold Leader races down the enormous trench that leads to the exhaust port. Laserbolts blast toward him in increasing numbers, occasionally exploding near the ship, causing it to bounce about.

GOLD LEADER: Switch all . . .

INT. GOLD TWO'S Y-WING

Gold Two is a younger pilot, about Luke's age.

GOLD LEADER: *(over headset)* . . . power to front deflector screens.

EXT. SURFACE OF THE DEATH STAR

Three Y-wings skim the Death Star surface deep in the trench as laserbolts streak past on all sides.

EXT. DEATH STAR SURFACE—GUN EMPLACEMENT

An exterior surface gun blazes away at the oncoming Rebel fighters.

INT. GOLD LEADER'S Y-WING—COCKPIT

GOLD LEADER: How many guns do you think, Gold Five?

INT. MASSASSI OUTPOST—WAR ROOM

GOLD FIVE: *(over speaker)* Say about twenty guns. Some on the surface, some on the towers.

Leia, Threepio, and the technicians view the projected target screen as target lights glow. The red target near the center blinks on and off.

Richard Chew: "For me, one of the biggest contributions I made to the film was a suggestion I made to George to intercut Princess Leia and the Rebels on their station with Luke making the run to destroy the Death Star. I had the idea that if we could put Princess Leia in jeopardy and then simultaneously have Luke try to destroy the Death Star in order to save her and the Rebels, it would just provide much more tension to the ending. Originally, these were not simultaneous events; they were separate. Without this crosscutting, whether Luke blew the Death Star on time or not wouldn't have had the same tension. If you look at the film, in the scenes with Leia, there's no dialogue that's on camera in synch because all the footage was taken from other scenes of the Rebels in the war room, and all the information that you're getting as to how close the Death Star is to the Rebels is either on animated screens or off-screen dialogue through a PA system. But in Leia's dialogue, for instance, there wasn't really any of the exposition that would indicate that they were in jeopardy. That was all created in the editing, as was the crosscutting between the action and the shots of Darth Vader before he got into his fighter and Tarkin, the Peter Cushing character."

MASSASSI INTERCOM VOICE: *(over speaker)* Death Star will be in range in five minutes.

EXT. SURFACE OF THE DEATH STAR

The three Y-wing fighters race toward camera and zoom past through a hail of laserfire.

INT. GOLD LEADER'S Y-WING—COCKPIT

Gold Leader pulls his computer targeting device down in front of his eyes. Laserbolts continue to batter the Rebel craft.

GOLD LEADER: Switch to targeting computer.

INT. GOLD LEADER'S Y-WING—COCKPIT

Gold Two's ship shudders under intense laser barrage.

GOLD TWO: Computer's locked. Getting a signal.

As the fighters begin to approach the target area, suddenly all the laserfire stops. An eerie calm clings over the trench as the surface whips past in a blur.

GOLD TWO: The guns . . . they've stopped!

EXT. SURFACE OF THE DEATH STAR

Two Y-wings zoom down the Death Star trench.

INT. GOLD FIVE'S COCKPIT

Gold Five looks behind him.

GOLD FIVE: Stabilize your rear deflectors. Watch for enemy fighters.

INT. GOLD LEADER'S Y-WING—COCKPIT

GOLD LEADER: They're coming in! Three marks at two ten.

EXT. SPACE AROUND THE DEATH STAR

Three Imperial TIE ships, Darth Vader in the center flanked by two wingmen, dive in precise formation almost vertically toward the Death Star surface.

INT. DARTH VADER'S COCKPIT

Darth Vader calmly adjusts his control stick as the stars zoom by.

VADER: I'll take them myself! Cover me!

INT. THE WINGMAN'S COCKPIT

WINGMAN: Yes, sir.

EXT. SPACE AROUND THE DEATH STAR

Three TIE fighters zoom across the surface of the Death Star.

INT. DARTH VADER'S COCKPIT

Vader lines up Gold Two in his targeting computer. Vader's hands grip the control stick as he presses the button.

INT. GOLD TWO'S Y-WING—COCKPIT

The cockpit explodes around Gold Two. His head falls forward.

EXT. SPACE AROUND THE DEATH STAR

As Gold Two's ship explodes, debris is flung out into space.

INT. GOLD LEADER'S Y-WING—COCKPIT

Gold Leader looks over his shoulder at the scene.

EXT. DEATH STAR TRENCH

The three TIE fighters race along in the trench in a tight formation.

INT. GOLD LEADER'S Y-WING—COCKPIT

Gold Leader begins to panic.

EXT. DEATH STAR TRENCH

The three TIE fighters are closing.

INT. GOLD LEADER'S Y-WING—COCKPIT

GOLD LEADER: *(into mike)* It's no good; I can't maneuver!

INT. GOLD FIVE'S Y-WING—COCKPIT

Gold Five, the old veteran, tries to calm Gold Leader.

GOLD FIVE: Stay on target!

INT. GOLD LEADER'S Y-WING—COCKPIT

The Death Star races by outside the cockpit window as he adjusts his targeting device.

GOLD LEADER: We're too close.

INT. GOLD FIVE'S Y-WING—COCKPIT

The older pilot remains calm.

GOLD FIVE: Stay on target!

EXT. DEATH STAR TRENCH

The TIE fighters close in.

INT. GOLD LEADER'S Y-WING—COCKPIT

Now he's really panicked.

GOLD LEADER: Loosen up!

INT. DARTH VADER'S COCKPIT

Vader calmly adjusts his targeting computer and pushes the fire button.

INT. GOLD LEADER'S Y-WING—COCKPIT

Gold Leader's ship is hit by Vader's lasers.

EXT. SURFACE OF THE DEATH STAR

Gold Leader explodes in a ball of flames, throwing debris in all directions.

INT. GOLD FIVE'S Y-WING—COCKPIT

Gold Five moves in on the exhaust port.

GOLD FIVE: Gold Five to Red Leader . . .

INT. LUKE'S X-WING FIGHTER—COCKPIT

Luke looks over his shoulder at the action outside of his cockpit.

GOLD FIVE: *(over headset)* Lost Tiree, lost Hutch.

INT. RED LEADER'S COCKPIT

RED LEADER: I copy, Gold Leader.

INT. GOLD FIVE'S Y-WING—COCKPIT

GOLD FIVE: They came from behind . . .

EXT. SURFACE OF THE DEATH STAR

One of the engines explodes on Gold Five's Y-wing fighter, blazing out of control. He dives past the horizon toward the Death Star's surface. Gold Five, a veteran of countless campaigns, spins toward his death.

INT. LUKE'S X-WING FIGHTER—COCKPIT

Luke looks nervously about him at the explosive battle.

INT. DEATH STAR—CONTROL ROOM

OFFICER: We've analyzed their attack, sir, and there is a danger. Should I have your ship standing by?

TARKIN: Evacuate? In our moment of triumph? I think you overestimate their chances!

Tarkin turns to the computer readout screen. Flames move around the green disk at the center of the screen; numbers read across the bottom.

VOICE: *(over speaker)* Rebel base, three minutes and closing.

INT. RED LEADER'S COCKPIT

Red Leader looks over at his wingmen.

RED LEADER: Red boys, this is Red Leader.

INT. MASSASSI OUTPOST—WAR ROOM

RED LEADER: *(over speaker)* Rendezvous at mark six point one.

WEDGE: *(over speaker)* This is Red Two. Flying toward you.

BIGGS: *(over speaker)* Red Three, standing by.

Dodonna moves to the intercom.

INT. RED LEADER'S COCKPIT

DODONNA: *(over headset)* Red Leader, this is Base One. Keep half your group out of range for the next run.

INT. BIGGS'S COCKPIT

Biggs listens in.

INT. LUKE'S X-WING FIGHTER—COCKPIT

RED LEADER'S VOICE: *(over headset)* Copy, Base One. Luke, take Red Two and Three.

INT. RED LEADER'S COCKPIT

RED LEADER: Hold up here and wait for my signal . . .

INT. LUKE'S X-WING FIGHTER—COCKPIT

RED LEADER'S VOICE: *(over headset)* . . . to start your run.

Luke nods his head.

EXT. SPACE AROUND THE DEATH STAR

The X-wing fighters of Luke, Biggs, and Wedge fly in formation high above the Death Star surface.

INT. LUKE'S X-WING FIGHTER—COCKPIT

Luke peers out from his cockpit.

EXT. SURFACE OF THE DEATH STAR

Two X-wings move across the surface of the Death Star. Red Leader's X-wing drops down to the surface leading to the exhaust port.

INT. RED LEADER'S COCKPIT

Red Leader looks around to watch for the TIE fighters. He begins to perspire.

RED LEADER: This is it!

EXT. SPACE

Red Leader roams down the trench of the Death Star as lasers streak across the black heavens.

EXT. DEATH STAR SURFACE—GUN EMPLACEMENT

A huge remote-control laser cannon fires at the approaching Rebel fighters.

EXT. DEATH STAR TRENCH

The Rebel fighters evade the Imperial laserblasts.

INT. RED TEN'S COCKPIT

RED TEN: We should be able to see it by now.

EXT. DEATH STAR TRENCH

From the cockpits of the Rebel pilots, the surface of the Death Star streaks by, with Imperial laserfire shooting toward them.

INT. RED LEADER'S COCKPIT

RED LEADER: Keep your eyes open for those fighters!

EXT. DEATH STAR TRENCH

The Rebel fighters fly in formation.

INT. RED TEN'S COCKPIT
RED TEN: There's too much interference!
EXT. SPACE—ABOVE DEATH STAR TRENCH
Three X-wing fighters move in formation above the Death Star trench.
RED TEN'S VOICE: Red Five, can you see them from where you are?
INT. LUKE'S X-WING FIGHTER—COCKPIT
Luke looks down at the Death Star surface below.
LUKE: No sign of any . . . Wait!
LUKE: *(over headset)* Coming in point three five.
Red Ten looks up and sees the Imperial fighters.
RED TEN: I see them.

Paul Hirsch: "I remember the studio wanted to eliminate the battle sequence from the script. They didn't want to shoot it because it was too expensive. They said, 'Well, they get to the Death Star, they rescue the princess, and that's it. You don't need an end battle.' But George was determined, and he said, 'We got to get going on the end battle before they really come down on cost, and we will do all the other shots later.' So there was a big deadline to get the battle done.

"The black-and-white footage was World War II fighter pilot stuff, and it was used to give a sense of motion. But very often the shots had nothing to do with what they represented. So you'd see a shot of a plane coming right toward you, and you'd look at the first frame and there'd be a number inscribed on it, and you'd look at this long list of special effects shots and you'd find the number, and it would say: 'Vader's ship moving left to right in trench.' So watching that didn't really tell you what the final film was going to look like, but what it said was that you cut to exterior at that point. It was a bit confusing because the directions weren't necessarily right, the size of the shot, the action weren't necessarily right . . . Sometimes the shots matched the action, but very often it was just guys sitting in front of a blue screen saying: 'Red One, this is Red Leader,' and you'd cut to a black-and-white shot of a Japanese plane, and then you'd have another guy in front of a blue screen saying: 'This is Red One, go ahead Red Leader,' and so on."

EXT. SURFACE OF THE DEATH STAR

Three TIE fighters, Vader flanked by two wingmen, dive in a tight formation. The sun reflects off their dominant solar fins as they loop toward the Death Star surface.

INT. RED LEADER'S COCKPIT

RED LEADER: I'm in range.

Red Leader moves his targeting device in front of his eyes.

EXT. SURFACE OF THE DEATH STAR

Red Leader's X-wing moves up the Death Star trench.

INT. RED LEADER'S COCKPIT

RED LEADER: Target's coming up!

Red Leader looks into his targeting device at his computer target readout screen.

RED LEADER: Just hold them off for a few seconds.

INT. DARTH VADER'S COCKPIT

Vader adjusts his control lever and dives on the X-wing fighters.

VADER: Close up formation.

The three TIE fighters move in formation across the Death Star surface.

INT. RED LEADER'S COCKPIT

RED LEADER: Almost there!

Red Leader lines up his target on the targeting device crosshairs.

EXT. SURFACE OF THE DEATH STAR

Vader and his wingmen zoom down the trench.

INT. DARTH VADER'S COCKPIT

Vader rapidly approaches the two X-wings of Red Ten and Red Twelve. The X-wings show in the center of Vader's computer screen. Vader's laser cannon flashes below the view of the front porthole.

EXT. SPACE

Red Twelve's X-wing fighter is hit by Vader's laserfire, and it explodes into flames against the trench.

INT. RED TEN'S COCKPIT

Red Ten works at his controls furiously, trying to avoid Vader's fighter behind him.

RED TEN: You'd better let her loose.

INT. RED LEADER'S COCKPIT

Red Leader is concentrating on his targeting device.

RED TEN: *(over headset)* They're right behind me.

RED LEADER: Almost there!

INT. RED TEN'S COCKPIT

Red Ten panics.

RED TEN: I can't hold them!

EXT. SURFACE OF THE DEATH STAR

Vader and his wingmen whip through the trench in pursuit of the Rebel fighters.

INT. RED TEN'S COCKPIT

Red Ten looks over his shoulder.

INT. DARTH VADER'S COCKPIT

Vader coolly pushes the fire button on his control stick.

INT. RED TEN'S COCKPIT

Darth Vader's well-aimed laserfire proves to be unavoidable and strikes Red Ten's ship. Red Ten screams in anguish and pain.

EXT. SPACE AROUND THE DEATH STAR

Red Ten's ship explodes and bursts into flames.

INT. RED LEADER'S COCKPIT

Grimly, Red Leader takes careful aim and watches his computer targeting device, which shows the target lined up in the crosshairs, and fires.

EXT. DEATH STAR TRENCH

Red Leader's missiles zoom down the trench.

RED LEADER: It's away!

EXT. DEATH STAR SURFACE

Red Leader's X-wing pulls up just before a huge explosion billows out of the trench.

INT. DEATH STAR

An armed Imperial stormtrooper is knocked to the floor by the attack explosion. Other troopers scurrying about the corridors are knocked against the wall and lose their balance.

INT. MASSASSI OUTPOST—WAR ROOM

Leia and the others stare at the computer screen.

RED NINE'S VOICE: *(over speaker)* It's a hit!

RED LEADER: *(over speaker)* Negative.

INT. RED LEADER'S COCKPIT

Tiny explosions are visible in the distance.

RED LEADER: Negative! It didn't go in, just impacted on the surface.

INT. MASSASSI OUTPOST—WAR ROOM

Leia shows her disappointment.

EXT. SPACE AROUND THE DEATH STAR—TIE FIGHTER

Darth Vader peels off in pursuit as Red Leader's X-wing passes the Death Star horizon.

INT. DARTH VADER'S COCKPIT

Vader swings his ship around for his next kill.

INT. RED LEADER'S COCKPIT

LUKE: *(over headset)* Red Leader, we're right above you. Turn to point . . .

INT. LUKE'S X-WING FIGHTER—COCKPIT

Luke tries to spot Red Leader. He looks down at the Death Star surface.

LUKE: . . . oh-five; we'll cover for you.

RED LEADER: *(over headset)* Stay there . . .

INT. RED LEADER'S COCKPIT

A wary Red Leader looks about nervously.

RED LEADER: . . . . I just lost my starboard engine.

INT. WEDGE'S COCKPIT

Wedge looks down out of his cockpit.

INT. LUKE'S X-WING FIGHTER—COCKPIT

RED LEADER: *(over headset)* Get set up . . .

INT. RED LEADER'S COCKPIT

RED LEADER: . . . for your attack run.

INT. DARTH VADER'S COCKPIT

Vader's gloved hand makes contact with the control sticks, and he presses their firing buttons.

EXT. SPACE AROUND THE DEATH STAR

Laserbolts are firing from Vader's TIE fighter, connecting with Red Leader's Rebel X-wing fighter.

INT. RED LEADER'S COCKPIT

Red Leader screams.

  Luke looks out the window of his X-wing at the explosion of Red Leader's fighter far below. For the first time, he feels the helplessness of his situation.

INT. DEATH STAR

DEATH STAR INTERCOM VOICE: Rebel base, one minute and closing.

Grand Moff Tarkin casts a sinister eye at the computer screen.

INT. MASSASSI OUTPOST—WAR ROOM

Dodonna and Princess Leia, with Threepio beside them, listen intently to the talk between the pilots. The room is grim after Red Leader's death. Princess Leia nervously paces the room.

LUKE: *(over speaker)* Biggs, Wedge, let's close it up. We're going in. We're going in full throttle.

INT. LUKE'S COCKPIT

LUKE: That ought to keep those fighters off our back.

INT. WEDGE'S COCKPIT

WEDGE: Right with you, boss.

EXT. SPACE AROUND THE DEATH STAR

The two X-wings peel off against a background of stars and dive toward the Death Star.

INT. BIGGS'S COCKPIT

BIGGS: Luke, at that speed will you be able to pull out in time?

LUKE: It'll be just like Beggar's Canyon back home.

EXT. SPACE AROUND THE DEATH STAR

The three X-wings move in toward the trench, unleashing a barrage of laserfire. Laserbolts are returned from the Death Star.

INT. BIGGS'S COCKPIT

Biggs struggles with his controls.

BIGGS: We'll stay back far enough to cover you.

INT. LUKE'S COCKPIT

WEDGE: *(over headset)* My scope shows the tower, but I can't see the exhaust port!

INT. WEDGE'S COCKPIT

WEDGE: Are you sure the computer can hit it?

EXT. DEATH STAR TRENCH

The two covering X-wings fly down the trench, dodging laserbolts.

EXT. DEATH STAR—GUN EMPLACEMENT

The Death Star laser cannon slowly rotates as it shoots laserbolts.

INT. LUKE'S X-WING FIGHTER—COCKPIT

LUKE: Watch yourself! Increase speed full throttle!

WEDGE: What about that tower?

INT. LUKE'S X-WING FIGHTER—COCKPIT

LUKE: You worry about those fighters! I'll worry about the tower!

EXT. DEATH STAR SURFACE

Luke's X-wing streaks through the trench, firing lasers.

INT. LUKE'S X-WING FIGHTER—COCKPIT

Luke breaks into a nervous sweat as the laserfire is returned, nicking one of his wings close to the engine.

LUKE: *(to Artoo)* Artoo . . . that, that stabilizer's broken loose again. See if you can't lock it down!

EXT. LUKE'S X-WING FIGHTER

Artoo works to repair the damage. The canyon wall rushes by in the background, making his delicate task seem more precarious.

EXT. DEATH STAR

Two laser cannons are firing on the Rebel fighters.

INT. BIGGS'S COCKPIT

Biggs looks around nervously for the TIE fighters.

INT. WEDGE'S COCKPIT

Wedge looks up and sees the TIE ships.

EXT. DEATH STAR TRENCH

Vader and his wingmen are closing in.

Rick McCallum: "We changed the shot of the planet Yavin during the restoration of the film. It moves better now, and it's a better reveal. The shots of the different spacecrafts have been cleaned up. For instance, the movements on the TIE fighters are less jerky . . . We added more ships in certain shots to make the chases more dynamic. The laserbolts also look better. There's only one reason why we did this, and that reason is archival. I'm serious when I say that two years ago it would have been impossible for this film to ever be released in the theaters again. It was gone, finished. Had this work not been done, in two or three years the picture would have completely disintegrated. Does an artist have the right to revisit his work? In the case of *Star Wars*, George didn't change anything that he didn't want or didn't originally conceive."

INT. WEDGE'S COCKPIT

WEDGE: Fighters. Coming in, point three.

Luke's targeting device marks off the distance to the target.

EXT. SPACE AROUND THE DEATH STAR

Vader and his wingmen zoom closer.

INT. WEDGE'S COCKPIT

Wedge looks over his shoulder at the closing TIE fighters.

INT. DARTH VADER'S COCKPIT

Vader adjusts his controls and fires laserbolts at the two X-wings flying down the trench. He scores a direct hit on Wedge.

INT. MASSASSI OUTPOST—WAR ROOM

Leia and the others are grouped around the computer board.

WEDGE: *(over headset)* I'm hit!

INT. WEDGE'S COCKPIT

WEDGE: I can't stay with you.

LUKE: *(over headset)* Get clear, Wedge.

INT. LUKE'S X-WING FIGHTER—COCKPIT

LUKE: You can't do any more good back there!

INT. WEDGE'S COCKPIT

WEDGE: Sorry!

EXT. SPACE AROUND THE DEATH STAR

Wedge pulls his crippled X-wing back away from the battle.
  Vader watches the escape but issues a command to his wingmen.

VADER: Let him go! Stay on the leader!

EXT. SPACE AROUND THE DEATH STAR

Luke's X-wing speeds down the trench; the three TIE fighters, still in perfect unbroken formation, tail close behind.

INT. BIGGS'S COCKPIT

Biggs looks around at the TIE fighters. He is worried.

BIGGS: Hurry, Luke, they're coming in much faster this time.

INT. LUKE'S COCKPIT

BIGGS: *(over headset)* We can't hold them!

EXT. SPACE AROUND THE DEATH STAR

The three TIE fighters move ever closer, closing in on Luke and Biggs.

INT. LUKE'S X-WING FIGHTER—COCKPIT

Luke looks back anxiously at little Artoo.

LUKE: Artoo, try and increase the power!

EXT. LUKE'S X-WING FIGHTER

Ignoring the bumpy ride, a beeping Artoo-Detoo struggles to increase the power, his dome swiveling.

EXT. SPACE AROUND THE DEATH STAR

Stealthily, the TIE formation creeps closer.

INT. DARTH VADER'S COCKPIT

Vader adjusts his control stick.

INT. BIGGS'S COCKPIT

Biggs looks around at the TIE fighters.

INT. LUKE'S X-WING FIGHTER—COCKPIT

Luke looks into his targeting device.

BIGGS: *(over headset)* Hurry up, Luke! Wait!

EXT. SPACE AROUND THE DEATH STAR

Vader and his wingmen race through the Death Star trench. Biggs moves in to cover for Luke, but Vader gains on him.

INT. BIGGS'S COCKPIT

Biggs sees the TIE fighters aiming at him.

INT. DARTH VADER'S COCKPIT

Vader squeezes the fire button on his controls.

INT. BIGGS'S COCKPIT

Biggs's cockpit explodes around him, lighting him in red.

EXT. SURFACE OF THE DEATH STAR

Biggs's ship bursts into a million flaming bits and scatters across the surface.

INT. MASSASSI OUTPOST—WAR ROOM

Leia and the others stare at the computer board.

INT. LUKE'S X-WING FIGHTER—COCKPIT

Luke is stunned by Biggs's death, but his anger is also growing.

INT. DEATH STAR—CONTROL ROOM

Grand Moff Tarkin watches the projected target screen with satisfaction.

DEATH STAR INTERCOM VOICE: Rebel base, thirty seconds and closing.

INT. DARTH VADER'S COCKPIT

Vader takes aim at Luke and talks to his wingmen.

VADER: I'm on the leader.

EXT. SURFACE OF THE DEATH STAR—LUKE'S SHIP

Luke's ship streaks through the trench of the Death Star.

INT. MASSASSI OUTPOST—WAR ROOM

Princess Leia glances at Threepio with a solid, grim determination. Threepio seems nervous.

THREEPIO: Hang on, Artoo!

Rick McCallum: "The battle sequence in the rough and first drafts is only five pages long; Han Solo has taught the Wookiees to operate starships, and they join General Skywalker in the final attack. They fire at the surface of the space fortress, causing chain reaction explosions; Vader and the governor are killed in the battle when the fortress explodes."

George Lucas: "The whole point was to show how a primitive culture like the Wookiees could overcome highly technical people. That was the theme; you have these woodland creatures that are completely nontechnical overcoming the Empire. But I used this instead in *Return of the Jedi* with the Ewoks."

INT. LUKE'S X-WING FIGHTER—COCKPIT
Luke concentrates on his targeting device.
EXT. SURFACE OF THE DEATH STAR
Three TIE fighters charge away down the trench toward Luke. Vader's fingers curl around the control stick.
INT. LUKE'S X-WING FIGHTER—COCKPIT
Luke adjusts the lens of his targeting device.
EXT. SURFACE OF THE DEATH STAR
Luke's ship charges down the trench.
INT. LUKE'S X-WING FIGHTER—COCKPIT
Luke lines up the yellow crosshair lines of the targeting device's screen. He looks into the targeting device, then starts at a voice he hears.
BEN'S VOICE: Use the Force, Luke.
EXT. SURFACE OF THE DEATH STAR
The Death Star trench zooms by.
INT. LUKE'S X-WING FIGHTER—COCKPIT
Luke looks up, then starts to look back into the targeting device. He has second thoughts.
BEN'S VOICE: Let go, Luke.
EXT. SURFACE OF THE DEATH STAR
Luke's fighter streaks through the trench.
INT. DARTH VADER'S COCKPIT
VADER: The Force is strong with this one!
Vader follows Luke's X-wing down the trench.
INT. LUKE'S X-WING FIGHTER—COCKPIT
Luke looks to the targeting device, then away as he hears Ben's voice.
BEN'S VOICE: Luke, trust me.
Luke's hand reaches for the control panel and presses the button. The targeting device moves away.
INT. MASSASSI OUTPOST—WAR ROOM
Leia and the others stand watching the projected screen.

BASE VOICE: *(over speaker)* His computer's off. Luke, you switched off your targeting computer. What's wrong?

LUKE'S VOICE: *(over speaker)* Nothing. I'm all right.

EXT. SURFACE OF THE DEATH STAR

Luke's ship streaks ever closer to the exhaust port.

INT. LUKE'S X-WING FIGHTER—COCKPIT

Luke looks at the Death Star surface streaking by.

INT. LUKE'S X-WING FIGHTER

Artoo-Detoo turns his head from side to side, beeping in anticipation.

EXT. SURFACE OF THE DEATH STAR

The three TIE fighters, manned by Vader and his two wingmen, follow Luke's X-wing down the trench.

Vader maneuvers his controls as he looks at his doomed target. He presses the fire buttons on his control sticks. Laserfire shoots toward Luke's X-wing fighter.

LUKE'S X-WING FIGHTER

A large burst of Vader's laserfire engulfs Artoo. The arms go limp on the smoking little droid as he makes a high-pitched sound.

INT. LUKE'S X-WING FIGHTER—COCKPIT

Luke looks frantically back over his shoulder at Artoo.

EXT. LUKE'S X-WING FIGHTER

Smoke billows out around little Artoo, and sparks begin to fly.

LUKE: I've lost Artoo!

Artoo's beeping sound dies out.

INT. MASSASSI OUTPOST—WAR ROOM

Leia and the others stare intently at the projected screen, while Threepio watches the princess.

MASSASSI INTERCOM VOICE: The Death Star has cleared the planet. The Death Star has cleared the planet.

Lights representing the Death Star and targets glow brightly.

INT. DEATH STAR—CONTROL ROOM

DEATH STAR INTERCOM VOICE: Rebel base, in range.

Lights representing the Death Star and targets glow brightly.

TARKIN: You may fire when ready.

DEATH STAR INTERCOM VOICE: Commence primary ignition.

An officer reaches up and pushes buttons on the control panel.

EXT. SURFACE OF THE DEATH STAR

The three TIE fighters zoom down the Death Star trench in pursuit of Luke, never breaking formation.

INT. LUKE'S COCKPIT

Luke looks anxiously at the exhaust port.

INT. DARTH VADER'S COCKPIT

Vader adjusts his control sticks, checking his projected targeting screen.

EXT. SURFACE OF THE DEATH STAR
Luke's ship barrels down the trench.
INT. LUKE'S COCKPIT
Luke continues determinedly down the trench.
INT. DARTH VADER'S COCKPIT
Vader's targeting computer swings around into position. Vader takes careful aim at Luke's X-wing fighter.
VADER: I have you now.
He pushes the fire buttons.
EXT. SURFACE OF THE DEATH STAR
The three TIE fighters move in on Luke. As Vader's center fighter unleashes a volley of laserfire, one of the TIE ships at his side is hit and explodes into flame. The two remaining ships continue to move on.
INT. LUKE'S X-WING FIGHTER—COCKPIT
Luke looks about, wondering whose laserfire destroyed Vader's wingman.
INT. DARTH VADER'S COCKPIT
Vader is taken by surprise and looks out from his cockpit.
VADER: What?
INT. DARTH VADER'S WINGMAN—COCKPIT
Vader's wingman searches around him, trying to locate the unknown attacker.
INT. *MILLENNIUM FALCON*—COCKPIT
Han grins from ear to ear.
HAN: *(yelling)* Yahoo!
EXT. SPACE AROUND THE DEATH STAR
The Millennium Falcon *heads right at the two TIE fighters. It's a collision course.*

Paul Hirsch: "During the sneak preview, the film started, the ship came over at the top of the screen, and the audience went wild. When they made the jump into hyperspace the first time, escaping from Tatooine, they all jumped out of their seats, and the whole screening was like that with people literally leaping out of their seats. So then we get to the moment in the end battle when Han knocks Darth Vader out, and the audience lets out a cheer . . . And the moment really worked for the audience. After the screening, I said to George, 'Anything you want to change?' and he said, 'I think we'll leave it alone.' So we never touched a frame."

INT. WINGMAN'S COCKPIT
The wingman spots the pirate ship coming at him and warns the Dark Lord.
WINGMAN: Look out!

EXT. DEATH STAR TRENCH

Vader's wingman panics at the sight of the oncoming pirate starship and veers radically to one side, colliding with Vader's TIE fighter in the process. Vader's wingman crashes into the side wall of the trench and explodes.

EXT. SPACE AROUND THE DEATH STAR

Vader's damaged ship has spun out of the trench with a damaged wing and continues to spin out of control with a bent solar fin, heading for deep space.

INT. DARTH VADER'S COCKPIT

Vader turns around and around in circles as his ship spins into space.

EXT. SURFACE OF THE DEATH STAR

Solo's ship moves in toward the Death Star trench.

INT. *MILLENNIUM FALCON*—COCKPIT

Solo, smiling, speaks to Luke over his headset mike.

HAN: *(into mike)* You're all clear, kid. Now let's . . .

INT. MASSASSI OUTPOST—WAR ROOM

Leia and the others listen to Solo's transmission.

HAN: *(over speaker)* . . . blow this thing and go home!

INT. LUKE'S X-WING FIGHTER—COCKPIT

Luke looks up and smiles. He concentrates on the exhaust port, then fires his laser torpedoes.

EXT. SURFACE OF THE DEATH STAR

Luke's torpedo shoots toward the port and seems to simply disappear into the surface and not explode. But the shots do find their mark and have gone into the exhaust port and are heading for the main reactor.

INT. LUKE'S X-WING FIGHTER—COCKPIT

Luke throws his head back in relief.

INT. DEATH STAR

An Imperial soldier runs to the control panel board and pulls the attack lever as the board behind him lights up.

INTERCOM VOICE: Stand by.

EXT. SPACE AROUND THE DEATH STAR

Two X-wings, a Y-wing, and the pirate ship race toward Yavin in the distance.

INT. DEATH STAR

Several Imperial soldiers, flanking a pensive Grant Moff Tarkin, busily push control levers and buttons.

INTERCOM VOICE: Stand by.

EXT. SPACE AROUND THE DEATH STAR

The Rebel ships have raced out of sight, leaving the moonlike Death Star alone against a blanket of stars. The Death Star bursts into a supernova, creating a spectacular heavenly display.

INT. *MILLENNIUM FALCON*—COCKPIT

HAN: Great shot, kid. That was one in a million.

INT. LUKE'S X-WING FIGHTER—COCKPIT

Luke is at last at ease, and his eyes are closed.

BEN'S VOICE: Remember, the Force will be with you . . . always.

The ship rocks back and forth.

EXT. DARTH VADER'S TIE FIGHTER

Vader's ship spins off into space.

INT. DARTH VADER'S TIE FIGHTER

Vader rights his ship.

EXT. SPACE

Vader's TIE fighter heads off into space.

EXT. SPACE

The Rebel ships race toward the fourth moon of Yavin.

INT. MASSASSI OUTPOST—MAIN HANGAR

Luke climbs out of his starship fighter and is cheered by a throng of ground crew and pilots. Luke climbs down the ladder as they all welcome him with laughter, cheers, and shouting.
   Princess Leia rushes toward him.

LEIA: Luke!

She throws her arms around Luke and hugs him as they dance around in a circle. Solo runs in toward Luke.

HAN: *(laughing)* Hey! Hey!

Han and Luke embrace one another.

LUKE: *(laughing)* I knew you'd come back! I just knew it!

HAN: Well, I wasn't gonna let you get all the credit and take all the reward.

Luke and Han look at one another as Solo playfully shoves at Luke's face. Leia moves in between them.

LEIA: *(laughing)* Hey, I knew there was more to you than money.

Luke looks toward the ship.

LUKE: Uh, no!

The fried little Artoo-Detoo is lifted off the back of the fighter and carried off under the worried eyes of Threepio.

THREEPIO: Oh, my! Artoo! Can you hear me? Say something! *(to mechanic)* You can repair him, can't you?

TECHNICIAN: We'll get to work on him right away.

THREEPIO: You must repair him! Sir, if any of my circuits or gears will help, I'll gladly donate them.

LUKE: He'll be all right.

EXT. MASSASSI OUTPOST

Trumpets are heard over the jungle setting.

INT. MASSASSI—MAIN THRONE ROOM

Luke, Han, and Chewbacca enter the huge ruins of the main temple. Hundreds of troops are lined up in neat rows. At the far end stands a vision in white, the beautiful young Senator Leia. Luke and the others solemnly march up the long aisle and kneel before Senator Leia.

Chewbacca is confused. Dodonna and several other dignitaries stand behind the Princess Leia. Leia is dressed in a long white dress and is staggeringly beautiful. She places a gold medallion around Han's neck. He winks at her. To one side a pristine Threepio stands, awestruck by the whole event. She then repeats the ceremony with Luke, who is moved by the event. They turn and face the assembled troops, who all applaud them. Chewbacca growls, and a shined-up and fully repaired Artoo beeps with happiness.

FADE OUT

END CREDITS OVER STARS

THE END

The story in the treatment ends with a huge parade on Ophuchi. The princess's uncle, the ruler of the planet, rewards the bureaucrats while Luke and the boys are commissioned into the princess's special guard. In the rough and first drafts Leia becomes the new queen. She designates the courageous warriors "Class A-4," and Annikin Starkiller is declared the new protector of Aquilae. The second draft ends after Luke comes back from the battle. His father, the Starkiller, congratulates him on his victory, and a roll appears, hinting at a possible sequel: ". . . And a thousand new systems joined the Rebellion, causing a significant crack in the great wall of the powerful Galactic Empire. The Starkiller would once again spark fear in the hearts of the Sith Knights, but not before his sons were put to many tests . . . the most daring of which was the kidnapping of the Lars family, and the perilous search for 'The Princess of Ondos.' " FADE OUT. In the third draft and all subsequent versions of the story Leia gives a medal to the heroes. In the third and fourth drafts Ben Kenobi is at her side for the ceremony. Ben dies in the revised fourth draft.

George Lucas: "There was a point when I was writing *Star Wars* where I just sat down and went through the entire story. I think it came around the third or fourth draft. I wrote a treatment or a book of notes that went through all the scripts, even the trilogy that I'm currently working on. It was reasonably loose, but it laid out the basic story of what happens, who does what to whom, and the various major issues. While I was writing the treatment, I decided to limit *Star Wars*. I said this is the stuff that happens later, this is the stuff that happens before, and this is the material that I need to make the script about. And that's how it came about that there was enough material for six scripts."

EPISODE V

The Empire Strikes Back

Star Wars. Episode V: *The Empire Strikes Back*
Annotations and Interviews by Laurent Bouzereau

Annotations on *Star Wars*, Episode V: *The Empire Strikes Back*, are based on the following materials:

Chapter II, *The Empire Strikes Back*, November 28 through December 2, 1977—story conference transcript, George Lucas and Leigh Brackett

The Empire Strikes Back, November 28, 1977—story treatment by George Lucas (handwritten original notes)

The Empire Strikes Back, November 28, 1977—story treatment by George Lucas (typed from original notes)

Star Wars Sequel, screenplay by Leigh Brackett, from *The Adventures of Luke Skywalker* by George Lucas, February 23, 1978—first draft

The following drafts were written by
George Lucas:

April 1978—second draft (handwritten version)

April 1978—second draft (typed from original notes)

April 1978—revised second draft (with George Lucas's handwritten notes)

April 1978—revised second draft (typed copy)

April 1978—third draft (handwritten notes)

Correspondence from Irvin Kerschner to George Lucas dated February 19, 1979, regarding revisions to pages 143–160

The following drafts were written by
Lawrence Kasdan:

Fourth draft revisions dated October 24, 1978 (Ext. Plain of Hoth—
Helicopter Shot—Day)

Fourth draft revisions dated October 24, 1978

Star Wars, Episode V: *The Empire Strikes Back*, by Leigh Brackett
and Lawrence Kasdan, from the novel by George Lucas, February 20, 1979—fifth draft

STAR WARS

A long time ago in a galaxy far, far away . . .

A vast sea of stars serves as the backdrop for the main title. War drums echo through the heavens as a roll-up slowly crawls into infinity.

EPISODE V
THE EMPIRE STRIKES BACK

It is a dark time for the
Rebellion. Although the Death
Star has been destroyed,
Imperial troops have driven the
Rebel forces from their hidden
base and pursued them across
the galaxy.

Evading the dreaded
Imperial Starfleet, a group of
freedom fighters led by Luke
Skywalker has established a
new secret base on the remote
ice world of Hoth.

The evil lord Darth Vader,
obsessed with finding young
Skywalker, has dispatched
thousands of remote probes into
the far reaches of space . . .

The crawl first appeared in the second draft.

The movie starts with a helicopter shot of a plain on Hoth: "A white snowscape racing to camera . . . The main title quickly recedes into the bleak horizon, followed by a roll-up."

Episode II: *The Empire Strikes Back*. "After the destruction of its most feared battle station, the Empire has declared martial law throughout the galaxy. A million worlds have felt the oppressive hand of the Emperor's stormtroopers in their attempt to crush the growing Rebellion. As the Imperial grip of tyranny tightens, a small band of freedom fighters search for a more secure base of operation . . ."

The crawl was subsequently modified and lengthened for the film.

EXT. GALAXY—PLANET HOTH

A Star Destroyer moves through space. It releases Imperial probe robots from its underside.

One of these probes zooms toward the planet Hoth and lands on its ice-covered surface. An explosion marks the point of impact.

EXT. HOTH—METEORITE CRATER—SNOW PLAIN—DAY

A weird mechanical sound rises above the whining of the wind. A strange probe robot with several extended sensors emerges from the smoke-shrouded crater. The ominous mechanical probe floats across the snow plain and disappears.

Ralph McQuarrie: "I did quite a lot of drawings of the Imperial probe robot. Joe Johnston and I both contributed to it . . . I kind of thought of it as a spidery thing with arms that could pick up stuff off the ground. I gave it these big round bulging lenses things that kind of looked like spider eyes and hanging legs."

EXT.—PLAIN OF HOTH—DAY

A small figure gallops across the windswept ice slope. The bundled rider is mounted on a large gray two-legged snow lizard, a tauntaun.

Joe Johnston: "Ralph McQuarrie and I did a lot of drawings for the tauntauns, but George wanted Phil Tippett to work on the design as well, since he was the one who was going to animate it. So it was his sculpture of the creature that really determined what it was going to look like."

The rider gallops up a slope and reins his lizard to a stop. Pulling off his protective goggles, Luke Skywalker notices something in the sky. He takes a pair of electrobinoculars from his utility belt and through them sees smoke rising from where the probe robot has crashed.

The wind whips at Luke's fur-lined cap, and he activates a comlink transmitter. His tauntaun shifts nervously beneath him.

LUKE: *(into comlink)* Echo Three to Echo Seven. Han, old buddy, do you read me?

After a little static a familiar voice is heard.

HAN: *(over comlink)* Loud and clear, kid. What's up?

LUKE: *(into comlink)* Well, I finished my circle. I don't pick up any life readings.

HAN: *(over comlink)* There isn't enough life on this ice cube to fill a space cruiser. The sensors are placed. I'm going back.

LUKE: *(into comlink)* Right. I'll see you shortly. There's a meteorite that hit the ground near here. I want to check it out. It won't take long.

Luke clicks off his transmitter and reins back on his nervous lizard. He pats the beast on the head to calm it.

LUKE: Hey, steady, girl. Hey, what's the matter? You smell something?

Suddenly he hears a monstrous howl and turns to see an eleven-foot-tall shape towering over him. It is a wampa ice creature, lunging at him ferociously.

Luke is hit by a huge white claw. He falls unconscious into the snow, and in a moment the terrified screams of the tauntaun are cut short by the horrible snap of a neck being broken.

The wampa ice creature grabs Luke by one ankle and drags him away across the frozen plain.

During the story conferences involving George Lucas and Leigh Brackett that took place November 28 through December 2, 1977, Hoth is referred to as the "Ice Planet." It is a planet completely covered by snow and has castles built into it. Hoth was originally going to be the name for the "Gas Planet" (which became Cloud City in the movie). During story conferences, several other planets were mentioned:

"The Water Planet": an underwater city.

"I'taz: The Rock/Desert Planet": gray, colorless with a civilization living in caves.

"The Garden Planet": Slightly fairy-tale–like; very lush environment with gardens rather than forests. Possible names for the planet were Bestpenkoluta, Bestpenkoleta, and Besspin-Kaaleita.

"Ton-mummd: The Grass Planet": with tall wheat fields, grass, and giant rolling hills as far as one can see.

"The City Planet": sort of like the Death Star, a completely built-over planet and possibly the home of the Empire.

The opening scene was discussed at length by Lucas and Brackett; a helicopter shot would reveal two men riding the snow dunes on some kind of giant snow lizard. One guy calls the other on his walkie-talkie but can't reach him; he hears all kinds of weird sounds. His friend eventually replies and says he's okay, but suddenly a beast attacks and kills him. The other man gets back to the base and reports that his friend has disappeared. Eventually the man attacked by the snow creature became Luke.

The opening envisioned in the treatment is similar to the way the movie begins, with Luke and Han riding their tauntauns. The first draft by Leigh Brackett also begins with Han and Luke on their "snow lizards" (they don't have a name in the script), riding the plains of the Ice Planet. There is no probe landing in the snow; instead, Luke tells Han via comlink that he has spotted a pretty ice formation and is going to check it out. Han reminds his friend that their orders specified that they go just to the ridge, not farther, but obviously Luke has made up his mind, and Solo returns to the base.

As for the wampa, the snow creature that attacks Luke in the movie, early discussions suggest that it should appear at the beginning of the movie as the Rebels are building their underground base, and that the creature should be fishlike, something that swims in the snow. The notes indicate that these beasts could possibly have supernatural powers and should be inside the building where the Rebels are hiding, creating chaos when Vader is approaching and beginning his attack on the base.

EXT. HOTH—REBEL BASE ENTRANCE—DAY
A stalwart figure rides his tauntaun up to the entrance of an enormous ice cave.
INT. HOTH—REBEL BASE—MAIN HANGAR DECK
Rebel troopers rush about unloading supplies and otherwise securing their new base. The rider, Han Solo, swings off his lizard and pulls off his goggles.

He walks into the main hangar deck toward the Millennium Falcon, which is parked among several fighters. Mechanics, R2 units, and various other droids hurry about. Han stops at the Millennium Falcon, where his Wookiee copilot, Chewbacca, is welding on a central lifter.

HAN: Chewie! Chewie! Chewie!

Chewie stops his work and lifts his face shield, growling an irritated greeting to his boss.

HAN: All right, don't lose your temper. I'll come right back and give you a hand.

Chewbacca puts his mask back on and returns to his welding as Han leaves.

Ralph McQuarrie: "George told me he wanted a castle, a big myste-rious castle on Hoth, and I did some paintings of that. It was the first drawing I did for *Empire*. It showed big towers with steel, silver, dif-ferent kinds of metal poking through the snow. It was meant to be the top of a huge cathedral-like structure."

In the first draft the Rebel base is described as an "ice castle," a natural structure of great beauty with fantastic domes and spires, hooded gun emplacements, and radar towers designed to be invisible from above. As Han arrives at the base, a blank wall slides open. Inside the structure ice has been hollowed into a series of chambers and halls with different levels and elevators.

Irvin Kershner: "Do you know why I had Chewbacca work with a welding torch on the *Falcon*? That was the only thing I could find where you could see what he was doing. If he was screwing some-thing with a tool, you wouldn't see anything. So whenever anything needs fixing, you'll notice the characters are welding!"

INT. HOTH—REBEL BASE—COMMAND CENTER
A makeshift command center has been set up in a blasted area of thick ice. The low-ceilinged room is a beehive of activity. Controllers, troopers, and droids move about setting up electronic equipment and monitoring radar signals.
   General Rieekan looks up from a console at Han's approach.
RIEEKAN: Solo?
HAN: No sign of life out there, General. The sensors are in place. You'll know if anything comes around.
RIEEKAN: Commander Skywalker reported in yet?
HAN: No. He's checking out a meteorite that hit near him.
RIEEKAN: With all the meteor activity in this system, it's going to be difficult to spot approaching ships.
Han blurts out what is on his mind.
HAN: General, I got to leave. I can't stay anymore.
Princess Leia, standing at a console nearby, is dressed in a short white combat jacket and pants. Her hair is braided and tied across her head in a Nordic fashion. She overhears their conversation and seems somewhat distressed.
RIEEKAN: I'm sorry to hear that.
HAN: Well, there's a price on my head. If I don't pay off Jabba the Hutt, I'm a dead man.
RIEEKAN: A death mark's not an easy thing to live with. You're a good fighter, Solo. I hate to lose you.

HAN: Thank you, General.

He turns to Leia as Rieekan moves away.

HAN: *(with feeling)* Well, Your Highness, I guess this is it.

LEIA: That's right.

Leia is angry. Han sees she has no warmth to offer him. He shakes his head and adopts a sarcastic tone.

HAN: *(coolly)* Well, don't get all mushy on me. So long, Princess.

Han walks away into the quiet corridor adjoining the command center. Leia stews a moment, then hurries after him.

In the first draft the war room has a three-dimensional rendition of the galaxy, "giving the impression that we're in space." Rebel Commander Willard explains: "We are here . . . The fourth planet of this detached system at the edge of Granita Clusta." Also present are General Dodonna, who appeared in *Star Wars: A New Hope*, Leia, and Threepio and Artoo, who are working at the panels, displaying calculations. Most of the map shifts to red, indicating the territories controlled by the Empire, and Willard explains that despite the destruction of the Death Star and the fact that many systems have joined the Rebellion, they're still weak and quite vulnerable. Interrupting his speech when Han walks in, Willard reprimands Han for being late. Leia tells Willard she'll handle Han, and they step out. Threepio watches this, gives "the robotic equivalent of a chuckle," and tells Artoo that Solo is as undisciplined as he is. In a more serious tone Threepio says that he is worried about the Empire and that the Rebellion has taken a huge chance with this new base.

INT. HOTH—REBEL BASE—ICE CORRIDOR

LEIA: Han!

Han stops in the corridor and turns to face Leia.

HAN: Yes, Your Highnessness?

LEIA: I thought you had decided to stay.

HAN: Well, the bounty hunter we ran into on Ord Mantell changed my mind.

LEIA: Han, we need you!

HAN: We need?

LEIA: Yes.

HAN: Oh, what about you need?

LEIA: *(mystified)* I need? I don't know what you're talking about.

HAN: *(shakes his head, fed up)* You probably don't.

LEIA: And what precisely am I supposed to know?

HAN: Come on! You want me to stay because of the way you feel about me.

LEIA: Yes. You're a great help to us. You're a natural leader . . .

HAN: No! That's not it. Come on. Aahhh—uh huh! Come on.

Leia stares at him, then understands.

LEIA: You're imagining things.

HAN: Am I? Then why are you following me? Afraid I was going to leave without giving you a good-bye kiss?

LEIA: I'd just as soon kiss a Wookiee.

HAN: I can arrange that. You could use a good kiss!

Angrily, Han strides down the corridor as Leia stares after him.

Many changes in Han's character were discussed during story meetings. In coming up with a possible mission for Han, George Lucas fleshed out the character's backstory. Han is an orphan and was raised by Wookiees on their planet. He left, flunked out of the Space Academy, and then met some kind of Ernest Hemingway character, a very powerful trader in the galaxy who took Han under his wing until they had a falling out. Han swore he'd never talk to him again.

When the story begins, the Rebel Alliance needs this man, this powerful trader, on its side; by now he controls all nonmilitary transports in the galaxy and is the head of some sort of transport guild. Leia tells Han that they've made contact with him and that he'll talk only to him. Another plot line suggests that Han is the only one who knows where this man is hiding and that the Rebellion wants Han to contact him. In either case the future of the Rebellion is in Han's hands. At first Han refuses to go, but eventually he agrees to take on the mission, although it is aborted when the Empire attacks the Rebel base. This concept appeared only in the first draft.

INT. HOTH—REBEL BASE—ANOTHER ICE CORRIDOR

A familiar stream of beeps and whistles heralds the approach of Artoo-Detoo and See-Threepio, who appear around a corner and move along an ice wall toward the main hangar.

THREEPIO: Don't try to blame me. I didn't ask you to turn on the thermal heater. I merely commented that it was freezing in the princess's chamber.

Artoo beeps a response.

THREEPIO: But it's supposed to be freezing. How are we going to dry out all her clothes? I really don't know.

Artoo beeps a stream of protesting whistles.

THREEPIO: Oh, switch off.

INT. HOTH—REBEL BASE—MAIN HANGAR DECK

The two robots stop at Han Solo's space freighter. Han and Chewie are still struggling with their central lifters.

HAN: *(to Chewie)* Why did you take this apart now? I'm trying to get us out of there, and you pull both of these—

THREEPIO: Excuse me, sir.

HAN: *(to Chewie)* Put them back together right now.

THREEPIO: Might I have a word with you, please?

HAN: What do you want?

THREEPIO: Well, it's Princess Leia, sir. She's been trying to get you on the communicator.

HAN: I turned it off. I don't want to talk to her.

THREEPIO: Oh. Well, Princess Leia is wondering about Master Luke. He hasn't come back yet. She doesn't know where he is.

HAN: I don't know where he is.

THREEPIO: Nobody knows where he is.

HAN: What do you mean, 'nobody knows'?

THREEPIO: Well, uh, you see . . .

Han walks off, as Threepio follows him.

HAN: Deck officer! Deck officer!

THREEPIO: Excuse me, sir. Might I inqu—

Han abruptly puts his hand over Threepio's mouth as the deck officer approaches.

DECK OFFICER: Yes, sir?

HAN: Do you know where Commander Skywalker is?

DECK OFFICER: I haven't seen him. It's possible he came in through the south entrance.

HAN: It's possible? Why don't you go find out? It's getting dark out there.

DECK OFFICER: Yes, sir.

The deck officer leaves hurriedly, as Han takes his hand off Threepio's mouth.

THREEPIO: Excuse me, sir. Might I inquire what's going on?

HAN: Why not?

THREEPIO: Impossible man. Come along, Artoo, let's find Princess Leia. Between ourselves, I think Master Luke is in considerable danger.

INT. HOTH—REBEL BASE—MAIN ICE TUNNEL

Deck officer and his assistant hurry toward Han as he enters the tunnel.

DECK OFFICER: Sir. Commander Skywalker hasn't come in the south entrance. He might have forgotten to check in.

HAN: Not likely. Are the speeders ready?

DECK OFFICER: Er, not yet. We're having some trouble adapting them to the cold.

HAN: Then we'll have to go out on tauntauns.

DECK OFFICER: Sir, the temperature's dropping too rapidly.

HAN: That's right. And my friend's out in it.

ASSISTANT OFFICER: I'll cover sector twelve. Have com control set to screen alpha.

Han pushes through the troops and mounts a tauntaun.

DECK OFFICER: Your tauntaun'll freeze before you reach the first marker.

HAN: Then I'll see you in hell!

Han maneuvers his mount out of the cave and races into the dark and bitter night.

EXT. HOTH—ICE GORGE—DUSK

The jagged face of a huge ice wall sits gloomily in the dim twilight of a Hoth day. Luke hangs upside down, ankles frozen into icy stalactites, his extended arms within a foot of the snow floor. He opens his eyes as a chilling moan of the hideous ice creature echoes off the gorge walls. Luke pulls himself up, grabs hold of his ankles, and futilely tries to unfasten the thongs.

Exhausted, he drops back into his hanging position. As he hangs there, he spies his lightsaber lying about three feet out of reach.

He focuses on the saber, and as his hand strains toward the weapon, he squeezes his eyes tight in concentration.

Just as the ice creature looms over Luke, the lightsaber jumps into Luke's hand.

The young warrior instantly ignites his sword, swings up, and cuts himself loose from the ice. He flops to the snow in a heap. Luke scrambles to his feet. He swings his lightsaber, and the beast screams in pain.

In the story treatment, after Luke escapes from the cave, George Lucas came up with the idea that he should be wearing some kind of talisman that used to belong to Ben. On the talisman would be markings giving him the name and location of a planet, and by instinct Luke would decide to go there.

In the first draft Luke is on the floor of the cave. In a recess in the cave he hears voices of aliens speaking an incomprehensible language. Luke gets up and goes out, when suddenly a huge white form appears in front of him. Luke hears Ben's voice saying to him: "Remember the Force, boy. Open your mind to it, open your heart." Luke pulls out his sword and slashes the creature with the beam. He steps out of the cave as other shapes are moving toward the entrance, but they stop, afraid to follow him.

In the second draft, as Luke is hanging upside down in the monster's cave, he sees his lasersword lying near a pile of his discarded gear; he suddenly hears Ben's voice saying to him: "Relax, Luke, use the Force. Think of the lightsaber in your hand. See it in your hand. Relax, Luke . . . Think of the saber." As Ben talks, Luke concentrates, and the saber jumps into Luke's hands. He frees himself and cuts the creature in half. The idea of having Ben talk to Luke inside the cave remained through the fourth draft. In the fifth draft Luke talks to himself, but eventually, in the film, Luke simply concentrates.

George Lucas: "In the restored version of *Empire*, we've added new shots of the wampa. Before you just heard him and barely saw him. Now you can actually see him when Luke turns around and looks. The original shot was not very good, and the wampa looked like a puppet. With today's computer technology, we were able to realize the shot properly."

From the Special Edition:

The jagged face of a huge ice wall sits gloomily in the dim twilight of a Hoth day. Luke hangs upside down, ankles frozen into icy stalactites, his extended arms within a foot of the snow floor. One side of his face is covered in a dried mask of frozen blood. He opens his eyes as a chilling moan of the hideous ice creature echoes off the gorge walls. The wampa creature is in the ice cave eating what appears to be carrion. It turns in Luke's direction and growls, then continues its meal. Luke pulls himself up, grabs hold of his ankles, and futilely tries to unfasten the thongs.

Exhausted, he drops back into his hanging position. The wampa continues eating, tearing away huge bites of carrion. As Luke hangs there, he spies his lightsaber stuck in the snow, about three feet out of reach.

Luke's motion distracts the creature. The wampa stops eating, stands upright, growls, and starts toward Luke. Finally, using the Force, Luke frees his lightsaber from the snow and it jumps to his hand. The wampa

> *continues to approach. Luke cuts his feet loose from the ice and drops down to the snow, sword blazing. The creature nears. Luke scrambles to his feet and swings his lightsaber, and the beast's right arm is left lying in the snow. The wampa screams in pain, and Luke flees.*

EXT. HOTH—ENTRANCE TO ICE GORGE—DUSK

Luke scrabbles out of the gorge into the dark and snowy twilight. Weak and exhausted, he tumbles down a snowbank.

Irvin Kershner: "We began shooting in March in Norway. When we got up the first day, it had snowed like crazy. The hotel where we were staying was completely snowed in. We had to cut our way out of the back door, and we looked and the snow was whirling around; it was twenty-six below zero. I needed to have shots of Luke running around in the snow without a coat on. I walked outside, and I said, 'How the hell are we going to shoot this?' And suddenly I got an idea: We put the camera in the doorway of the hotel, and I asked Mark to run outside. When I said cut, he would run back inside the hotel and we would warm him up."

EXT. HOTH—SNOW PLAIN—DUSK

A small, lone figure riding a tauntaun races through the hostile vastness of snow and cold. As it runs, the tauntaun's legs kick up large clouds of snow and ice into the snowy air.

EXT. HOTH—OUTSIDE ICE HANGAR—DUSK

Artoo stands in the falling snow, beeping worriedly. Threepio moves stiffly over to him.

THREEPIO: You must come along now, Artoo. There's really nothing more we can do. And my joints are freezing up.

Artoo beeps, long and low.

THREEPIO: Don't say things like that! Of course we'll see Master Luke again. And he'll be quite all right, you'll see. *(to himself)* Stupid little short-circuit. He'll be quite all right.

Threepio has turned to go back inside the main hangar as Artoo mournfully keeps his vigil.

EXT. HOTH—SNOWDRIFT—DUSK

The wind is blowing quite strongly now. Luke gets up and struggles to stay upright but falls over again. Meanwhile, the searching Han dismounts from his tauntaun.

INT. REBEL BASE—MAIN HANGAR DECK—ENTRANCE—NIGHT

A Rebel lieutenant moves to Major Derlin, an officer keeping watch.

LIEUTENANT: Sir, all the patrols are in. Still no . . . still no contact from Skywalker or Solo.

Princess Leia stands waiting for a sign of the two Rebel heroes. Threepio and Artoo approach.

THREEPIO: Mistress Leia, Artoo says he's been quite unable to pick up any signals, although he does admit that his own range is far too weak to abandon all hope.

DERLIN: Your Highness, there's nothing more we can do tonight. The shield doors must be closed.

Leia nods an acknowledgment, but she is lost in thought.

DERLIN: Close the doors.

LIEUTENANT: Yes, sir.

Chewie lets out a short moan. At the same moment, Artoo begins a complex series of efficient beeps.

Irvin Kershner: "When you're in the hangar and the doors are closing, I thought, The doors are closing and here is Chewbacca, who is like a dog, he is hurt, the one he loves is out there in the snow. So as the doors slam shut, I had him scream in agony. That wasn't in the original script; that was a decision I made during filming. Take out the yell and it's just doors closing. When you make a movie, you always have to think of the characters, and that little detail is the kind of thing that makes a film work."

THREEPIO: Artoo says the chances of survival are seven hundred and twenty-five . . . to one.

Leia stands praying to herself as the huge metal doors slam across the entrance of the ice cave. The loud booms echo throughout the huge cavern. Chewie lets out another suffering howl.

THREEPIO: Actually, Artoo has been known to make mistakes . . . from time to time. Oh, dear, oh, dear. Don't worry about Master Luke, I'm sure he'll be all right. He's quite clever, you know . . . for a human being.

EXT. HOTH—SNOWDRIFT—DUSK

Luke lies facedown in the snow, nearly unconscious.

BEN: Luke . . . Luke.

Slowly Luke looks up and sees Ben Kenobi, barely visible through the blowing snow. It is hard to tell if Kenobi is real or a hallucination.

LUKE: *(weakly)* Ben?

BEN: You will go to the Dagobah system.

LUKE: Dagobah system?

BEN: There you will learn from Yoda, the Jedi Master who instructed me.

LUKE: *(groaning faintly)* Ben . . . Ben.

In the story treatment, after escaping from the cave, Luke simply goes back to the base. In the first draft Luke escapes from the wampa's cave and starts walking in the snow; he gets on his hands and knees, praying to Ben and telling him that the Force is gone. A search party headed by Han and Leia finds Luke semiconscious. In the second draft and as in the movie a ghostlike image of Ben appears in front of Luke as he is struggling in the snow. Ben keeps telling Luke that he must survive and go to the Dagobah system to find Yoda, the Jedi Master.

Irvin Kershner: "I thought that Ben's shimmering image might be a break in form, but there is a mystical element to the film, and therefore I was able to rationalize it. Having Ben come back is almost like Zen, a Buddhist notion that you don't die, that you come back and have to suffer again until you do enough good and decide you don't want to come back. All cultures have a mythic world that they deal with in some way, either in their religion or in their art. So Ben in the story is still alive but not corporeal."

The image of Ben fades, revealing a lone tauntaun rider approaching from the windswept horizon.
Luke drops into unconsciousness.
Han hurries to his snow-covered friend. Han's tauntaun lets out a low, pitiful bellow. But Han's concern is with Luke, and he holds him urgently.

HAN: Luke! Luke! Don't do this, Luke. Come on, give me a sign here.

Luke doesn't respond. Han hears a rasping sound behind him. He turns just in time to see his tauntaun stagger and then fall over into the snow.
Han drags Luke to the beast.

HAN: Not much time.

He pushes Luke's inert form against the belly of the now-dead beast.

LUKE: *(moaning)* Ben . . . Ben . . .

Han ignites Luke's saber and cuts the beast from head to toe.

George Lucas: "Unless it's something that you absolutely have to have in order to motivate a character, unless it's actually a plot point, just personal history is not something that you need to put into a script. A script starts off big because you're trying to define the characters and the plot, but the work you do after the first draft is to make sure that you tell a very precise story and that you take out everything that's not relevant to your plot."

Lawrence Kasdan: "There's a very interesting thing that hap-

HAN: Hang on, kid.

LUKE: *(mumbling)* Dagobah system . . . You will go to Dagobah . . .

HAN: This may smell bad, kid . . .

LUKE: *(moaning)* Yoda . . .

HAN: *(struggling to get Luke inside the carcass)* . . . but it will keep you warm . . . till I can get the shelter built. Agh! Agh . . . I thought they smelled bad on the outside! Agh!

pened that I often refer to. At one point in the script the characters were doing something, and I had Han say: 'This is boring,' and George said, 'We never want to tell people it's boring. If a character in a movie says something is boring, then the audience will begin to think that the film is boring.' "

The wind has picked up considerably, making it difficult to move. Han removes a pack from the dead creature's back, taking out a shelter container. He begins to set up what can only be a pitiful protection against a bitter Hoth night.

EXT. HOTH—SNOWDRIFT—DAWN

Four snub-nosed armored snowspeeders race across the white landscape.

INT. SNOWSPEEDER—COCKPIT

There is only one pilot, Zev, in the enclosed two-man craft. He concentrates on the scopes that ring his cockpit. He hears a low beep from one of his monitors.

ZEV: *(into transmitter)* Echo Base . . . I've got something! Not much, but it could be a life-form . . .

EXT. HOTH—SNOWDRIFT

The small craft banks and makes a slow arc, then races off in a new direction.

INT. SNOWSPEEDER—COCKPIT

The pilot switches over to a new transmitter.

ZEV: *(into transmitter)* Commander Skywalker, do you copy? This is Rogue Two. This is Rogue Two. Captain Solo, do you copy?

EXT. HOTH—SNOWDRIFT

The snowspeeder races across the white landscape.

INT. SNOWSPEEDER—COCKPIT

ZEV: Commander Skywalker, do you copy? This is Rogue Two.

There is a sharp crackle of static, then a faint voice.

HAN: *(filtered over Zev's receiver)* Good morning. Nice of you guys to drop by.

ZEV: *(switching transmitters)* Echo Base . . . this is Rogue Two. I found them. Repeat, I found them.

EXT. HOTH—SNOWDRIFT—DAY

Standing outside the small shelter he has set up, Han spots Zev's snowspeeder approaching in the distance and waves at the tiny craft.

INT. REBEL BASE—MAIN HANGAR DECK

The snowspeeder returns.

INT. REBEL BASE—MEDICAL CENTER

Strange robot surgeons adjust a mass of electronic equipment. Luke is submerged in a bacta tank, thrashing about in his delirium.

INT. REBEL BASE—MEDICAL CENTER—RECOVERY ROOM

Luke sits up in a recovery room bed, weak but smiling. His face shows terrible wounds from the wampa's attack.

THREEPIO: Master Luke, sir, it's so good to see you fully functional again.

Artoo beeps his good wishes.

THREEPIO: Artoo expresses his relief also.

Han and Chewie make their entrance, the Wookiee growling his greetings.

HAN: How you feeling, kid? You don't look so bad to me. In fact, you look strong enough to pull the ears off a gundark.

LUKE: Thanks to you.

HAN: That's two you owe me, junior.

Han turns as Leia enters the room. He looks at her with a big, devilish grin.

HAN: Well, Your Worship, looks like you managed to keep me around for a little while longer.

LEIA: *(haughtily)* I had nothing to do with it. General Rieekan thinks it's dangerous for any ships to leave the system until we've activated the energy shield.

HAN: That's a good story. I think you just can't bear to let a gorgeous guy like me out of your sight.

LEIA: I don't know where you get your delusions, laserbrain.

Chewie is amused; he laughs in his manner. Han, enjoying himself, regards Chewie good-humoredly.

HAN: Laugh it up, fuzzball. But you didn't see us alone in the south passage. *(looking pointedly at Luke)* She expressed her true feelings for me.

Leia is flushed, eyes darting between Luke and Han.

LEIA: My . . . ! Why, you stuck-up . . . half-witted . . . scruffy-looking . . . nerf herder!

HAN: Who's scruffy-looking? *(to Luke)* I must have hit pretty close to the mark to get her all riled up like that, huh, kid?

Leia looks vulnerable for a moment, then the mask falls again, and she focuses on Luke.

LEIA: Why, I guess you don't know everything about women yet.

With that she leans over and kisses Luke on the lips. Then she turns on her heel and walks out, leaving everyone in the room slightly dumbstruck. With some smugness, Luke puts his hand behind his head and grins.

Meanwhile, in the distance, the muffled sound of an alarm has been heard.

ANNOUNCER: *(over loudspeaker)* Headquarters personnel, report to command center.

The voice repeats the order, and Han, Chewie, Artoo, and Threepio hurry out of the room, bidding farewell to Luke.

HAN: Take it easy.

THREEPIO: Excuse us, please.

The aspect of a possible romance between Leia and Luke was a lot more obvious in the earlier drafts. In the treatment and the first draft, Luke declares his love but Leia explains that a relationship is impossible because of her duties. In the second draft Luke's declaration is interrupted when Han walks into the sick bay, and in the revised fourth draft the droids come in as Luke is about to kiss Leia passionately.

In the first draft, as Luke is recovering, he finds a crystal in the hilt of his lasersword. He plugs it into Artoo, and Threepio translates that the crystal gives the coordinates to a star system.

INT. HOTH—REBEL BASE—COMMAND CENTER

Rieekan looks up grimly from a console screen. He calls over to Leia and Han.

RIEEKAN: Princess . . . we have a visitor.

The group hurries over to Rieekan.

RIEEKAN: We've picked up something outside the base of zone twelve, moving east.

SENIOR CONTROLLER: It's metal.

LEIA: Then it couldn't be one of those creatures.

HAN: It could be a speeder, one of ours.

SENIOR CONTROLLER: No. Wait—there's something very weak coming through.

Threepio has stepped up to the control panel and listens intently to the strange signal.

THREEPIO: Sir, I am fluent in six million forms of communication. This signal is not used by the Alliance. It could be an Imperial code.

The transmission ends in static.

HAN: It isn't friendly, whatever it is. Come on, Chewie, let's check it out.

RIEEKAN: Send Rogues Ten and Eleven to station three-eight.

EXT. HOTH—SNOW PLAIN—DAY

The dark probe robot lowers its large antennae from the top of its head and moves away from the smoldering ruins of station three-eight and down a ridge toward the Rebel base.

The probe droid spots Chewbacca, who, not thirty feet away, has popped his head over a snowbank. Instantly, the probe robot swings around, firing its deadly ray. But before it can get a shot off, it is hit from behind by a laserbolt from Han Solo's blaster and explodes in a million pieces.

INT. HOTH—REBEL BASE—COMMAND CENTER

Leia and Rieekan listen to Han on the comlink.

HAN: *(over comlink)* 'Fraid there's not much left.

LEIA: *(into comlink)* What was it?

HAN: *(over comlink)* Droid of some kind. I didn't hit it that hard. It must have had a self-destruct.

LEIA: *(into comlink)* An Imperial probe droid.

HAN: *(over comlink)* It's a good bet the Empire knows we're here.

RIEEKAN: We'd better start the evacuation.

EXT. SPACE—IMPERIAL FLEET

Darth Vader's Star Destroyer, larger and more awesome than the five Imperial Star Destroyers that surround it, sits in the vastness of space. The six huge ships are surrounded by a convoy of smaller spacecraft. TIE fighters dart to and fro.

INT. DARTH VADER'S STAR DESTROYER—BRIDGE—MAIN CONTROL DECK

Darth Vader, Lord of the Sith, surveys his fleet from the bridge. As the squat, evil-looking Admiral Ozzel and the younger, powerfully built General Veers approach him, Captain Piett hurries up to Ozzel.

PIETT: Admiral.

OZZEL: Yes, Captain?

PIETT: I think we've got something, sir. The report is only a fragment from a probe droid in the Hoth system, but it's the best lead we've had.

OZZEL: *(irritated)* We have thousands of probe droids searching the galaxy. I want proof, not leads!

PIETT: The visuals indicate life readings.

OZZEL: It could mean anything. If we followed up every lead . . .

PIETT: But sir, the Hoth system is supposed to be devoid of human forms.

Controllers working the vast complex of electronic controls hear ominous approaching footsteps and look up from their controls. Darth Vader moves across the wide bridge like a chill wind.

VADER: You found something?

PIETT: Yes, my lord.

Vader moves to a large screen showing an image of the Rebel snow base. Rebel speeders can be seen approaching the base in the distance.

VADER: *(studying the image on the console screen)* That's it. The Rebels are there.

OZZEL: My lord, there are so many uncharted settlements. It could be smugglers, it could be . . .

VADER: That is the system. And I'm sure Skywalker is with them. Set your course for the Hoth system. General Veers, prepare your men.

VEERS: Admiral?

Ozzel nods.

Irvin Kershner: "All the Americans in the film play the good guys, and all the characters who speak with a British accent are the bad guys. I did that on purpose. Vader, of course, has an American accent, but you see, he was a good guy before he turned to the dark side!"

INT. HOTH—REBEL BASE—TRANSPORT BAY

A captain issues instructions to two of his men at the entrance to the main transport bay. The Rebels are moving to evacuate quickly, but not in panic.

REBEL CAPTAIN: Groups seven and ten will stay behind to fly the speeders. As soon as each transport is loaded, evacuation control will give clearance for immediate launch.

REBEL FIGHTER: Right, sir.

INT. HOTH—REBEL BASE—MAIN HANGAR DECK

Han is welding on the lifters of the Millennium Falcon.
He finishes his work and stands up straight.

HAN: *(shouting to Chewie)* All right, that's it. Try it . . .

Smoke rises from a minor explosion of the lifter.

HAN: Off! Turn it off! Turn it off! Off!

INT. REBEL BASE—MEDICAL CENTER

Luke dresses in readiness for the evacuation as his attending medical droid stands by.

MEDICAL DROID: Sir, it will take quite a while to evacuate the T-forty-sevens.

LUKE: Well, forget the heavy equipment. There's plenty of time to get the smaller modules on the transports.

MEDICAL DROID: Take care, sir.

LUKE: Thanks.

INT. REBEL BASE—MAIN HANGAR DECK

Pilots and gunners scurry about. Luke is headed toward a row of armored speeders. He stops at the rear of the Millennium Falcon, *where Han and Chewie are still trying to repair the right lifter.*

LUKE: Chewie, take care of yourself, okay?

As Luke pats Chewie on the arm, Chewie puts his arms around Luke and gives him a tight hug. Han is discussing the lifter with a repair droid when he sees Luke.

HAN: Hi, kid. *(to droid)* There's got to be a reason for it. Check it at the other end. Wait a second. *(to Luke)* You all right?

LUKE: Yeah.

Luke nods, smiles, then walks on. He and Han have exchanged a silent communication, each wishing the other safety, happiness—many things, all difficult to verbalize.

HAN: Be careful.

LUKE: You, too.

INT. REBEL BASE—CONTROL ROOM

In the control room a controller urgently gestures for General Rieekan to check a computer scan.

CONTROLLER: General, there's a fleet of Star Destroyers coming out of hyperspace in sector four.

RIEEKAN: Reroute all power to the energy shield. We've got to hold them till all transports are away. Prepare for ground assault.

EXT. SPACE—IMPERIAL FLEET

Six huge Star Destroyers move through space into the Hoth system.

INT. VADER'S STAR DESTROYER—VADER'S CHAMBER—MEDITATION CUBICLE

In the cubicle the brooding Dark Lord sits in meditation. General Veers has come to see Vader. Although seemingly very sure of himself, Veers is still not bold enough to interrupt the meditating lord. The young general stands quietly at attention until the evil presence speaks.

VADER: What is it, General?

VEERS: My lord, the fleet has moved out of lightspeed. Com-scan has detected an energy field protecting an area of the sixth planet of the Hoth system. The field is strong enough to deflect any bombardment.

VADER: *(angrily)* The Rebels are alerted to our presence. Admiral Ozzel came out of lightspeed too close to the system.

VEERS: He felt surprise was wiser . . .

VADER: He is as clumsy as he is stupid. General, prepare your troops for a surface attack.

VEERS: Yes, my lord.

Veers turns smartly and leaves as Vader activates a large viewscreen showing the bridge of his mighty ship. Admiral Ozzel appears on the viewscreen, standing slightly in front of Captain Piett.

OZZEL: Lord Vader, the fleet has moved out of lightspeed, and we're preparing to . . . Aaagh!

VADER: You have failed me for the last time, Admiral. Captain Piett.

Piett steps forward as the admiral moves away, slightly confused, gasping and touching his throat as it begins to constrict painfully.

PIETT: Yes, my lord.

VADER: Make ready to land our troops beyond their energy field and deploy the fleet so that nothing gets off the system. You are in command now, Admiral Piett.

PIETT: Thank you, Lord Vader.

Piett's pleasure about his unexpected promotion is not an unmixed emotion. He glances warily at the struggling Admiral Ozzel, who, with a final choke, has stumbled and fallen in a lifeless heap before him.

INT. REBEL BASE—MAIN HANGAR DECK

With a sense of urgency Leia quickly briefs a group of pilots gathered in the center of the hangar.

LEIA: All troop carriers will assemble at the north entrance. The heavy transport ships will leave as soon as they're loaded. Only two fighter escorts per ship. The energy shield can only be opened for a short time, so you'll have to stay very close to your transports.

HOBBIE: Two fighters against a Star Destroyer?

LEIA: The ion cannon will fire several shots to make sure that any enemy ships will be out of your flight path. When you've gotten past the energy shield, proceed directly to the rendezvous point. Understood?

PILOTS: *(in unison)* Right. Yeah.

LEIA: Good luck.

DERLIN: Okay. Everybody to your stations. Let's go!

The pilots hurry away.

Irvin Kershner: "If you look closely at the picture, you'll see giant sets, but you see them only briefly. Usually, in Hollywood pictures, when you have giant sets, you pull back and show them. But here the sets were not important; it was the people in the sets that were important. If you look at the scene in the big hangar where Leia is briefing the Rebel soldiers, it's huge, yet you see it for just a few seconds. I never wanted to say, 'I'm going to show the sets.' I wanted to show a piece here, a piece there, and eventually the audience would put it all together in their heads. You see more of a set if you show it in pieces around the actors than if you show it in a long shot. If I ever used a long shot, it was for an emotional effect, not to show the sets."

EXT. HOTH—ICE PLAIN—SNOW TRENCH—DAY

Rebel troops carry heavy bazooka-type weapons and position them along a snow trench. Men hurriedly respond to their officers' yelled orders.

Other troops swing a gun turret into position.

INT. REBEL BASE—COMMAND CENTER

Princess Leia and General Rieekan are tense but trying very hard not to show any fear.

RIEEKAN: Their primary target will be the power generators. Prepare to open shield.

EXT. ICE PLAIN

The Rebel transport and two escort fighters begin their departure from the ice planet.

EXT. SPACE—IMPERIAL STAR DESTROYER

George Lucas: "Writing has never been something I have enjoyed, and so, ultimately, on the second film I hired Leigh Brackett. Unfortunately, it didn't work out; she turned in the first draft, and then she passed away. I didn't like the first script, but I gave Leigh credit because I liked her a lot. She was sick at the time she wrote the script, and she really tried her best. During the story conferences I had with Leigh, my thoughts weren't fully formed and I felt that her script went in a completely different direc-

A huge Imperial Star Destroyer rests against a sea of stars far above the white surface of the planet Hoth.

INT. IMPERIAL STAR DE-STROYER—BRIDGE

An Imperial controller approaches his commander.

CONTROLLER: Sir. Rebel ships are coming into our sector.

CAPTAIN: Good. Our first catch of the day.

INT. REBEL BASE—COMMAND CENTER

WOMAN CONTROLLER: Stand by, ion control . . . Fire!

EXT. REBEL BASE—ICE CAVE—ION CANNON

The giant ball-shaped ion cannon blasts two red energy beams skyward.

EXT. SPACE—HOTH—REBEL TRANSPORT

The Rebel transport and its escorts race away from the white planet, closely followed by the two red energy beams.

As the Rebel transport races toward the waiting Imperial Star Destroyer, it is overtaken by the two scarlet energy bolts. The Imperial Star Destroyer is hit in the conning tower by the powerful bolts, which set up fiery explosions on its metal hull.

The big destroyer veers out of control. As the Imperial ship careens into deep space, the Rebel transport races away to safety.

INT. REBEL BASE—MAIN HANGAR DECK

Pilots, gunners, and troopers hurry to their stations and their vehicles.

ANNOUNCER: *(over loudspeaker)* "The first transport is away."

Everyone cheers at the announcement, which echoes through the hangar. Luke runs toward his snowspeeder. His gunner, Dack, a fresh-faced, eager kid, is already aboard

tion. Anyway, I had no script, and we were starting production, and I didn't have anybody to hire to write the damn thing. That's when I sat down and wrote two drafts, which are closer to the film. Larry Kasdan had just delivered *Raiders of the Lost Ark*, and I said to him, 'I need a writer.' And he said, 'But George, you haven't even read *Raiders*, you don't know if I'm a good writer.' I said, 'I'm desperate, here is a draft, just rewrite it for me, and if I don't like *Raiders*, you're fired!' So Larry rewrote the script, but we sort of all worked on it. No matter how much I wanted to get out of writing, I was somehow always forced to sit down and work on the script."

Lawrence Kasdan: We had meetings with Kersh [Irvin Kershner]. George walked us through the story, and I took notes like crazy."

George Lucas: "Those movies were so big and they were so hard to do that I just felt that I couldn't deal with all the issues and be on the set every day at the same time. I decided not to direct so that I could get an *and glad to see him. Luke climbs in.*

DACK: Feeling all right, sir?

LUKE: Just like new, Dack. How about you?

DACK: Right now I feel like I could take on the whole Empire myself.

LUKE: *(quietly, strapping in)* I know what you mean.

EXT. HOTH—ICE PLAIN

A thin horizon line cuts across the bleak landscape. Small dot-size objects begin to appear on the horizon, moving in the direction of the Rebel base.

EXT. HOTH—ICE PLAIN—SNOW TRENCH

A Rebel officer lifts a pair of electrobinoculars to his eyes. Through the lens he sees a very close view of a giant Imperial snow walker. He adjusts the view, which then zooms back to reveal two more of the ominous lumbering battle machines.

The officer lowers his binoculars as the regular rhythmic pounding begins to make the ground vibrate. The pounding grows louder and is accompanied by a high-pitched metallic rattling. The officer speaks into his comlink.

TRENCH OFFICER: Echo Station Three-T-Eight.

INT. REBEL BASE—CORRIDOR

Pilots and gunners race to their waiting snowspeeders.

TRENCH OFFICER: *(over comlink)* We have spotted Imperial walkers!

Ice and snow begin falling from the walls of the corridor, shaken by the pounding Imperial snow walkers as they draw ever nearer.

CONTROLLER: Imperial walkers on the north ridge.

EXT. HOTH—ICE PLAIN—SNOW TRENCH

The Rebel troops aim their weapons

overview of the whole thing, which meant I could oversee the shooting but didn't have to be on the set all the time. There was a lot of work with these movies, and you really need to take a step back in order to make it work."

Irvin Kershner: "I got a phone call from George, and he asked me to meet him at Universal Studios, where his office was. We had lunch, and he said, 'Would you like to do the second *Star Wars*?' I knew George from USC, and at first I was reluctant to do it because the first film was such a successful picture and it was such an original notion, how could you make a second one that would in any way be as good, and if not as good, at least be something original? So at first I thought, No, I don't want to do this, and my agent talked to me and said you must do it, you know, the way agents are . . . I did ask George why he wanted me, and he said, 'I want somebody who knows what a Hollywood director knows but is not Hollywood,' and I guess I never really considered myself Hollywood; you know, I don't at the horizon as explosions erupt all around them. They are nervous, and their grip on their weapons tightens from the cold and from fear.

INT. LUKE'S SNOWSPEEDER, ROGUE LEADER—COCKPIT

LUKE: *(into comlink)* Echo Station Five-seven. We're on our way.

EXT. HOTH—ICE PLAIN—BATTLEFIELD

The fleet of snowspeeders races above the ice field at full throttle. They accelerate away from the base and head toward the distant walkers.

INT. LUKE'S SNOWSPEEDER, ROGUE LEADER—COCKPIT

LUKE: *(into comlink)* All right, boys, keep tight now.

DACK: Luke, I have no approach vector. I'm not set.

LUKE: Steady, Dack. Attack pattern delta. Go now.

EXT. HOTH—ICE PLAIN—BATTLEFIELD

Four speeders race away past an enormous walker and bank to the right.

INT. LUKE'S SNOWSPEEDER, ROGUE LEADER—COCKPIT

LUKE: All right, I'm coming in.

He turns his speeder and heads directly at one of the walkers, flying toward its towering legs. The horizon twists as the speeder banks between the legs.

LUKE: *(into comlink)* Hobbie, you still with me?

EXT. HOTH—ICE PLAIN—BATTLEFIELD

Two speeders race directly at a walker, then split and fly past it.

Three other walkers march onward, firing all cannons.

EXT. HOTH—ICE PLAIN—SNOW TRENCH

Rebel troops fire on the approaching

run with the pack. And so I asked him, 'How am I going to make a picture that's as good as *Star Wars?*' and he said he wanted a picture that was going to be better. He didn't want to direct anymore, and I felt kind of flattered in one way, scared in another, and finally I said yes. After the script was finished, I took off for England, and the next year I sat for about six hours a day in a room and drew storyboards. I then took my drawings to an artist, who made them larger, more elaborate. But I figured out how the scenes were going to work, and in the late afternoon I would meet with the art directors, the costume people, and everyone else involved in the production, but most of the day for a year was spent storyboarding. So by the time I was finished, every single shot in the film was in my head because I had had the experience of doing it, of figuring out how it was going to work. I then took the good drawings, and I made up a book, and I sent a copy of it to George. He was in California, and I would call him from the set in England and walkers as snow and ice explode all around them.

EXT. HOTH—ICE PLAIN—BATTLE-FIELD

A speeder banks through and away from the legs of a walker. Two other speeders pass the first speeder from the opposite direction.

A giant walker head swivels and fires, striking a snowspeeder and sending it crashing in a ball of flames.

INT. IMPERIAL SNOW WALKER—COCKPIT

General Veers and two walker pilots keep a careful eye on the racing Rebel speeders as they maneuver their lumbering war machine forward.

Luke's speeder banks in from the side of Veers's walker and heads straight for its viewport, blasting away. An explosion hits the walker window but dissipates, doing no harm. The speeder roars up and over the impregnable war machine.

INT. LUKE'S SNOWSPEEDER, ROGUE LEADER—COCKPIT

LUKE: That armor's too strong for blasters.

EXT. HOTH—ICE PLAIN—BATTLE-FIELD

Another walker lumbers on as two snowspeeders bank past it.

INT. LUKE'S SNOWSPEEDER, ROGUE LEADER—COCKPIT

LUKE: (into comlink) Rogue Group, use your harpoons and tow cables. Go for the legs. It might be our only chance of stopping them.

EXT. HOTH—ICE PLAIN—BATTLE-FIELD

Two snowspeeders streak by.

INT. LUKE'S SNOWSPEEDER, ROGUE LEADER—COCKPIT

LUKE: (to Dack) All right, stand by, Dack.

say, 'I shot scene number 7 on page 12, the next one that ties in I'm not going to shoot, I don't need it; I'm going to skip to scene number 9, etc. . . .' And we had perfect communication thanks to the book. In any film, communication is the key; miscommunication is a curse. And the book helped us or else we would have gotten lost, and thanks to it, I had something to go by, and even though I didn't shoot the film exactly the way I drew it, I basically knew the sets, the scale, where to place the actors . . ."

Joe Johnston: "George said the Imperial weapons attacking Hoth should look like walking tanks. The intention with the walker was to make it more frightening and anthropomorphic so it would look like a big robot. The idea of having a head and shapes that looked like big eyes and a big jaw was really to make it look more frightening."

George Lucas: "I definitely thought I was taking a chance by having the big battle at the beginning of the film. But the whole idea was that the major confrontation at the end be-

Dack is at the gunner's controls.

DACK: Oh, Luke, we've got a mal-function in fire control. I'll have to cut in the auxiliary.

LUKE: Just hang on. Hang on, Dack. Get ready to fire that tow cable.

Dack, sitting behind his harpoon gun, is hit by a volley of fire.

EXT. HOTH—ICE PLAIN—BATTLE-FIELD

Rogue Leader flies under the walker.

INT. LUKE'S SNOWSPEEDER, ROGUE LEADER—COCKPIT

Luke turns around to see if Dack is all right.

LUKE: Dack? Dack!

Dack is lost. His forehead rests on his smoldering controls.

EXT. HOTH—ICE PLAIN—SNOW TRENCH AREA

Rebel troops fire the dishlike ray gun while explosions erupt around them.

EXT. HOTH—ICE PLAIN—BATTLE-FIELD

Two walkers lumber toward the Rebel base as a speeder flies behind them, emitting a plume of smoke.

INT. IMPERIAL SNOW WALKER—COCKPIT

Through the cockpit window Veers watches the approach to the Rebel power generators in the distance.

EXT. HOTH—ICE PLAIN—SNOW TRENCH

The dishlike ray gun is hit by a laser-bolt and instantly explodes.

INT. IMPERIAL SNOW WALKER—COCKPIT

A hologram of Darth Vader appears on a control panel screen.

VEERS: Yes, Lord Vader. I've reached the main power genera-tors. The shield will be down in moments. You may start your landing.

tween Vader and Luke was going to be a personal battle, and I wanted to use a simple sword fight instead of pyrotech-nics. So I had to put the big battle in the front; I was relying on the emotional content of Luke and Vader's confronta-tion. I wanted it to have another dimension and to be more interesting than just a basic battle."

Irvin Kershner: "The Empire Strikes Back was the second act of a three-act play. Now, the second act never has a grand climax; it leads to the climax, it deals with the characters, it deals with the problems of your characters. I wanted the audience to anticipate the cli-max for the next film. We had to have action, though, so we showed it in the first part of the film, and then we got more into the characters. I was very worried that the second part would be dull, so we had to keep it moving, have surprises so that you wouldn't feel let down at the end, you'd feel you wanted to know what hap-pened to these people."

*Paul Hirsch: "It was a very courageous choice to have the

EXT. HOTH—ICE PLAIN—BATTLEFIELD

Two snowspeeders bank sharply.

INT. LUKE'S SNOWSPEEDER, ROGUE LEADER—COCKPIT

LUKE: *(into comlink)* Rogue Three.

INT. WEDGE'S SNOWSPEEDER, ROGUE THREE—COCKPIT

WEDGE: *(into comlink)* Copy, Rogue Leader.

LUKE: *(over comlink)* Wedge, I've lost my gunner. You'll have to make this shot. I'll cover for you.

INT. LUKE'S SNOWSPEEDER, ROGUE LEADER—COCKPIT

LUKE: Set your harpoon. Follow me on the next pass.

EXT. HOTH—ICE PLAIN—BATTLEFIELD

Two snowspeeders bank sharply.

INT. WEDGE'S SNOWSPEEDER, ROGUE THREE—COCKPIT

WEDGE: *(into comlink)* Coming around, Rogue Leader.

Wedge's young gunner, Janson, grimaces behind his harpoon.

INT. LUKE'S SNOWSPEEDER, ROGUE LEADER—COCKPIT

LUKE: *(into comlink)* Steady, Rogue Two.

EXT. HOTH—BATTLEFIELD

Wedge's speeder races through the legs of one of the monstrous walkers.

INT. WEDGE'S SNOWSPEEDER, ROGUE THREE—COCKPIT

WEDGE: *(to gunner)* Activate harpoon.

Wedge's gunner reaches for a firing switch to activate the harpoon. The harpoon flashes out and speeds toward the receding legs of the walker.

EXT. HOTH—BATTLEFIELD

The harpoon hurtles toward the walker. In an instant it is embedded in one of the walker's legs.

INT. WEDGE'S SNOWSPEEDER, ROGUE THREE—COCKPIT

WEDGE: *(to gunner)* Good shot, Janson.

EXT. HOTH—BATTLEFIELD

The speeder Rogue Three races around one of the giant walker's feet, trailing the cable behind it. Continuing around the back foot, Rogue Three then circles the walker around the tail end.

INT. WEDGE'S SNOWSPEEDER, ROGUE THREE—COCKPIT

Janson grimaces.

EXT. HOTH—ICE PLAIN—BATTLEFIELD

Wedge's snowspeeder continues to circle the giant walker.

big battle at the beginning of the film. *The Empire Strikes Back* was not intended as being a remake/sequel. You can see the *Rocky* movies, they're all the same; they're not really sequels, they're remakes of the first film. As George explained it to me, he didn't want *Empire* to be a remake/sequel. I think that Irvin Kershner did a great job with the actors; he got the most out of the characters."

INT. WEDGE'S SNOWSPEEDER, ROGUE LEADER—COCKPIT

Wedge checks his controls and banks around the front of the walker.

WEDGE: One more pass.

JANSON: Coming around. Once more.

EXT. HOTH—BATTLEFIELD

The speeder sweeps left to right in front of the giant legs, towing the cable behind it.

INT. WEDGE'S SNOWSPEEDER, ROGUE THREE—COCKPIT

Wedge has swung the speeder between the legs of the giant walker.

JANSON: Cable out! Let her go!

WEDGE: Detach cable.

EXT. WEDGE'S SNOWSPEEDER, ROGUE THREE

The cable release on the back of the speeder snaps loose, and the cable drops away.

INT. WEDGE'S SNOWSPEEDER, ROGUE THREE—COCKPIT

JANSON: Cable detached.

EXT. HOTH—BATTLEFIELD

The speeder zooms away into the distance. The tangled legs of the enormous war machine attempt a step, but as they do, the giant Imperial walker begins to topple. It teeters for a moment and then crashes onto the icy ground, sending snow flying.

EXT. HOTH—ICE PLAIN—SNOW TRENCH

The troops in the trenches cheer at the sight of the crashing walker.
An officer gives a signal to his men.

TRENCH OFFICER: Come on!

The Rebel troops charge toward the doomed walker, followed by two Rebel speeders flying overhead, which fire at it; it explodes, snowing lumps of metal onto the frozen ground.

INT. WEDGE'S SNOWSPEEDER, ROGUE THREE—COCKPIT

Wedge lets out a triumphant yell, banking his speeder away from the fallen walker.

WEDGE: *(into comlink)* Whooha! That got him!

INT. LUKE'S SNOWSPEEDER, ROGUE LEADER—COCKPIT

LUKE: *(into comlink)* I see it, Wedge. Good work.

INT. REBEL BASE—COMMAND CENTER

Leia and General Rieekan monitor computer screens as the command center is shaken by the continuing battle.

RIEEKAN: I don't think we can protect two transports at a time.

LEIA: It's risky, but we can't hold out much longer. We have no choice.

RIEEKAN: Launch patrols.

LEIA: *(to an aide)* Evacuate remaining ground staff.

INT. REBEL BASE—MAIN HANGAR

Muffled distant explosions are creating widening cracks in the ice roof of the hangar. Trying to ignore the noise and falling bits of snow, Han works on one of the Falcon's lifters while Chewie works on one of the wings. Noticing Chewie attach a wrong part, Han grows impatient.

HAN: No, no! No! This one goes there, that one goes there. Right?

In another area of the hangar Threepio watches as Artoo is raised up into Luke's X-wing fighter.

THREEPIO: Artoo, you take good care of Master Luke now, understand? And . . . do take good care of yourself. Oh, dear, oh, dear.

EXT. HOTH—BATTLEFIELD

The fierce battle on the vast snow plains of Hoth rages on. The Imperial walkers continue their slow, steady assault on the Rebel base, firing lasers as they lumber ever onward. In the snow trench Rebel troops fire large bazookalike guns and dish-like ray guns as explosions erupt around them. A gun tower is hit by a laserbolt and instantly explodes. Another blast destroys a ray gun.

INT. IMPERIAL SNOW WALKER—COCKPIT

General Veers is surveying the battlefield.

VEERS: All troops will debark for ground assault. Prepare to target the main generator.

EXT. HOTH—BATTLEFIELD

Luke's speeder and Rogue Two fly in formation, banking and flying above the erupting battlefield.

INT. LUKE'S SNOWSPEEDER, ROGUE LEADER—COCKPIT

Luke, glancing over, sees Rogue Two on his left.

LUKE: *(into comlink)* Rogue Two, are you all right?

ZEV: *(over comlink)* Yeah.

INT. ZEV'S SNOWSPEEDER, ROGUE TWO—COCKPIT

ZEV: *(into comlink)* I'm with you, Rogue Leader.

INT. LUKE'S SNOWSPEEDER, ROGUE LEADER—COCKPIT

LUKE: *(into comlink)* We'll set harpoon. I'll cover for you.

EXT. HOTH—BATTLEFIELD

The two speeders race across the horizon toward the giant walkers.

INT. ZEV'S SNOWSPEEDER, ROGUE TWO—COCKPIT

ZEV: *(into comlink)* Coming around.

INT. LUKE'S SNOWSPEEDER, ROGUE LEADER—COCKPIT

LUKE: *(into comlink)* Watch that crossfire, boys.

INT. ZEV'S SNOWSPEEDER, ROGUE TWO—COCKPIT

ZEV: *(into comlink)* Set for position three. *(to gunner)* Steady.

INT. LUKE'S SNOWSPEEDER, ROGUE LEADER—COCKPIT

LUKE: *(into comlink)* Stay tight and low.

INT. ZEV'S SNOWSPEEDER, ROGUE TWO—COCKPIT

Zev is hit.

EXT. ZEV'S SNOWSPEEDER, ROGUE TWO

Suddenly Zev's speeder is hit by a laserbolt, and the cockpit explodes in a ball of flame.

INT. LUKE'S SNOWSPEEDER, ROGUE LEADER—COCKPIT

Desperately, Luke works the controls of his flak-buffeted ship. Suddenly the speeder is rocked by an explosion. Luke struggles with the controls with a look of terror on his face. Electric sparks jump about the cockpit.

LUKE: *(into comlink)* Hobbie, I've been hit!

INT. LUKE'S SNOWSPEEDER, ROGUE LEADER

Luke's snowspeeder crash-dives toward the legs of the giant walker.

INT. LUKE'S SNOWSPEEDER, ROGUE LEADER—COCKPIT

Luke's snowspeeder crash-lands.

INT. LUKE'S SNOWSPEEDER, ROGUE LEADER

Luke struggles to escape from the cockpit as a walker bears down on him and throws himself clear just in time.

INT. REBEL BASE—COMMAND CENTER

Laserblasts can be heard thundering above. Han appears, running. Cracks have appeared in some of the walls, and some pipes have broken, sending hot steam billowing into the underground hallways. Han hurries into the command center. It is a shambles—a gigantic cave-in has almost obliterated the room, but some people are still at their posts. He finds Leia and Threepio near one of the control boards.

HAN: You all right?

Leia is surprised to see him.

LEIA: Why are you still here?

HAN: I heard the command center had been hit.

LEIA: You got your clearance to leave.

HAN: Don't worry, I'll leave. First I'm going to get you to your ship.

THREEPIO: Your Highness, we must take this last transport. It's our only hope.

LEIA: *(to controller)* Send all troops in sector twelve to the south slope to protect the fighters.

A blast rocks the command center, throwing Threepio backward into Han's arms.

ANNOUNCER: *(over loudspeaker)* Imperial troops have entered the base. Imperial troops have entered . . .

HAN: Come on . . . that's it.

LEIA: *(to head controller)* Give the evacuation code signal. And get to your transports!

Leia looks exhausted. Han has grabbed her arm and starts to lead her out.

As Han, Leia, and Threepio run out of the command center, the code signal can be heard echoing off the corridor walls.

HEAD CONTROLLER: K-one-zero . . . all troops disengage.

THREEPIO: *(to Han and Leia)* Oh! Wait for me!

EXT. BATTLEFIELD—SNOW TRENCH

Rebel troops retreat under the awesome Imperial onslaught.

OFFICER: Begin retreat!

SECOND OFFICER: Fall back! Fall back!

Troops flee from the battle, the ground exploding around them.

EXT. HOTH—BATTLEFIELD

The giant walkers, firing lasers, advance toward the Rebel headquarters.

EXT. HOTH—SNOW TRENCH

Continuing their retreat, the Rebels see the walkers looming ever nearer.

EXT. HOTH—BATTLEFIELD—ICE PLAIN

On the battlefield Luke is running, too. He looks up at the underbelly of a huge walker passing by overhead.

Luke fires his harpoon gun at the walker's underside. A thin cable follows the projectile from the gun. The magnetic head and cable attach firmly to the metal hull.

Soon he is pulled up the cable and hangs dangling underneath the walker.

The walker's giant feet continue to pound onward across the frozen snow. Stray laserbolts whistle by Luke as he reaches a small hatch. Hanging precariously, Luke cuts the solid metal hatch with his laser sword.

He takes a land mine from his belt and throws it inside the Imperial machine. Quickly, Luke starts down the cable and crashes onto the icy ground far below.

The giant walker stops in midstep. A muffled explosion comes from within— followed by several more. The machine topples over, smoking thickly.

EXT. HOTH—BATTLEFIELD

Veers's walker continues to advance toward the Rebel base.

INT. IMPERIAL SNOW WALKER—COCKPIT

Inside his walker General Veers prepares to fire on the Rebel power generators.

VEERS: Distance to power generators?

PILOT: One-seven, decimal two-eight.

EXT. HOTH—BATTLEFIELD

The walker shoots down a snowspeeder.

INT. IMPERIAL SNOW WALKER—COCKPIT

Veers reaches for the electrorangefinder and lines up the main generator.

VEERS: Target. Maximum firepower.

EXT. HOTH—BATTLEFIELD

The Rebel troops continue their desperate retreat, pushed back by the relentless Imperial assault.

INT. IMPERIAL SNOW WALKER—COCKPIT

From the cockpit of Veers's snow walker the Rebel main generator can be seen exploding in a ball of flame.

INT. HOTH—REBEL BASE—ICE CORRIDORS

With Threepio lagging behind, Han and Leia race through the crumbling ice corridors. Suddenly there is an explosion. Han turns, grabs the princess, and shields her with his body as a tremendous cave-in blocks their path.

He takes the comlink from his pocket.

HAN: *(into comlink)* Transport, this is Solo. Better take off—I can't get to you. I'll get her out on the *Falcon.*

Han and Leia turn and race down the corridor.

THREEPIO: But . . . but . . . but . . . where are you going? Oh . . . come back!!

INT. HOTH—REBEL BASE—COMMAND CENTER

Imperial troops have reached the base. As they push through the blocked passageway, Darth Vader strides behind them.

INT. HOTH—REBEL BASE—ICE CORRIDOR

Han and Leia run toward the entrance of the main hangar, where the Millennium Falcon is docked. Threepio still lags behind.

THREEPIO: Wait! Wait for me! Wait! Stop!

The door to the hangar closes in his face.

THREEPIO: *(exasperated)* How typical.

Quickly the door reopens as Han reaches out and pulls the golden droid through.

HAN: Come on.

INT. HOTH—REBEL BASE—MAIN HANGAR

Chewie has been pacing under the shelter of the Millennium Falcon's *landing gear. The giant Wookiee lets out a relieved grunt at seeing Han and Leia running toward the ship.*

HAN: Hurry up, Goldenrod, or you're going to be a permanent resident!

THREEPIO: Wait! Wait!

Han and Leia run up the ramp after Chewie, closely followed by Threepio.

INT. HOTH—REBEL BASE—ICE CORRIDOR

Vader strides through the base corridors, surveying the place.

INT. REBEL BASE—MAIN HANGAR—*MILLENNIUM FALCON*

On the hangar deck, the Millennium Falcon *struggles to start up.*

INT. MAIN HANGAR—*MILLENNIUM FALCON*—MAIN HOLD

A worried Leia observes as Chewie watches a troublesome gauge and Han, standing before a control panel, is busy flipping switches.

HAN: *(to Chewie)* How's this?

The Wookiee barks a negative reply.

LEIA: Would it help if I got out and pushed?

Threepio hurries into the hold.

THREEPIO: Captain Solo, Captain Solo . . .

HAN: It might.

THREEPIO: Sir, might I suggest that you . . .

Han gives the gold robot a devastating look.

THREEPIO: It can wait.

INT. MAIN HANGAR—*MILLENNIUM FALCON*—COCKPIT

They move to the cockpit, where Han flips some more switches. Leia, impatient, is disbelieving.

LEIA: This bucket of bolts is never going to get us past that blockade.

HAN: This baby's got a few surprises left in her, sweetheart.

INT. HOTH—REBEL BASE—MAIN HANGAR

A squad of stormtroopers rushes into the far side of the hangar.

INT. MAIN HANGAR—*MILLENNIUM FALCON*

A laser gun appears on the Falcon *and swings around to fire at the Imperial troops.*

INT. HOTH—REBEL BASE—MAIN HANGAR

The stormtroopers are hit by the Falcon's *fire and are thrown about in all directions.*

INT. MAIN HANGAR—*MILLENNIUM FALCON*—COCKPIT

Chewie rushes into the cockpit.

HAN: Come on! Come on! Switch over. Let's hope we don't have a burnout.

Chewie settles into his chair.

INT. HOTH—REBEL BASE—MAIN HANGAR

The stormtroopers hurriedly set up a large bazookalike weapon.

INT. MAIN HANGAR—*MILLENNIUM FALCON*—COCKPIT

Han gets the engine to fire.

HAN: See?

LEIA: Someday you're going to be wrong, and I just hope I'm there to see it.

INT. REBEL BASE—MAIN HANGAR

The Falcon's *laser gun continues to exchange fire with Imperial stormtroopers.*

INT. MAIN HANGAR—*MILLENNIUM FALCON*—COCKPIT

Han looks at Chewie.

HAN: Punch it!

The roar of the Falcon's *main engines blasts out everything as the ice-cave wall rushes by outside the cockpit window.*

INT. REBEL BASE—MAIN HANGAR

Vader enters the hangar, closely followed by more stormtroopers. Hearing the loud roar of the Millennium Falcon's *engines, Vader looks toward the main hangar doors just in time to see the* Falcon *lift up and disappear outside the cave.*

EXT. HOTH—ICE SLOPE—DAY

Luke looks up as the Millennium Falcon *races above him, flying very close to the ground.*

He and two other pilots trudge toward their X-wing fighters. Luke waves to fighters overhead, then heads toward his own fighter.

LUKE: Artoo!

Artoo, seated in his cubbyhole, chirps an excited greeting.

LUKE: Get her ready for takeoff.

WEDGE: Good luck, Luke. See you at the rendezvous.

Luke lowers himself into the cockpit of his X-wing while Artoo waits in the cubbyhole, beeping impatiently.

LUKE: Don't worry, Artoo. We're going, we're going.

The canopy over the X-wing lowers and snaps shut.

EXT. SPACE—LUKE'S X-WING

Luke's fighter, its wings closed, speeds away from the icy planet. Then it banks sharply.

INT. LUKE'S X-WING—COCKPIT

The monitor screen on Luke's control panel prints out a question from the concerned Artoo.

LUKE: *(into comlink)* There's nothing wrong, Artoo. Just setting a new course.

EXT. LUKE'S X-WING

Artoo beeps once again.

INT. LUKE'S X-WING—COCKPIT

LUKE: *(into comlink)* We're not going to regroup with the others.

Artoo begins a protest, whistling an unbelieving "What?!"

LUKE: *(into comlink)* We're going to the Dagobah system.

EXT. LUKE'S X-WING

Artoo chirps up again.

LUKE: *(into comlink)* Yes, Artoo?

INT. LUKE'S X-WING—COCKPIT

Artoo utters a soft, carefully phrased stream of whistles.

Luke reads Artoo's exclamation on his control panel.

LUKE: *(into comlink, chuckling)* That's all right. I'd like to keep it on manual control for a while.

EXT. LUKE'S X-WING

The little droid lets out a defeated whimper. Luke continues on his course.

In the story treatment and the first draft, before the Empire attacks the Rebels, the snow creatures create chaos inside the base. In both cases the stories establish the fact that Luke is weak and is making the wrong decisions; in the treatment Han is assaulted by a creature and is nearly killed when Luke tries to use the Force instead of his weapon. In the first draft, Luke is the one who is attacked and Han has to save him. In both situations Luke is humiliated, and Han obviously thinks less of him.

The scene where wampas attack the base was simplified in later drafts and eventually was dropped altogether for the film and never shot.

Irvin Kershner: "You see, my theory is it's better not to shoot something than to shoot it and cut it out. If you know that you're too long or if you know that the story may not need it, then it's better to give yourself more time for the scenes that you really need. The scenes with the wampas attacking the base would have been very difficult to realize because we couldn't show too much of the creatures; they wouldn't have looked real."

The snowspeeders flown by the Rebels first appeared in the second draft and are described as being "more powerful than the ones Luke used on the farm on Tatooine. They can go up to sixty or seventy feet in the air and can make banking turns sharper than a skyhopper."

In all the different drafts Leia, Chewie, Han, and Threepio escape together aboard the *Falcon*, while Luke goes off on his own with Artoo. In the first draft an interesting concept has Threepio encased in ice after an overhead pipe breaks over him.

EXT. SPACE—*MILLENNIUM FALCON*

The Millennium Falcon *speeds away from Hoth, closely followed by one huge Star Destroyer and four tiny TIE fighters.*

INT. *MILLENNIUM FALCON*—COCKPIT

Inside the cockpit, Chewie lets out a loud howl. Han checks the deflectors as the ship is buffeted by exploding flak. He appears to be doing six things at once.

HAN: *(harried)* I saw 'em! I saw 'em!

LEIA: Saw what?

HAN: Star Destroyers. Two of them, coming right at us.

Threepio bumps and bangs his way into the cockpit.

THREEPIO: Sir, sir! Might I suggest . . .

HAN: *(to Leia)* Shut him up or shut him down! *(to Chewie)* Check the deflector shields!

Chewie barks a reply as he readjusts an overhead switch.

HAN: Oh, great. Well, we can still outmaneuver them.

EXT. SPACE—*MILLENNIUM FALCON*—STAR DESTROYERS

The Millennium Falcon *has been racing toward one of the huge oncoming Star Destroyers. Suddenly the* Falcon *starts into a steep dive straight down, closely followed by TIE fighters. The underside of the Star Destroyer continues on a collision course with the two oncoming Star Destroyers.*

INT. STAR DESTROYER—BRIDGE

Out of the front window the two approaching Star Destroyers can be seen veering to the left.

IMPERIAL OFFICER: Take evasive action!

Alarms sound all over the huge ship. The two other Star Destroyers get closer, one of them moving over the bridge so close that it makes brushing contact with it.

EXT. SPACE—*MILLENNIUM FALCON*—TIE FIGHTERS

The Millennium Falcon *races away from the colliding Star Destroyers, still followed by four TIE fighters. Laserbolts spark the pitch-black skies.*

Things have calmed down a bit, but the race isn't over yet.

HAN: Prepare to make the jump to lightspeed!

Chewie barks at Han. The ship is buffeted by laserblasts.

THREEPIO: But sir!

LEIA: They're getting closer!

The buffeting of the lasers becomes louder and stronger.

HAN: *(with a gleam in his eye)* Oh, yeah? Watch this.

Expectantly, they look out the cockpit window as stars do not go into hyperspace but just sit there.

LEIA: Watch what?

HAN: I think we're in trouble.

THREEPIO: If I may say so, sir, I noticed earlier, the hyperdrive motivator has been damaged. It's impossible to go to lightspeed!

HAN: We're in trouble!

The explosions become heavier.

EXT. SPACE—*MILLENNIUM FALCON*—TIE FIGHTERS—STAR DESTROYER

The Falcon *races into the starry vastness, followed by the four Imperial TIE fighters and an Imperial Star Destroyer.*

INT. *MILLENNIUM FALCON*—HOLD

Han works furiously at some control panels while giving various orders to Chewie.

HAN: Horizontal boosters . . . ! *(Chewie barks)* Alluvial dampers . . . ! *(Chewie barks)* Now? That's not it. Bring me the hydrospanners! *(Chewie barks)*

Chewie hurries over to the pit and places the tools on the edge.

HAN: I don't know how we're going to get out of this one.

Suddenly, a loud thump hits the side of the Falcon, *causing it to lurch radically. Chewie barks. The tools fall into the pit on top of Han.*

HAN: Oww! Chewie!

More turbulence rocks the ship.

HAN: Those were no laserblasts! Something hit us.

Irvin Kershner: "The bit with the toolbox falling on Harrison was improvised on the set. But of course, I didn't want the audience to think that he was hurt, so I immediately had a close-up of him to show that he is all right. Another thing we improvised was when Harrison hits the control panels of the *Falcon* to make them work. We were afraid to do it, but I finally said, 'Come on, this is fun, let's do it!' "

INT. *MILLENNIUM FALCON*—COCKPIT.

LEIA: *(into comlink)* Han, get up here!

INT. *MILLENNIUM FALCON*—HOLD

HAN: Come on, Chewie!

Han climbs out of the hold like a shot. Both he and Chewie run out of the hold and toward the cockpit.

INT. *MILLENNIUM FALCON*—COCKPIT

Out of the front cockpit window they see hundreds of asteroids.

LEIA: Asteroids!

Han changes places with Leia, who has been at the controls. Han works his controls.

HAN: Oh, no! Chewie, set two-seven-one.

A chunk of rock crosses in front of the ship.

LEIA: What are you doing? You're not actually going into an asteroid field?

Another asteroid bumps against the ship.

HAN: They'd be crazy to follow us, wouldn't they?

EXT. *MILLENNIUM FALCON*

The Millennium Falcon weaves through the asteroid field.

INT. *MILLENNIUM FALCON*—COCKPIT

LEIA: You don't have to do this to impress me.

THREEPIO: Sir, the possibility of successfully navigating an asteroid field is approximately three thousand seven hundred and twenty to one.

HAN: Never tell me the odds!

EXT. ASTEROID BELT—*MILLENNIUM FALCON*

A large asteroid tumbles away from the Falcon's path. Other asteroids of all sizes pass by in every direction. The tiny Millennium Falcon veers around the big asteroid and races past it through the rain of rocks, followed by four TIE fighters, which bob and weave around the asteroids.

One of the pursuing TIE fighters connects with an asteroid and explodes. Another fighter is pelted and explodes.

INT. *MILLENNIUM FALCON*—COCKPIT

Asteroids race by the cockpit window as Han pilots his trusty craft through the dangerous field.

Looking out the cockpit window, the Falcon crew sees a big asteroid drop past the window, narrowly missing the ship.

Chewie moans in terror as a slightly smaller asteroid comes especially close— too close—and bounces off the Falcon with a loud crunch. Princess Leia sits stone-faced, staring at the action. Threepio cries out in alarm and covers his eyes with his hands.

HAN: *(to Leia)* You said you wanted to be around when I made a mistake; well, this could be it, sweetheart.

LEIA: I take it back. We're going to get pulverized if we stay out here much longer.

HAN: I'm not going to argue with that.

The group watches as more asteroids race by outside the window.

THREEPIO: Pulverized?

HAN: I'm going in closer to one of those big ones.

LEIA: Closer?

THREEPIO: Closer?

Chewbacca barks the same word, only louder.

EXT. *MILLENNIUM FALCON*—ASTEROID BELT

The Millennium Falcon *dives toward the surface of one of the moon-sized asteroids. The two remaining TIE fighters follow the* Falcon *to the large asteroid, firing laserbolts. The* Falcon *skims the surface of the giant asteroid as, all the while, small asteroids explode on the surface of the ship.*

The TIE fighters follow the Falcon *down the canyons of the moon-sized asteroid until they crash into the canyon walls and explode.*

INT. *MILLENNIUM FALCON*—COCKPIT

Rattled by the violent rocking of the starship, Threepio is nearly in hysterics.

THREEPIO: Oh, this is suicide!

Han notices something on his main scope and nudges his faithful Wookiee, pointing.

HAN: There. That looks pretty good.

LEIA: What looks pretty good?

HAN: Yeah. That'll do nicely.

THREEPIO: *(to Leia)* Excuse me, ma'am, but where are we going?

Out of the cockpit windows they see that they are skimming the surface of the enormous asteroid and nearing a large crater.

EXT. *MILLENNIUM FALCON*—GIANT ASTEROID CRATER

The Millennium Falcon *dives into the huge crater.*

INT. *MILLENNIUM FALCON*—COCKPIT

LEIA: I hope you know what you're doing.

HAN: Yeah, me, too.

INT. GIANT ASTEROID CRATER

The walls are barely visible as the Falcon *speeds through the tunnel-like opening.*

In the story treatment the *Falcon* jumps to lightspeed and escapes from the Imperial Star Destroyers. But when the *Falcon* comes out of lightspeed at the Rebel rendezvous point, Leia and Han find themselves in the middle of the Imperial fleet. The *Falcon* is chased by Imperial forces into an asteroid field and hides in the cave of one of the larger asteroids. In the first draft, as the *Falcon* is being pursued by an Imperial Destroyer, Leia suggests that they jump to lightspeed. Han asks about the rendezvous point, and Leia pulls a small metal container from around her neck, "programmed to explode if it got in the wrong hands." She extracts a metal clip that will set them on the rendezvous course, but just as she is about to give it to Han, red lights glow on the panel indicating that the overdrive generator has been hit.

Han goes to repair the damage, passing Threepio, who has been encased in dripping ice since they left the Ice Planet. Finally, the red light goes off and Chewie inserts the metal clip; the *Falcon* goes into hyperdrive. The scene ends with Leia cracking the mask of ice covering Threepio's face and the robot asking her to oil his joints before they rust. Later, the *Falcon* reaches the rendezvous point. As was established in the treatment, Imperial ships are already there; a voice asks them to identify themselves, and Han says he's a trader. An Imperial cruiser tries to board, but the *Falcon* makes an escape into an asteroid field. Leia gets in the turret guns; she misses her targets but manages to slow down the fighters. Finally, the *Falcon* hides in a cave on one of the asteroids.

The idea of the *Falcon* not being able to jump to lightspeed first appeared in the second draft.

EXT. SPACE—LUKE'S X-WING
The tiny X-wing speeds toward the planet Dagobah.
INT. LUKE'S X-WING—COCKPIT
Artoo whistles. His words are translated and screened on the computer scope.
LUKE: *(into comlink)* Yes, that's it. Dagobah.
EXT. LUKE'S X-WING
Artoo beeps a hopeful inquiry.
INT. LUKE'S X-WING—COCKPIT
LUKE: *(into comlink)* No, I'm not going to change my mind about this.
EXT. LUKE'S X-WING
Artoo listens as Luke, getting a little nervous, continues.
LUKE: *(over comlink)* I'm not picking up any cities or technology.
INT. LUKE'S X-WING—COCKPIT
LUKE: Massive life-form readings, though. There's something alive down there . . .
EXT. LUKE'S X-WING
Again Artoo beeps, this time a slightly worried question.
INT. LUKE'S X-WING—COCKPIT
LUKE: *(into comlink)* Yes, I'm sure it's perfectly safe for droids.

In the story treatment Luke gives directions to Artoo, using the planet described on the talisman that belonged to Ben and that Luke now wears around his neck. In the first draft Luke and Artoo escape while Vader and his men walk inside the Rebel base; one of his officers tells him that Luke Skywalker is not among the prisoners and that he might have been buried in one of the tunnels. Vader says he is alive and asks to be left alone. His breathing changes, and he whispers the name of Luke Skywalker. In space Luke suddenly can't breathe. In a last effort he releases the crystal he discovered earlier in his saber and gives it to Artoo. The robot places it in the proper slot and punches in some coordinates on the navigational computer, and the ship vanishes into hyperspace. At the base Vader realizes that once again Luke has escaped him.

EXT. SPACE—DAGOBAH—LUKE'S X-WING

The X-wing continues its flight down through the twilight above the cloud-covered planet.

EXT. LUKE'S X-WING

Artoo beeps and whistles frantically as clouds race by.

INT. LUKE'S X-WING—COCKPIT

Luke must operate his controls carefully since the cloud cover has completely obscured his vision.

LUKE: *(into comlink)* I know, I know! All the scopes are dead. I can't see a thing! Just hang on. I'm going to start the landing cycle . . .

EXT. LUKE'S X-WING

Artoo continues to squeal electronically.

INT. LUKE'S X-WING—COCKPIT

The blast of the retrorockets is deafening, drowning out Artoo's electronic squeals. Suddenly there is a cracking sound as if limbs were being broken off trees and then a tremendous jolt as the spacecraft stops. Luke looks out of the cockpit.

EXT. DAGOBAH—DUSK

The mist-shrouded X-wing fighter is almost invisible in the thick fog. Luke climbs out onto the long nose of the spacecraft as Artoo pops out of his cubbyhole on the back. The young warrior surveys the fog, which is barely pierced by the ship's landing lights. About all he can make out are some giant twisted trees nearby. Artoo whistles anxiously.

Ralph McQuarrie: "There were going to be lots of weird snakelike, octopuslike creatures on Dagobah. It was going to be a spooky jungle place with threatening things. I thought of all kinds of creatures, like a giant white spider, a crablike monster, a giant slug. I imagined that everything on the planet was petrified except for funguslike things that grew on the floor, food basically for the creatures that lived there."

George Lucas: "You always want to have something fantastic, but when you get down to the level of actually realizing your vision, you may find out that it's impossible to do, that you don't have the time or that it's just too expensive. So you have to take out of the script some of the most amazing and eccentric elements. In the new movies, thanks to digital technology, I hope that I will be able to realize some of the fantastical things that I couldn't have done in the past."

LUKE: No, Artoo, you stay put. I'll have a look around.

Artoo lets out a short beep. As Luke moves along the nose, Artoo loses his balance and disappears with a splash into the boggy lake.

LUKE: Artoo?

Luke kneels and leans over the plane, looking for Artoo, but the water is still and reveals no sign of the little droid.

LUKE: Artoo! Where are you? Artoo!

A small periscope breaks the surface of the water, and a gurgly beep is heard. The periscope starts to move to shore. Luke is relieved.

LUKE: You be more careful, Artoo—that way!

Luke jumps off the plane into the water. The periscope still steadily moves toward shore.

Suddenly, through the thick fog layer, a dark shape appears, moving toward the little droid. The droid disappears from sight, uttering a pathetic electronic scream as Luke scrambles ashore. The dark, sinuous bog beast dives beneath the swampy water.

LUKE: Artoo!

The black surface is still as death itself . . . until PHHEEWAAT!! The runt-size robot is spit out of the water, makes a graceful arc, and comes crashing down into a patch of soft gray moss.

LUKE: Oh, no! Are you all right? Come on. *(helping Artoo to his feet)* You're lucky you don't taste very good. Anything broken?

Artoo responds with feeble, soggy beeps.

LUKE: If you're saying coming here was a bad idea, I'm beginning to agree with you. Artoo, what are we doing here? It's like . . . something out of a dream or, I don't know. *(wiping the mud and roots from Artoo's round metal body)* Maybe I'm just going crazy.

As Luke glances around at the spooky swamp jungle that surrounds him, Artoo ejects a stream of muddy water from one of his cranial ports.

EXT. SPACE

The Imperial Starfleet moves through space, seeking its prey.

INT. VADER'S STAR DESTROYER—VADER'S CHAMBER

Admiral Piett hesitates in the entryway to Vader's private chamber.

After a moment he steps into the room and pauses at the surprising sight before him.

Darth Vader, his back turned, is on the far side of the chamber. A droid attends him. Among the various apparatuses surrounding them, a respirator tube now retracts from Vader's uncovered head. The head is bald with a mass of ugly scar tissue covering it. The droid lowers the mask and helmet onto Vader's head. When it is in place, the Dark Lord turns to face Piett.

The idea of the chamber for the Emperor was originally conceived during story meetings and was described as a "gray, macabre, cold steel box." In the second draft Veers visits Vader in his chamber, "a dark cubicle illuminated by a single shaft of light from above." Vader sits on a raised meditation cube. The reveal of the back of Vader's head first appeared in the fifth draft, and in the scene a "black insect-looking droid" attends Vader.

Irvin Kershner: "I shot this scene very carefully. When the captain comes in and Vader is sitting in his capsule with his back toward us, all you see are scars on the back of his neck for half a second. I didn't want the audience to see anything else. I imagined that beneath the mask Vader was hideous; his mouth was cut away, and he had one eye hanging low. I was very surprised to see that he was an ordinary man in the third film."

VADER: Yes, Admiral?

PIETT: Our ships have sighted the *Millennium Falcon*, Lord. But . . . it has entered an asteroid field, and we cannot risk—

VADER: *(interrupting)* Asteroids do not concern me, Admiral. I want that ship, not excuses.

PIETT: Yes, Lord.

EXT. ASTEROID CAVE—*MILLENNIUM FALCON*

The pirate starship rests in a dark, dripping asteroid cave. It is so dark that the cave's exact dimensions are impossible to determine.

INT. *MILLENNIUM FALCON*—COCKPIT

HAN: I'm going to shut down everything but the emergency power systems.

Han and Chewie busily shut down the engine and all electronic systems. Threepio and Leia watch worriedly.

THREEPIO: Sir, I'm almost afraid to ask, but . . . does that include shutting me down, too?

HAN: No. I need you to talk to the *Falcon*, find out what's wrong with the hyperdrive.

Suddenly the ship lurches, causing all the loose items in the cockpit to go flying. Chewie howls.

THREEPIO: Sir, it's quite possible this asteroid is not entirely stable.

HAN: Not entirely stable? I'm glad you're here to tell us these things. Chewie, take the professor in the back and plug him into the hyperdrive.

THREEPIO: Oh! Sometimes I just don't understand human behavior. After all, I'm only trying to do my job in the most . . .

The sliding door closes behind the indignant Threepio as he and Chewie move back to the hold. Suddenly the ship lurches again, throwing Leia across the cabin into Han's arms. Then, abruptly, the motion stops as suddenly as it started. With some surprise, Leia realizes she is in Han's arms.

LEIA: Let go.

HAN: Sshh!

LEIA: Let go, please.

Leia flushes, averting her eyes. She's not exactly fighting to get free. But of course Han blows it . . .

HAN: Don't get excited.

The anger rises in Leia.

LEIA: Captain, being held by you isn't quite enough to get me excited.

HAN: Sorry, sweetheart. We haven't got time for anything else.

Han grins wickedly at Leia as he turns and exits through the door. Leia's confused emotions show clearly on her lovely face.

EXT. DAGOBAH—BOG CLEARING—DUSK

The mist has dispersed a bit, but it is still a very gloomy-looking swamp.

Luke carries an equipment box from the shore to the clearing.

LUKE: What? Ready for some power? Okay. Let's see now. Put that in there. *(taking a power cable, he plugs it into Artoo's noselike socket)* There you go.

The droid whistles his appreciation.

LUKE: *(sighs)* Now all I got to do is find this Yoda . . . *(nervously, he looks around at the foreboding jungle)* if he even exists. It's really a strange place to find a Jedi Master.

Luke then opens a container of processed food and sits before the thermal heater.

LUKE: This place gives me the creeps.

Artoo beeps in agreement with that sentiment.

LUKE: Still . . . there's something familiar about this place. I don't know . . . I feel like . . .

STRANGE VOICE: Feel like what?

Luke jumps out of his skin. Artoo beeps in terror. The young warrior grabs for his blaster as he spins around, looking for the speaker. Mysteriously standing right in

front of Luke is a strange, bluish creature not more than two feet tall. The wizened
little thing is dressed in rags. It covers its face.

The idea of using another person, perhaps an alien, for Luke to play off of came up during story meetings. George Lucas and Leigh Brackett thought that the alien could be an Indian desert type, very childlike even though he's an old man. He at first should be repulsive and slimy but then should become kind and wise. He appears as a crazy little nitwit that goes around scurrying like a rat but ultimately teaches Luke a great deal about the Force. It was suggested that he should be very small, about twenty-eight inches high. He should be slightly froglike, with slick skin, a wide mouth, no nose, bulbous eyes, thin spidery arms, and little thin hands. He should have a round body with short legs but very large, floppy webbed feet, almost like swim fins, and a big mouth with two tiny nostrils. Basically he would have the personality of a Muppet, only with almost human and realistic behavior.

At that point Yoda did not have a name and was referred to as "The Critter." In the story treatment the little creature is named Minch Yoda. In the first draft Yoda is referred to only as Minch. In his introductory scene Luke asks the creature if he knows of the Jedi Knights, and Minch says he used to serve them. He knew Luke's father and Obi-Wan Kenobi. The bog planet is where they trained. In the second draft Yoda is described as a "strange froglike creature no more than two feet high." The wizened little thing is totally unhuman, although it is dressed in rags of somewhat human design. The creature lets out another long giggle as it brushes gray hair out of its eyes. In the third draft Yoda is described as a strange blue creature not more than two feet tall and dressed in rags.

George Lucas: "I wanted Yoda to be the traditional kind of character you find in fairy tales and mythology. And that character is usually a frog or a wizened old man on the side of the road. The hero is going down the road and meets this poor and insignificant person. The goal or the lesson is for the hero to learn to respect everybody and to pay attention to the poorest person because that's where the key to his success will be. I wanted Yoda to be perceived at first as a funny critic, not as the most powerful of all the Jedi. I wanted him to be the exact opposite of what you might expect, since the Jedi is based on a philosophical idea rather than a physical idea."

LUKE: *(looking at the creature)* Like we're being watched!

CREATURE: Away put your weapon! I mean you no harm. I am wondering, why are you here?

After some hesitation Luke puts away his weapon, although he really doesn't understand why.

LUKE: I'm looking for someone.

CREATURE: Looking? Found someone, you have, I would say, hmmm?

The little creature laughs.

LUKE: *(trying to keep from smiling)* Right.

CREATURE: Help you I can. Yes, mmmm.

LUKE: I don't think so. I'm looking for a great warrior.

CREATURE: Ahhh! A great warrior. *(laughs and shakes his head)* Wars not make one great.

With the aid of a walking stick the tiny stranger moves over to one of the cases of supplies. He begins to rummage around.

Their tiny visitor picks up the container of food Luke was eating from and takes a bite.

LUKE: Put that down! Now . . . Hey! That's my dinner!

The creature spits out the bite he has taken. He makes a face.

CREATURE: How you get so big, eating food of this kind?

LUKE: Listen, friend, we didn't mean to land in that puddle, and if we could get our ship out, we would, but we can't, so why don't you just . . .

George Lucas: "As you go along, you're constantly trying to balance the elements in a movie so that you have all the issues that you're trying to deal with, but you don't overindulge in one particular area. In the kind of movies I make, I tend to stress the plot side of things. The nature of the characters is pivotal to the way they react to things. Usually the characters are archetypes to such a degree that it's not necessary to go into a lot of detail because I'm not dealing with deep psychological problems. My films are storytelling movies, not character movies. So with that in mind, I try to get to the cleanest, to the most simple way of portraying things."

Lawrence Kasdan: "We tried to avoid expressions like 'I'll be there in a minute,' or 'It will take us an hour,' as much as possible. George wanted the characters to have their own time, something that would have nothing to do with ours."

CREATURE: *(teasing)* Aww, can't you get your ship out?

The creature starts rummaging through one of Luke's supply cases.

LUKE: Hey, get out of there!

CREATURE: Ahhh! *(as Luke rescues an item from his clasp)* No! Oh!

LUKE: Hey, you could have broken this.

The creature begins to throw the contents of the case out behind him, finally spotting something of interest—a tiny power lamp—and examines it with delight.

LUKE: Don't do that. Ohhh . . . you're making a mess. Hey, give me that!

CREATURE: *(retreating with the lamp)* Mine! Or I will help you not.

Clutching its treasure, the creature backs away from Luke, drawing closer to Artoo. As Luke and the creature argue, one of Artoo's little arms slowly moves out toward the power lamp, completely unnoticed by the creature.

Irvin Kershner: "I wanted to reveal Yoda gradually. First you see him from the back, then from the front, and then you have the close-up. In that first scene I had to give a sense to the audience of how short Yoda was. So I had this shot of Luke in the foreground standing in front of Yoda. Then Luke bends down, and you have a real sense of scale. We had three different Yodas. Frank Oz and several other operators were literally underground operating Yoda, and they had a little video monitor that showed them what the camera saw. In the long shot, when Yoda is walking, we used a little person walking on his knees."

LUKE: I don't want your help. I want my lamp back. I'm gonna need to get out of this slimy mudhole.

CREATURE: Mudhole? Slimy? My home this is.

Artoo grabs hold of the lamp, and the two little figures are immediately engaged in a tug-of-war over it.

Artoo beeps a few angry "Give me thats."

CREATURE: Ah, ah, ah!

LUKE: Oh, Artoo, let him have it!

CREATURE: Mine! Mine!

LUKE: Artoo!

CREATURE: Mine!

Artoo lets go. The creature pokes Artoo lightly with his stick.

LUKE: *(fed up)* Now will you move along, little fella? We've got a lot of work to do.

CREATURE: No! No, no! Stay and help you, I will. *(laughs)* Find your friend.

LUKE: I'm not looking for a friend. I'm looking for a Jedi Master.

CREATURE: Oohhh, Jedi Master. Yoda. You seek Yoda.

LUKE: You know him?

CREATURE: Mmm. Take you to him, I will. *(laughs)* Yes, yes. But now we must eat. Come. Good food. Come.

With that, the creature scurries out of the clearing, laughing merrily. Luke stares after him.

CREATURE: *(in the distance)* Come, come.

Luke makes his decision.

LUKE: Artoo, stay and watch after the camp.

Luke starts for the creature. Artoo, very upset, whistles a blue streak of protests.

    Artoo beeps even more frantically. But as Luke disappears from view, the worried little droid grows quieter and utters a soft electronic sigh.

INT. *MILLENNIUM FALCON*—MAIN HOLD AREA

Threepio is at the control panel, which emits a few mystifying beeps.

THREEPIO: Oh, where is Artoo when I need him?

Han enters the hold area and kneels on the floor near the control box.

THREEPIO: Sir, I don't know where your ship learned to communicate, but it has the most peculiar dialect. I believe, sir, it says that the power coupling on the negative axis has been polarized. I'm afraid you'll have to replace it.

HAN: Well, of course I'll have to replace it.

He hands a wire coil up to Chewie, who is working near the ceiling.

HAN: Here! And Chewie . . .

Chewie brings his head back through the trapdoor in the ceiling and whines. Han glances back at Threepio, then speaks quietly to Chewie so only he can hear.

HAN: *(continuing)* . . . I think we'd better replace the negative power coupling.

Leia finishes welding the valve she has been working on and attempts to reengage the system by pulling a lever attached to the valve. It doesn't budge. Han notices her struggle and moves to help her. She rebuffs him.

HAN: Hey, Your Worship, I'm only trying to help.

LEIA: *(still struggling)* Would you please stop calling me that?

Han hears a new tone in her voice. He watches her pull on the lever.

HAN: Sure, Leia.

LEIA: Oh, you make it so difficult sometimes.

HAN: I do, I really do. You could be a little nicer, though. *(he watches her reaction)* Come on, admit it. Sometimes you think I'm all right.

She lets go of the lever and licks her sore hand.

LEIA: Occasionally, maybe . . . *(a little smile, haltingly)* . . . when you aren't acting like a scoundrel.

HAN: Scoundrel? Scoundrel? I like the sound of that.

Han has taken her hand and starts to massage it.

LEIA: Stop that.

HAN: Stop what?

Leia is flushed, confused.

LEIA: Stop that! My hands are dirty.

HAN: My hands are dirty, too. What are you afraid of?

LEIA: *(looking right into his eyes)* Afraid?

Han looks at her with a piercing look. He's never looked more handsome, more dashing, more confident.

HAN: You're trembling.

LEIA: I'm not trembling.

Then, with an irresistible combination of physical strength and emotional power, the space pirate begins to draw Leia toward him . . . very slowly.

HAN: You like me because I'm a scoundrel. There aren't enough scoundrels in your life.

Leia is now very close to Han, and as she speaks, her voice becomes an excited whisper, a tone completely in opposition to her words.

LEIA: I happen to like nice men.

HAN: I'm a nice man.

LEIA: No, you're not. You're . . .

He kisses her now with slow, hot lips. He takes his time, as though he had forever, bending her body backward. She has never been kissed like this before.

Suddenly Threepio appears in the doorway, speaking excitedly.

THREEPIO: Sir, sir! I've isolated the reverse power flux coupling.

Han turns slowly, icily, from their embrace.

HAN: Thank you. Thank you very much.

THREEPIO: Oh, you're perfectly welcome, sir.

The moment is spoiled.

In the story treatment and as in the movie, Han and Leia have their first kiss after they've hidden in the asteroid cave. In the first draft Han tries to seduce Leia, and she tells him that she is not in love with him or Luke. Later Han tries again and wants Leia to say that she loves him. They finally kiss, but their embrace is interrupted by Chewie, who seems annoyed by the relationship. Threepio guesses that the Wookiee is afraid that Leia is going to distract Han from their adventures. Chewie grunts, resenting the droid's insight into his character. Threepio says he doesn't understand the pleasure of kissing and is grateful for the fact that he is not human.

Lawrence Kasdan: "I wanted Chewbacca to be jealous of Han's relationship with Leia so that each time you cut to him watching them, you'd begin to read into his character. I was always looking to add things that would make the story more detailed. I wanted everybody in the script to have reactions to everything. Of course, when you make a movie, you tend to have to lose those things."

Irvin Kershner: "We didn't need to spend too much time on the love story. When Han tried to kiss her, that was enough. In the *Star Wars* series a kiss is the equivalent of a sex scene. Han is always after her, he's always looking at her and she is always looking at him, and you have this right from the beginning. Basically, that's all you need. Larry Kasdan did a great job with the love scene. We rehearsed it and we made changes, but the essence was always there. Larry is a good dialogue writer because he has a sense of rhythm.

You know if the dialogue is good when you're working with the actors. If the rhythm is right, they have no problem with the lines; if it's bad, they have problems learning the dialogue. Incidentally, it was essential to have Threepio interrupt the kiss between Leia and Solo because he is so taken with himself that it makes sense that he would walk in and say, 'Hey, what are you doing here?' He is not human; he doesn't understand emotions."

EXT. SPACE—ASTEROID FIELD
The Imperial fleet moves through the asteroid-filled void, intently seeking its prey.
INT. VADER'S STAR DESTROYER—BRIDGE
Before Darth Vader are the hologram images of battleship commanders. One of these images, the commander of a ship that has just exploded, is fading quickly away. Another image is faded and continually disrupted by static. It is the image of Captain Needa, commander of the Star Destroyer most hotly on the tail of the Millennium Falcon. Admiral Piett and an aide stand behind the Dark Lord.
NEEDA: *(in hologram)* . . . and that, Lord Vader, was the last time they appeared in any of our scopes. Considering the amount of damage we've sustained, they must have been destroyed.
VADER: No, Captain, they're alive. I want every ship available to sweep the asteroid field until they are found.
The Imperial star captain fades out as Admiral Piett approaches Vader.
PIETT: Lord Vader.
VADER: Yes, Admiral, what is it?
The admiral is scared, his face white as a sheet.
PIETT: The Emperor commands you to make contact with him.

VADER: Move the ship out of the asteroid field so that we can send a clear transmission.

PIETT: Yes, my lord.

EXT. ASTEROID FIELD—VADER'S STAR DESTROYER

Vader's Imperial Star Destroyer moves against the vast sea of stars away from the rest of the fleet.

INT. VADER'S STAR DESTROYER—VADER'S CHAMBER

The Dark Lord, Darth Vader, is alone in his chamber. Vader kneels as a strange sound enters the room.

VADER: What is thy bidding, my master?

A twelve-foot hologram of the Galactic Emperor materializes before Vader. The Emperor's dark robes and monk's hood are reminiscent of the cloak worn by Ben Kenobi. His voice is even deeper and more frightening than Vader's.

EMPEROR: There is a great disturbance in the Force.

VADER: I have felt it.

EMPEROR: We have a new enemy—Luke Skywalker.

VADER: Yes, my master.

EMPEROR: He could destroy us.

VADER: He's just a boy. Obi-Wan can no longer help him.

EMPEROR: The Force is strong with him. The son of Skywalker must not become a Jedi.

VADER: If he could be turned, he would become a powerful ally.

EMPEROR: Yes. Yes. He would be a great asset. Can it be done?

VADER: He will join us or die, Master.

Vader bows.

During meetings George Lucas and Leigh Brackett decided that the Emperor and the Force had to be the two main concerns in the film; the Emperor had barely been dealt with in the first movie, and the intention in the sequel was to deal with him on a more concrete level. Eventually this idea was used later on, in the third film. The Emperor, however, was then envisioned as a bureaucrat, Nixonian in his outlook and sort of a Wizard of Oz–type person.

It was suggested that after the battle on the ice planet Vader would go into isolation, maybe in a cave with demons or in a tall, dark tower surrounded by lava, sort of like in hell. Vader would have gremlins or goblintype gargoyles with him. In the first draft the scene with Vader in his castle is intercut with Luke beginning his training. Vader lives in what's described as a grim castle of black iron that squats on a rock in the midst of a crimson sea. He is feeding gargoyles from a golden bowl, and he suddenly stiffens, frightening even the creatures; he has felt a disturbance in the Force. Later Vader has a discussion with the Emperor, who appears on a communication screen, "caped and hooded in a cloth of gold." He tells Vader that he also felt the disturbance in the Force and that Luke must be eliminated.

Joe Johnston: "When we were doing *Star Wars,* I remember I had done a series of sketches of Vader's home, and there was a sea of lava that his house looked out on. I remember having trouble drawing it because everything was either orange or a shadow; it was very intense. But before we got too far, George said we would save this for somewhere down the line, and I stopped working on it."

In the second draft Vader talks on the video screen to Sate Molock, "Grand Vizier to his eminence the Emperor," in his holograph chamber. Molock tells Vader that the Emperor is in a bad mood. Vader reports that the base on Hoth has been destroyed and that he is tracking down the survivors. Later Vader has his talk with the Emperor. The Emperor tells Vader to turn Luke to the dark side, and before his image fades away, he passes his hand over Vader's head.

In the revised second draft Sate Molock is called Sate Pestage. This character was ultimately deleted.

EXT. DAGOBAH—CREATURE'S HOUSE—NIGHT
A heavy downpour of rain pounds through the gnarled trees. A strange baroque mud house sits on a moss-covered knoll on the edge of a small lagoon. The small, gnomish structure radiates a warm glow from its thick glass windows. As the rain tap-dances a merry tune on Artoo's head, the stubby little droid rises up on his tiptoes to peek into one of the glowing portals.

Irvin Kershner: "I figured that a robot rising up on his tiptoes had never been shown before, so I put it in the movie. It was improvised on the set. You can't think of those things until you see the set."

INT. CREATURE'S HOUSE
Artoo, peeking in the window, sees the inside of the house—a very plain but cozy dwelling. Everything is in the same scale as the creature. The only thing out of

place in the miniature room is Luke, whose height makes the four-foot ceiling seem even lower.

The creature is in an adjoining area—his little kitchen—cooking up an incredible meal. Luke watches impatiently.

LUKE: Look, I'm sure it's delicious. I just don't understand why we can't see Yoda now.

CREATURE: Patience! For the Jedi it is time to eat as well. Eat, eat. Hot.

Moving with some difficulty in the cramped quarters, Luke sits down near the fire and serves himself from the pot. Tasting the unfamiliar concoction, he is pleasantly surprised.

CREATURE: Good food, hm? Good, hmmm?

LUKE: How far away is Yoda? Will it take us long to get there?

CREATURE: Not far. Yoda not far. Patience. Soon you will be with him. Rootleaf, I cook. Why wish you become Jedi? Hm?

LUKE: Mostly because of my father, I guess.

CREATURE: Ah, father. Powerful Jedi was he, mmm, powerful Jedi, mmm.

LUKE: *(a little angry)* Oh, come on. How could you know my father? You don't even know who I am. *(fed up)* Oh, I don't know what I'm doing here. We're wasting our time.

The creature is turned away from Luke and speaks to a third party.

CREATURE: *(irritated)* I cannot teach him. The boy has no patience.

Luke's head turns in the direction the creature faces. But there is no one there. The boy is bewildered, but it gradually dawns on him that the little creature is Yoda, the Jedi Master, and that he is speaking with Ben.

BEN'S VOICE: He will learn patience.

YODA: Hmmm. Much anger in him, like his father.

BEN'S VOICE: Was I any different when you taught me?

YODA: Hah. He is not ready.

LUKE: Yoda! I am ready. I . . . Ben! I, I can be a Jedi. Ben, tell him I'm ready.

Trying to see Ben, Luke starts to get up but hits his head on the low ceiling.

YODA: Ready, are you? What know you of ready? For eight hundred years have I trained Jedi. My own counsel will I keep on who is to be trained! A Jedi must have the deepest commitment, the most serious mind. *(to the invisible Ben, about Luke)* This one a long time have I watched. All his life has he looked away . . . to the future, to the horizon. Never his mind on where he was. Hmm? What he was doing. Hmph. Adventure. Heh! Excitement. Heh! A Jedi craves not these things. *(turning to Luke)* You are reckless!

Luke knows it is true.

BEN'S VOICE: So was I, if you remember.

YODA: He is too old. Yes, too old to begin the training.

Luke thinks he detects a subtle softening in Yoda's voice.

LUKE: But I've learned so much.

Yoda turns his piercing gaze on Luke, as though the Jedi Master's huge eyes could somehow determine how much the boy has learned. After a long moment the little Jedi turns toward where he alone sees Ben.

YODA: *(sighs)* Will he finish what he begins?
LUKE: I won't fail you. *(as Yoda turns back toward him)* I'm not afraid.
YODA: Yeah. You will be. You will be.

George Lucas: "After I had killed Ben in *Star Wars*, I had to figure out a way to replace him. I didn't want another human being, and that's when I decided to make him tiny and green and very odd and eight hundred years old and a whole different level of Jedi than Ben was. Then I created the backstory that he was Ben's teacher."

Irvin Kershner: "The concept of Yoda, which is a Zen concept, is for adults, but kids can get something out of it, too. I used to study Zen and Buddhism, and I found many ideas there. Also, after I read the script, I started reading fairy tales and the analysis of fairy tales. You see, this is not really science fiction, and I wanted to know what makes a fairy tale work for people so that it stays in their culture for so many years."

Lawrence Kasdan: "I remember that George had a feeling about the kind of speech he wanted Yoda to have. It had to do with inversion and with a kind of medieval feeling with religious overtones. Once we figured that out, it became very logical to have Yoda say things like 'Good it will be . . .' Inverting everything did the trick."

In the story treatment Yoda tells Luke that Ben gave him the talisman he wears around his neck so that he could find him. Luke is starving, and Yoda says he has food but won't give him any until Luke starts learning about the Force. In the first draft Luke thinks he has come to the wrong place and gets ready to leave. Minch reveals that he taught Ben, and to convince Luke of his power, he grabs Luke's lasersword and calls Ben; Obi-Wan appears, and the two Jedi begin to fence. Finally, Luke sees that Minch is clearly better and even more powerful than Ben. Minch takes Luke to his house, which is scaled to his size and is described as "a small gem, beautifully constructed of reeds rather in the fashion of the Marsh Arabs."

In the second draft Yoda's dwelling is described as a baroque mud house with thick glass windows. Yoda reveals that he is the Jedi Master Luke is looking for and that *he trained both his father and Ben Kenobi*. In the revised second draft Yoda says that *he trained Obi-Wan, who then trained Luke's father*. In the third draft Luke explains to Yoda that he wants to be a Jedi as his father was. Yoda has trained Jedi Knights for eight hundred years and says that he has been watching Luke for a long time; he cannot be his teacher because Luke wants adventure and excitement. To prove him wrong Luke closes his eyes and concentrates. Ben appears and tells Yoda that the boy called him, that he deserves a chance, that he will finish what he begins. Yoda decides to train Luke despite the fact that he thinks Ben is wrong about the boy's potential.

EXT. SPACE—STAR DESTROYERS—ASTEROID FIELD

The Imperial fleet around Vader's ship is surrounded by the asteroid storm. Smaller Imperial vessels search for their prey.

EXT. ASTEROID CAVE—*MILLENNIUM FALCON*

The Millennium Falcon *continues to lie low.*

INT. ASTEROID CAVE—*MILLENNIUM FALCON*—COCKPIT

The cockpit is quiet and lit only by the indicator lights on the control panel. Princess Leia sits in the pilot's seat, thinking of Han and the confusion he has created within her. Suddenly, something outside the cockpit window catches her eye. The reflection of the panel lights obscures her vision until a soft suctionlike cup attaches itself to the windscreen and large, yellow eyes flash open and stare back at her. Startled, the young Princess races from the cockpit.

INT. ASTEROID CAVE—*MILLENNIUM FALCON*—HOLD AREA

The lights go bright for a second, then go out again. Threepio and Chewbacca watch as Han finishes with some wires.

THREEPIO: Sir, if I may venture an opinion—

HAN: I'm not really interested in your opinion, Threepio.

Leia rushes into the cabin just as Han drops the final floor panel into place.

LEIA: *(out of breath)* There's something out there.

HAN: Where?

LEIA: Outside, in the cave.

As she speaks, there comes a sharp banging on the hull.

THREEPIO: There it is! Listen! Listen!

Chewie looks up and moans anxiously.

HAN: I'm going out there.

LEIA: Are you crazy?

HAN: I just got this bucket back together. I'm not going to let something tear it apart.

He grabs his breath mask off a rack and hurries out.

LEIA: Oh, then I'm going with you.

Chewie and Leia follow suit.

THREEPIO: I think it might be better if I stay behind and guard the ship. *(hears another mysterious noise)* Oh, no.

EXT. ASTEROID CAVE—*MILLENNIUM FALCON*

It is very dark and dank inside the huge asteroid cave, too dark to see what is attacking the ship.

LEIA: This ground sure feels strange. It doesn't feel like rock.

Han kneels and studies the ground, then attempts to study the outline of the cave.

HAN: There's an awful lot of moisture in here.

LEIA: I don't know. I have a bad feeling about this.

HAN: Yeah.

HAN: *(to Leia)* Watch out!

Han has seen a five-foot-long shape moving across the top of the Falcon. The leathery creature lets out a screech as Han blasts it with a laserbolt. Chewie barks through his face mask.

The black shape tumbles off the spaceship and onto the ground.

HAN: *(to Chewie)* It's all right. It's all right.

Han looks down to investigate the dead creature.

HAN: Yeah, what I thought. Mynock. Chewie, check the rest of the ship, make sure there are no more attached. They're chewing on the power cables.

LEIA: Mynocks?

HAN: Go on inside. We'll clean them off if there are any more.

Just then a swarm of the ugly creatures swoops through the air. Leia puts her arms over her head to protect herself as she runs toward the ship. Several of the batlike creatures flap their wings loudly against the cockpit window of the Falcon. Inside, Threepio shudders at their presence.

THREEPIO: Ohhh! Go away! Go away! Beastly thing. Shoo! Shoo!

As Chewie shoos a mynock away with his blaster, the cave rocks. Han looks around the strange cave.

HAN: Wait a minute . . .

He unholsters his blaster and fires at the far side of the huge cave. The cavern begins to shake, and the ground starts to buckle.

Leia and Han move for the ship, followed closely by a barking Chewie.

INT. ASTEROID CAVE—*MILLENNIUM FALCON*—ENTRY AREA

The ship continues to shake and heave.

HAN: Pull her up, Chewie, let's get out of here!

The Wookiee heads for the cockpit as Han, followed by Threepio, rushes to the hold area and checks the scopes on the control panel. Leia hurries after.

LEIA: The Empire is still out there. I don't think it's wise to . . .

Han rushes past her and heads for the cockpit.

HAN: *(interrupting)* No time to discuss this in committee.

And with that he is gone. The main engines of the Falcon *begin to whine. Leia races after him, bouncing around in the shaking ship.*

LEIA: *(angry)* I am not a committee!

INT. ASTEROID CAVE—*MILLENNIUM FALCON*—COCKPIT

Han reaches the pilot's seat and pulls back on the throttle.

LEIA: You can't make the jump to lightspeed in this asteroid field . . .

HAN: Sit down, sweetheart. We're taking off!

As the ship begins to move forward, Chewie barks. He notices something outside the window ahead. Threepio sees it, too.

THREEPIO: Look!

HAN: I see it, I see it.

Suddenly a row of jagged white stalagmites and stalactites can be seen surrounding the entrance. And as the Falcon *moves forward, the entrance to the cave grows ever smaller. Han pulls hard on the throttle, sending his ship surging forward.*

THREEPIO: We're doomed!

LEIA: The cave is collapsing!

HAN: This is no cave.

LEIA: What?

Leia sees that the rocks of the cave entrance are not rocks at all but giant teeth, quickly closing around the tiny ship.

INT. SPACE SLUG MOUTH

The Millennium Falcon, *zooming through the monster's mouth, rolls on its side and barely makes it between two of the gigantic white teeth before the huge jaw slams closed.*

EXT. CAVE ENTRANCE—GIANT ASTEROID

The enormous space slug moves its head out of the cave as the Falcon *flies out of its mouth. The monster tilts its head, watching the starship fly away.*

EXT. *MILLENNIUM FALCON*—GIANT ASTEROID

The Falcon *races out of the asteroid crater and into the deadly rain of the asteroid storm.*

EXT. CAVE ENTRANCE—GIANT ASTEROID

The monstrous slug withdraws its head back into its crater.

The scene with "large leathery creatures with yellow eyes" attacking the *Falcon* inside the cave on the asteroid first appeared in the second draft. In the fifth draft the yellow eyes became "something like a soft suction cup" that attaches itself to the windscreen of the *Falcon;* Leia, not Han as in the movie, says that they look like some kind of "mynock," and Threepio explains that they usually travel in groups of five.

Irvin Kershner: "The mynocks were just pieces of plastic on fishing poles. You'll notice that I cut away from them very quickly because they didn't look great. I wanted the actors to wear oxygen masks in this sequence, but I didn't want the masks to cover their faces entirely. So I had to make the masks really small. The *Falcon* of course never moved. It was all done with the camera and with the actors. I would shout to the actors, 'Move right,' and the camera would go the opposite way, and vice versa."

The space slug was first introduced in the fifth draft and was described as a monstrous moray eel.

EXT. DAGOBAH—DAY

With Yoda strapped to his back, Luke climbs up one of the many thick vines that grow in the swamp. Panting heavily, he continues his course—climbing, flipping through the air, jumping over roots, and racing in and out of the heavy ground fog.

YODA: Run! Yes. A Jedi's strength flows from the Force. But beware of the dark side. Anger . . . fear . . . aggression. The dark side of the Force are they. Easily they flow, quick to join you in a fight. If once you start down the dark path, forever will it dominate your destiny, consume you it will, as it did Obi-Wan's apprentice.

LUKE: Vader. Is the dark side stronger?

YODA: No . . . no . . . no. Quicker, easier, more seductive.

LUKE: But how am I to know the good side from the bad?

Lawrence Kasdan: "I'm a big Samurai movie fan, as is George. The stories I find most interesting are stories of Zen education and the Zen master teaching a pupil how to transcend physical prowess into some kind of mental prowess. That's what all the training sequences are about. My favorite director is Akira Kurosawa, and *Star Wars* was inspired by his film *The Hidden Fortress*, so George and I had an immediate connection there. All through Kurosawa's movies you have the idea that it's one thing to be physically adept and something else to be spiritually adept."

YODA: You will know. When you are calm, at peace. Passive. A Jedi uses the Force for knowledge and defense, never for attack.

LUKE: But tell me why I can't . . .

YODA: *(interrupting)* No, no, there is no why. Nothing more will I teach you today. Clear your mind of questions. Mmm. Mmmmmmm.

Artoo beeps in the distance as Luke lets Yoda down to the ground. Breathing heavily, he takes his shirt from a nearby tree branch and pulls it on.

Yoda sits on a large root, poking his gimer stick into the dirt.

Luke turns to see a huge dead black tree, its base surrounded by a few feet of water. Giant twisted roots form a dark and sinister cave on one side. Luke stares at the tree, trembling.

LUKE: There's something not right here. I feel cold, death.

YODA: That place . . . is strong with the dark side of the Force. A domain of evil it is. In you must go.

LUKE: What's in there?

YODA: Only what you take with you.

Luke looks warily between the tree and Yoda. He starts to strap on his weapon belt.

YODA: Your weapons . . . you will not need them.

Luke gives the tree a long look, then shakes his head no. Luke reaches up to brush aside some hanging vines and enters the tree.

INT. DAGOBAH—TREE CAVE

Luke moves into the almost total darkness of the wet and slimy cave. The youth can barely make out the edge of the passage. He sees a lizard crawling up the side of the cave and a snake wrapped around the branches of a tree. Luke draws a deep breath, then pushes deeper into the cave.

The space widens around him, but he feels that rather than sees it. It is very quiet here.

Then Darth Vader appears across the blackness. They cross lightsabers, but Luke parries perfectly and slashes at Vader with his sword.

Vader is decapitated. His helmet-encased head flies from his shoulders as his body disappears into the darkness. The helmet containing Vader's head spins and bounces and finally stops. For an instant it rests on the floor, then it explodes. The black helmet and breath mask fall away to reveal . . . Luke's head.

Across the space the standing Luke stares at the sight, wide-eyed in terror.

George Lucas and Leigh Brackett had lengthy discussions about Luke's training with Yoda and decided to turn the lessons into proverbs and commandments. Through the lessons, Luke should learn to respect Yoda and Yoda should realize that the boy is a great warrior. The Force also was discussed in great detail. In the story meeting transcripts George Lucas defined the Force as follows: The act of living generates a force field, an energy. That energy surrounds us; when we die, that energy joins with all the other energy. There is a giant mass of energy in the universe that has a good side and a bad side. We are part of the Force because we generate the power that makes the Force live. When we die, we become part of that Force, so we never really die; we continue as part of the Force.

It was decided that learning the ways of the Force had to be a constant struggle for Luke and that he would always have to prove himself. In regard to the dark side of the Force, the story meeting transcripts suggest that although one can't see it, it should be the real villain of the story. In his training Luke discovers the roots of the evil Force. The danger, the jeopardy is that Luke will become Vader, will be taken over. He has to fight the bad side and learn to work with the good side. Lucas felt that at one point during the training Ben should explain to Luke that he should use his powers with moderation. If he uses too much of the Force, it will start using him. For example, to lift objects Luke has to use the bad side of the Force, so if he overuses this power, the dark side will start taking him over as it did with Vader. When Luke fights, he has to use the dark side, but he is also using the good side for protection. In this episode Luke should embody the classic tale of the ugly duckling who becomes a hero, and by the end of the film Luke should have become Ben.

In the first draft, during his training Luke calls Obi-Wan Kenobi; Ben appears and explains what has happened to him since he was struck by Vader. He is now in a different part of the universe. Ben says that he's brought someone else with him, and Luke's father appears (obviously, in this draft Vader is not Luke's father). He is described as a tall, fine-looking man and is referred to as Skywalker. Skywalker tells Luke that he has a sister; he won't reveal where she is for fear that Vader might then be able to find her. This concept of Luke's sister was discussed during story conferences: The idea was that Luke's father had twin children and took one of them to an uncle and the second one to the other side of the universe so that if one was killed, another would survive. It was suggested that Luke's twin sister would be going through training at the same time that he was and become a Jedi Master as well. Eventually, in another episode the story could deal with both Luke and his sister as Jedi Knights.

In the first draft Luke takes the oath of a Jedi from his father. Later Minch tells Luke that facing Vader and the dark side is the real test for him. Luke concentrates, and suddenly two shapes rise from the swamp: one looks like Vader, and the other one is smaller, featureless but reminiscent of Luke. In ghostly voices they talk to each other. Vader says he wants Luke as an ally. The two shapes now seem to stand in space. Vader tells Luke that he knows that he loves Leia and that Han is standing between them. If he joins him, no one will ever be in his way and one day they will rule the universe. Vader tells Luke to reach out for stars; Luke tries, but the stars burn his fingers and he says that he's taken an oath. Vader tells him that the dark side won't let him rest even if he runs. Luke comes out of the trance and sobs, saying that he couldn't fight Vader.

In the second draft Yoda tells Luke that he lacks concentration; Luke says he feels the Force the most when he is angry. Yoda warns him that anger is a dangerous path to the dark side. The dark side is aggressive while the good side is passive, and a Jedi must use the Force only for defense and for knowledge, never for attack. They continue the training with Luke trying to deflect bolts coming from four seeker balls with his lasersword. Later Yoda and Luke reach a tree with giant twisted roots near a dark sinister cave. Yoda says that the tree is strong with the dark side of the Force and tells Luke he must face it. Luke feels he is not ready but eventually goes inside the cave. At one point he sees a shape and instinctively swings his weapon, only to realize that there is nothing. He comes out shaking and scared, and the scene ends with Yoda telling him to go back inside the cave.

In the third draft Luke's training is presented in several montages that show the boy learning how to jump, run, concentrate, and fight without ever using anger. As in the movie, Luke faces the dark side in the tree cave; Vader appears, and Luke decapitates him with his saber. Luke's face appears in Vader's mask, and it suddenly "fades away as in a vision."

In the fourth draft, during the training Yoda is always smoking from his "gimer stick," a short twig with three little branches at the far end. At one point Luke tries to leap over the pond but falls short; he surfaces, looking a bit dazed. Behind him the water monster that tried to swallow Artoo earlier appears. Artoo sees the danger and rushes to Yoda, who won't help. Luke swims frantically and finally makes it safely back to shore. The scene inside the tree cave is a bit different from the scene in the film: In this draft Luke reaches up to brush aside some hanging vines, and "they snap at him like lobster claws." Luke looks up and sees that they are attached to a monstrous tree that stares down at him. Luke enters the tree and is enveloped by a thick spiderweblike membrane. There's also a beetle the size of Luke's hand that scurries up the wall to join its mate. All of this was simplified in the film.

Irvin Kershner: "I don't like explanation of anything. The beauty of film is that you see it and you hear it and the audience goes along with you. The confrontation between Luke and Vader in the cave is very simple, for instance. Luke goes down into a hole that becomes a cave, and it's totally real. If it wasn't done totally real, it would have no power, no tension."

EXT. SPACE—VADER'S STAR DESTROYER

Vader's Imperial Star Destroyer moves through space, guarded by its convoy of TIE fighters.

INT. VADER'S STAR DESTROYER—BRIDGE—CONTROL DECK

Vader stands in the back control area of his ship's bridge with a motley group of men and creatures. Admiral Piett and two controllers stand at the front of the bridge and watch the group with scorn.

PIETT: Bounty hunters. We don't need that scum.

FIRST CONTROLLER: Yes, sir.

PIETT: Those Rebels won't escape us.

A second controller interrupts.

SECOND CONTROLLER: Sir, we have a priority signal from the Star Destroyer *Avenger*.

PIETT: Right.

The group standing before Vader is a bizarre array of galactic fortune hunters: There is Bossk, a slimy, tentacled monster with two huge, bloodshot eyes in a soft baggy face; Zuckuss and Dengar, two battle-scarred, mangy human types; IG-88, a battered, tarnished chrome war droid; 4-LOM, a bounty hunter; and Boba Fett, a man in a weapon-covered armored spacesuit.

VADER: There will be a substantial reward for the one who finds the *Millennium Falcon*. You are free to use any methods necessary, but I want them alive. No disintegrations.

BOBA FETT: As you wish.

Joe Johnston: "I designed the final version of Boba Fett. Ralph and I both worked on preliminary designs, and we traded ideas back and forth. Originally, Boba Fett was part of a force we called Super Troopers, and they were these really high-tech fighting units, and they all looked alike. That eventually evolved into a single bounty hunter. I painted Boba's outfit and tried to make it look like it was made of different pieces of armor. It was a symmetrical design, but I painted it in such a way that it looked like he had scavenged parts and had done some personalizing of his costume; he had little trophies hanging from his belt, and he had little braids of hair, almost like a collection of scalps."

At that moment Admiral Piett approaches Vader in a rush of excitement.

PIETT: Lord Vader! My lord, we have them.

EXT. IMPERIAL STAR DE-STROYER *AVENGER*—ASTEROID BELT

The Millennium Falcon *speeds through deep space, closely followed by a firing Imperial Star Destroyer.*

INT. *MILLENNIUM FALCON*—COCKPIT

The ship shudders as flak explodes near the cockpit window. Threepio checks a tracking scope on the side control panel while Leia watches tensely out the window.

THREEPIO: Oh, thank goodness we're coming out of the asteroid field.

EXT. *MILLENNIUM FALCON*—STAR DESTROYER *AVENGER*—ASTEROID FIELD

The Falcon *is hit hard by a bolt from the Star Destroyer that creates a huge explosion near the cockpit of the smaller ship. The* Falcon *tilts steeply, then rights itself.*

George Lucas: "I was very nervous about the scenes involving Luke's training with Yoda. I knew that Yoda had to be a very strong character in order to sustain the middle part of the movie. I obviously used the other device of inter-cutting Luke's training with the progression of the situation with Han and Leia so that I could have them in action and contrast that with Luke's training. And I tried to indicate that Luke's training was going to link up with their pending jeopardy so that you would have some kind of interest that would carry through the whole piece."

INT. *MILLENNIUM FALCON*—COCKPIT

Han corrects the angle of his ship.

HAN: Let's get out of here. Ready for lightspeed? One . . . two . . . three!

Han pulls back on the hyperspace throttle and—nothing happens.

HAN: *(frantic)* It's not fair!

Chewie is very angry and starts to growl and bark at his friend and captain. Again Han desperately pulls back on the throttle as flak bursts continue to rock the ship.

HAN: The transfer circuits are all working. It's not my fault!

Chewie puts his head in his hands, whining.

LEIA: *(almost expecting it)* No lightspeed?

HAN: It's not my fault.

EXT. *MILLENNIUM FALCON*—STAR DESTROYER *AVENGER*—ASTEROID FIELD

The Millennium Falcon is closely pursued by the firing Star Destroyer.

INT. *MILLENNIUM FALCON*—COCKPIT

THREEPIO: Sir, we just lost the main rear deflector shield. One more direct hit on the back quarter and we're done for.

Han makes a decision.

HAN: Turn her around.

Chewie barks in puzzlement.

HAN: I said turn her around! I'm going to put all power in the front shield.

LEIA: You're going to attack them?!

THREEPIO: Sir, the odds of surviving a direct assault on an Imperial Star Destroyer—

LEIA: Shut up!

EXT. SPACE—*MILLENNIUM FALCON*—ASTEROID FIELD

The Falcon banks, making a steep, twisting turn.

INT. STAR DESTROYER *AVENGER*—BRIDGE

The Imperials stationed on the Avenger's bridge are stunned to see the small spaceship headed directly at them. The Destroyer's commander, Captain Needa, can scarcely believe his eyes.

NEEDA: They're moving to attack position!

EXT. SPACE—*MILLENNIUM FALCON*—ASTEROID FIELD

The Millennium Falcon is racing toward the Star Destroyer, looking very small against the massive surface of the Imperial ship. As it moves across the surface of the Star Destroyer, the Falcon weaves to avoid the numerous flak bursts.

INT. STAR DESTROYER *AVENGER*—BRIDGE

NEEDA: Shields up!

EXT. SPACE—*MILLENNIUM FALCON*—ASTEROID FIELD

The Falcon sweeps past.

INT. STAR DESTROYER *AVENGER*—BRIDGE

Needa and his men duck as the Falcon nears the bridge window. At the last minute the Falcon veers off and out of sight. All is quiet.

NEEDA: Track them. They may come around for another pass.

TRACKING OFFICER: Captain Needa, the ship no longer appears on our scopes.

NEEDA: They can't have disappeared. No ship that small has a cloaking device.

TRACKING OFFICER: Well, there's no trace of them, sir.

COMMUNICATIONS OFFICER: Captain, Lord Vader demands an update on the pursuit.

NEEDA: *(drawing a breath)* Get a shuttle ready. I shall assume full responsibility for losing them and apologize to Lord Vader. Meanwhile, continue to scan the area.

COMMUNICATIONS OFFICER: Yes, Captain Needa.

EXT. DAGOBAH—BOG—DAY

Luke's face is upside down and showing enormous strain. He stands on his hands, with Yoda perched on one of his feet. Luke lifts one hand from the ground. His body wavers, but he maintains his balance.

Artoo, standing nearby, is whistling and beeping frantically.

YODA: Use the Force, yes. Now . . . the stone.

Near Luke and Yoda are two rocks the size of bowling balls. Luke stares at the rocks and concentrates. One of the rocks lifts from the ground and floats up to rest on the other.

YODA: Feel it.

But distracted by Artoo's frantic beeping, Luke loses his balance.

YODA: Concentrate!

Luke finally collapses. Yoda jumps clear. Annoyed by the disturbance, Luke looks over at Artoo, who is rocking urgently back and forth in front of him.

Catching on, Luke moves to the swamp's edge. The X-wing fighter has sunk, and only the tip of its nose shows above the lake's surface.

LUKE: Oh, no. We'll never get out now.

YODA: So certain are you. Always with you it cannot be done. Hear you nothing that I say?

Luke looks uncertainly out at the ship.

LUKE: Master, moving stones around is one thing. This is totally different.

YODA: No! No different! Only different in your mind. You must unlearn what you have learned.

LUKE: *(focusing, quietly)* All right. I'll give it a try.

YODA: No! Try not. Do. Or do not. There is no try.

Luke closes his eyes and concentrates on thinking the ship out.

Slowly, the X-wing's nose begins to rise above the water. It hovers for a moment and then slides back, disappearing once again.

LUKE: *(panting heavily)* I can't. It's too big.

YODA: Size matters not. Look at me. Judge me by my size, do you? Mm? Mmmm.

Luke shakes his head.

YODA: And well you should not. For my ally is the Force. And a powerful ally it is. Life creates it, makes it grow. Its energy surrounds us and binds us. Luminous beings are we . . . *(Yoda pinches Luke's shoulder)* . . . not this crude matter. You must feel the Force around you. *(gesturing)* Here, between you . . . me . . . the tree . . . the rock . . . everywhere! Yes, even between the land and the ship!

LUKE: *(discouraged)* You want the impossible.

Quietly Yoda turns toward the sunken X-wing fighter. With his eyes closed and his head bowed he raises his arm and points at the ship.

Soon the fighter rises above the water and moves forward as Artoo beeps in terror and scoots away.

The entire X-wing moves majestically, surely, toward the shore. Yoda, perched on a tree root, guides the fighter carefully down toward the beach.

Luke stares in astonishment as the fighter settles gently onto the shore. He walks toward Yoda.

LUKE: I don't . . . I don't believe it.

YODA: That is why you fail.

Irvin Kershner: "At first I thought Yoda should be eight feet, nine feet tall with a big beard, like an oversized Moses, because after all, he is a Zen master, he is almost Godlike. But that was too much of a cliché. At one point we thought of using a monkey to play Yoda; we would have animated his lips later like in the movie *Babe* [1995], but that didn't work. Then we started looking for a face—what does he look like?—and then we thought, Well, he is amphibious, he can live underwater, he is on a wet planet, therefore his skin is not affected by water, he's like a lizard. But we couldn't get a good image of the head, and Stuart Freeborn, the makeup man, who was also sort of an engineer and made props, said, 'I think I can make the face.' So he went away and came back a few weeks later, and here was this head draped with a cloth.

We sat there, and he said, 'Now I'll show you what Yoda could look like, and he pulled the cover off, and I thought it was a joke because it looked exactly like him. He was very small, had a large head, a round face . . . It was a self-portrait. In regard to Yoda's clothes, I wanted him to wear something that looked homemade, but none of the fabrics we selected looked right. Finally we found this raw silk from India, and it was just perfect. It hung nicely, and it . looked homemade. We had a piece left over, and I had a jacket made out of it for myself."

The scene with Yoda raising Luke's X-wing from the swamp was introduced in the story treatment. In the first draft that particular scene appears earlier in the story, right after Luke meets Minch.

Luke tries to use the Force to pull his ship from the mud; Minch steps to the side, his eyes begin to glow, and he seems to grow in stature. The fighter rises; Luke at this point is unaware that it is Minch, not himself, who miraculously pulls the vehicle from the mud. In the second draft Yoda raises Luke's X-wing from the swamp right after the crash. In the third draft, as in the movie, this sequence comes later, after Luke has gone through training. In this particular draft Luke's training is also a lot longer than what it ended up being in the movie.

EXT. SPACE—IMPERIAL FLEET

The fleet around Vader's Star Destroyer now includes Needa's Star Destroyer, the Avenger. Needa's shuttle departs for Vader's Star Destroyer.

INT. VADER'S STAR DESTROYER—BRIDGE

Clutching desperately at his throat, Captain Needa slumps down, then falls over on his back at the feet of Darth Vader.

VADER: Apology accepted, Captain Needa.

Two stormtroopers pick up the lifeless body and carry it quickly away as Admiral Piett and two of his captains hurry up to the Dark Lord.

PIETT: Lord Vader, our ships have completed their scan of the area and found nothing. If the *Millennium Falcon* went into lightspeed, it'll be on the other side of the galaxy by now.

VADER: Alert all commands. Calculate every possible destination along their last known trajectory.

PIETT: Yes, my lord. We'll find them.

VADER: Don't fail me again, Admiral.

Vader exits as the admiral turns to an aide, a little more uneasy than when he arrived.

PIETT: Alert all commands. Deploy the fleet.

EXT. SPACE—IMPERIAL FLEET

Vader's ship moves away, flanked by its fleet of smaller ships. The Avenger glides off into space in the opposite direction. No one on that ship or on Vader's is aware that, clinging to the side of the Avenger, is the pirate ship the Millennium Falcon.

INT. *MILLENNIUM FALCON*—COCKPIT

THREEPIO: Captain Solo, this time you have gone too far. *(Chewie growls)* No, I will not be quiet, Chewbacca. Why doesn't anyone listen to me?

HAN: *(to Chewie)* The fleet is beginning to break up. Go back and stand by the manual release for the landing claw.

Chewie barks, struggles from his seat, and climbs out of the cabin.

THREEPIO: I really don't see how that is going to help. Surrender is a perfectly acceptable alternative in extreme circumstances. The Empire may be gracious enough—

Leia reaches over and shuts off Threepio in midsentence.

HAN: Thank you.

Leia slips out of her chair and moves next to the handsome pilot.

LEIA: What did you have in mind for your next move?

HAN: Well, if they follow standard Imperial procedure, they'll dump their garbage before they go to lightspeed, and then we just float away.

LEIA: With the rest of the garbage. Then what?

HAN: Then we've got to find a safe port somewhere around here. Got any ideas?

LEIA: No. Where are we?

HAN: The Anoat system.

LEIA: Anoat system. There's not much there.

HAN: No. Well, wait. This is interesting. Lando.

He points to a computer mapscreen on the control panel.

LEIA: Lando system?

HAN: Lando's not a system, he's a man. Lando Calrissian. He's a card player, gambler, scoundrel. You'd like him.

LEIA: Thanks.

HAN: Bespin. It's pretty far, but I think we can make it.

LEIA: *(reading from the computer)* A mining colony?

HAN: Yeah. A Tibanna gas mine. Lando conned somebody out of it. We go back a long way, Lando and me.

LEIA: Can you trust him?

HAN: No. But he has got no love for the Empire, I can tell you that.

Chewie barks over the intercom. Han quickly changes his readouts and stretches to look out the cockpit window.

HAN: *(into intercom)* Here we go, Chewie. Stand by. Detach!

Leia thinks for a moment; a grin creeps across her face.

LEIA: You do have your moments. Not many of them, but you do have them.

Leia gives Han a quick kiss.

EXT. SPACE—IMPERIAL STAR DESTROYER

As the Avenger *Star Destroyer moves slowly into space, the hatch on its underbelly opens, sending a trail of junk floating behind it. Hidden among the refuse, the* Falcon *tumbles away. In the next moment, the* Avenger *roars off into hyperspace. The* Falcon's *engines are ignited, and it races off into the distance. Amidst the slowly drifting junk, Boba Fett's ship appears and moves after the* Falcon.

INT. BOBA FETT'S SHIP—COCKPIT

Boba Fett is tailing the Millennium Falcon.

In the first draft Han remembers his friend Lando Kadar, a refugee from the Clone Wars. Solo refers to him as an honest smuggler who lives on a planet called Hoth. This discussion takes place inside the cave on the asteroid; the *Falcon* comes out of hiding (remember, in this draft there's no space slug), and the ship jumps to lightspeed before the Imperial fighters catch on.

In the second draft, as in the film, the *Falcon* hides along the side of the Imperial starship. Han says his friend Lando Calrissian won the gas mine in a "sabacca game," or "so he claims." The scene with Boba Fett following the *Falcon* first appeared in the third draft.

EXT. DAGOBAH—BOG—CLEARING—DAY
In the clearing behind Yoda's house Luke again stands upside down, but his face shows less strain and more concentration than before. Yoda stands beside the young warrior.
YODA: Concentrate.
An equipment case slowly rises into the air.
YODA: Feel the Force flow. Yes.
Nearby Artoo watches, humming to himself, when suddenly he, too, rises into the air. His head turns frantically, looking for help.
YODA: Good. Calm, yes. Through the Force, things you will see. Other places. The future . . . the past. Old friends long gone.
Luke suddenly becomes distressed.
LUKE: Han! Leia!
The packing box and Artoo fall to the ground with a crash, then Luke himself tumbles over.
YODA: *(shaking his head)* Hmm. Control, control. You must learn control.
LUKE: I saw . . . I saw a city in the clouds.
YODA: Mmm. Friends you have there.
LUKE: They were in pain.
YODA: It is the future you see.
LUKE: Future? Will they die?
Yoda closes his eyes and lowers his head.
YODA: Difficult to see. *(looking up)* Always in motion is the future.
LUKE: I've got to go to them.
YODA: Decide you must how to serve them best. If you leave now, help them you could. But you would destroy all for which they have fought and suffered.
Luke is stopped cold by Yoda's words. Glooms shrouds him as he nods his head sadly.

Irvin Kershner: "We tried to move Yoda's eyes apart, make them extralarge, but we realized that the creature didn't look real, didn't look intelligent. All human eyes are within a few millimeters in size and in distance apart. Even though we might say that someone has big eyes or that they're far apart, like Jackie Onassis, they're only maybe a half millimeter farther apart. When Yoda closed his eyes halfway, it looked like he was smiling. I also had him look up each time I wanted him to look spiritual. And of course we wanted to use the traditional three fingers from comics ... You'll notice that in comic books all the anthropomorphized animals always have three fingers."

In the second draft Ben's shimmering image appears for the first time just before Luke has the vision of his friends in danger. He is by a campfire, and Yoda tells him to relax; through the Force he'll be able to see the past, the future, and old friends long gone from the material world. Ben's image appears, and he asks Yoda how Luke is doing; the Jedi Master replies that Luke would be his most gifted apprentice if he would only concentrate. When Luke turns around to look at Ben, his image disappears. Yoda explains that Ben has become part of the Force and is always with them; if Luke concentrates enough, Ben will come back.

EXT. BESPIN SURFACE—*MILLENNIUM FALCON*

It is dawn on the soft pink gaseous planet of Bespin. Huge billowing clouds form a canyon as the ship banks around them, headed toward the system's Cloud City.

Suddenly, two twin-pod cars appear and move toward the Falcon.

INT. *MILLENNIUM FALCON*—COCKPIT

HAN: No, I don't have a landing permit. I'm trying to reach Lando Calrissian.

One of the cloud cars opens fire on the Falcon, *its flak rocking the ship.*

HAN: *(into transmitter)* Whoa! Wait a minute! Let me explain.

Ralph McQuarrie: "Originally, we talked about another planet that was going to be a Rebel stronghold, a grass planet with the Rebels riding flying beasties. And then somehow those beasties got incorporated into my drawings for Bespin. Because they were operating in a medium like water or air, only thinner, I decided to make them look like giant flying fish."

INTERCOM VOICE: You will not deviate from your present course.

THREEPIO: Rather touchy, aren't they?

LEIA: I thought you knew this person.

Chewie barks and growls at his boss.

HAN: *(to Chewie)* Well, that was a long time ago. I'm sure he's forgotten about that.

INTERCOM VOICE: Permission granted to land on Platform Three-two-seven.

HAN: *(into transmitter)* Thank you.

Angry, Han snaps off the intercom.

HAN: *(to the worried Princess and her droid)* There's nothing to worry about. We go way back, Lando and me.

Leia doesn't look convinced.

LEIA: Who's worried?

EXT. CLOUD CITY—*MILLEN-NIUM FALCON*—CLOUD CARS

Joe Johnston: "We had determined that the style of the city was Deco or some other-worldly form of Deco, and I concentrated on designing vistas that you might see out a window or that might be incorporated into a matte painting, different buildings, interesting plazas, details basically. Cloud City was originally created for *Star Wars*, and we had a painting by Ralph of this city floating in the clouds. The shape of the city, which is basically a giant dish on a stick with a reactor at the bottom, had been determined, and all I had to do was create detail and the architectural elements. Cloud City was fun for me because it was different from doing spaceships and crea-tures."

The clouds part to reveal a full view of the city as it bobs in and out of the cloud surface. The cloud cars and the Falcon head for the gleaming white metropolis.

From the Special Edition:
The clouds part to reveal a full view of the city as it bobs in and out of the cloud surface. The cloud cars and the Falcon head for the gleaming white metropolis. As the Falcon and the cloud cars approach the city, they bank around a large structure and fly in toward the landing platform.

EXT. CLOUD CITY—LANDING PLATFORM—*MILLENNIUM FALCON*
With the cloud cars still guarding it, the Falcon lands on one of the Cloud City's platforms.
EXT. LANDING PLATFORM—DOOR OF *MILLENNIUM FALCON*

Han and Chewie stand at the open door, armed, surveying the scene warily. Leia follows behind them.

THREEPIO: Oh. No one to meet us.

LEIA: I don't like this.

HAN: Well, what would you like?

THREEPIO: Well, they did let us land.

HAN: Look, don't worry. Everything's going to be fine. Trust me.

A small group appears in the doorway to the landing platform.

HAN: See? My friend. (to Chewie) Keep your eyes open, huh?

Chewie growls as Han walks down the ramp. Lando and his men head across the bridge to meet the space pirate.

HAN: Hey?

Lando Calrissian, a suave, dashing black man in his thirties, leads a group of aides and some Cloud City guards toward the landing platform.

The group, like the other citizens of the city, is a motley collection of aliens, droids, and humans of all descriptions.

Lando stops ten feet from Han. The two men eye each other carefully. Lando shakes his head. He has a grim expression on his face.

LANDO: Why, you slimy, double-crossing, no-good swindler! You've got a lot of guts coming here after what you pulled.

Han points to himself innocently, mouthing "Me?"

Lando moves threateningly toward Han. Suddenly, he throws his arms around his startled, long-lost friend and embraces him.

LANDO: (laughs) How you doing, you old pirate? So good to see you! I never thought I'd catch up with you again. Where you been?

EXT. LANDING PLATFORM—DOOR OF MILLENNIUM FALCON

THREEPIO: Well, he seems very friendly.

LEIA: (wary) Yes . . . very friendly.

The two old friends embrace, laughing and chuckling.

LANDO: What are you doing here?

HAN: (gestures toward the Falcon) Ahh . . . repairs. I thought you could help me out.

LANDO: (in mock panic) What have you done to my ship?

HAN: Your ship? Hey, remember, you lost her to me fair and square.

Chewie, Leia, and Threepio have made their way down the ramp.

LANDO: And how are you doing, Chewbacca? You still hanging around with this loser?

Chewie growls a reserved greeting. Lando suddenly notices the Princess and smiles admiringly.

LANDO: Hello. What have we here? Welcome. I'm Lando Calrissian. I'm the administrator of this facility. And who might you be?

LEIA: Leia.

LANDO: Welcome, Leia.

Lando kisses her hand.

HAN: All right, all right, you old smoothie.

Han takes Leia by the hand and steers her away from Lando.

THREEPIO: Hello, sir. I am See-Threepio, Human Cyborg Relations. My facilities are at your . . .

Before Threepio can finish his self-introduction, Lando has turned to follow Han and Leia, who are walking toward the city.

THREEPIO: Well, really!

Lando, his aide, Lobot, and Han lead the way across the bridge, followed by Threepio, Chewie, and Leia.

LANDO: What's wrong with the *Falcon*?

HAN: Hyperdrive.

LANDO: I'll get my people to work on it.

HAN: Good.

Lando turns to Leia.

LANDO: You know, that ship saved my life quite a few times. She's the fastest hunk of junk in the galaxy.

HAN: How's the gas mine? Is it still paying off for you?

INT. CLOUD CITY—CORRIDOR

The group has crossed the narrow bridge and entered the city. They walk down the lovely Art Deco passageway, rounding several corners and passing many small plazas as they go. Threepio lags a bit behind.

LANDO: Oh, not as well as I'd like. We're a small outpost and not very self-sufficient. And I've had supply problems of every kind. I've had labor difficulties . . . *(Han laughs)* What's so funny?

HAN: You. Listen to you—you sound like a businessman, a responsible leader. Who'd have thought that, huh?

LANDO: You know, seeing you brings back a few things.

Lando is reflective. He stops and looks at Han a moment.

HAN: Yeah.

LANDO: *(shakes his head)* Yeah. I'm responsible these days. It's the price you pay for being successful.

The group moves on through the corridor.

During story conferences George Lucas and Leigh Brackett referred to Cloud City as "Ketbrae or Kettlebrae: The Gas Planet"; in early notes this planet is described as "nothing but clouds with cities that sit on giant piers that go down into gases." The story meetings suggest that maybe the planet has a force field that makes it invisible until one passes through a certain distance, and all of a sudden it becomes visible. Han, Leia, Chewbacca, and Threepio arrive on the Gas Planet and are attacked by the Whatnots, aliens that live in the center of the fog; they retreat back to the *Falcon* and take off. A patrol finds them and guides them to Han's friend, who lives in another part of the system. The notes indicate that the aliens should be semistoic creatures, sort of tall, thin, white, maybe similar to the aliens in Steven Spielberg's *Close Encounters of the Third Kind* (1977). They should be very noble but threatening; they carry a spear or a pneumatic dart gun or a long pole with a beam that comes out of it. There's an alien chief described as fair, wise, and noble.

Lando was discussed as "a new Han Solo character." He is described as a slick, riverboat gambler dude. Unlike Han Solo, this guy should be elegant, sort of like James Bond. There were discussions about getting this new character a sidekick, a girl or female alien or a matched set of girls . . . possibly something odd and outrageous. This man should be charming so it will not occur to the audience that he could betray Han and Leia.

Another permutation had Lando be a gambler who runs a general store on a Wookiee planet or a trader, some sort of businessman who works with smugglers. He is pro-Empire but thinks that he's smarter than the Empire. He doesn't care about the Rebellion until the end of the story, when he makes a complete turn against the Empire. Even Vader should be intimidated by this man's political power. During another discussion the character took on a whole new approach: In *Star Wars* Leia mentioned "the Clone Wars" in her holographic message to Ben, and Han's friend could be a clone. The princess doesn't trust him because of the war that practically wiped out his species. He could be one of the last clones, and in another episode he could run across a clan of clones who are all exactly like him. He came from a planet of clones; the planet had maybe seven hundred different countries, and each country was composed of a clone clan and he was the ruler of one of the clans.

In the second draft Lando is a black man, and a description of the city's crowd indicates that half the citizens are black.

George Lucas: "At one point in the original *Star Wars*, Han Solo was going to be black. I was in the casting, and one of the finalists was a black actor, and I just decided that I liked Harrison the best. It didn't have to do with race at all. I had a lot of different ideas. At one point Luke, Leia, and Ben were all going to be little people, and we did screen tests to see if I could do that. At one point Luke and Leia were going to be Oriental. I played with various ethnic groups, but when there are four main characters, it seemed better to have them all be the same race. But I had been interested right from the very beginning to get ethnic diversity into the project. So when I got to adding the Lando character, who was not originally written as a black man, there was a chance to put in variety. You know, at the time *Star Wars* came out, a lot of critics attacked the film for not having one of the characters be a black person. They also said that it was a chauvinistic movie. And I thought, Wait a minute, Leia is not a man, she is tough and independent, how can that be chauvinistic? The film got attacked for everything."

Irvin Kershner: "The idea of Lando communicating with his aide, Lobot, through his headset did not exist in the script. I added that on the set."

The lagging Threepio passes a Threepio-type silver droid who is coming out of a door.
THREEPIO: Oh! Nice to see a familiar face.
SECOND THREEPIO: *(mumbles)* E chu ta!
THREEPIO: How rude!
Threepio stops, watching the silver droid move away. Then he hears the muffled beeping and whistling of an R2 unit coming from within the room.
THREEPIO: That sounds like an R2 unit in there.
INT. CLOUD CITY—ANTEROOM
Curious, Threepio enters the room.
THREEPIO: I wonder if . . .
Threepio walks through the doorway to the main room. He looks in.
THREEPIO: Hello? Hello? How interesting.
MAN'S VOICE: *(from within)* Who are you?
THREEPIO: Who am I? Oh, I'm terribly sorry. I . . . I didn't mean to intrude. No, no, please don't get up. No!
A laserbolt to Threepio's chest sends him flying in twenty directions. Smoldering mechanical arms and legs bounce off the walls as the door whooshes closed behind him.

The concept of Threepio being completely torn apart was conceived during story meetings as a way to create sympathy for the robot: "He becomes a box full of parts . . . He is the robot that can't stay together." Another intriguing idea was to have Vader take the robot's heart out and smash it.

INT. CLOUD CITY—CORRIDOR

Lando, Han, and Leia have continued down the corridor, unaware of Threepio's dreadful accident. Chewbacca glances around, sniffs the air, but shrugs his shoulders and follows the group.

EXT. DAGOBAH—BOG—DUSK

In the bright lights of the fighter, Luke inspects the cockpit of the ship. Artoo sits on top of the X-wing, settling down into his cubbyhole. Yoda perches nearby on a log.

YODA: Luke! You must complete the training.

LUKE: I can't keep the vision out of my head. They're my friends. I've got to help them.

YODA: You must not go!

LUKE: But Han and Leia will die if I don't.

BEN'S VOICE: You don't know that.

Luke looks toward the voice in amazement. Ben has materialized as a real, slightly shimmering image near Yoda. The power of his presence stops Luke.

BEN: Even Yoda cannot see their fate.

LUKE: But I can help them! I feel the Force!

BEN: But you cannot control it. This is a dangerous time for you, when you will be tempted by the dark side of the Force.

YODA: Yes, yes. To Obi-Wan you listen. The cave. Remember your failure at the cave!

LUKE: But I've learned so much since then, Master Yoda. I promise to return and finish what I've begun. You have my word.

BEN: It is you and your abilities the Emperor wants. That is why your friends are made to suffer.

George Lucas: "When *Star Wars* became a hit and I had a chance to make the other movies, I had to figure out a way to bring Ben back, but a lot of the issues he had to deal with were carried by Yoda. In a sense, I combined Yoda with the spirit of Ben. I wanted Ben to have some kind of influence, but I didn't want it to be a direct influence where he could help Luke. So Ben has managed to keep his identity after he became one with the Force. One of the things he was doing on Tatooine besides watching over Luke was learning how to keep his identity after he became part of the Force."

LUKE: That's why I have to go.

BEN: Luke, I don't want to lose you to the Emperor the way I lost Vader.

LUKE: You won't.

YODA: Stopped they must be. On this all depends. Only a fully trained Jedi Knight with the Force as his ally will conquer Vader and his Emperor. If you end your training now, if you choose the quick and easy path, as Vader did, you will become an agent of evil.

BEN: Patience.

LUKE: And sacrifice Han and Leia?

YODA: If you honor what they fight for . . . yes!

BEN: If you choose to face Vader, you will do it alone. I cannot interfere.

Luke is in great anguish. He struggles with the dilemma, a battle raging in his mind.

LUKE: I understand. *(he climbs up his X-wing)* Artoo, fire up the converters.

Artoo whistles a happy reply. Luke climbs into his ship.

BEN: Luke, don't give in to hate—that leads to the dark side.

YODA: Strong is Vader. Mind what you have learned. Save you it can.

LUKE: I will. And I'll return. I promise.

Artoo closes the cockpit.

YODA: *(sighs)* Told you, I did. Reckless is he. Now matters are worse.

BEN: That boy is our last hope.

YODA: *(looks up)* No. There is another.

The roar of the engines and the wind engulfs Ben and Yoda.

Irvin Kershner: "We had a few Yodas on the set, and when they were lying there, they were just plastic and rubber and wires, and I didn't relate to it at all. But when Frank Oz was underneath the floor holding it up and it was talking, I related to it as an individual. I was the only one who could hear his voice because I was wearing earphones. Even Mark Hamill when he was talking to Yoda couldn't hear his voice. We'd rehearse it with a speaker so Mark could get the timing, and then he'd have to do it blank with nothing coming out of Yoda's mouth. He did a good job, Mark; he is a good actor."

In the story treatment, Luke dreams of Vader and Ben says it's time for him to leave. Luke and Artoo climb aboard the X-wing and take off. In the first draft Luke explains to Minch that he ran away from Vader and the dark side during his training because he couldn't trust himself. Minch tells him to remember that he is now a Jedi Knight. Using their lightsabers, they salute each other. Luke and Artoo get in the ship and take off. Luke concentrates and is able to locate Leia, and he knows that Vader will be there, too. In the second draft and as in the movie, Luke has the vision of his friends in danger and decides to save them; Ben and Yoda warn him against Vader and the dark side. Luke says he'll come back and takes off. In this draft there's no hint that there may be another hope if Luke fails. In the revised second draft a few lines of dialogue were added as Luke's X-wing disappears in the sky: Yoda says: "Now we must find another." Ben replies: "He is our only hope." And in the third draft, after Luke takes off, Ben says: "The boy is our last hope." Yoda replies: "No . . . We must search for another."

George Lucas: "My feeling about Luke being the last hope was really done in an effort to make sure that he was in some jeopardy, that he might not succeed. I was trying to set up subliminally in the audience's mind that something is going on here, that he could fail. And if he does fail, 'there is another hope.' So the audience is saying, 'Don't go, finish your training.' "

Irvin Kershner: "Instead of showing Luke's ship overhead, I just showed the light on Yoda's face. I felt it was more powerful than having another special effects shot of the spaceship."

EXT. SPACE—PLANET DAGOBAH
Luke's tiny X-wing rockets away from the green planet of Dagobah and off into space.

EXT. BESPIN—CLOUD CITY
Within the quarters assigned her on Cloud City, Leia paces in agitation.

From the Special Edition:
EXT. BESPIN SURFACE—CLOUD CAR
A twin-pod cloud car flies forward away from the suspended Cloud City. Another cloud car banks along Cloud City's surface, between buildings and behind and around the tower room. Through a window, Leia can be seen pacing.

INT. CLOUD CITY—LIVING QUARTERS—DAY
Leia has changed from her cold-weather pants and jacket to a lovely dress. Her hair is down, tied back with ribbons. She moves from a large, open window and turns to see Han entering through the doorway.

HAN: The ship's almost finished. Two or three more things and we're in great shape.

LEIA: The sooner the better. Something's wrong here. No one has seen or knows anything about Threepio. He's been gone too long to have gotten lost.

Han takes Leia by the shoulders and gently kisses her forehead.

HAN: Relax. I'll talk to Lando. See what I can find out.

LEIA: I don't trust Lando.

HAN: Well, I don't trust him, either. But he is my friend. Besides, we'll soon be gone.

LEIA: And then you're as good as gone, aren't you?

Not speaking, Han considers her words and gazes at her troubled face.

INT. CLOUD CITY—JUNK ROOM

The room is piled high with broken and discarded machine parts. Ugnaughts, small hoglike creatures, separate the junk and throw some pieces onto a conveyor belt, which moves briskly toward a pit of molten metal. Pieces of Threepio's golden body move down the belt. Chewie enters the room and spots an Ugnaught picking up and inspecting Threepio's head. The Wookiee barks a command, startling the Ugnaught, then reaches to grab the head. But the Ugnaught tosses it away from him to another Ugnaught. This game of keep-away goes on until Threepio's head falls from their grip and bounces with a clang on to the ground.

INT. CLOUD CITY—LIVING QUARTERS—DAY

The door zaps open. Chewbacca walks in, carrying a packing case of Threepio, arms and legs hanging over the edges.

LEIA: What happened?

Chewie sets the case on a table, grunting and groaning an explanation.

HAN: Where? Found him in a junk pile?

LEIA: Oh, what a mess. Chewie, do you think you can repair him?

The giant Wookiee studies the array of robot parts. He looks at the princess and moans sadly.

HAN: Lando's got people who can fix him.

LEIA: No, thanks.

Lando enters.

LANDO: I'm sorry. Am I interrupting anything?

LEIA: Not really.

LANDO: You look absolutely beautiful. You truly belong here with us among the clouds.

LEIA: *(coolly)* Thank you.

LANDO: Will you join me for a little refreshment?

Chewie barks at the mention of food and licks his lips.

LANDO: Everyone's invited, of course.

Leia takes Lando's proffered arm, and the group turns to go. Lando spots Threepio's remains.

LANDO: Having trouble with your droid?

HAN: No.

Han and Leia exchange a quick glance.

HAN: No problem. Why?

Han and Leia move arm in arm through the door, followed by Lando and Chewie.

INT. CLOUD CITY—CORRIDOR—DAY

Leia walks between Han and Lando as Chewie follows a short distance behind. Long shafts of light pour across a corridor between tall, pure-white columns.

LANDO: So, you see, since we're a small operation, we don't fall into the . . . uh . . . jurisdiction of the Empire.

LEIA: So you're part of the mining guild, then?

LANDO: No, not actually. Our operation is small enough not to be noticed . . . which is advantageous for everybody since our customers are anxious to avoid attracting attention to themselves.

The group walks into another corridor and heads for a huge doorway at the far end.

HAN: Aren't you afraid the Empire's going to find out about this little operation and shut you down?

LANDO: It's always been a danger, but it looms like a shadow over everything we've built here. But things have developed that will ensure security. I've just made a deal that will keep the Empire out of here forever.

INT. CLOUD CITY—DINING ROOM

The mighty doors to the dining room slide open, and the group enters the dining room. At the far end of a huge banquet table sits Darth Vader.

Faster than the wink of an eye, Han draws his blaster and pops off a few shots directly at Vader. The Dark Lord quickly raises his hand, deflecting the bolts into one of the side walls, where they explode harmlessly. Just as quickly, Han's weapon zips into Vader's hand.

VADER: We would be honored if you would join us.

Boba Fett, the bounty hunter, steps out from behind Vader. Imperial stormtroopers cut off the adventurers' escape.

LANDO: I had no choice. They arrived right before you did. I'm sorry.

HAN: I'm sorry, too.

In the story treatment, as Leia tells Han that she doesn't trust Lando, city guards bring a box full of Threepio's parts. They say he must have bumped into a power field. As in the movie, Lando delivers the Rebels to Vader and explains that he had no other choice. In the first draft Lando brings the remains of Threepio, saying that he was found "jammed in the gears of a recycling chute." Leia asks if Lando can have him repaired, but he says that his workshops are already running overtime. He reassures her that the *Falcon*, however, will soon be ready. Leia doesn't trust Lando and suspects he might be a clone.

Later Lando invites the group to dinner. On their way he admits to being a clone of the Ashandi family: His great-grandfather wanted many sons and produced them from the cells of his own body. His sister produced many daughters the same way. Since the war, not many clones are left. Lando confesses that he feels alone now that he walks among people who all look different. When Lando delivers the group to Vader, he says that he knew all along who Leia was (in this draft she gave Lando a fake name) and that he owes his comfort to the Empire; he had no other choice. They all sit with Vader at the dinner table. Because of his physical condition, Vader doesn't eat; no one except Lando has an appetite.

Vader says he knows that Luke is alive and that he is in love with Leia. He wants nothing from them, just Luke. The group returns to its quarters. In the third draft Vader is a lot more menacing toward Han, Leia, and Chewie. It's not just about using them as bait to get Luke; he also threatens them, which as in the movie creates a lot more tension and jeopardy for the characters.

EXT. LUKE'S X-WING—BESPIN SYSTEM
Luke's X-wing races through thick clouds toward Cloud City.
INT. LUKE'S X-WING—COCKPIT
Luke is grim-faced as he pilots his course toward Bespin's shining city. Artoo's beeps and whistles are transmitted onto the scope.
LUKE: *(into comlink)* No. Threepio's with them.
EXT. LUKE'S X-WING
Artoo whistles another worried inquiry.
INT. LUKE'S X-WING—COCKPIT
LUKE: *(into comlink)* Just hang on. We're almost there.
EXT. LUKE'S X-WING—BESPIN SYSTEM
Luke's X-wing closes on Cloud City.

In the story treatment and the first draft Luke arrives in Cloud City via the ruined city. He has an encounter with the aliens, who eventually take him and Artoo to Lando. In the first draft Lando turns against the Empire when troopers kill his friend Bahiri, the alien chief.

INT. CLOUD CITY—LARGE CELL

Chewbacca is in a Cloud City prison cell. The stark room is flooded with hot light. To add to Chewie's misery, a high-pitched whistle screeches loudly. Chewie is going mad. He paces across the floor and shakes the bars of his cell. The whistle stops abruptly. Moaning to himself, the prisoner moves to a platform where the disassembled pieces of Threepio lie. He picks up the golden droid's head and meditates on it for a moment, barking a few philosophical remarks. Chewie sticks the robot's head on its torso and starts adjusting wires and circuits.

Suddenly the lights in Threepio's eyes spark to life as Chewie touches two connectors together. Threepio immediately begins to speak, but his voice is so uneven as to be nearly unintelligible.

THREEPIO: Mmm. Oh, my. Uh, I, uh— Take this off! I, uh, don't mean to intrude here. I, don't, no, no, no . . . Please don't get up. No!

Chewie looks at Threepio in bewilderment. He gets an idea and adjusts some connections, whereupon Threepio immediately begins speaking normally.

THREEPIO: Stormtroopers? Here? We're in danger. I must tell the others. Oh, no! I've been shot!

In the second draft an angry, short, and fat alien shows up in the prison area with a Bespin salesman to buy Chewie. The Wookiee barks at them. The salesman argues that at the price they're asking for Chewie, the alien should be able to afford having him trained. But the alien turns down the deal. In the revised second draft the character of the salesman has been replaced by an Imperial guard.

Irvin Kershner: "When Chewbacca is trying to put Threepio back together and he's got his head in his hands, that's like in Shakespeare's *Hamlet*; it's the grave digger staring down at the skull. That was my inspiration for this scene. I felt that Threepio was not as interesting as Artoo in *Star Wars*. Artoo was the important one in the first film. So I tried to make Threepio more important in *Empire*."

INT. CLOUD CITY—PRISON ENTRY AREA

Darth Vader strides through the room as two stormtroopers prepare an elaborate torture mechanism. Han is strapped to a rack that tilts forward onto the torture device. Vader activates the mechanism, creating two bursts of sparks, which strike Han.

INT. CLOUD CITY—HOLDING CHAMBER

The door opens, and Vader leaves the torture room just as Han screams a sharp, piercing cry of agony. In the holding chamber Lando and Boba Fett await Vader.

Irvin Kershner: "I originally filmed more shots of Solo as he is being tortured. There were flashes of electricity everywhere. But it was cut out because we were afraid it might be too intense for children. We also took out some of his screaming offscreen when Vader is talking to Lando outside the cell."

LANDO: Lord Vader.

VADER: *(to Fett)* You may take Captain Solo to Jabba the Hutt after I have Skywalker.

Han's screams filter through the torture room door.

BOBA FETT: He's no good to me dead.

VADER: He will not be permanently damaged.

LANDO: Lord Vader, what about Leia and the Wookiee?

VADER: They must never again leave this city.

LANDO: That was never a condition of our agreement, nor was giving Han to this bounty hunter!

VADER: Perhaps you think you're being treated unfairly.

LANDO: No.

VADER: Good. It would be unfortunate if I had to leave a garrison here.

The doors of the elevator close on Vader. Lando walks swiftly down another corridor, muttering to himself.

LANDO: This deal is getting worse all the time.

INT. CLOUD CITY—LARGE CELL

Chewie now has a little more of Threepio back together. One arm is connected, but the legs are yet to be attached. There is one small problem, however: It seems the Wookiee has managed to put the droid's head on backward.

THREEPIO: Oh, yes, that's very good. I like that. Oh! Something's not right because now I can't see. Oh. Oh, that's much better. Wait. Wait! Oh, my! What have you done? I'm backwards, you flea-bitten furball. Only an overgrown mophead like you would be stupid enough—

Threepio is cut off in midsentence as Chewie angrily deactivates a circuit and the droid shuts down. The door to the chamber slides open, and a ragged Han Solo is shoved into the room by two stormtroopers. Barking his concern, the huge Wookiee picks Han up. Han is very pale, with dark circles under his eyes.

HAN: I feel terrible.

Chewie helps Han to a platform and then turns as the door slides open, revealing Leia. She, too, looks a little worse for wear. The troopers push her into the cell, and the door slides closed. She moves to Han, who is lying on the platform, and kneels next to him, gently stroking his head.

LEIA: Why are they doing this?

HAN: They never even asked me any questions.

The cell door slides open. Lando and two of his guards enter.

LEIA: Lando.

HAN: Get out of here, Lando!

LANDO: Shut up and listen! Now, Vader has agreed to turn Leia and Chewie over to me.

HAN: Over to you?

LANDO: They'll have to stay here, but at least they'll be safe.

LEIA: What about Han?

LANDO: Vader's giving him to the bounty hunter.

LEIA: Vader wants us all dead.

LANDO: He doesn't want you at all. He's after somebody called Skywalker.

HAN: Luke?

LANDO: Lord Vader has set a trap for him.

Leia's mind is racing.

LEIA: And we're the bait.

LANDO: Yeah, well, he's on his way.

Han's rage peaks.

HAN: Perfect. You fixed us all real good, didn't you? *(spits it out)* My friend!

Han has hauled himself up and punches Lando. One of the guards hits Han with his rifle butt, and he falls to the floor. Chewie growls and starts for the other guard. He points his laser weapon at the giant Wookiee, but Lando stops him.

LANDO: Stop! I've done all I can. I'm sorry I couldn't do better, but I got my own problems.

HAN: Yeah, you're a real hero.

Lando and his guards leave. Leia and Chewie help Han sit up.

LEIA: You certainly have a way with people.

INT. CLOUD CITY—CARBON-FREEZING CHAMBER

Armor-suited stormtroopers stand at the ready in the large chamber, which is filled with pipes and chemical tanks. In the middle of the room is a round pit housing a hydraulic platform. Darth Vader and Lando stand near the platform.

VADER: This facility is crude, but it should be adequate to freeze Skywalker for his journey to the Emperor.

An Imperial soldier appears.

IMPERIAL SOLDIER: Lord Vader, ship approaching, X-wing class.

VADER: Good. Monitor Skywalker and allow him to land.

The soldier bows and leaves the chamber.

LANDO: Lord Vader, we only use this facility for carbon freezing. You put him in there . . . it might kill him.

VADER: I do not want the Emperor's prize damaged. We will test it . . . on Captain Solo.

Lando's face registers dismay.

EXT. SPACE—BESPIN SYSTEM—LUKE'S X-WING

Luke's X-wing moves through the clouds as it nears the city.

INT. LUKE'S X-WING—COCKPIT

Encountering no city guards, Luke scans his display panels with concern.

EXT. CLOUD CITY

Luke's X-wing approaches the city.

INT. CLOUD CITY—CARBON-FREEZING CHAMBER

There has been great activity on the carbon-freezing platform. Six Ugnaughts have frantically prepared the chamber for use. A special coffinlike container has been put in place. With Boba Fett in the lead, a squad of six stormtroopers brings in Han, Leia, and Chewie. Strapped to Chewie's back, with only his head, torso, and one arm assembled, is Threepio. Threepio's head faces the opposite direction from Chewie's. The remaining pieces of his body are randomly bundled to the Wookiee's back so that his legs and other arm stick out at odd angles from the pack.

THREEPIO: If only you had attached my legs, I wouldn't be in this ridiculous position. Now, remember, Chewbacca, you have a responsibility to me, so don't do anything foolish.

HAN: *[to Lando]* What's going on . . . buddy?

LANDO: You're being put into carbon freeze.

Boba Fett moves away from the group to Darth Vader.

BOBA FETT: What if he doesn't survive? He's worth a lot to me.

VADER: The Empire will compensate you if he dies. Put him in!

Realizing what is about to happen, Chewie lets out a wild howl and attacks the stormtroopers surrounding Han.

From the instant of Chewie's first move Threepio begins to scream in panic while he tries to protect himself with his one arm.

THREEPIO: Oh, no! No, no, no! Stop!

HAN: Stop, Chewie, stop! Stop!

THREEPIO: Yes, stop, please! I'm not ready to die.

Han breaks away from his captors. Vader has evidently nodded to the guards to let him go, and the pirate breaks up the fight.

HAN: Hey, hey! Listen to me. Chewie! Chewie, this won't help me. Hey! Save your strength. There'll be another time. The princess—you have to take care of her. You hear me? Huh?

The Wookiee wails a doleful farewell.

Han turns to Princess Leia. They look sorrowfully at one another, then Han moves toward her and gives her a final, passionate kiss.

LEIA: I love you!

HAN: I know.

The idea of putting Han in carbon freeze first appeared in the second draft. Before Han gets frozen, Leia tells him: "I love you. I was afraid to tell you before, but it's true." Han replies: "I'll be back." In the third draft Han replies: "Just remember that, 'cause I'll be back."

Irvin Kershner: "The only difference I ever had with George on the cutting happened when Han is about to go into the freezing chamber and Leia tells him, 'I love you.' When I was shooting the scene, Han was supposed to reply: 'I love you, too.' So we did a take, and I said, 'Wait a minute, Harrison, I don't like the dialogue.' It's like she wins, she said it first, and 'I love you, too' is pretty weak stuff for Han Solo because he is too smart, too arrogant for that. So Harrison asked, 'What do you want?' And I said, 'I don't know; let's improvise.' So Leia says: 'I love you,' and he goes: 'Yeah, yeah.' And we tried it again and again with different lines, and finally Harrison says, 'I give up, I don't know what the hell to say.' The crew is hating me by now; it's hot, we're way up high on this set, they're all hungry, it was a nightmare. Finally Harrison says, 'Let's do it one more time and that's it.' So she says, 'I love you,' and he replies, 'I know.' And it just came out of him, and I said, 'Cut!' The assistant turns to me and says, 'You're not going to use this, are you?' And I said, 'Why not? It's perfect.' When I cut the film, George looked at the scene and said, 'In the script it was something like "I love you, too," wasn't it?' I told him, 'Yes, but it's such a stinky line for Han Solo that we had to change it.' George was worried that the audience was going to laugh and that it would break the tension. I felt very strongly about this, and George said, 'All right, when we show the film the first time, we'll show it your way, and then we'll show it the way it was written.' So we sneak previewed the film in North Beach, and when the line came, the audience roared. George turns to me and says, 'You see, it's a mistake.' Now the picture is over, people start coming out, and they're all talking about the line, saying how great it was. They all noticed it. So we kept it in the film. George is very flexible; he knows what he wants, but he is flexible, and that's why I like him so much."

Helpless, Leia watches the dashing pirate on the hydraulic platform. Han looks one final time at his friends—and then, suddenly, the platform drops. Chewie howls. Leia turns away in agony.

Lando winces in sorrow; it makes a life-changing impression on him.

Instantly, smoke begins to pour forth. Holding Leia, Chewie half turns away from the sight, giving Threepio a view of the procedure.

THREEPIO: What . . . what's going on? Turn around. Chewbacca, I can't see.
Chewie howls.

A huge mechanical tong lifts the steaming metal-encased space pirate out of the vat and stands him on the platform. Some Ugnaughts rush over and push the block over onto the platform.

Lando kneels and adjusts some knobs, measuring the heat. He shakes his head in relief.

Irvin Kershner: "When the cast of Solo in carbon freeze was created the first time, he was standing straight up, looking normal. That's what the prop department thought I wanted. I said, 'No, he's got to be looking like he is fighting to get out; he has to look like he is in agony.' So we changed it to the way it looks in the film."

THREEPIO: Oh . . . they've encased him in carbonite. He should be quite well protected—if he survived the freezing process, that is.

VADER: Well, Calrissian, did he survive?

LANDO: Yes, he's alive. And in perfect hibernation.

Vader turns to Boba Fett.

VADER: He's all yours, bounty hunter. Reset the chamber for Skywalker.

IMPERIAL OFFICER: Skywalker has just landed, my lord.

VADER: Good. See to it that he finds his way in here. Calrissian, take the princess and the Wookiee to my ship.

LANDO: You said they'd be left in the city under my supervision.

VADER: I am altering the deal. Pray I don't alter it any further.

Lando's hand instinctively goes to his throat as he turns to Leia, Chewie, and Threepio.

INT. CLOUD CITY—CORRIDOR—DAY

As Luke and Artoo move carefully down a deserted corridor, they hear a group of people coming down a side hallway.

Boba Fett enters from a side hallway, followed by two guards pushing the floating, encased body of Han Solo. Two stormtroopers follow. The two guards whisk Han into another hallway as Artoo lets out an excited series of beeps and whistles. Luke glares at the tiny droid, who stops in his tracks with a feeble squeak. But the noise has drawn the attention of Fett, who fires a deadly laser at Luke, which explodes to one side and tears up a huge chunk of wall.

Leia, Chewie, Threepio, and Lando are herded down a second hallway by several other stormtroopers. Leia turns just in time to see Luke. Surreptitiously, Lando sends a signal to his aide, Lobot.

LEIA: Luke! Luke, don't—it's a trap! It's a trap!

Before she can finish, she is pulled through a doorway and disappears from sight. Luke races after the group, leaving little Artoo trailing behind.

INT. CLOUD CITY—ANTEROOM

Luke runs into an anteroom and stops to get his bearings. Leia and the others are nowhere to be seen. Behind Luke, Artoo scoots down the corridor toward the anteroom, when suddenly a giant metal door comes slamming down, cutting off Luke's exit.

INT. CLOUD CITY—CARBON-FREEZING CHAMBER

Luke rises into the chamber, borne by the platform. The room is deathly quiet. Very little steam escapes from the pipes, and no one else seems to be in the large room. Warily, Luke walks toward the stairway.

Steam begins to build up in the chamber. Looking up through the steam, Luke sees a dark figure standing on a walkway above him.

VADER: The Force is with you, young Skywalker. But you are not a Jedi yet.

Luke moves up the stairs to face Vader. He feels confident, eager to engage his enemy.

Luke ignites his sword in answer. In an instant, Vader's own sword is lit. Luke lunges, but Vader repels the blow. Again Luke attacks, and the swords of the two combatants clash in battle.

During story meetings George Lucas and Leigh Brackett decided that it would be important to turn Luke into a very good swordsman and that that would pay off during his fight with Vader. The challenge with the confrontation between Luke and Vader was to play it like a seduction, a temptation; the audience knows that Luke is not going to die, so the ultimate hook is the fear that Luke might turn to the dark side.

INT. CLOUD CITY—CORRIDOR

Leia, Lando, and Chewie, with Threepio on his back, march along, guarded by stormtroopers. The group reaches an intersection where Lobot and a dozen of Lando's guards stand at attention.

The guards immediately aim their weapons at the startled stormtroopers. Taking the stormtroopers' weapons from them, Lando hands one to Leia.

LANDO: *(to Lobot)* Well done. Hold them in the security tower—and keep it quiet. Move.

As Lando's guards quickly march the stormtroopers away, Lando begins to undo Chewie's binding.

LEIA: What do you think you're doing?

LANDO: We're getting out of here.

THREEPIO: I knew all along it had to be a mistake.

Chewie turns on Lando and starts to choke him.

LEIA: Do you think that after what you did to Han we're going to trust you?

Lando tries to free himself from Chewie.

LANDO: *(choking)* I had no choice . . .

Chewie barks ferociously.

THREEPIO: *(to Chewie)* What are you doing? Trust him, trust him!

LEIA: Oh, so we understand, don't we, Chewie? He had no choice.

LANDO: I'm just trying to help . . .

LEIA: We don't need any of your help.

LANDO: *(choking)* H-a-a-a . . .

LEIA: What?

THREEPIO: It sounds like Han.

LANDO: There's still a chance to save Han . . . At the East Platform . . .

LEIA: Chewie.

Chewie finally releases Lando, who fights to get his breath back.

THREEPIO: *[to Lando]* I'm terribly sorry about all this. After all, he's only a Wookiee.

In the second draft, after Lando has turned against the Empire and rescued Chewie, Leia, and the droids, the group tries to make an escape in an elevator and gets stuck. The main lights go out, and Lando goes through the top of the lift and tries to rewire the shaft. Artoo accesses the central control and attempts to reroute the braking mechanism. Suddenly, the elevator rockets through the shaft and Artoo tries to stop it, but the cabin keeps on going. Finally Lando fires his laser pistol at the huge brake, and the elevator stops.

Irvin Kershner: "Obviously, there was no dialogue written for Chewbacca or Artoo. Body language was the key for all the creatures and the robots, even for Threepio, because his mouth didn't move. Gestures conveyed everything. It was interesting one day when Peter Mayhew, who played Chewbacca, was sick and I used someone else his size in the suit. I had to throw out all the footage and reshoot with Peter because the gestures and body movements were all wrong. The scene when Chewbacca is choking Lando and has Threepio on his back was difficult to shoot. We had an electronic head and arm for Threepio, and I manipulated the mechanism with a joystick. But it wasn't working. The propman said, 'Give me fifteen minutes.' We all went to get coffee, and when we came back, Threepio's head turned perfectly and his arm moved naturally. I looked up and realized that the prop man had a fishing pole with a fine nylon string attached to Threepio's arm. He had rigged another string around the head, which Chewbacca was holding. As Chewie moved his hands, Threepio's head turned!"

EXT. CLOUD CITY—EAST LANDING PLATFORM—BOBA FETT'S SHIP

BOBA FETT: Put Captain Solo in the cargo hold.

The two guards slide Han's enclosed body into an opening in the side of the bounty hunter's ship. Boba Fett climbs aboard on a ladder next to the side opening.

INT. CLOUD CITY—CORRIDOR

Lando, Leia, and Chewie run down a Cloud City corridor. Artoo rushes after them, beeping wildly.

THREEPIO: Artoo! Artoo! Where have you been?

Chewie turns around to see the stubby droid, causing Threepio to be spun out of sight of his friend.

THREEPIO: Wait, turn around, you woolly . . . ! (to Artoo) Hurry, hurry! We're trying to save Han from the bounty hunter!

Whistling frantically to Threepio, Artoo scoots along with the racing group.

THREEPIO: Well, at least you're still in one piece! Look what happened to me!

EXT. EAST LANDING PLATFORM—SIDE BAY

An elevator door slides open, and Leia, Chewbacca, and Lando race for a large bay overlooking the East Landing Platform.

Just as they arrive, Boba Fett's ship takes off against the cloudy sunset sky.

In wild anguish, Chewie howls and starts firing at the ship.

Nilo Rodis-Jamero: "Joe Johnston showed me some of the ideas he had for Boba Fett, and I remember asking myself what his spaceship would look like. I remember seeing a radar dish and stopping to sketch it very quickly to see if I could get something out of it. The original design I had was round, but when you looked at it from the side, it became elliptical. For some reason, when I drew it, George thought it was elliptical, so that's what it became. When we were building the ship at ILM, somebody looked at street lamps and pointed out that they looked like Boba's ship. So everyone began to think that was where I got the idea for the design."

THREEPIO: Oh, no! Chewie, they're behind you!

A laserbolt explodes near the princess. Everyone turns to see what Threepio has already spotted coming from the other direction: stormtroopers.

Laserbolts continue to explode around the princess and the Wookiee, but they barely notice. They seem possessed, transported, as all the frustration of captivity and anger of loss pour out through their death-dealing weapons.

After a few moments the group begins to move through the rain of laserfire.

INT. CLOUD CITY—CARBON-FREEZING CHAMBER

Luke and Vader are locked in combat on the platform overlooking the chamber. Their swords clash; the platform sways.

VADER: You have learned much, young one.

LUKE: You'll find I'm full of surprises.

Vader makes two quick moves, hooking Luke's sword out of his hands and sending it flying. Another lightning move at Luke's feet forces the youth to jump back to protect himself. Losing his balance, Luke rolls down the stairs to the circular carbon-freezing platform. There he sprawls on the floor, surprised and shaken. Just in time he looks up to see Vader, like a giant black bird, flying right at him. Luke rolls away as Vader lands. Crouching, Luke keeps his gaze steadily on his enemy.

VADER: Your destiny lies with me, Skywalker. Obi-Wan knew this to be true.

LUKE: No!

Behind Luke the hydraulic elevator cover has opened noisily. All the while Luke slowly, cautiously moves back, away from the Dark Lord.

Suddenly, Luke loses his balance and falls back into the opening.

VADER: All too easy. Perhaps you are not as strong as the Emperor thought.

There is a rumble, and in an instant freezing steam rises to obscure Vader's vision. Vader turns aside and deactivates his sword.

Through the steam behind Vader something blurs upward.

Vader turns around—and then looks up. He sees Luke, who has leapt fifteen feet straight up and who now hangs from some hoses on the carbonite outlet.

VADER: Impressive . . . most impressive.

Luke jumps down to the platform, where he is separated from Vader by the steaming carbonite pit. He raises his hand. His sword, which had fallen on another part of the platform, swiftly jumps into his outstretched hand and is instantly ignited. Vader and he clash swords.

VADER: Obi-Wan has taught you well. You have controlled your fear . . . now release your anger. Only your hatred can destroy me.

Luke is more cautious, controlling his anger. He begins to retreat as Vader goads him on. As Luke takes a defensive position, he realizes he has been foolhardy.

Breathing hard, Luke jumps in the air, turning a somersault over Vader. He lands on the floor and slashes at Vader as the room continues to fill up the screen. A quick sword exchange and Luke forces Vader back. Another exchange and Vader retreats. Luke presses forward.

Vader retreats before Luke's skillful sword. Vader blocks the sword but loses his balance and falls into the outer rim of pipes. The energy Luke has used to stop Vader has brought him to the point of collapse. Luke moves to the edge and looks down but sees no sign of Vader. He then deactivates his sword, hooks it on his belt, and moves down into the pit.

INT. CLOUD CITY—TUNNEL AND REACTOR CONTROL ROOM

Moving through a tunnel-like entrance, Luke cautiously approaches the reactor room. He ignites his sword and moves into the room and toward a large window as Vader enters.

Luke raises his sword and moves forward to attack.

Behind Luke a large pipe detaches itself from the wall and comes smashing forward toward his back. Luke turns and cuts it in half.

As Luke and Vader cross swords, another piece of equipment detaches and comes flying at Luke. Small tools and equipment come flying at him. Bombarded from all sides, Luke does his best to deflect everything, but soon he is bloodied and bruised. Finally, one machine glances off him and goes flying out the large window. A fierce wind blows into the room, whipping everything about and creating a horrendous noise. In the center of the room, unmoving, stands the dark, rocklike figure of Vader.

A piece of machinery hits Luke, and he is sucked out the window.

The idea of Vader using telekinetic powers during his fight with Luke was created during story meetings. There was concern, however, that the audience might think back to the first film and wonder why Vader didn't use all his powers on Ben; this was easily explained by the fact that Ben was possibly stronger than Vader. George Lucas and Leigh Brackett also discussed the different levels of the Force; maybe Ben was a six, Vader was a four, and Luke is now at level two.

Another idea that came out of story meetings was to have Luke wedged up against a wall; there's a pipe next to him, and Vader and Luke duel, trying to bend it until it buckles and ties itself up.

INT. GANTRY—OUTSIDE CONTROL ROOM—REACTOR SHAFT

Luke has fallen onto the gantry and hangs over the edge. He begins to scramble up.

INT. CLOUD CITY—CORRIDOR LEADING TO LANDING PLATFORM

Leia, Lando, Chewie, and the droids are fighting a running battle with storm-troopers. They come around a corner and head for the door to the landing platform. Lando punches desperately at the door's control panel.

LANDO: The security code has been changed!

THREEPIO: Artoo, you can tell the computer to override the security system. Artoo, hurry!

Threepio has pointed to a computer socket on the control panel. Artoo beeps and scoots toward it. Lando meanwhile has connected up to the panel's intercom.

LANDO: Attention! This is Lando Calrissian. The Empire has taken control of the city. I advise everyone to leave before more Imperial troops arrive.

From the Special Edition:

LANDO: Attention! This is Lando Calrissian.

The citizens of Cloud City stop their activities to listen to Lando's announcement.

LANDO: The Empire has taken control of the city. I advise everyone to leave before more Imperial troops arrive.

Artoo takes off a connector cover and sticks his computer arm into the socket. Suddenly, a short beep turns into a wild scream. Artoo's circuits light up, his head spins wildly, and smoke begins to seep out underneath him. Quickly, Chewie pulls him away.

LANDO: This way.

Lando, Leia, Artoo, and Chewie flee down the corridor. As he scoots along with them, Artoo sends some angry beeps Threepio's way.

THREEPIO: Well, don't blame me. I'm an interpreter. I'm not supposed to know a power socket from a computer terminal.

INT. CLOUD CITY—CORRIDOR

In a panic, Cloud City residents are trying to get out of the city. Some carry boxes, others packages. They run, then change direction.

Stormtroopers pursue Lando, Leia, and Chewie, who are firing back at them. Artoo works on another door to the landing platform while Threepio berates him for his seeming ineptitude.

THREEPIO: Ah. We're not interested in the hyperdrive on the *Millennium Falcon.* It's fixed! Just open the door, you stupid lump.

A triumphant beep from Artoo—and the door snaps open.

THREEPIO: *(to Artoo)* I never doubted you for a second. Wonderful!

Chewie, Leia, and Lando retreat along the corridor.

Artoo lays down a cloud of fog, obscuring everything, as the group dashes outside.

EXT. LANDING PLATFORM—CLOUD CITY—DUSK

They race for the Millennium Falcon as a battalion of stormtroopers reaches the main door. Lando and Leia hold off the troops as the droids get on board with Chewie. As Chewie bounds to the ship with Threepio on his back, Threepio hits his head on the top of the ramp.

THREEPIO: Ouch! Oh! Ah! That hurt. Bend down, you thoughtless . . . Ow!

LANDO: Leia! Go!

Lando and Leia race up the ramp under a hail of laserfire as Chewie starts up the ship.

INT. *MILLENNIUM FALCON*—CORRIDOR

Artoo drags the partially assembled Threepio down the corridor of the Falcon.

THREEPIO: I thought that hairy beast would be the end of me. Of course I've looked better.

Artoo beeps understandingly.

EXT. CLOUD CITY—LANDING PLATFORM—DUSK

Troops fire after it as the Millennium Falcon lifts gracefully into the twilight sky and roars away from the city.

Remember, Han being put into carbon freeze first appeared in the second draft. So in the story treatment and the first draft Han, Leia, Chewie, and the droids make it back to the *Falcon* while Lando eludes the stormtroopers. Leia wants to go back to save Luke, but Han tells her that Skywalker would want them to escape. In a sense, the situation from the first film is re-created here, with Luke risking his life against the Empire's stormtroopers to allow his friends to escape. As the *Falcon* takes off, a large blastshield comes crashing down in front of the ship. It looks as if they're trapped, but Han blasts his way out.

INT. GANTRY—OUTSIDE CONTROL ROOM—REACTOR SHAFT

Luke moves along the railing and up to the control room. Vader lunges at him, and Luke immediately raises his lit sword to meet Vader's. Sparks fly as they duel, Vader gradually forcing Luke backward toward the gantry.

VADER: You are beaten. It is useless to resist. Don't let yourself be destroyed as Obi-Wan did.

Luke answers by rolling sideways and thrusting his sword at Vader so viciously that he nicks Vader on the shoulder. The black armor sparks and smokes, and Vader seems to be hurt but immediately recovers.

Luke has backed off along the narrow end of the gantry as Vader comes at him, slashing at the young Jedi with his sword. Luke makes a quick move around the instrument complex attached to the end of the gantry. Vader's sword comes slashing down, cutting the complex loose; it begins to fall.

Then Vader's sword comes down across Luke's right forearm, cutting off his hand and sending his sword flying. In great pain, Luke squeezes his forearm under his left armpit and moves back along the gantry to its extreme end. Vader follows. The wind subsides. Luke holds on. There is nowhere else to go.

VADER: There is no escape. Don't make me destroy you, Luke. You do not yet realize your importance. You have only begun to discover your power. Join me and I will complete your training. With our combined strength, we can end this destructive conflict and bring order to the galaxy.

LUKE: I'll never join you!

VADER: If you only knew the power of the dark side. Obi-Wan never told you what happened to your father.

LUKE: He told me enough! He told me you killed him.

VADER: No. I am your father.

Shocked, Luke looks at Vader in utter disbelief.

LUKE: No. No. That's not true! That's impossible!

VADER: Search your feelings. You know it to be true.

LUKE: No! No!

VADER: Luke. You can destroy the Emperor. He has foreseen this. It is your destiny. Join me, and together we can rule the galaxy as father and son.

Vader has put away his sword and holds his hand out to Luke.

VADER: Come with me. It is the only way.

A calm comes over Luke, and he makes a decision. In the next instant he steps off the gantry platform into space. The Dark Lord looks over the platform and sees Luke falling far below. The wounded Jedi begins to drop fast, unable to grab onto anything to break his fall.

INT. REACTOR SHAFT

Suddenly Luke is sucked into an exhaust pipe in the side of the shaft.

INT. EXHAUST PIPE

Luke tumbles through the exhaust pipe.

He slides to the end of the slickly polished pipe and stops, then falls through a circular grille.

EXT. BOTTOM OF CLOUD CITY—WEATHER VANE—DUSK

Luke tumbles out, emerging at the undermost part of Cloud City. Reaching out desperately, he manages to grab onto an electronic weather vane.

George Lucas: "I didn't discuss the notion of Vader being Luke's father with Leigh Brackett. At that point I wasn't sure if I was going to include it in that script or reveal it in the third episode. I was going back and forth, and rather than confuse things for Leigh, I decided to keep the whole issue out of the mix. I figured I would add it later on."

The notion of Vader being Luke's father first appeared in the second draft. Vader became attracted to the dark side while he was training to become a Jedi. He became a Jedi and killed most of the Jedi Knights; very few escaped. Ben fought Vader and pushed him down a nuclear reactor shaft. One of his arms was severed, and Ben believed he had killed Vader; in fact, Vader survived and became a mutant.

In the story treatment, Luke gets trapped on a narrow ledge and Vader tries to win him over to the dark side. Vader wants Luke to use his anger to fight, knowing that if he gets angry enough, he'll give in. Finally, Vader tries to kill Luke, but Luke jumps off the ledge into a debris chute on the side of the main shaft. He comes out on the side of the city from a drainpipe, gets caught on a grate, and dangles above the exit port of the city.

Remember, in the first draft Luke had a vision of his confrontation with Vader in Minch's house. For the climax, Leigh Brackett created a surrealistic scene where we see the blackness of space and the large black shadow of Vader towering against the starfields. Luke's shadow is almost as dark as Vader's. Vader asks Luke to join him. Luke's form starts to glow lighter as he says that he'd rather die than join Vader; as in the movie, Vader and Luke reach the main shaft and Luke jumps. Vader cutting Luke's arm first appeared in the second draft.

George Lucas: "I contemplated for a while whether or not I was going to reveal that Vader was Luke's father in the second film. I was afraid the scene when Vader says 'I am your father' and then cuts off his son's arm might be too intense. That is a pretty intense moment and basically a castration scene. I also asked people I knew how they felt about ending the film that way, and most opinions were that it was okay, that it wouldn't be detrimental to anyone. But I conceived the scene so that you would not know if Vader was lying or telling the truth, so the audience could walk away saying, 'He is a bad guy, he lied.' You have to have an escape hatch for kids psychologically so they can deny it."

Lawrence Kasdan: "When we started to work on *Empire*, George said Darth was Luke's father. I thought that was really cool. Writing their confrontation was difficult because the language had to be on the nose."

Irvin Kershner: "The confrontation between Luke and Vader was very difficult to shoot. First of all, we had to show something spectacular, so we had these giant sets. Then, when Luke climbs out on that ledge, Mark Hamill was actually hanging with a harness about thirty-five feet above the ground, plus there was a huge fan blowing, plus the whole thing was moving. The actor who played Vader did not know that Luke was his son; when we did the scene, the only one who knew was Mark, and I told him right before we shot it. We didn't want anybody to know, so I had the page with the real dialogue put away. So the actor playing Vader was saying other words; I gave him other words. He was saying something totally different, which of course we replaced later.

What I did was mime with him, told him to lean forward, to bring his arm up so that he would say the lines, but all I used were the movements. Mark knew that when Vader said 'You will come with me,' he was really saying 'I'm your father.' Now, I was talking to kids, and I discovered that children below the age of nine say, 'No, no, he's not his father, he's lying.' They can't accept it. About ten on, they accept it. Ambiguity is a necessary part of a good story; if you eliminate ambiguity, you're not touching the unconscious of the audience. What you want is the audience doing their own film while they're watching it so that everybody is having a slightly different experience."

LUKE: Ben . . . Ben, please!

Luke tries to pull himself up on the weather vane but slips back down. He hooks one of his legs around the fragile instrument. All the while, a powerful current of air rushes out at him from the exhaust pipe.

LUKE: "Ben. Leia!"

EXT. CLOUD CITY—*MILLENNIUM FALCON*—DUSK

The Millennium Falcon *is leaving Cloud City.*

INT. *MILLENNIUM FALCON*—COCKPIT

Leia seems to be lost in a fog, her expression troubled.

EXT. BOTTOM OF CLOUD CITY—WEATHER VANE—DUSK

LUKE: Hear me! Leia!

INT. *MILLENNIUM FALCON*—COCKPIT

LEIA: Luke . . . We've got to go back.

Chewie is busy operating the ship. Lando stands next to the Wookiee, watching a readout on the control panel.

Chewie growls in surprise.

LANDO: What?

LEIA: I know where Luke is.

LANDO: But what about those fighters?

Chewie barks in agreement with Lando.

LEIA: Chewie, just do it.

LANDO: But what about Vader?

Chewie turns on Lando, the newcomer, with an ominous growl.

LANDO: All right, all right, all right.

EXT. CLOUD CITY—*MILLENNIUM FALCON*—DUSK

The Falcon *makes a graceful banking turn back toward Cloud City.*

EXT. CLOUD CITY—CORRIDOR

Vader strides toward the landing platform, followed by an aide and stormtroopers.

VADER: Bring my shuttle.

EXT. BOTTOM OF CLOUD CITY—WEATHER VANE

Nearly unconscious, Luke hangs upside down on the weather vane.

EXT. *MILLENNIUM FALCON*—BOTTOM OF CLOUD CITY

The Falcon *dives to the underside of the floating city.*

INT. *MILLENNIUM FALCON*—COCKPIT

Leia tries to remain calm.

LANDO: *(pointing out the cockpit window)* Look, someone's up there.

LEIA: It's Luke. Chewie, slow down. Slow down and we'll get under him. Lando, open the top hatch.

Lando rushes out of the cockpit.

EXT. BOTTOM OF CLOUD CITY—WEATHER VANE

Luke hangs by one arm from the crossbar of the weather vane. He slips from the bar and grabs onto the pole of the vane as the Falcon *banks toward him.*

The Falcon *positions itself under Luke as Lando moves up through the opening of the hatch. Luke begins to slide and finally falls from the vane into space.*

INT. *MILLENNIUM FALCON*—COCKPIT

Out of the cockpit window Leia sees Luke.

LEIA: Okay. Easy, Chewie.

The Falcon *closes in on Luke.*

EXT. BOTTOM OF CLOUD CITY

The Falcon *positions itself under Luke.*

INT. *MILLENNIUM FALCON*—HATCH

The hatch pops open with a hiss of pressure. Lando has gone up to help the battered warrior inside the ship.

EXT. BOTTOM OF CLOUD CITY

As Lando appears in the hatchway, Luke falls toward the Falcon *and TIE fighters appear.*

INT. *MILLENNIUM FALCON*—COCKPIT

Flak bursts all around it as the Falcon *banks away from the city. Leia and Chewie struggle with the controls.*
LEIA: *(into intercom)* Lando?
LANDO: *(over intercom)* Okay, let's go.
EXT. BOTTOM OF CLOUD CITY
The Falcon *races away.*
INT. *MILLENNIUM FALCON*—HOLD
Lando helps Luke into the Falcon.

In the story treatment and in the first draft Han has blasted the large shield door, and as the *Falcon* is about to leave, Solo notices Luke, who is hanging from a grate. Luke is rescued, and the *Falcon* zooms into hyperdrive. In the second draft Leia hears Ben's voice telling her to save Luke. She orders Lando to go back, and they find Luke hanging from the weather vane. Luke lets himself drop on top of the ship and tries to work his way to a hatch near the gun turret. The hatch opens, and Lando reaches out to help Luke. Suddenly there's an explosion, causing the ship to bobble, almost throwing Luke overboard, but Lando grabs him in time. The *Falcon* immediately jumps to lightspeed after that.

In the revised second draft Luke is almost unconscious, hanging onto the weather vane. He sees the *Falcon* approaching, and in his attempt to wave, he breaks the weather vane. Leia and Lando see Luke falling and get the ship under him. Luke lands with a thud on top of the ship. In the revised fourth draft, after Luke's rescue, the *Falcon* is attacked by TIE fighters. Vader realizes that Luke has escaped and, defeated, he calls back his fighters. The idea of Luke still struggling with Vader and the dark side after he's been brought aboard the *Falcon* first appeared in the fifth draft, as did the concept of the *Falcon* not being able to jump to lightspeed.

EXT. BOTTOM OF CLOUD CITY
The Falcon *is closely followed by the three TIE fighters, all of which keep up a heavy laser assault on the fleeing starship.*
INT. *MILLENNIUM FALCON*—COCKPIT
Explosions erupt all around the cockpit, buffeting the ship wildly. Chewie howls as he frantically tries to control the ship.
   Luke, bloody and battered, enters the cockpit, supported by Lando. Leia jumps up and hugs him while Chewie barks in joyous relief.

LUKE: Oh, Leia.

LANDO: All right, Chewie. Let's go.

Leia helps Luke from the cockpit as another huge blast rocks the ship.

EXT. SPACE—CLOUD CITY—DAY

The Falcon, *still followed by the three TIE fighters, races away from the cloud-covered city.*

INT. *MILLENNIUM FALCON—* SLEEPING QUARTERS

Luke rests on a cot, his injured arm wrapped in a protective cuff. Leia gently wipes his face. The ship lurches again. She kisses him. Then Leia leaves the quarters.

LEIA: I'll be back.

EXT. SPACE

The Millennium Falcon *is relentlessly pursued by TIE fighters.*

INT. *MILLENNIUM FALCON—*HOLD

Chewie enters through the doorway, grunting to himself.

Beeping while he works, Artoo is busy connecting some wires to Threepio, who now has one leg attached.

THREEPIO: Noisy brute. Why don't we just go into lightspeed?

Artoo beeps in response.

THREEPIO: We can't? How would you know the hyperdrive is deactivated?

Artoo whistles knowingly.

THREEPIO: The city's central computer told you? Artoo-Detoo, you know better than to trust a strange computer. Ouch! Pay attention to what you're doing!

Chewie is in the pit. He is trying to loosen something with an enormous wrench.

INT. *MILLENNIUM FALCON—*COCKPIT

Leia is seated in front of the control panel. Lando is working on some other controls. Sparks fly.

EXT. SPACE

The Millennium Falcon *is pursued around the Star Destroyer by the three firing TIE fighters.*

INT. VADER'S STAR DESTROYER—BRIDGE

Vader stands on the bridge, watching as the Millennium Falcon *is chased by the TIE fighters. As the* Falcon *draws nearer, Vader's breathing gets slightly faster.*

VADER: Luke.

INT. *MILLENNIUM FALCON—*SLEEPING QUARTERS

Luke realizes that Vader's ship is very near. He feels resigned to his fate. He senses that he is beaten, more emotionally than physically.

LUKE: Father.

INT. VADER'S STAR DESTROYER—BRIDGE

VADER: Son, come with me.

INT. *MILLENNIUM FALCON*—SLEEPING QUARTERS

LUKE: *(moaning)* Ben, why didn't you tell me?

INT. *MILLENNIUM FALCON*—COCKPIT

Lando and Leia are at the controls of the Falcon. *Meanwhile, in the ship's hold, Chewie continues to work frantically on the hyperdrive mechanism.*

LANDO: *(into intercom)* Chewie!

Frustrated, Chewie uses his wrench like a club and hits the panel . . .

EXT. SPACE

The Falcon *races past the huge Imperial Star Destroyer, followed very closely by the TIE fighters.*

INT. *MILLENNIUM FALCON*—COCKPIT

Luke enters the cockpit and looks out the window. He is almost unconscious with pain and depression.

LUKE: It's Vader.

INT. VADER'S STAR DESTROYER—BRIDGE

VADER: Luke . . . it is your destiny.

INT. *MILLENNIUM FALCON*—COCKPIT

LUKE: Ben, why didn't you tell me?

EXT. SPACE

TIE fighters pursue the Millennium Falcon.

INT. VADER'S STAR DESTROYER—BRIDGE

PIETT: Alert all commands. Ready for the tractor beam.

INT. *MILLENNIUM FALCON*—HOLD

Artoo races to a control panel and starts working on a circuit board. Furious, Threepio stands on one leg, yelling.

THREEPIO: Artoo, come back at once! You haven't finished with me yet! You don't know how to fix the hyperdrive. Chewbacca can do it. I'm standing here in pieces, and you're having delusions of grandeur!

Artoo moves a circuit on a control panel. Suddenly the control panel lights up.

INT. *MILLENNIUM FALCON*—COCKPIT

Leia and Lando are thrown back into their seats as the Millennium Falcon *unexpectedly shoots into hyperdrive.*

Irvin Kershner: "It was essential to have Artoo be the one who fixes the hyperdrive. If it had been Lando, for instance, it would have been flat. But the fact that they're all desperate and little Artoo goes over calmly to rig the thing and changes the code makes the scene work."

INT. *MILLENNIUM FALCON*—HOLD

The ship tilts up, and Artoo topples into the pit on top of Chewie.

THREEPIO: You did it!

INT. *MILLENNIUM FALCON*—COCKPIT

Stars stream past as the Millennium Falcon *shoots into lightspeed.*

EXT. SPACE

The Falcon *soars into infinity and away from the huge Star Destroyer.*

INT. VADER'S STAR DESTROYER—BRIDGE

Admiral Piett looks at Vader in terror. Vader turns slowly and walks off the bridge, his hands held behind his back in a contemplative gesture.

EXT. SPACE—REBEL STAR CRUISER

The Millennium Falcon *is attached to a huge Rebel cruiser by a docking tube. Rebel fighters move about the giant cruiser, and a Rebel transport ship hovers near the fleet.*

INT. *MILLENNIUM FALCON*—COCKPIT

Lando sits in the pilot's seat as he talks into the comlink.

LANDO: *(into comlink)* Luke, we're ready for takeoff.

Chewie enters, barking.

LUKE: *(over comlink)* Good luck, Lando.

EXT. SPACE—REBEL STAR CRUISER

LANDO: *(into comlink)* When we find Jabba the Hutt and that bounty hunter, we'll contact you.

INT. STAR CRUISER—MEDICAL CENTER

Luke speaks into the comlink as a medical droid works on his hand. Leia stands near him.

LUKE: *(into comlink)* I'll meet you at the rendezvous point on Tatooine.

INT. *MILLENNIUM FALCON*—COCKPIT

LANDO: *(into comlink)* Princess, we'll find Han. I promise.

INT. STAR CRUISER—MEDICAL CENTER

LUKE: *(into comlink)* Chewie, I'll be waiting for your signal.

Chewie's wail comes over the comlink.

LUKE: *(into comlink)* Take care, you two.

INT. *MILLENNIUM FALCON*—COCKPIT

LUKE: *(over comlink)* May the Force be with you.

Chewie wails.

INT. STAR CRUISER—MEDICAL CENTER

Chewie's wail comes over the comlink.

   Luke looks down at his hand. A metalized type of bandage has been wrapped around his wrist. The medical droid makes some adjustments in a tiny electronic unit, then pricks each one of Luke's fingers.

LUKE: Ow!

Luke wriggles his fingers, makes a fist, and relaxes it. His hand is completely functional.

It was Irvin Kershner's idea to spend a moment showing the new hand being fitted on Luke with a probe touching his fingers and the fingers reacting. "Whenever I see an amputee," Irvin Kershner wrote in a letter to George Lucas dated February 19, 1979, "and I am sure most people feel this way, they wonder how it is not to have any feel, any sensitivity in the fingertips." Irvin Kershner wanted to show that advanced technology gave Luke a feeling in his new hand. This of course also was an attempt to take away some of the potential horror of what has happened to Luke.

Irvin Kershner: "The audience had to know that Luke had feeling in his hand. That way, even though he has a mechanical hand, when he puts his arm around Leia, it isn't creepy."

He gets up and walks over to Leia. There is a new bond between them, a new understanding. Leia is thinking about Han; Luke is thinking about his uncertain and newly complicated future. Together they stand at the large window of the medical center, looking out on the Rebel star cruiser and a dense, luminous galaxy swirling in space.

Luke puts his arm around Leia. The droids stand next to them, and Threepio moves closer to Artoo, putting his arm on him.

INT. *MILLENNIUM FALCON*—COCKPIT

Lando and Chewie are at the controls.

EXT. SPACE

The Millennium Falcon turns away from the Rebel cruiser and blasts into space.

INT. STAR CRUISER—MEDICAL CENTER

Luke, Leia, Threepio, and Artoo watch as the Millennium Falcon moves into view and zooms away into space.

EXT. SPACE

The Millennium Falcon recedes into space.

INT. STAR CRUISER—MEDICAL CENTER

Threepio looks emotional. Artoo beeps.

EXT. SPACE—REBEL STAR CRUISER

While Luke, Leia, and the droids stand, looking out the window of the star cruiser, slowly the cruiser moves away into space.

DISSOLVE TO:

EXT. GALAXY—SPACE

END CREDITS FADE IN AND OUT OVER BACKGROUND.

THE END

In the story treatment the *Falcon* has landed in a beautiful jungle garden. Han, Chewie, and Lando are getting ready to leave; the Wookiee hugs everyone, even Threepio, who thanks him for putting him back together. Han gives Leia a long kiss. The *Falcon* takes off at sunset: "Twin suns low on the horizon as the *Falcon* becomes a tiny speck, then disappears behind the silhouettes of Luke, Leia, and the robots." In the first draft the *Falcon* lands on Besspin Kaalida, the garden planet. Han kisses the princess and says goodbye to his friends; he is off to persuade his stepfather, Ovan Marekal, to join the Rebellion (remember, in this draft Han was about to leave on the mission at the beginning of the story, but had to change his plans after the Empire attacked the Rebels' secret base). Leia, Luke, Lando, and the robots watch the *Falcon* take off from a garden balcony. Luke holds his saber in a position of salute as the *Falcon* disappears in the sky.

In the second draft the last scene takes place on the bridge of a Rebel star cruiser as Lando and Chewie are about to leave to search for Han. Lando shakes hands with generals, admirals, Rebel senators, and officers. Artoo beeps to Chewie, and Threepio translates that he hopes he finds Han; Threepio also thanks the Wookiee for putting him back together. Luke offers to go with them, but Chewie "barks negative." Lando promises that he'll come back with Han or die trying. As the *Falcon* takes off, Luke tells Leia that he'll be leaving soon, too; there's something he's got to finish. Leia thinks he's upset because he realizes that she loves Han, but Luke says: "I have been swept into another sphere. Han is better for you . . . Don't worry, they'll find him." Luke kisses her on the forehead, and they watch from the viewport as the *Falcon* disappears into a sea of stars.

In the revised second draft Rebel generals bow before Lando and Chewie as they're about to depart on the *Falcon* to look for Han. "Luke's left lower arm is exposed, revealing metal struts and electronic circuits similar to Threepio's." Leia bows before the two heroes, and then she gives a big hug to Chewie. Luke shakes Lando's hand and scratches Chewie's chest, "which the Wookiee loves"; he barks with enjoyment. In this draft Threepio just hugs Chewie, and the Wookiee is embarrassed but manages a friendly pat on the droid's back and another on little Artoo's dome head. There's no dialogue about Leia being in love with Han anymore; in this draft Luke just says: "They'll find him. I know they will."

In a letter to George Lucas, Irvin Kershner indicated that there should be nothing more important for Luke than going with Lando and Chewie to find Han. Irvin Kershner felt that in the script the fact that Luke doesn't go with them makes us dislike him. Luke must not be able to go. In the fifth draft Luke tells Lando and Chewie: "I'll see you on Tatooine," leaving no doubt that as soon as he recovers, he'll help rescue Han Solo.

George Lucas: "At the end of the second movie, Han Solo is in carbon freeze and Luke has this terrible piece of information about his father. That's a hard thing to try to pull off; it's not a formula kind of idea where you just take a hit movie and remake a different version of the same thing. This is a bigger story, and since this was the middle, nothing really gets resolved. It was a real challenge, and there was a good chance that people were going to reject it. To defy the convention that you have to have a happy ending was very challenging, but I felt that I had to tell the story and I had no choice. I'm dealing with the same dilemma in the first three movies; they're not what you might expect, but that's the story I want to tell and I've committed myself to it, so I'm just going to continue regardless of whether it's the wisest thing to do in terms of conventions. These films aren't sequels; they're the continuation of a grand story. Therefore, some end up and some end down."

EPISODE VI
Return of the Jedi

Star Wars. Episode VI: *Return of the Jedi*
Annotations and Interviews by Laurent Bouzereau

Annotations on *Star Wars*, Episode VI: *Return of the Jedi*, are based on the following materials:

Handwritten notes, February 24, 1995

Star Wars, Episode VI: *Revenge of the Jedi*, by George Lucas, first draft, handwritten, February 20, 1981

Star Wars, Episode VI: *Revenge of the Jedi*, by George Lucas, rough draft, February 24, 1981

Revised rough draft with original notes, June 12, 1981

Star Wars, Episode VI: *Revenge of the Jedi*, by George Lucas, revised rough draft, June 12, 1981, typed

Revenge of the Jedi story conference transcript, July 13, 1981, through July 17, 1981, George Lucas, Howard Kazanjian, Richard Marquand, Larry Kasdan

Second draft, September 21, 1981

Handwritten changes to Scene 61 from Howard Kazanjian

Star Wars, Episode VI: *Revenge of the Jedi*, story by George Lucas, screenplay by Lawrence Kasdan, second draft, September 21, 1981

Return of the Jedi by Lawrence Kasdan and George Lucas, revised second draft, November 1, 1981, including handwritten notes

Star Wars, Episode VI: *Return of the Jedi*, screenplay by Lawrence Kasdan and George Lucas, story by George Lucas, revised second draft, November 11, 1981

Star Wars, Episode VI: *Return of the Jedi*, screenplay by Lawrence

Kasdan and George Lucas, story by George Lucas, third draft, December 1, 1981—Larry and George's changes.

Star Wars, Episode VI: *Return of the Jedi*, screenplay by Lawrence Kasdan and George Lucas, story by George Lucas, third draft, December 1, 1981 (Larry's version)

Wookiee Doodle Pad, miscellaneous notes (Han changes [hand-written] from Larry, December 15, 1981)

(29a–29b) Jedi scene order as of July 30, 1981—scene breakdowns.

Lucas revisions dated January 4, 1982

(31a–31g) various memos

STAR WARS

A long time ago in a galaxy far, far away . . .

The boundless heavens serve as a backdrop for the main title, followed by a roll-up, which crawls into infinity.

EPISODE VI
RETURN OF THE JEDI

Luke Skywalker has returned to his home planet of Tatooine in an attempt to rescue his friend Han Solo from the clutches of the vile gangster Jabba the Hutt.

Little does Luke know that the GALACTIC EMPIRE has secretly begun construction on a new armored space station even more powerful than the first dreaded Death Star.

When completed, this ultimate weapon will spell certain doom for the small band of Rebels struggling to restore freedom to the galaxy . . .

As in the first two movies, the crawl went through many changes and variations. The rough draft mentioned two Death Stars and spoke of the situation in general terms. With each new draft, the text became more focused on the heroes of the story, drawing the audience into the film on a more personal level.

George Lucas: "By the time we got down to doing the third film, we'd had so many difficulties with people trying to report stuff with the media and the press and everything that we called the film *Revenge of the Jedi* to throw people off. The title was always intended to be

Return of the Jedi, but we made the film under the code name *Revenge of the Jedi*. Unfortunately, what happened is Fox started promoting the film before we could tell them not to use the title. We were lucky that they didn't start promoting the film under the title *Blue Harvest*, because we were also using that as a bogus title."

PAN DOWN *to reveal a monstrous half-completed Death Star, its massive superstructure curling away from the completed section like the arms of a giant octopus.*
An Imperial Star Destroyer moves overhead toward the massive armored space station, followed by two zipping TIE fighters. A small Imperial shuttle rockets from the main bay of the ship and hustles toward the Death Star.

INT. IMPERIAL SHUTTLE—COCKPIT
The shuttle captain makes contact with the Death Star.

SHUTTLE CAPTAIN: Command station, this is ST Three-twenty-one. Code Clearance Blue. We're starting our approach. Deactivate the security shield.

INT. DEATH STAR CONTROL ROOM

DEATH STAR CONTROLLER: The security deflector shield will be deactivated when we have confirmation of your code transmission. Stand by. You are clear to proceed.

INT. IMPERIAL SHUTTLE—COCKPIT

SHUTTLE CAPTAIN: We're starting our approach.

EXT. SPACE
The shuttle and its two escorting TIE fighters approach, and the shuttle enters the Death Star.

INT. DEATH STAR CONTROL ROOM
Operators move about among the control panels.
A control officer addresses a shield operator.

OFFICER: Inform the commander that Lord Vader's shuttle has arrived.
OPERATOR: Yes, sir.

The Imperial shuttle has landed in the massive docking bay. A squad of Imperial stormtroopers moves into formation before the craft.

INT. DEATH STAR—MAIN DOCKING BAY
The Death Star commander, Moff Jerjerrod, a tall, confident technocrat, strides through the assembled troops to the base of the shuttle ramp. The troops stand to attention; many are uneasy about the new arrival. Even the arrogant Death Star commander swallows nervously.
The exit hatch of the shuttle opens with a whoosh, revealing only darkness. Then, heavy footsteps and mechanical breathing. From this black void appears Darth Vader, Lord of the Sith. Vader looks over the assemblage as he walks down the ramp.

JERJERROD: Lord Vader, this is an unexpected pleasure. We're honored by your presence.

VADER: You may dispense with the pleasantries, Commander. I'm here to put you back on schedule.

The commander turns ashen and begins to tremble.

JERJERROD: I assure you, Lord Vader, my men are working as fast as they can.

VADER: Perhaps I can find new ways to motivate them.

JERJERROD: I tell you, this station will be operational as planned.

VADER: The Emperor does not share your optimistic appraisal of the situation.

JERJERROD: But he asks the impossible. I need more men.

VADER: Then perhaps you can tell him when he arrives.

JERJERROD: *(aghast)* The Emperor's coming here?

VADER: That is correct, Commander. And he is most displeased with your apparent lack of progress.

JERJERROD: We shall double our efforts.

VADER: I hope so, Commander, for your sake. The Emperor is not as forgiving as I am.

EXT. ROAD TO JABBA'S PALACE—TATOOINE

A lonely, windswept road meanders through the desolate Tatooine terrain. Artoo-Detoo and See-Threepio are making their way along the road toward the ominous palace of Jabba the Hutt. Artoo beeps.

THREEPIO: Of course I'm worried. And you should be, too. Lando Calrissian and poor Chewbacca never returned from this awful place.

Artoo whistles timidly.

THREEPIO: Don't be so sure. If I told you half the things I've heard about this Jabba the Hutt, you'd probably short-circuit.

The two droids fearfully approach the massive gate to the palace.

EXT. JABBA'S PALACE—GATE

THREEPIO: Artoo, are you sure this is the right place?

Threepio looks around for some kind of signaling device.

THREEPIO: I'd better knock, I suppose.

He timidly knocks on the iron door.

THREEPIO: *(instantly)* There doesn't seem to be anyone here. Let's go back and tell Master Luke.

A small hatch in the middle of the door opens, and a spidery mechanical arm with a large electronic eyeball on the end pops out and inspects the two droids.

STRANGE VOICE: Tee chuta hhat yudd!

THREEPIO: Goodness gracious me!

The eye continues to jabber in its strange language.
Threepio points to Artoo, then to himself.

THREEPIO: Artoo Detoowha bo Seethreepiowha ey toota odd mishka Jabba du Hutt.

The eye pokes forward toward Threepio, there is a laugh, then the eye zips back into the door. The hatch slams shut.

THREEPIO: I don't think they're going to let us in, Artoo. We'd better go.

Artoo bleeps his reluctance as Threepio turns to leave. Suddenly, the massive door starts to rise with a horrific metallic screech. The robots turn back and face an endless black cavity.

Artoo starts forward into the gloom.

THREEPIO: Artoo, wait. Oh, dear! Artoo, Artoo, I really don't think we should rush into all this.

Threepio rushes after his stubby companion. Artoo continues down the corridor, with Threepio following.

THREEPIO: Oh, Artoo! Artoo, wait for me!

INT. JABBA'S PALACE—HALLWAY

The frightened robots are met by two giant green Gamorrean guards. One guard grunts an order. Artoo beeps nervously.

THREEPIO: Just you deliver Master Luke's message and get us out of here. Oh, my!

The door slams shut with a loud crash that echoes throughout the dark passageway.

THREEPIO: Oh, no.

In the rough draft, after the crawl, a pan down reveals the planet of Had Abbadon, capital of the Galactic Empire. The planet is completely covered by cities and is shrouded in a sickly brown haze. Orbiting the polluted planet is the Green Moon. The film begins with the arrival of Grand Moff Jerjerrod, Vader's rival. Vader joins Jerjerrod aboard his Imperial shuttle, and they discuss the activity taking place on the Green Moon; apparently, Had Abbadon is over-populated, and according to Jerjerrod, the Green Moon is being cleaned to eventually become a new "paradise." Vader says that he's felt a Rebel presence on the Green Moon; Jerjerrod is offended by this remark, which undermines his authority, and refuses to believe it.

Meanwhile, Leia, a scruffy old pilot, and a young copilot are aboard a stolen Imperial transport and nearly hit Jerjerrod's shuttle. They've come to set up on the Green Moon in preparation for the arrival of the Rebel fleet. They wait anxiously for clearance, afraid that the code they gave might not be current. Leia seems concerned; she heard from Lando that Han is alive, but she still doesn't know how difficult it will be to free him. They identify themselves as "equipment and construction personnel for Moon Base 7" and finally get clearance to get through.

In the revised rough draft, after the opening and the reveal of two Death Stars in construction, we cut to Wedge, the Rebel pilot from the two previous films, who is undercover, flying one of the TIE fighters escorting Vader's Super Star Destroyer. Suddenly his ship begins to wobble; Wedge struggles with the controls and starts panicking. He calls Leia, who is aboard the stolen Imperial transport. Wedge gets out of range, and despite the fact that this may attract attention to them, Leia decides to go after him. The controller from Vader's Star Destroyer calls them, saying that they're moving out of their flight path. The controller is suspicious and asks for the security code. While they wait for clearance, Wedge's fighter is towed in. As in the previous draft, Leia and the Rebel pilot have a discussion about Han. There's a tense moment when Grand Moff Jerjerrod's shuttle approaches at great speed and Leia thinks it's a boarding party that has come to inspect them.

The sequence involving Vader and Jerjerrod now occurs right after Leia and her party have been given clearance. Their exchange is different from the one in the previous draft; Vader complains that the Emperor has not answered any of his transmissions. Jerjerrod tries to avoid an argument, but Vader wants to know why he has been ordered to return to his home system. Jerjerrod explains that the Emperor is disturbed by Vader's failure to deal with young Skywalker and has decided to handle the matter personally; Vader will now supervise the construction of the battle stations. Of course, Vader is furious. Jerjerrod tells him that it appears he still has feelings for Luke and that the Emperor is the only one who will be able to turn Skywalker to the dark side. In fact, the Emperor already knows that the entire Rebel force is on its way to them. Vader tells Jerjerrod that Luke would not be so foolish as to fall into such a trap; the Grand Moff says that Luke is on his home planet of Tatooine but will soon be in the hands of the Emperor. The Grand Moff leaves Vader standing alone on the bridge.

During story conferences, to simplify things Lawrence Kasdan suggested that there be only one Death Star as opposed to two. George Lucas eventually decided that the idea of Had Abbadon be dropped and that the Emperor should come to the Death Star to supervise its completion and direct the attack on the Rebel fleet.

In the second draft and as suggested during the story meetings, there's only one Death Star; there's no more Had Abbadon, and the Green Moon is called Jus-Endor. In this draft the Death Star commander doesn't have a name (he eventually became Jerjerrod in the revised second draft) and is described as a tall, confident technocrat.

Walking toward them out of the darkness is Bib Fortuna, a humanlike alien with long tentacles protruding from his skull.
BIB: Die Wanna Wanga!

Nilo Rodis-Jamero: "Bib Fortuna is one of those people I consider someone who aspires to have power but who in reality doesn't have any. He wears metal on his costume to let people know that he is powerful. In my drawings I gave him a refined, feminine posture, and he wears a cloak and some kind of armor. Then [makeup and creature designer] Phil Tippett gave him a brain that kind of hangs around. I thought the marriage between the two concepts was perfect. I think it was also Phil who gave him those weird teeth, you know, like a saw."

THREEPIO: Oh, my! Die Wanna Wauaga. We—we bring a message to your master, Jabba the Hutt.
Artoo lets out a series of quick beeps.
THREEPIO: *(continuing)* . . . and a gift. *(thinks for a moment, then to Artoo)* Gift, what gift?
Bib shakes his head negatively.
BIB: Nee labba no badda. Me chaade su goodie.
Bib holds out his hands toward Artoo, and the tiny droid backs up a bit, letting out a protesting array of squeaks. Threepio turns to the strange-looking alien.
THREEPIO: He says that our instructions are to give it only to Jabba himself!
Bib thinks about this for a moment.
THREEPIO: I'm terribly sorry. I'm afraid he's ever so stubborn about these sort of things.
Bib gestures for the droids to follow.
BIB: Nudd Chaa.
The droids follow the tall, tentacled alien into the darkness, trailed by the two guards.
THREEPIO: Artoo, I have a bad feeling about this.
INT. JABBA'S THRONE ROOM
The throne room is filled with the vilest, most grotesque creatures ever conceived in the universe. Artoo and Threepio seem very small as they pause in the doorway to the dimly lit chamber.

Light shafts partially illuminate the drunken courtiers as Bib Fortuna crosses the room to the platform upon which rests the leader of this nauseating crowd: Jabba the Hutt. The monarch of the galactic underworld is a repulsive blob of bloated fat with a maniacal grin.

Ralph McQuarrie: "In my sketches Jabba was huge, agile, sort of an apelike figure. But then the design went in another direction, and Jabba became more like a worm kind of creature."

Nilo Rodis-Jamero: "My vision of Jabba was literally Orson Welles when he was older. I saw him as a very refined man. Most of the villains we like are very smart people. But Phil Tippett kept imagining him as some kind of slug, almost like in *Alice in Wonderland*. At one time he sculpted a creature that looked like a slug that's smoking. I kept thinking I must be really off, but eventually that's where it led up to."

Phil Tippett: "There was a lot of talk about Jabba, but I think that the initial direction from George was something like a very big Sydney Greenstreet. There were at least eight different designs that I played around with before George settled on what finally became the Jabba you see in the film."

Duwayne Dunham: "During filming, [director] Richard Marquand [1938–1987] did the voice for Jabba with that Shakespearean voice of his. So we had a guide track for the editing, but we had to be careful to make the shots long enough so that the audience would have time to read the subtitles. At the same time we had to make sure that the sequence had some internal rhythm to it. I remember George saying one day, 'Threepio is out of synch.' I said, 'What do you mean Threepio is out of synch? He doesn't even have a mouth!' But you know, it was true, and it was very important to George that every little inflection, any kind of body movement coming from the robots and the different creatures, be put with the right syllables."

Chained to the horrible creature is the beautiful alien dancer named Oola. At the foot of the dais sits an obnoxious birdlike creature, Salacious Crumb. Bib whispers something in the slobbering degenerate's ear. Jabba laughs horribly at the two terrified droids before him. Threepio bows politely.

THREEPIO: Good morning. The message, Artoo, the message.

JABBA: Bo Shuda!

*Artoo whistles, and a beam of light projects from his domed head, creating a holo-
gram of Luke on the floor.*

*The image grows to over ten feet tall, and the young Jedi towers over the space
gangsters.*

LUKE: Greetings, Exalted One. Allow me to introduce myself. I am Luke Skywalker, Jedi Knight and friend to Captain Solo. I know that you are powerful,
mighty Jabba, and that your anger with Solo must be equally powerful. I seek
an audience with Your Greatness to bargain for Solo's life. *(Jabba's crowd
laughs)* With your wisdom, I'm sure that we can work out an arrangement
which will be mutually beneficial and enable us to avoid any unpleasant confrontation. As a token of my goodwill, I present to you a gift: these two droids.

Threepio is startled by this announcement.

THREEPIO: What did he say?

LUKE: *(continuing)* Both are hardworking and will serve you well.

THREEPIO: This can't be! Artoo, you're playing the wrong message.

Luke's hologram disappears.
  Bib speaks to Jabba in Huttese.

JABBA: *(in Huttese subtitled)* There will be no bargain.

THREEPIO: We're doomed.

JABBA: *(in Huttese subtitled)* I will not give up my favorite decoration. I like
Captain Solo where he is.

*Jabba looks toward an alcove beside the throne. Hanging high, flat against the
wall, exactly as we saw him last, is a carbonized Han Solo.*

THREEPIO: Artoo, look! Captain Solo. And he's still frozen in carbonite.

INT. DUNGEON CORRIDOR

*One of Jabba's Gamorrean guards marches Artoo and Threepio down a dark,
shadowy passageway lined with holding cells. The cries of unspeakable creatures
bounce off the cold stone walls. Occasionally a repulsive arm or tentacle grabs
through the bars at the hapless droids.*

THREEPIO: What could possibly have come over Master Luke? Is it something I did? He never expressed any unhappiness with my work. Oh! Oh! How
horrid!

A large tentacle wraps around Threepio's neck.

THREEPIO: Ohh!

*He manages to break free. Artoo beeps pitifully, and they move on to a door at the
end of the corridor.*

INT. BOILER ROOM

*The door slides open, revealing a room filled with steam and noisy machinery.
The guard has motioned them into the boiler room, where a power droid is upside
down. As smoking brands are pressed into his feet, the stubby robot lets out an
agonized electronic scream. Threepio cringes. They are met by a tall, thin humanlike robot named EV-9D9 (Eve-Ninedenine).*

NINEDENINE: Ah, good. New acquisitions. You are a protocol droid, are you not?

THREEPIO: I am See-Threepio, Human Cy—

NINEDENINE: Yes or no will do.

THREEPIO: Oh. Well, yes.

NINEDENINE: How many languages do you speak?

THREEPIO: I am fluent in over six million forms of communication and can readily—

NINEDENINE: Splendid! We have been without an interpreter since our master got angry with our last protocol droid and disintegrated him.

THREEPIO: Disintegrated?

NINEDENINE: *(to a Gamorrean guard)* Guard! This protocol droid might be useful. Fit him with a restraining bolt and take him back up to His Excellency's main audience chamber.

The guard shoves Threepio toward the door.

THREEPIO: *(disappearing)* Artoo, don't leave me! Ohhh!

Artoo lets out a plaintive cry as the door closes. Then he beeps angrily.

NINEDENINE: You're a feisty little one, but you'll soon learn some respect. I have need for you on the master's sail barge. And I think you'll fill in nicely.

The poor work droid in the background lets out another tortured electronic scream.

In the rough draft Luke is asleep and struggling with thoughts of Vader and the dark side. Yoda and Ben are also present in the dream, and Luke berates Ben for not telling him that Vader is his father. Yoda explains that soon he'll be joining Ben in the Netherworld, and therefore he'll become stronger and will be better able to help Luke. Vader's voice reappears, and Luke awakes. He has been staying on Tatooine in a peasant hovel with two strange-looking creatures (Del Andues). Suddenly the droids, Chewie, and Lando enter. Lando explains that many travelers have arrived for Han's execution. Han has obviously been taken out of carbon freeze and it's time for Luke to plan Han's rescue; he kneels before Artoo and records a message for Jabba. The idea is for the droids to deliver the message to Jabba and later Chewie and Lando will bring him a phony "spice extractor" and promise him more in exchange for Han Solo.

As in the movie, the droids get to the iron gates of Jabba's palace, and the spidery mechanical arm with a large electronic eyeball inspects them and lets them in. They're escorted by two green giant scaly guards to Bib Fortuna, the High Beeser of Hoth, a wizened old man dressed in a dark cloak and tall hat. Bib takes them to Jabba, who is described as the godfather of the galactic crime world; he is a repulsively fat, sultanlike monster and is surrounded by the most grotesque and vile creatures in the universe. A note explains that Jabba speaks in Huttese, but his actual dialogue on the page is in English. Artoo delivers the message, and Jabba refuses to let Han Solo go, but he takes the droids anyway.

Artoo and Threepio are taken to the boiler room; there a tall, thin humanlike robot named U-8D8 (Eue-Atedeate), chief of cyborg operations, hires Threepio to be Jabba's protocol droid. Artoo will dispense drinks and clean (the robot became EV-8D8 [EVE-ATE-DATE] in the revised second draft and was called EV-9D9 [EVE-NINEDNINE] in the third draft).

In the revised rough draft we left Vader alone on the bridge of his ship after his confrontation with Grand Moff Jerjerrod, and he reaches Luke in his sleep. There is, however, no dream sequence in this version of the script. Instead, Luke wakes up in a small, run-down tavern and the Del Andue creatures from the previous draft have been replaced by "two vile, little dirty Jawas, Atetu and Tweetu." The sequence is very similar to the previous draft except for Lando's dialogue: He explains to Luke that Han survived the unfreezing process but that he couldn't get any report on Han's condition. They must hurry to save Han before his execution, which has been set for the following day.

INT. JABBA'S THRONE ROOM

The court of Jabba the Hutt is in the midst of a drunken, raucous party. Sloppy, smelly monsters cheer and make rude noises as Oola and a fat female dancer perform in front of Jabba's throne.

Jabba leers at the dancers and with a lustful gleam in his eye beckons Oola to come and sit with him. She stops dancing and backs away, shaking her head. Jabba gets angry and points to a spot next to him.

From the Special Edition:

The court of Jabba the Hutt is in the midst of a drunken, raucous party. Sloppy, smelly monsters cheer and make rude noises as Oola and a large six-breasted female dancer perform in front of Jabba's throne. Jabba's alien band plays a wildly rhythmic tune on reeds, drums, and other exotic instruments. The Hutt rocks and swings in time with the music and toys with Oola's leash. The song comes to a close, and the audience applauds.

George Lucas: "The scene in Jabba's palace was supposed to have a big musical number, but unfortunately, we ended up with only a couple of shots. Now, thanks to digital technology, we're able to turn this scene into the real musical number that it was supposed to be in the first place. John Williams is doing a new score for the end music and felt it was okay to have someone else do the musical number because it is so different from the rest of the score."

Rick McCallum: "We've added more musicians to the band; we have about eleven of them now. We have three backup singers, Sy Snootles moves like Mick Jagger, and there's an alien male singer next to her who sounds like Joe Cocker. We have a drummer with eight arms, a guitar player, etc. . . . The whole number is about two minutes now."

There's no party in the rough draft; in its place, Jabba is holding court and Threepio translates for a weathered old star captain who has come to collect money. Jabba refuses to pay him, and the old captain pulls out his gun, but before he can fire, he falls through a trapdoor in the floor: "A rumble is heard, then muffled growls and a hideous scream." Next on line are Chewie and Lando, who bring to Jabba the "Durellian spice extractor." Jabba takes Luke's gift but takes both Lando and Chewie prisoner, saying that now he can ask for twice the ransom. The two prisoners are taken to a cell and are reunited with a bearded Han Solo. (Remember, here Solo has already been taken out of carbon freeze.) Han wants to strangle Lando until Lando explains that he rescued Leia and Chewie and now has come to rescue Han; Luke will soon arrive. Like in the film, Solo makes a snide comment, wondering how a kid who can't take care of himself could rescue them from this mess. The party at Jabba's palace first appeared in the revised second draft.

JABBA: Da Eitha!
The lovely alien shakes her head again and screams.
OOLA: Na Chuba negtorie Na! Na! Natoota . . .
Jabba is furious and pulls her toward him, tugging on the chain.
JABBA: Boscka!

He pushes a button, and before the dancer can flee, a trapdoor in the floor springs open and swallows her up. As the door snaps shut, a muffled growl is followed by a hideous scream. Jabba and his monstrous friends laugh hysterically, and several revelers hurry over to watch her fate through a grate.

From the Special Edition:
Jabba slams his fist down on a button, and before the dancer can flee, a trapdoor in the floor springs open and swallows her up. As the door snaps shut, a muffled growl is followed by a hideous scream. Jabba and his monstrous friends laugh hysterically, and several revelers hurry over to watch her fate through a grate. Oola tumbles down a chute and sprawls on the floor of the rancor cage.

Threepio cringes and glances wistfully at the carbonite form of Han Solo but is distracted by a gunshot offscreen. An unnatural quiet sweeps the boisterous gathering.

On the far side of the room the crush of debauchers moves aside to allow the approach of Boushh, an oddly cloaked bounty hunter, leading his captive, Han Solo's copilot, Chewbacca the Wookiee.

The bounty hunter bows before the gangster and speaks a greeting in a strange, electronically processed tongue (Ubese).

BOUSHH: *(in Ubese subtitled)* I have come for the bounty on this Wookiee.
THREEPIO: Oh, no! Chewbacca!
JABBA: *(in Huttese subtitled)* At last we have the mighty Chewbacca.
Jabba calls for Threepio. The reluctant droid obeys.
THREEPIO: Oh, uh, yes, uh, I am here, Your Worshipfulness. Uh . . . yes!
Jabba continues speaking, as Threepio nervously translates.
THREEPIO: Oh. The illustrious Jabba bids you welcome and will gladly pay you the reward of twenty-five thousand.

BOUSHH: *[in Ubese subtitled]* I want fifty thousand. No less.

THREEPIO: Fifty thousand. No less.

Jabba immediately flies into a rage, knocking the golden droid off the raised throne into a clattering heap on the floor.

Boushh adjusts his weapon as Jabba raves in Huttese and Threepio struggles back onto the throne. The disheveled droid tries to compose himself.

THREEPIO: Oh, oh . . . but what, what did I say? *[to Boushh]* Uh, the mighty Jabba asks why he must pay fifty thousand.

The bounty hunter holds up a small silver ball in his hand.

THREEPIO: Because he's holding a thermal detonator.

Threepio is very nervous. The guards instantly back away, as do most of the other monsters in the room. But Boba Fett raises his gun. The room has fallen into a tense hush. Jabba begins to laugh.

JABBA: *[in Huttese subtitled]* This bounty hunter is my kind of scum, fearless and inventive.

Jabba continues.

THREEPIO: Jabba offers the sum of thirty-five. And I do suggest you take it.

Bib and the other monsters study the bounty hunter and wait for his reaction.

BOUSHH: Zeebuss.

Boushh releases a switch on the thermal detonator, and it goes dead.

THREEPIO: He agrees!

The raucous crowd of monsters erupts in a symphony of cheers and applause as the party returns to its full noisy pitch. Chewbacca growls and is led away. The band starts up, and dancing girls take the center of the floor, to the hoots of the loudly appreciative creatures.

Boushh leans against a column with gunfighter cool and surveys the scene, his gaze stopping only when it connects with a glare from across the room: Boba Fett is watching him.

During story meetings Richard Marquand came up with the idea that both Lando and Leia should arrive at Jabba's palace in disguise. He specifically suggested that Leia be dressed up as a bounty hunter but said that the audience should know who she is; Lawrence Kasdan pushed the concept further and suggested that her identity be kept secret from the audience. George Lucas then came up with the idea that the bounty hunter/Leia should have a mechanical voice and speak an alien language. Also, during this sequence Lucas mentioned that he wanted to hint at some kind of jealousy and rivalry between the bounty hunter and Boba Fett.

In an effort to develop the bond between Threepio and Chewie, one of Lucas's ideas was to have Chewie be tortured.

In the second draft Leia is disguised as a bounty hunter by lethal-looking armor that she wears with a helmet. She speaks in electronically processed English and explains to Jabba that she captured Chewbacca in Mos Eisley while he was trying to buy a secret entrance into his palace. Jabba asks the bounty hunter where he is from; Leia/the bounty hunter replies that he is from a place to which he can never return and that this is none of Jabba's business anyway. Jabba laughs, saying this is his kind of scum, and invites the bounty hunter to join the party, hinting that he may have some work for him later on. In the shadows, Boba Fett is watching. In the revised second draft the bounty hunter is now called Boushh and speaks "Ubese." In this sequence Jabba refers to Threepio as a "Talkdroid." The scene is now comparable to the way it was filmed, with Boushh pulling out the thermal detonator.

INT. DUNGEON CORRIDOR AND CELL

Gamorrean guards lead Chewie down the same hallway we saw before. As he is led away, we spot Lando Calrissian disguised as a skiff guard in a partial face mask. When a tentacle reaches out at the Wookiee, Chewie's ferocious roar echoes against the walls and the tentacle snaps back into its cell in terror. It takes both guards to hurl Chewie roughly into a cell, slamming the door behind him.

EXT. JABBA'S PALACE

The palace is sitting in the light of the double sunset. On the road in front a large toadlike creature flicks its tongue out for a desert rodent and burps in satisfaction.

JABBA'S THRONE ROOM—NIGHT

Silence. The room is deserted, only the awful debris of the alien celebration giving mute witness to the activity here before. Several drunk creatures lie unconscious around the room, snoring loudly.

A shadowy figure moves stealthily among the columns at the perimeter of the room and is revealed to be Boushh, the bounty hunter. He picks his way carefully through the snoring, drunken monsters.

Han Solo, the frozen space pirate, hangs spotlighted on the wall, his coffinlike case suspended by a force field. The bounty hunter deactivates the force field by flipping a control switch to one side of the coffin.

The heavy case slowly lowers to the floor of the alcove.

Boushh steps up to the case, studying Han, then turns to the controls on the side of the coffin. He activates a series of switches and slides the decarbonization lever. The case begins to emit a sound as the hard shell covering the contours of Han's face begins to melt away. The bounty hunter watches as Han's body is freed of its metallic coat and his forearms and hands, previously raised in reflexive protest, drop slackly to his side. His face muscles relax from their mask of horror. He appears quite dead.

Boushh's ugly helmet leans close to Han's face, listening for the breath of life.

Nothing. He waits. Han's eyes pop open with a start, and he begins shaking. The bounty hunter steadies the staggering newborn.

BOUSHH: Just relax for a moment. You're free of the carbonite.

Han touches his face with his hand.

BOUSHH: Shhh. You have hibernation sickness.

HAN: I can't see.

BOUSHH: Your eyesight will return in time.

HAN: Where am I?

BOUSHH: Jabba's palace.

HAN: Who are you?

The bounty hunter reaches up and lifts the helmet from his head, revealing the beautiful face of Princess Leia.

LEIA: Someone who loves you.

HAN: Leia!

The idea of showing Han coming out of carbon freeze first appeared in the second draft, but the scene was played differently: first Han falls, looking quite dead. Then Leia takes off her helmet and kisses Han, who then awakes suddenly.

LEIA: I gotta get you out of here.

As Leia helps her weakened lover stand up, the relative quiet is pierced by an obscene Huttese cackle from the other side of the alcove.

HAN: What's that? I know that laugh.

The curtain on the far side of the alcove opens, revealing Jabba the Hutt, surrounded by Bib and other aliens. He laughs again, and his gross cronies join in a cacophony of alien glee.

HAN: Hey, Jabba. Look, Jabba. I was just on my way to pay you back, but I got a little sidetracked. It's not my fault.

Jabba laughs.

JABBA: *(in Huttese subtitled)* It's too late for that, Solo. You may have been a good smuggler, but now you're bantha fodder.

HAN: Look—

JABBA: *(continuing; in Huttese subtitled)* Take him away.

The guards grab Han and start to lead him away.

HAN: Jabba . . . I'll pay you triple! You're throwing away a fortune here. Don't be a fool!

Han is dragged off.

JABBA: *(in Huttese subtitled)* Bring her to me.

Jabba chuckles as Lando and a second guard lead the beautiful young princess toward him.

LEIA: We have powerful friends. You're gonna regret this.

JABBA: *(in Huttese subtitled)* I'm sure.

Inexorably her lovely face moves to within a few inches of Jabba's ugly blob of a head.

LEIA: *(turning away in disgust)* Ugh!

THREEPIO: Ohhh, *(quickly turning away in disgust)* I can't bear to watch.

INT. DUNGEON CELL

The blinded star captain is thrown into the dungeon, and the door slams behind him, leaving only a thin sliver of light from a crack in the ceiling. Han is trying to collect himself, when suddenly a growl is heard from the far side of the cell. He listens.

HAN: Chewie? Chewie, is that you?

The shadowy figure of Chewie lets out a crazy yell and races toward Han, hugging him.

HAN: Chew—Chewie!

The giant Wookiee barks with glee.

HAN: Wait, I can't see, pal. What's goin' on?

Chewie barks an excited blue streak.

HAN: Luke? Luke's crazy. He can't even take care of himself, much less rescue anybody.

Chewie barks a reply.

HAN: A—a Jedi Knight? I'm out of it for a little while, everybody gets delusions of grandeur.

Chewie growls insistently. He holds Han to his chest and pets his head.

HAN: I'm all right, pal. I'm all right.

INT. MAIN GATE AND HALL—JABBA'S PALACE

Noisily, the main gate lifts to flood the blackness with blinding light and reveal the silhouetted figure of Luke Skywalker. He is clad in a robe similar to Ben's and wears neither pistol nor lasersword.

Nilo Rodis-Jamero: "I remember George telling me that in samurai movies costumes say a lot about the characters; the way the costume is folded, the way it's tucked in is very important. So I thought, Luke has become a Jedi; he is more distant, more serious. I thought, What do gunslingers wear when they mean business? They wear black. If you look at Luke's costume, it's all derivative of Japanese designs . . . Ben also wore some kind of Japanese kimono. So I tailored the costume in a way that would allow Luke to fight in the action sequences."

Luke strides purposefully into the hallway. Two giant guards move to block Luke's path. Luke halts.

Luke raises his hand and points at the puzzled guards, who immediately lower their spears and fall back. The young Jedi lowers his hand and moves on down the hallway.

INT. JABBA'S THRONE ROOM

Jabba is asleep on his throne, with Leia lying in front of him. Salacious sits by Jabba's tail, watching it wriggle. Leia is now dressed in the skimpy costume of a dancing girl; a chain runs from a manacle/necklace at her throat to her new master, Jabba the Hutt.

Nilo Rodis-Jamero: "George always talked about a slave girl outfit. I kept thinking, How am I going to do this in style? I mean, this is Leia. I actually struggled with that for a long time, and all I kept coming up with was clunky, Ben Hur kind of stuff. And one day I happened to see a sculpture that I really liked, and as soon as I saw it, I thought my problem was solved. I did full-size wax pieces of the costume, taking dimensions from Carrie Fisher. We tested it on her, it looked great, and that was it."

Threepio stands behind Jabba.

    Bib Fortuna appears out of the gloom. He speaks to Luke as they approach each other.

LUKE: I must speak with Jabba.

Bib answers in Huttese, shaking his head in denial.

INT. JABBA'S THRONE ROOM

Leia looks up in recognition of Luke's voice.

INT. MAIN GATE AND HALL— JABBA'S PALACE

Luke stops and stares at Bib; he raises his hand slightly.

LUKE: You will take me to Jabba now!

Bib turns in hypnotic response to Luke's command, and Luke follows him into the gloom.

LUKE: You serve your master well.

Bib responds.

LUKE: And you will be rewarded.

INT. JABBA'S THRONE ROOM

Bib comes up to the gangster slug.

THREEPIO: At last! Master Luke's come to rescue me!

George Lucas: "Usually, if I like something and I have to drop it, I put it on the shelves and very often end up using it somewhere else later on. The thing about writing is that ideas aren't precious; you have to get over the thought that everything you think up is brilliant. When you think of something, you have to be willing to throw it away. More important than to think up an idea in the first place is to be able to reject it if it doesn't work, if it doesn't fit. You have to be very hard on yourself when you write a script and only use things that are symmetrical to the center of your story. You should never use

BIB: Master.

Jabba awakens with a start, and Bib continues in Huttese.

BIB: Luke Skywalker, Jedi Knight.

JABBA: *(in Huttese subtitled)* I told you not to admit him.

LUKE: I must be allowed to speak.

BIB: *(in Huttese subtitled)* He must be allowed to speak.

Jabba, furious, shoves Bib away. Luke stares hard at Jabba.

JABBA: *(in Huttese subtitled)* You weak-minded fool! *(turning)* He's using an old Jedi mind trick.

LUKE: You will bring Captain Solo and the Wookiee to me.

JABBA: *(laughing) (in Huttese subtitled)* Your mind powers will not work on me, boy.

LUKE: Nevertheless, I'm taking Captain Solo and his friends. You can either profit by this . . . or be destroyed! It's your choice. But I warn you not to underestimate my powers.

an idea just because it's a cute idea."

Duwayne Dunham: "George had a bulletin board in the cutting room where Sean Barton and I were editing the film. The script had been broken down into scenes, and each scene was an index card with a brief description saying, for example, 'Yoda dies' or 'Luke tells Leia she's his sister.' So these cards were on that board, and it wouldn't be uncommon either first thing in the morning or at some point in the day to find George just staring at the board and moving cards around. Basically, the story kept evolving and changing."

Jabba smiles. Threepio attempts to warn Luke about the pit.

THREEPIO: Master Luke, you're standing on . . .

JABBA: *(in Huttese subtitled)* There will be no bargain, young Jedi. I shall enjoy watching you die.

Luke reaches out, and a pistol jumps out of the guard's holster and flies into Luke's hand. The bewildered guard grabs for it as Jabba raises his hand.

JABBA: Boscka!

The floor suddenly drops away, sending Luke and the hapless guard into the pit. The pistol goes off, blasting a hole in the ceiling.

INT. RANCOR PIT

Luke and the guard have dropped twenty-five feet from a chute into the dungeon-like cage. Luke gets to his feet as the guard yells hysterically for help.

INT. JABBA'S THRONE ROOM

Jabba laughs, and his courtiers join him. Leia starts forward but is comforted by a human guard — Lando, recognizable behind his mask.

INT. RANCOR PIT

A crowd has gathered around the edge of the pit as a door in the side of the pit starts to rumble open.

THREEPIO: Oh, no! The rancor!

At the side of the pit, an iron door rumbles upward and a giant fanged rancor emerges. The guard runs to the side of the pit and tries futilely to scramble to the top. The hideous beast closes in on him.

INT. JABBA'S THRONE ROOM

The spectators look on.

INT. RANCOR PIT

The rancor moves past Luke, and as the guard continues to scramble, the rancor picks him up and pops him into its slavering jaws. A few screams, and the guard is swallowed with a gulp.

INT. JABBA'S THRONE ROOM

The audience cheers and laughs at the guard's fate.

INT. RANCOR PIT

The monster turns and starts for Luke.

INT. JABBA'S THRONE ROOM

Jabba smiles.

INT. RANCOR PIT

The young Jedi dashes away just ahead of the monster's swipe at him and picks up the long arm bone of an earlier victim. The monster grabs Luke.

INT. JABBA'S THRONE ROOM

The audience cheers.

INT. RANCOR PIT

The monster brings him up to his salivating mouth.

INT. JABBA'S THRONE ROOM

Leia can hardly bear to watch.

INT. RANCOR PIT

At the last moment Luke wedges the bone in the monster's mouth and is dropped to the floor. The monster bellows in rage and flails about.

The monster crunches the bone in its jaws and sees Luke, who squeezes into a crevice in the pit wall. Luke looks past the monster to the holding cave beyond. On the far side of the holding cave is a utility door—if only he can get to it. The rancor spots Luke and reaches into the crevice for him. Luke grabs a large rock and raises it, smashing it down on the rancor's finger.

INT. HOLDING TUNNEL—RANCOR PIT

The rancor lets out a howl as Luke makes a run for the holding cave. He reaches the door and pushes a button to open it. When he succeeds, he sees a heavy barred gate between him and safety. Beyond the gate two guards have looked up from their dinner. Luke turns to see the monster heading for him and pulls with all his might on the gate. The guards move to the gate and start poking at the young Jedi with spears, laughing.

INT. JABBA'S THRONE ROOM

The audience is mad with excitement.

INT. HOLDING TUNNEL—RANCOR PIT

Luke crouches (against the wall) as the monster starts to reach for him. Suddenly he notices a main door control panel halfway up the wall. As the rancor moves in *for the kill, Luke picks up a skull from the cave floor and hurls it at the panel. A split second before the rancor reaches Luke, the panel explodes. The giant overhead door comes crashing down on the beast's head, squashing it.*

In the second draft, as in the movie, Luke arrives at Jabba's chamber. Jabba is not intimidated and says that in his time he's killed many Jedi Knights. Luke reaches out his hand, and a pistol jumps out of one of the guard's holsters, flying magically into Luke's hand. But before he can use the weapon, he falls through the floor into the rancor pit; the creature is described as a giant brown fanged monster. Luke tries to get out through a grate, but "two filthy little Jawas" hit his fingers with the butts of their laser rifles. Luke falls back in the pit and manages to hit a switch, and the heavy door comes crashing down on the rancor.

In the second draft, as in the movie, Lando is in disguise among Jabba's guards. After Luke has arrived in the throne room, Threepio recognizes Lando and draws attention to him. Immediately, Luke raises his hands and Threepio's voice degenerates to garbled static. Jabba, of course, realizes that something is wrong and gets suspicious. Luke reaches out, and a pistol jumps out of a guard's holster and flies into his hands. A trapdoor opens, and as in the film, both Luke and the guard fall into the pit.

INT. THRONE ROOM

A startled gasp is heard from the stunned court. There's consternation at this turn of events. Heads look to Jabba, who is actually turning red with anger.

INT. HOLDING TUNNEL—RANCOR PIT

The beast breathes its last.

INT. THRONE ROOM

Leia cannot suppress her joy.

INT. RANCOR PIT

The rancor keepers have come into the cage and are examining their dead beast. One of them breaks down and weeps. The other glares menacingly at Luke, who is unworried. Several guards rush into the holding tunnel and take Luke away.

INT. THRONE ROOM

Jabba utters harsh commands to his guards, and they hurry off.

JABBA: (in Huttese subtitled) Bring me Solo and the Wookiee. They will all suffer for this outrage.

INT. RANCOR PIT

The weeping rancor keeper is consoled and led away.

INT. THRONE ROOM

The crowd of creepy courtiers parts as Han and Chewie are brought into the throne room, and other guards, including Lando, drag Luke up the steps.

LUKE: Han!

HAN: Luke!

LUKE: Are you all right?

HAN: Fine. Together again, huh?

LUKE: Wouldn't miss it.

HAN: How are we doing?

LUKE: The same as always.

HAN: That bad, huh? Where's Leia?

LEIA: I'm here.

Threepio is standing behind the grotesque gangster as he strokes Leia like a pet cat.

Threepio steps forward and translates for the captives.

THREEPIO: Oh, dear. His High Exaltedness, the great Jabba the Hutt, has decreed that you are to be terminated immediately.

HAN: Good. I hate long waits.

THREEPIO: You will therefore be taken to the Dune Sea and cast into the Pit of Carkoon, the nesting place of the all-powerful Sarlacc.

HAN: *(to Luke)* Doesn't sound so bad.

THREEPIO: In his belly you will find a new definition of pain and suffering as you are slowly digested over a thousand years.

Chewie barks.

HAN: On second thought, let's pass on that, huh?

LUKE: You should have bargained, Jabba. That's the last mistake you'll ever make.

Jabba cackles evilly at this.

As the guards drag the prisoners from the throne room, Leia looks concerned, but Luke Skywalker, Jedi warrior, cannot suppress a smile.

In the rough draft Han, Chewie, and Lando are in their cell. Before they're brought to Jabba, Artoo discreetly opens one of his small doors and reveals two small blasters. Solo and Lando grab the weapons, hide them, and are taken to Jabba. They're put on trial with Luke, and Jabba orders that they be taken to the "Sloth Pit." Han is upset at Luke and calls his plan stupid; now, he says, they're all going to die. The only difference in the revised rough draft is that Artoo doesn't carry hidden weapons. In the second draft, however, the scene is a bit longer, with more humorous dialogue between

Luke and Han. Luke, for example, says that the only reason he managed to kill the rancor is that it was a "small one." Also, Han, who can't see anything as a result of being in carbon freeze, says, "I'll believe it when I see it, if you'll excuse the expression," about Luke having supposedly become a strong Jedi warrior.

From the Special Edition:
EXT. TATOOINE DUNE SEA
A herd of wild banthas trek across Tatooine's dunes.

EXT. TATOOINE DUNE SEA
Jabba's huge sail barge moves above the desert surface, accompanied by two smaller skiffs.
INT. BARGE OBSERVATION DECK
Jabba's entire retinue is traveling with him, drinking, eating, and having a good time.
EXT. TATOOINE DUNE SEA
The sail barge and skiffs continue their journey.

Joe Johnston: "On one level, the barge and the skiffs are very archaic. They had to look almost as if they were pleasure craft with decorative elements, yet they had to be high-tech vehicles that could float over land. The barge was designed before the skiffs, and the skiffs are almost like lifeboats from the barge. I wanted both vehicles to look alike, to have similar designs . . . They had to look like they had been built by the same culture."

INT. BARGE OBSERVATION DECK
Jabba the Hutt rides like a sultan in the massive antigravity ship. Leia is watching her friends in one of the skiffs.
EXT. TATOOINE DUNE SEA—SKIFF
The skiff glides close, revealing Luke, Han, and Chewie—all in bonds—surrounded by guards, one of whom is Lando in disguise.
HAN: I think my eyes are getting better. Instead of a big dark blur, I see a big light blur.
LUKE: There's nothing to see. I used to live here, you know.
HAN: You're gonna die here, you know. Convenient.
LUKE: Just stick close to Chewie and Lando. I've taken care of everything.
HAN: Oh . . . great!
INT. BARGE OBSERVATION DECK

The chain attached to Leia's neck is pulled tight, and Jabba tugs the scantily clad princess to him.

JABBA: *(in Huttese subtitled)* Soon you will learn to appreciate me.

Threepio wanders among the sail barge aliens, bumping into a smaller droid serving drinks, spilling them all over the place. The stubby droid lets out an angry series of beeps and whistles.

THREEPIO: Oh, I'm terribly sor . . . Artoo! What are you doing here?

Artoo beeps a quick reply.

THREEPIO: Well, I can see you're serving drinks, but this place is dangerous. They're going to execute Master Luke and, if we're not careful, us, too!

Artoo whistles a singsong response.

THREEPIO: Hmm. I wish I had your confidence.

In the second draft there's a brief scene with Threepio translating for two drunken aliens; the larger of the two aliens is called Ephant Mon and has a small monkeylike reptile sitting on his shoulder called Salacious Crumb, who repeats everything the monster says. The other alien, Ree-Yees, is a three-eyed creature. Ephant Mon insults Ree-Yees, whose three eyes narrow angrily; Ree slugs Ephant in the snout, knocking him over and sending his partner, Salacious, flying. Threepio, who has been translating for the two droids, takes this as a sign to leave and bumps into Artoo, who is serving drinks.

EXT. SARLACC PIT

The convoy moves up over a huge sand pit. The sail barge stops to one side of the depression, as does the escort skiff. But the prisoners' skiff moves out directly over the center and hovers. A plank is extended from the edge of the prisoners' skiff. At the bottom of the deep cone of sand is a repulsive, mucous-lined hole surrounded by thousands of needle-sharp teeth. This is the Sarlacc. Guards release Luke's bonds and shove him out onto the plank above the Sarlacc's mouth.

INT. SAIL BARGE OBSERVATION DECK

Jabba and Leia are now by the rail, watching.

Lawrence Kasdan: "When I wrote the script for *Raiders of the Lost Ark*, I took a lot of pride in making everything make sense, and you could follow the action as you read it. It didn't just say on the page: 'They fight.' In both *Empire* and *Jedi* the production was well along in the model making when I started writing. But once I had written an action scene, George would go through it and decide what special ef-

EXT. SAIL BARGE

Threepio's voice is amplified across loudspeakers.

THREEPIO: Victims of the almighty Sarlacc: His Excellency hopes that you will die honorably. But should any of you wish to beg for mercy . . .

INT. SAIL BARGE OBSERVATION DECK

Bib listens gleefully.

EXT. SAIL BARGE

THREEPIO: . . . the great Jabba the Hutt will now listen to your pleas.

INT. SAIL BARGE OBSERVATION DECK

Jabba waits as Artoo zips unnoticed up the ramp to the upper deck.

EXT. SKIFF

Han steps forward arrogantly and begins to speak.

HAN: Threepio, you tell that slimy piece of worm-ridden filth he'll get no such pleasure from us. Right?

Chewie growls his agreement. Artoo appears on the upper deck of the sail barge.

LUKE: Jabba! This is your last chance. Free us or die.

INT. SAIL BARGE OBSERVATION DECK

The assembled monsters rock with mocking laughter. Jabba's laughter subsides as he speaks into the com-link.

JABBA: *(in Huttese subtitled)* Move him into position.

EXT. SKIFF—PLANK

Luke is prodded by a guard to the edge of the plank over the gaping Sarlacc! He exchanges nods with Lando.

EXT. BARGE—UPPER DECK

Artoo is at the rail, facing the pit.

fects they were capable of doing. Very often George would describe to me what the battles were going to look like and give me a lot of details for the script."

Duwayne Dunham: "The scene at the Sarlacc pit was very difficult to edit. Everybody had their hands in it. Sean Barton put it together, I worked on it, George worked on it. There was a lot going on in the sequence; you had Han regaining his eyesight, you had Leia chained to Jabba . . . Then you also had to show what was going on with the droids, Luke, Lando, Chewie, and Boba Fett. A sequence like this has to be put together like a puzzle, and you have to make sure that you pay attention to each of the pieces but that you keep the momentum going. By the time we finished the sequence and sent it to the negative cutter, I remember we got this call from the lab saying that the reel had more cuts in it than most movies!"

George Lucas: "When you're editing, you're dealing with the reality of the film. And cinematically, things are very

EXT. SKIFF—PLANK

Han looks around for a way out of their plight.

INT. SAIL BARGE OBSERVATION DECK

Leia looks worried.

EXT. SKIFF PLANK

Luke looks up at Artoo, then gives a jaunty salute: the signal the little droid has been waiting for.

EXT. BARGE—UPPER DECK

A flap opens in Artoo's domed head.

INT. SAIL BARGE OBSERVATION DECK

JABBA: *(in Huttese subtitled)* Put him in.

EXT. SKIFF—PLANK

Luke is prodded and jumps off the plank to the cheers of the bloodthirsty spectators. But before anyone can even perceive what is happening, he spins around and grabs the end of the plank by his fingertips. The plank bends wildly from his weight and catapults him skyward.

EXT. BARGE—UPPER DECK

Artoo sends Luke's lightsaber arcing toward him.

EXT. SKIFF

In midair he does a complete flip and drops down into the skiff. He casually extends an open palm—and his lightsaber drops into his hand.

With samurai speed, Luke ignites it and attacks the guards. The other guards swarm toward Luke. He wades into them, lightsaber flashing.

EXT. SARLACC PIT

A guard falls overboard, lands in the soft, sandy slope of the pit, and begins sliding into the pit.

INT. SAIL BARGE

Jabba watches this and explodes in rage. He barks commands, and the guards around him rush off to do his bidding. The scuzzy creatures watch-

different from the way you originally had them on the page. Words and images are two different things because cinema really involves movement and sound and there're a lot of elements that you can't express on paper because you're dealing with two different mediums. It's not the same grammar. For example, on the barge there's a sequence where Boba Fett gets knocked over, and we didn't really have the right shot to make the sequence work, so I reversed one shot of Boba Fett falling down and made it look like he was getting up."

Lawrence Kasdan: "In the Sarlacc sequence I thought we should have one of the heroes go down to prove the Sarlacc was for real. I suggested that Lando be killed, but George didn't want anyone to die except for the villains. I thought it would have been a real surprise to the audience if someone we cared about died and had been killed by the Empire."

Duwayne Dunham: "The explosion of the barge was a great moment, and during the editing we kept trying to extend

ing the action from the window are in
an uproar.

the scene; we kept adding tail to it to make sure it had a lot of impact."

EXT. SKIFF

Luke knocks another guard off the skiff and into the waiting mouth of the Sarlacc. He starts to untie Chewie's bonds.

LUKE: Easy, Chewie.

EXT. UPPER DECK—SAIL BARGE

The deck gunmen on the barge set up a cannon on the upper deck.

EXT. SKIFF

Lando struggles with a guard at the back of the skiff.

EXT. UPPER DECK—SAIL BARGE

At that moment a deck gunman unleashes a blast from his cannon.

EXT. SKIFF

Lando is tossed from the deck of the rocking skiff. He manages to grab a rope and dangles desperately above the Sarlacc pit.

LANDO: Whoa! Whoa! Help!

EXT. UPPER DECK—SAIL BARGE

With two swift strides the dangerous Boba Fett ignites his rocket pack, leaps into the air, and flies from the barge down to the skiff.

EXT. SKIFF

Boba lands on the skiff and starts to aim his laser gun at Luke, who has freed Han and Chewie from their bonds. But before Boba can fire, the young Jedi spins on him, lightsaber sweeping, and hacks the bounty hunter's gun in half.
　　Immediately, the skiff takes another direct hit from the barge's deck gun. Shards of skiff deck fly. Chewie and Han are thrown against the rail.

HAN: Chewie, you okay? Where is he?

The Wookiee is wounded, and he howls in pain.
　　For a moment Luke is distracted, and in that moment Boba fires a cable out of his armored sleeve. Instantly, Luke is wrapped in a strong cable, his arms pinned against his sides.

EXT. UPPER DECK—SAIL BARGE

The deck gunman continues to blast the skiff with his cannon.

EXT. SKIFF

Luke's sword arm is free only from the wrist down. He bends his wrist so the light-saber points straight up to reach the wire lasso and cuts through. Luke shrugs away the cable and stands free.
　　Another blast from the barge's deck gun hits near Boba, and he is knocked unconscious to the deck, next to where Lando is hanging.

LANDO: Han! Chewie?

HAN: Lando!

Luke is a little shaken but remains standing as a fusillade brackets him. The second skiff, loaded with guards firing their weapons, moves in on Luke fast. Luke

*leaps toward the incoming second skiff. The young Jedi leaps into the middle of
the second skiff and begins decimating the guards from their midst.*

*Chewie, wounded, has barked directions to Han, guiding him toward a spear
that has been dropped by one of the guards. Finally, Han grabs hold of the spear.*

*Boba Fett, badly shaken, rises from the deck. He looks over at the other skiff,
where Luke is whipping a mass of guards. Boba raises his arm and aims his lethal
appendage.*

Chewie barks desperately to Han.

HAN: Boba Fett?! Where?

*The space pirate turns around blindly, and the long spear in his hand whacks
squarely in the middle of Boba's rocket pack.*

*The impact of the swing causes the rocket pack to ignite. Boba blasts off, flying
over the second skiff like a missile, smashing against the side of the huge sail
barge, and sliding away into the air. He screams as his armored body makes its
last flight past Lando and directly into the mucous mouth of the Sarlacc. The Sarlacc burps.*

Originally George Lucas envisioned a fight between Boba Fett and
Lando but eventually suggested instead that the power pack on
Boba's back should be hit and thrown around, as if he had "a bal-
loon on his back that got air out of it."

INT. SAIL BARGE

*Leia wrecks the power supply, throwing the observation deck into darkness, then
leaps onto Jabba's throne and throws the chain that enslaves her over his head,
around his bulbous neck. Then she dives off the other side of the throne, pulling
the chain violently in her grasp. Jabba's flaccid neck contracts beneath the tight-
ening chain. His huge eyes bulge from the sockets, and his scum-coated tongue
flops out.*

During story conferences Lawrence Kasdan suggested that Leia
should kill Jabba, and George Lucas came up with the idea that she
should strangle him with the chain in a scene reminiscent of *The
Godfather*, in which a large man is garroted.

EXT. SKIFF

*Luke continues to destroy the aliens on the guards' skiff as Han extends his spear
downward to Lando, who is still dangling precariously from a rope on the prisoners' skiff.*

HAN: Lando, grab it!

LANDO: Lower it!

HAN: I'm trying!

INT. SAIL BARGE

The Exalted Hutt's huge tail spasms through its death throes and then slams down into final stillness.

EXT. SKIFF

A major hit from the barge deck gun knocks the skiff on its side. Han and almost everything else on board slides overboard. The rope breaks, and Lando falls to the side of the Sarlacc pit. Luckily, Han's foot catches on the skiff railing, and he dangles above Lando and the pit. The wounded Wookiee holds on to the skiff for dear life.

HAN: Whoa! Whoa! Whoa! Grab me, Chewie! I'm slipping.

Chewie grabs hold of Han's feet, holding him upside down as Han extends the spear toward Lando, who is clutching the side of the pit.

    Luke has finished off the last guard on the second skiff. He sees the deck gun blasting away at his helpless companions.

EXT. UPPER DECK—SAIL BARGE

The deck gunner continues to blast away.

EXT. SKIFF

Luke leaps from the skiff, across the chasm of air, to the sheer metallic side of the sail barge. Barely able to get a fingerhold, he is about to begin a painful climb up the hull, when suddenly an alien comes through a hatch inches from his head. With Jedi agility, Luke grasps the wrist holding the gun and yanks the helpless guard through the hatch and into the deadly pit.

    The injured Chewie is still reaching over the rail for the dangling Han, who is, in turn, still blindly reaching down toward the desperate Lando. The Baron has stopped his slippage down the sandy slope of the Sarlacc pit by lying very still.

HAN: Grab it! Almost . . . You almost got it!

EXT. UPPER DECK—SAIL BARGE

The deck gunner fires again.

EXT. SKIFF

The blast hits the front of the tilted skiff, causing Lando to let go of the spear.

LANDO: Hold it! Whoa!

EXT. UPPER DECK

The deck gunners have Chewie and the desperate dangling human chain in the gun sights when something up on deck commands their attention. Luke, standing before them like a pirate king, ignites his lightsaber. The deck gunners have barely reached for their pistols before the young Jedi has demolished them.

EXT. SKIFF

Again Han extends the spear toward Lando.

HAN: Gently now. All . . . all right. Easy. Hold me, Chewie.

Lando screams. One of the Sarlacc's tentacles has wrapped itself tightly around his ankle, dragging him down the side of the pit.

HAN: Chewie!

EXT. UPPER DECK—SAIL BARGE

Luke continues to hold the upper deck against all comers.

EXT. SKIFF

HAN: Chewie, give me the gun. Don't move, Lando.

LANDO: No, wait! I thought you were blind!

HAN: It's all right. Trust me. Don't move.

LANDO: A little higher! Just a little higher!

Han adjusts his aim as Lando lowers his head, and the fuzzy-eyed pirate fires at the tentacle. Direct hit. The tentacle releases Lando.

HAN: Chewie, pull us up! All right . . . up, Chewie, up!

Chewie starts to pull them on board the skiff.

INT. SAIL BARGE—OBSERVATION DECK

Artoo extends a small laser gun and blasts Leia's chain apart.

LEIA: Come on. We gotta get out of here.

Artoo and Leia race for the exit, passing Threepio, who is kicking and screaming as Salacious Crumb, the reptilian monkey-monster, picks out one of the golden droid's eyes.

In the second draft, while Artoo is dealing with Salacious Crumb, Threepio struggles with a huge monster called Hermi Odle who is sitting on him.

THREEPIO: Not my eyes! Artoo, help! Quickly, Artoo. Oh! Ohhh!

Artoo zips over and zaps Salacious, sending him skyward, with a scream, into the rafters.

THREEPIO: Beast!

EXT. SKIFF

On board the skiff Chewie and Lando are helping Han up.

EXT. UPPER DECK—SAIL BARGE

Luke is warding off laser blasts with his lightsaber, surrounded by guards and fighting like a demon. Leia emerges on to the deck as Luke turns to face another guard.

LUKE: *(to Leia)* Get the gun! Point it at the deck!

Leia turns toward the barge cannon, climbs on the platform, and swivels the gun around.

LUKE: Point it at the deck!

A laserblast hits Luke's mechanical hand, and he bends over in pain but manages to swing his lightsaber upward and take out the last of the guards.

Near the rail of the upper deck Artoo and Threepio steady themselves as Threepio gets ready to jump. Artoo beeps wildly.

THREEPIO: Artoo, where are we going? I couldn't possibly jump . . .

Artoo butts the golden droid over the edge and steps off himself, tumbling toward the sand.

Luke runs along the empty deck toward Leia and the barge gun, which she has brought around to point down at the deck.

LUKE: Come on!

Luke has hold of one of the rigging ropes from the mast. He gathers Leia in his other arm and kicks the trigger of the deck gun. The gun explodes into the deck as Luke and Leia swing out toward the skiff.

EXT. SKIFF

Han is tending to the wounded Chewie as Luke and Leia land on the skiff with flair.

LUKE: Let's go! And don't forget the droids.

LANDO: We're on our way.

The sail barge is exploding in stages in the distance. Half of the huge craft is on fire.

EXT. SAND DUNE

Artoo's periscope sticks up from the dune where he landed. Next to it, Threepio's legs are the only things above sand. As the skiff floats above them, two large electromagnets dangle down on a wire. Both droids are pulled from the sand.

EXT. SAND DUNE

The burning sail barge continues its chain of explosions. As the skiff sails off across the desert, the barge settles to the sand and disappears in one final conflagration.

In the rough draft, aboard one of the skiffs, the guards have found the weapons concealed on Han and Lando. At their most desperate hour, Luke reaches out and a blaster flies from the holster of one of the guards into his hands. From his barge Jabba orders his guards to shoot the prisoners, and during the battle Chewie is hit and falls unconscious in the back of the skiff. Luke and Han fall overboard when the vehicle is hit by a blast, and Lando throws them a cable just as the creature is about to grab Han. Meanwhile, Artoo has opened all the power connectors aboard Jabba's ship, and he and Threepio jump out a window into the sand dunes below. The ship explodes, throwing Jabba, Bib, and company into the mouth of the sloth. With a giant magnet, the droids are brought aboard the skiff, and they take off.

EXT. SPACE ABOVE TATOOINE

The desolate yellow planet fills the screen. The Falcon *appears and grows huge, to roar directly over camera, followed by Luke's X-wing, which peels off to the left.*

INT. X-WING COCKPIT

Luke is at the controls. He speaks into his comlink to the others in the Millennium Falcon.

LUKE: Meet you back at the fleet.

LEIA: *(over comlink)* Hurry. The Alliance should be assembled by now.

LUKE: I will.

HAN: *(over comlink)* Hey, Luke, thanks. Thanks for comin' after me. Now I owe you one.

EXT. X-WING

Artoo, who is attached to Luke's X-wing outside the canopy, beeps a message.

INT. X-WING—COCKPIT

The message from Artoo appears on the small monitor screen in front of Luke. He smiles at the monitor and speaks to Artoo as he pulls a black glove on to cover his wounded mechanical hand.

LUKE: That's right, Artoo. We're going to the Dagobah system. I have a promise to keep . . . to an old friend.

EXT. SPACE

Luke's X-wing soars off.

In the rough draft Luke, Han, Lando, Chewie, and the droids all get aboard the *Falcon* at the spaceport of Hutt and take off (in this draft Leia is already setting up the Rebel base in the forest of the Green Moon). The *Falcon* zooms to lightspeed and reaches a Rebel base in the Sice system. During the trip Luke falls asleep and dreams of Vader and Yoda. Yoda tells Luke that he must destroy Vader. Luke doesn't think he can go through with this, and Ben's image appears. Ben reveals that Luke has a sister; the Force is strong in her, but she is untrained. Luke suddenly understands that Leia is his sister.

Meanwhile, on the Green Moon, Leia and the Rebel commander, Captain Jode, are setting up two cannons to destroy the shield generator and a communications disk to facilitate the Rebels' attack on Had Abbadon.

In the revised rough draft, after they escape from Jabba, Luke, Han, Lando, and Chewie reach an underground starship hangar at the Hutt Spaceport, where the *Falcon* is parked. As the group is about to board, Threepio comes running in and explains that Artoo has been captured. Luke and Han go to look for him, and soon they realize that this was a trap to capture Luke. Imperial officers take Luke while Han, Lando, Chewie, and the droids go back to the *Falcon* and take off to rescue their friend.

In the second draft, after escaping from Jabba, a sequence with the group caught in a sandstorm was created and filmed.

Duwayne Dunham: "The sandstorm sequence was the first scene to be shot in London. And basically, it was just the group getting together at the *Millennium Falcon* and Luke saying, 'I'm going someplace else, and I'll meet you later on Endor.' As it turned out, the scene was simply not needed, and it was better to go from the big explosion of the barge to the *Falcon* and the X-wing in space. The scene in the sandstorm was one of those shoelaces scenes that just was not needed. But you know, the script was so tightly written that I can't really recall any other scene that had to be deleted that way."

EXT. DEATH STAR
Squads of TIE fighters escort an Imperial shuttle toward the half-completed Death Star.
INT. DOCKING BAY—DEATH STAR
Thousands of Imperial troops in tight formation fill the mammoth docking bay. Vader and the Death Star commander wait at the landing platform, where the shuttle has come to rest.
The Emperor's Royal Guards come down the shuttle's ramp and create a lethal perimeter. Then, in the huge silence that follows, the Emperor appears. He is a rather small, shriveled old man. His bent frame slowly makes its way down the ramp with the aid of a gnarled cane. He wears a hooded cloak similar to the one Ben wears, except that it is black. The Emperor's face is shrouded and difficult to see. Commander Jerjerrod and Darth Vader are kneeling to him.
EMPEROR: *(to Vader)* Rise, my friend.
The Supreme Ruler of the galaxy beckons to the Dark Lord. Vader rises and falls in next to the Emperor as he slowly makes his way along the rows of troops. Jerjerrod and the other commanders will stay kneeling until the Supreme Ruler and Vader, followed by several Imperial dignitaries, pass by; only then do they join in the procession.
VADER: The Death Star will be completed on schedule.
EMPEROR: You have done well, Lord Vader. And now I sense you wish to continue your search for young Skywalker.
VADER: Yes, my master.
EMPEROR: Patience, my friend. In time he will seek you out. And when he does, you must bring him before me. He has grown strong. Only together can we turn him to the dark side of the Force.
VADER: As you wish.
EMPEROR: Everything is proceeding as I have foreseen.
He laughs to himself as they pass along the vast line of Imperial troops.

In the rough draft Vader's audience with the Emperor occurs at the beginning of the movie, right after Leia has been given clearance to land on the Green Moon. Vader and Grand Moff Jerjerrod arrive on Had Abbadon, descend into a vast steaming pit, and reach the level of the throne room, which looks out over a fuming lake of red lava. They approach a small, shrouded figure sitting on an island in the middle of the volcanic lake. This is the Emperor, Supreme Ruler of the Galactic Empire and Master of the dark side of the Force. Both Vader and Jerjerrod kneel before him. The Emperor tells Vader that he's been away too long, that his power has weakened. Luke Skywalker is more powerful than ever and must be destroyed. Vader means to reply, but suddenly his breathing stops and he starts choking. He collapses to the ground; the Emperor lowers his hand, and Vader starts breathing again. He struggles and gets back on his knees. Finally, the Emperor says that Luke is his to destroy and asks Vader to leave. Once the Dark Lord is gone, the Emperor tells Jerjerrod to watch Vader closely; he wants him to think that Luke is to be destroyed when in fact he will take Vader's place at his side. The Emperor also reveals that he knows that the Rebels are getting ready to attack.

In the revised rough draft, on his Star Destroyer Vader asks Admiral Piett where he can find Grand Moff Jerjerrod. Piett explains that he is in the private communication chamber; all surveillance in the room has been cut off, and his coded transmission is undecipherable. Piett also informs Vader that the extra patrol has arrived on the Sanctuary Moon with General Veers under command to search for Rebels. In the communication chamber Jerjerrod kneels before a huge holographic image of the Emperor, who orders him to bring Skywalker directly to him and says that Vader should know nothing of their conversation. Jerjerrod says that the Rebel attack should distract him from Luke and enable the Emperor to take control of the new Jedi Knight.

Lawrence Kasdan: "My sense of the relationship is that the Emperor is much more powerful than Vader and that Vader is very much intimidated by him. Vader has dignity, but the Emperor in *Jedi* really has all the power."

George Lucas: "I didn't want Vader to be all-powerful. In the first film it was very easy to make him into some kind of superhero. But I decided not to do that. In fact, he is one of the Dark Lords who is working for the Emperor, and he has to do the Emperor's bidding. You will see at some point in the future that the Jedi have the same relationship to the Republic; they're like public servants, they're like marshals or policemen. They basically do what they're told to do. They're not independent agents who can do whatever they want. In the case of the Jedi, they work for the Republic, and in the case of the Sith Lords, they work for the Empire. So I obviously didn't want to make Vader too weak, but I didn't want to make him so you thought that he was in charge of everything. That's why I had Tarkin in the first film, although he was more of a bureaucrat."

EXT. YODA'S HOUSE—DAGOBAH

Once again Artoo finds himself waiting around in the damp environs of the swamp planet, and he's none too happy about it. He beeps disconsolately to himself and turns to look at Yoda's cottage. Warm yellow light escapes from the oddly shaped windows to fight the gloom.

INT. YODA'S HOUSE

A walking stick taps hesitantly across the earthen floor of the cottage. The small green hand that clutches it is followed by the familiar face of Yoda, the Jedi Master. His manner is frail, and his voice, though cheerful, seems weaker.

YODA: Hmm. That face you make? Look I so old to young eyes?

Luke is sitting in a corner of the cramped space, and indeed, his look has been woeful. Caught, he tries to hide it.

LUKE: No . . . of course not.

YODA: *(tickled, chuckles)* I do, yes, I do! Sick have I become. Old and weak. *(points a crooked finger)* When nine hundred years old you reach, look as good you will not. Hmm?

Yoda chuckles at this, coughs, and hobbles over toward his bed.

YODA: Soon will I rest. Yes, forever sleep. Earned it, I have.

Yoda sits himself on his bed with great effort.

LUKE: Master Yoda, you can't die.

YODA: Strong am I with the Force . . . but not that strong! Twilight is upon me, and soon night must fall. That is the way of things . . . the way of the Force.

LUKE: But I need your help. I've come back to complete the training.

YODA: No more training do you require. Already know you that which you need.

Yoda sighs, lying back on his bed.

LUKE: Then I am a Jedi.

YODA: *(shakes his head)* Ohhh. Not yet. One thing remains: Vader. You must confront Vader. Then, only then, a Jedi will you be. And confront him you will.

Luke is in agony. He is silent for a moment, screwing up his courage. Finally he is able to ask.

LUKE: Master Yoda . . . is Darth Vader my father?

Yoda's eyes are full of weariness and compassion. An odd, sad smile creases his face. He turns painfully on his side, away from Luke.

YODA: Mmm . . . rest I need. Yes . . . rest.

Luke watches him, each moment an eternity.

LUKE: Yoda, I must know.

YODA: Your father he is. Told you, did he?

LUKE: Yes.

A new look of concern crosses Yoda's face. He closes his eyes.

YODA: Unexpected this is, and unfortunate . . .

LUKE: Unfortunate that I know the truth?

YODA: No.

Yoda opens his eyes again and studies the youth.

YODA: *(gathering all his strength)* Unfortunate that you rushed to face him . . . that incomplete was your training. That not ready for the burden were you.

LUKE: I'm sorry.

YODA: Remember, a Jedi's strength flows from the Force. But beware. Anger, fear, aggression. The dark side are they. Once you start down the dark path, forever will it dominate your destiny. *(faintly)* Luke . . . Luke . . .

The young Jedi moves closer to him.

YODA: Do not . . . Do not underestimate the powers of the Emperor or suffer your father's fate you will. Luke, when gone am I . . . the last of the Jedi will you be. Luke, the Force runs strong in your family. Pass on what you have learned, Luke . . . *(with great effort)* There is . . . another . . . Sky . . . walker.

The ancient green creature catches his breath and dies. Luke stares at his dead master as he disappears in front of his eyes.

George Lucas: "As you're building to the climax of an endeavor such as this, you want the situation to get more and more desperate and you want the hero to lose whatever crutches he or she has helping along the way. One of the challenges here is that Luke should be completely on his own. He has to face the Emperor one on one."

EXT. DAGOBAH SWAMP—X-WING
Luke wanders back to where his ship is sitting. Artoo beeps a greeting but is

ignored by his depressed master. Luke kneels down, begins to help Artoo with the ship, then stops and shakes his head dejectedly.

LUKE: I can't do it, Artoo. I can't go on alone.

BEN: *(offscreen)* Yoda will always be with you.

Luke looks up to see the shimmering image of Ben Kenobi.

LUKE: Obi-Wan!

The ghost of Ben Kenobi approaches him through the swamp.

LUKE: Why didn't you tell me? You told me Vader betrayed and murdered my father.

BEN: Your father was seduced by the dark side of the Force. He ceased to be Anakin Skywalker and became Darth Vader. When that happened, the good man who was your father was destroyed. So what I told you was true . . . from a certain point of view.

LUKE: *(derisive)* A certain point of view!

BEN: Luke, you're going to find that many of the truths we cling to depend greatly on our own point of view.

Luke is unresponsive. Ben studies him in silence for a moment.

BEN: Anakin was a good friend.

As Ben speaks, Luke settles on a stump, mesmerized.

BEN: When I first knew him, your father was already a great pilot. But I was amazed how strongly the Force was with him. I took it upon myself to train him as a Jedi. I thought that I could instruct him just as well as Yoda. I was wrong.

Luke is entranced.

LUKE: There is still good in him.

BEN: He's more machine now than man. Twisted and evil.

LUKE: I can't do it, Ben.

BEN: You cannot escape your destiny. You must face Darth Vader again.

LUKE: I can't kill my own father.

BEN: Then the Emperor has already won. You were our only hope.

LUKE: Yoda spoke of another.

BEN: The other he spoke of is your twin sister.

LUKE: But I have no sister.

BEN: Hmm. To protect you both from the Emperor, you were hidden from your father when you were born. The Emperor knew, as I did, if Anakin were to have any offspring, they would be a threat to him. That is the reason why your sister remains safely anonymous.

LUKE: Leia! Leia's my sister.

BEN: Your insight serves you well. Bury your feelings deep down, Luke. They do you credit. But they could be made to serve the Emperor.

Luke looks into the distance, trying to comprehend all this.

During story conferences George Lucas suggested that Lawrence Kasdan write a great scene for Alec Guinness with powerful Shakespearean dialogue. Lucas referred to the fact that in *The Empire Strikes Back* Guinness had wanted most of his own dialogue to be delivered by Yoda to make it sound more special. It was decided that in *Jedi*, just as in the previous film, Ben would appear only as a shimmering image.

Lawrence Kasdan: "You see, in my own philosophy or religion, such as it is, I believe there is so much more going on than we can see or perceive, that we're not alone in this space, that everything that has happened in this space is still there. So for me, Ben always related to this notion, to a Force that all humans contribute to. The Force is the combined vibrations of all living things."

George Lucas: "One of the things that will never get explained in the films is how Ben was able to retain his identity, because it happened somewhere in between the third and fourth movies. I set up that this is a discipline that he learned from Yoda; Yoda told him how to do that. We don't ever get to see how he does it, but the idea of retaining your identity after you've passed on is something that Ben learned as a Jedi."

It was decided during story meetings that Uncle Owen was in fact Ben's brother. Owen always resented Ben for imposing Luke on them, and now Ben is taking the blame for what is happening and is feeling guilty.

In the revised rough draft Luke has been taken prisoner and is being taken to the Emperor. He is inside the Imperial shuttle, sitting in a small metallic cell; he is begging Ben to help him face his father, saying that he might be able to resist the dark side. Yoda's image appears for the first time in this draft. He tells Luke that Ben can no longer help him; his power to stay in the Netherworld has been spent, and he will soon be one with the Force, his identity lost forever. Only Luke can draw him back to the material world, but Luke is unsure of himself, and his anger toward Ben for not telling him that Vader is his father could prevent him from coming back to the real world. Yoda then reveals to Luke that he has a twin sister — Leia. If Luke fails to destroy Vader, she'll be the only hope left.

In the second draft, Luke wanders in the swamp and Ben's shimmering image appears. At first Luke is furious at Ben for not telling him that Vader is his father. Ben then talks in detail about his friendship with Luke's father before Anakin became Darth Vader: "When I first encountered your father he was already a great pilot. But what amazed me was how strongly the Force was with him. I had never seen anything like it and did not again . . . until you. With foolish pride I took it upon myself to train Anakin in the ways of the Jedi. My mistake was thinking I could be as good a teacher as Yoda. I was not. And so, when the Emperor sensed Anakin's power, he was able to gradually lure him to the dark side. Your father began betraying his fellow Jedi Knights." Ben explains that he fought Anakin; he thought he had destroyed him, but the Emperor was able to save him, making him half man and half machine. The Emperor knew, as Ben did, that the Force is strong in the Skywalker line, and he began to search for Anakin's offspring. Ben reveals to Luke that he has a twin sister and that they were separated; Luke was sent to stay with Ben's brother, Owen, on Tatooine, while his sister and mother were sent to the protection of friends in a distant system. The mother died shortly thereafter, and Luke's sister was adopted by Ben's friends, the governor of Alderaan and his wife.

At that point Luke guesses that his sister is Leia. Ben feels tremendous responsibility and guilt for what happened to Vader, and unfortunately, because of the circumstances, it is now up to Luke to deal with Vader. Ben explains that Yoda is going to pass on; Luke is crushed, but Ben tells him that to the contrary, this is going to be a great relief for Yoda and that all his former students are waiting for him. Luke is still angry at Ben and ignites his lasersword as if to attack him. He then throws the sword into the woods. Ben tells Luke that he can't really help him but will always be with him. Luke resolves his anger and looks in the direction where he threw his weapon; suddenly the sword flies out of the woods and jumps into his hand. The scene ends with Ben and Luke looking deep into each other's eyes.

In the third draft the notion that Ben feels responsible for Anakin turning to the dark side is stronger than it was in the previous screenplays. He uses himself as a bad example to help Luke learn patience; if he had been more patient, he would have trained Anakin better. Ben's mistake was to believe that he could be as good a teacher as Yoda.

George Lucas: "The part I am working on now is mostly about Darth Vader, who he is, where he came from, how he became Luke and Leia's father, what his relationship to Ben is. In *Jedi* the film is really about the redemption of this fallen angel. Ben is the fitting good angel, and Vader is the bad angel who started off good. All these years Ben has been waiting for Luke to come of age so that he can become a Jedi and redeem his father. That's what Ben has been doing, but you don't know this in the first film."

EXT. SPACE—REBEL FLEET

The vast Rebel fleet stretches as far as the eye can see. Overhead a dozen small Corellian battleships fly in formation. Fighters and battlecruisers surround the largest of the Rebel star cruisers, the headquarters frigate.

INT. HEADQUARTERS FRIGATE—MAIN BRIEFING ROOM

Hundreds of Rebel commanders of all races and forms are assembling in the war room. Wedge is among them. In the center of the room is a holographic model depicting the half-completed Imperial Death Star, the nearby moon of Endor, and the protecting deflector shield.

Moving through the crowd, Han finds Lando. He peers at the new insignia on his chest and is amused.

HAN: Well, look at you, a general, huh?

LANDO: Someone must have told them about my little maneuver at the Battle of Taanab.

HAN: *(sarcastic)* Well, don't look at me, pal. I just said you were a fair pilot. I didn't know they were lookin' for somebody to lead this crazy attack.

LANDO: *(smiling)* I'm surprised they didn't ask you to do it.

HAN: Well, who says they didn't? But I ain't crazy. You're the respectable one, remember?

Mon Mothma, the leader of the Alliance, has entered the room. She is a stern but beautiful woman in her fifties. Mon Mothma signals for attention, and the room falls silent.

MON MOTHMA: The Emperor has made a critical error, and the time for our attack has come.

This causes a stir. Mon Mothma turns to a holographic model of the Death Star, the nearby Endor moon, and the protecting deflector shield in the center of the room.

MON MOTHMA: The data brought to us by the Bothan spies pinpoints the exact location of the Emperor's new battle station. We also know that the weapon systems of this Death Star are not yet operational. With the Imperial fleet spread throughout the galaxy in a vain effort to engage us, it is relatively unprotected. But most important of all, we've learned that the Emperor himself is personally overseeing the final stages of the construction of this Death Star. Many Bothans died to bring us this information. Admiral Ackbar, please.

Admiral Ackbar (a salmon-colored Mon Calamari) steps forward, indicating the Death Star's force field and the moon of Endor.

ACKBAR: You can see here the Death Star orbiting the forest moon of Endor. Although the weapon systems on this Death Star are not yet operational, the Death Star does have a strong defense mechanism. It is protected by an energy shield which is generated from the nearby forest moon of Endor. The shield must be deactivated if any attack is to be attempted. Once the shield is down, our cruisers will create a perimeter, while the fighters fly into the superstructure and attempt to knock out the main reactor. General Calrissian has volunteered to lead the fighter attack.

Han turns to Lando with a look of respect.

HAN: Good luck.

Lando returns his look.

HAN: You're gonna need it.

ACKBAR: General Madine.

Madine moves center stage.

GENERAL MADINE: We have stolen a small Imperial shuttle. Disguised as a cargo ship and using a secret Imperial code, a strike team will land on the moon and deactivate the shield generator.

The assembly begins to mumble among themselves.

THREEPIO: Sounds dangerous.

LEIA: *(to Han)* I wonder who they found to pull that off.

GENERAL MADINE: General Solo, is your strike team assembled?

Leia, startled, looks up at Han, surprise changing to admiration.

HAN: Uh, my team's ready. I don't have a command crew for the shuttle.

Chewbacca raises his hairy paw and volunteers. Han looks up at him.

HAN: Well, it's gonna be rough, pal. I didn't want to speak for you.

Chewie waves that off with a huge growl.

HAN: *(smiles)* That's one.

LEIA: Uh, General . . . count me in.

VOICE: *(offscreen)* I'm with you, too!

They turn in that direction and peer into the crowd, which parts to admit Luke. Han and Leia are surprised and delighted.

Leia moves to Luke and embraces him warmly. She senses a change in him and looks into his eyes questioningly.

LEIA: What is it?

LUKE: *(hesitant)* Ask me again sometime.

Han, Chewie, and Lando crowd around Luke as the assembly breaks up.

HAN: Luke.

LUKE: Hi, Han . . . Chewie.

Artoo beeps a singsong observation to a worried Threepio.

THREEPIO: "Exciting" is hardly the word I would choose.

INT. HEADQUARTERS FRIGATE—MAIN DOCKING BAY

The Millennium Falcon *rests beyond the stolen Imperial shuttle, which looks anomalous among all the Rebel ships in the vast docking bay crowded now with the Rebel strike team loading weapons and supplies. Lando turns to face Han.*

HAN: Look: I want you to take her. I mean it. Take her. You need all the help you can get. She's the fastest ship in the fleet.

LANDO: All right, old buddy. You know, I know what she means to you. I'll take good care of her. She—she won't get a scratch. All right?

HAN: Right. I got your promise. Not a scratch.

LANDO: Look, would you get going, you pirate.

Han and Lando pause, then exchange salutes.

LANDO: Good luck.

HAN: You, too.

Han goes up the ramp. Lando watches him go and then slowly turns away.

In the rough draft the war room sequence takes place in the city of Sicemon, where General Madine updates Luke, Solo, Lando, Chewie, and the droids on Leia's situation. Solo is not too pleased with the risks the princess is taking and wants to join her immediately on the Green Moon. Jokingly, Luke displays his powers and has Han magically locked with a pair of handcuffs to one of the control panels. Later, Luke tries to repair his lightsaber. Threepio doesn't think he can succeed because the knowledge needed to construct lightsabers has long been lost. When Luke finally manages to fix the weapon, Yoda's image appears. He tells Luke that now that he has mastered the secret of the lightsaber, his training is complete and he is ready for the final test: his father. When Luke says that he can't do it, Yoda tells him to concentrate, and he suddenly sees that Leia is in danger. The attack on Had Abbadon will fail, and he's got to help; now he has no choice but to face Vader. Luke takes off aboard the *Falcon* with Solo, Chewie, and the droids, while Lando and General Madine will wait for their signal.

In the revised rough draft the *Falcon* arrives at a Rebel rendezvous point and lands on one of the star cruisers. Han, Chewie, Lando, and the robots are greeted by Captain New and several of his officers. Lando tells them about Luke's capture on Tatooine. They're taken to the war room, where they meet with General Madine, who is standing next to a large electronic table. Madine explains that Leia has succeeded in setting up two cannons on the moon sanctuary of Had Abbadon. Lando says that the odds of the plan succeeding aren't too good unless the Rebel fleet can be brought out of hyperspace on one side of the moon. Han doesn't have much patience during the discussion and says he is going to get Leia, and together they'll save Luke. Han, Chewie, and the robots take off aboard the *Falcon*.

In the second draft, the briefing room sequence is slightly different from the way it ended up in the film. Mon Mothma has only a few lines of dialogue, and Admiral Akbar is introduced and described as "a pale blue nonhuman." Lando has been named a general and is going to lead the attack on the new Death Star aboard the *Falcon*. Akbar explains that they've stolen an Imperial shuttle and have purchased the current shield clearance code from a reliable source. Leia has agreed to lead the strike team, but she needs pilots to fly the shuttle. Chewie immediately volunteers. Han reluctantly joins the team. As in the film, Luke shows up, and the scene ends with Han saying: "Well, this is it, gang . . . We've all chosen to die young."

INT. IMPERIAL SHUTTLE—COCK-PIT

Luke is working on a back control panel as Han comes in and takes the pilot's seat. Chewie, in the seat next to him, is trying to figure out all the Imperial controls.

HAN: You got her warmed?

LUKE: Yeah, she's comin' up.

Chewie growls a complaint.

HAN: I don't think the Empire had Wookiees in mind when they designed her, Chewie.

INT. HEADQUARTERS FRIGATE—MAIN DOCKING BAY

The shuttle warms up.

George Lucas: "In the first film Luke takes on the responsibility of his father; he is given his father's lightsaber. In the second film the father destroys that. In the first movie Luke wants to go off on an adventure, but he doesn't really have a purpose. He doesn't have a real cause that he is emotionally connected to. In the second film he gets this cause; he gets emotionally involved and

INT. IMPERIAL SHUTTLE COCK-PIT

Leia comes in from the hold and puts a hand on Han's shoulder.

Han's glance has stuck on something out the window: the Millennium Falcon. *Leia nudges him gently.*

LEIA: Hey, are you awake?

HAN: Yeah. I just got a funny feeling. Like I'm not gonna see her again.

Chewie, on hearing this, stops his activity and looks longingly out at the Falcon, *too.*

LEIA: *(softly)* Come on, General, let's move.

Han snaps back to life.

HAN: Right. Chewie, let's see what this piece of junk can do. Ready, everybody?

LUKE: All set.

THREEPIO: Here we go again.

EXT. SPACE—THE REBEL FLEET

The stolen Imperial shuttle leaves the main docking bay of the headquarters frigate and lowers its wings into flight position.

INT. IMPERIAL SHUTTLE—COCKPIT

HAN: All right, hang on.

EXT. SPACE—THE REBEL FLEET

The Imperial shuttle zooms off into space.

EXT. SPACE—DEATH STAR

TIE fighters patrol the surface of the Death Star.

INT. EMPEROR'S THRONE ROOM

The converted control room is dimly lit. The Emperor stands before a large window that looks out across the half-completed Death Star to the giant Green Moon of Endor.

Darth Vader stands with other members of the Imperial council. The ruler's back is to Vader.

VADER: What is thy bidding, my master?

EMPEROR: *(turning)* Send the fleet to the far side of Endor. There it will stay until called for.

VADER: What of the reports of the Rebel fleet massing near Sullust?

philosophically attached to a particular idea. The new lightsaber that Luke built himself in Jedi symbolizes that he has detached himself completely from his father and now is on his own. The central issue is that Luke confronts his demons, and his demons basically revolve around whether he will follow in his father's footsteps, whether he will succumb to the dark side. The ultimate issue here is, Will he make the same mistake that his father made? The major emotional conflict is that the audience has to feel that he is not completely ready yet to face Vader and the Emperor."

EMPEROR: It is of no concern. Soon the Rebellion will be crushed and young Skywalker will be one of us! Your work here is finished, my friend. Go out to the command ship and await my orders.

VADER: Yes, my master.

Vader bows, then turns and exits the throne room as the Emperor walks toward the waiting council members.

EXT. SPACE—DEATH STAR—MOON

The Imperial shuttle approaches the Death Star.

INT. STOLEN IMPERIAL SHUTTLE—COCKPIT

There is a great deal of Imperial traffic in the area as construction proceeds on the Death Star. TIE fighters and a few Star Destroyers move about.

As Chewie flips switches, through the viewscreen the Death Star and the huge Super Star Destroyer can be seen.

HAN: If they don't go for this, we're gonna have to get outta here pretty quick, Chewie.

Chewie growls his agreement.

CONTROLLER: *(over radio)* We have you on our screen now. Please identify.

HAN: Shuttle *Tydirium* requesting deactivation of the deflector shield.

EXT. SPACE—DEATH STAR—MOON

The shuttle approaches the Super Star Destroyer.

INT. SUPER STAR DESTROYER—BRIDGE

CONTROLLER: *(into radio)* Shuttle *Tydirium*, transmit the clearance code for shield passage.

INT. STOLEN IMPERIAL SHUTTLE—COCKPIT

HAN: Transmission commencing.

LEIA: Now we find out if that code is worth the price we paid.

HAN: It'll work. It'll work.

Chewie whines nervously. They listen tensely as the sound of a high-speed transmission begins. Luke stares at the huge Super Star Destroyer that looms ever larger before them.

LUKE: Vader's on that ship.

HAN: Now don't get jittery, Luke. There are a lot of command ships. Keep your distance, though, Chewie, but don't look like you're trying to keep your distance.

Chewie barks a question.

HAN: I don't know. Fly casual.

Chewie barks his worries as the Super Star Destroyer grows larger out the window.

INT. VADER'S STAR DESTROYER—BRIDGE

Lord Vader walks down the row of controllers to where Admiral Piett is looking over the tracking screen of the controller we've seen earlier. Piett looks round at Vader's approach.

VADER: Where is that shuttle going?

PIETT: *(into comlink)* Shuttle *Tydirium*, what is your cargo and destination?

PILOT VOICE (HAN): *(filtered)* Parts and technical crew for the forest moon.

The bridge commander looks to Vader for a reaction.

VADER: Do they have code clearance?

PIETT: It's an older code, sir, but it checks out. I was about to clear them.

Vader looks upward as he senses Luke's presence.

INT. STOLEN IMPERIAL SHUTTLE—COCKPIT

LUKE: I'm endangering the mission. I shouldn't have come.

HAN: It's your imagination, kid. Come on. Let's keep a little optimism here.

EXT. SPACE—STOLEN IMPERIAL SHUTTLE—DEATH STAR

The shuttle continues on its way.

INT. VADER'S STAR DESTROYER—BRIDGE

PIETT: Shall I hold them?

VADER: No. Leave them to me. I will deal with them myself.

PIETT: *(surprised)* As you wish, my lord. *(to controller)* Carry on.

INT. STOLEN IMPERIAL SHUTTLE—COCKPIT

The group waits tensely.

HAN: They're not goin' for it, Chewie.

CONTROLLER: *(filtered)* Shuttle *Tydirium*, deactivation of the shield will commence immediately. Follow your present course.

Everyone breathes a sigh of relief. Everyone but Luke, who looks worried.

HAN: Okay! I told you it was gonna work. No problem.

EXT. SPACE—STOLEN IMPERIAL SHUTTLE—ENDOR

The stolen Imperial shuttle moves off toward the green Sanctuary Moon.

INT. VADER'S STAR DESTROYER—BRIDGE

Vader watches from the bridge.

EXT. ENDOR—FOREST CANOPY

The shuttle comes in to land.

EXT. FOREST LANDING SITE—ENDOR

In the moon's dark primeval forest, dwarfed by the ancient, towering trees, the helmeted Rebel contingent makes its way up the steep trail. Leia and Han are slightly ahead of Luke and Chewie. The troops of the strike team squad follow, with Artoo and Threepio bringing up the rear.

Up ahead Han and Leia reach a crest in the hill and drop suddenly to the ground, signaling the rest of the group to stop.

THREEPIO: Oh, I told you it was dangerous here.

Their POV: Not far below them two Imperial scouts are wandering through bushes in the valley below. Their two rocket bikes are parked nearby.

Nilo Rodis-Jamero: "Han's costume actually resulted from a discussion that came about when we were fitting Harrison Ford. He suggested a duster, and we did a mock-up of one immediately. It seemed like the right choice, and we went for it. The helmets Luke and Leia wear were modeled after World War II helmets that had fabric on them. I used to go to a surplus store, and I had seen a lot of helmets that were made out of cloth. So I bought some of them and adapted them to a new and original design. When we started working on *Jedi*, George said he didn't like the original helmets the stormtroopers wore in the first two films; from a design point of view they were great, but when they turned their heads, the helmets would follow only a bit later. They weren't very practical. So we reengineered the design of the helmets so that they would fit the head properly. Part of the idea behind the new design was to convey that, like racing horses, the helmets have blinders; the stormtroopers are like kamikazes, and all they need to see is what's in front of them. They're like Formula One drivers! I still like the original helmet the best, but you had to be tall to make it look proportionate; what I did with the new one is that I made it narrower so that anyone can wear it, but whoever is wearing it still looks threatening."

LEIA: Should we try and go around?

HAN: It'll take time. This whole party'll be for nothing if they see us. Chewie and I will take care of this. You stay here.

LUKE: Quietly; there might be more of them out there.

HAN: *(grins)* Hey . . . it's me.

Han and Chewie turn and start through the bushes toward the scouts. Luke and Leia exchange smiles.

Han sneaks up behind one of the scouts and steps on a twig, and the scout whirls, knocking Han into a tree. The scout shouts for his companion.

SCOUT #1: Go for help! Go!

LUKE: *(sarcastic)* Great! Come on.

The second scout jumps on his speeder bike and takes off, but Chewie gets off a shot on his crossbow laser weapon, causing the scout to crash into a tree. Han and Scout #1 are in a rousing fistfight.

Luke starts for the scuffle, followed by Leia. As they run through the bushes, Leia stops and points to where two more scouts are sitting on their speeder bikes, with an unoccupied bike parked nearby.

LEIA: Over there! Two more of them!

LUKE: I see them. Wait, Leia.

But Leia doesn't hear him and races for the remaining speeder bike. She starts it and takes off as Luke jumps on the bike behind her.

Luke and Leia speed into the dense foliage in hot pursuit, barely avoiding two huge trees.

Joe Johnston: "The rocket bikes were built entirely in three dimensions. There were some preliminary sketches done, but once the final design was set, it was all done in model, you know, kit bashing. You'd take model kits, and you'd chop them off, and you'd get the pieces and use them to build the bikes. There're a lot of different pieces on the bikes; there's a space shuttle nose that is part of the exhaust flaring at the back; there's a part of a formula car that's up front; there's a Ferrari engine as part of the rocket engine, etc. . . . So in a way the rocket bikes were pretty unique because the design was determined more in three dimensions than it was on paper. More than any other machines or vehicles in the film, they really look like they might actually work!"

HAN: Hey, wait! Ahhh!

He flips the remaining scout to the ground.

LUKE: *(pointing to the controls)* Quick! Jam their comlink. Center switch!

EXT. FOREST—THE BIKE CHASE

The two fleeing Imperial scouts have a good lead as Luke and Leia pursue them through the giant trees at two hundred miles an hour.

LUKE: Move closer!

Leia guns it, closing the gap, as the two scouts recklessly veer through a narrow gap in the trees.

LUKE: Get alongside that one!

Leia pulls her speeder bike up so close to the scout's bike that they scrape noisily. Luke leaps from his bike to the back of the scout's, grabs the Imperial warrior around the neck, and flips him off the bike into a thick tree trunk. Luke gains control of the bike and follows Leia, who has pulled ahead. They tear off after the remaining scout.

The speeding chase passes two more Imperial scouts. These two swing into pursuit, chasing Luke and Leia, firing away with their laser cannon. The two Rebels look behind them just as Luke's bike takes a glancing hit.

LUKE: *(indicating the one ahead)* Keep on that one! I'll take these two!

With Leia shooting ahead, Luke suddenly slams into braking mode. Luke's bike is a blur to the two pursuing scouts as they zip by him on either side. Luke slams his bike into forward and starts firing away, having switched places with his pursuers in a matter of seconds. Luke's aim is good, and one scout's bike is blasted out of control. It explodes against a tree trunk.

The scout's cohort takes one glance back at the flash and shifts into turbo drive, going even faster. Luke keeps on his tail.

Far ahead, Leia and the first scout are doing a high-speed slalom through the death-dealing trunks. Now Leia aims her bike skyward and rises out of sight.

The scout turns in confusion, unable to see his pursuer. Suddenly Leia dives down upon him from above, cannon blasting.

Leia moves in alongside him. The scout eyes her beside him, reaches down, and pulls out a handgun. Before Leia can react, the scout has blasted her bike, sending it out of control. The happy scout looks back at the explosion. But when he turns forward again, he is on a collision course with a giant fallen tree. He hits his brakes to no avail and disappears in a conflagration.

ANOTHER PART OF THE FOREST: Luke and the last remaining scout continue their weaving chase through the trees. Now Luke moves up close. The scout responds by slamming his bike into Luke's.

Both riders look ahead—a wide trunk looms directly in Luke's path, but the scout's bike beside him makes it almost impossible for him to avoid it. Luke reacts instinctively and dives off the bike. It explodes against the tree. The scout sweeps out and circles back to find Luke.

Luke rises from the undergrowth as the scout bears down on him and opens fire with his laser cannon. Luke ignites his lasersword and begins deflecting the bolts. The scout's bike keeps coming, and it appears that in a second it will cut Luke in half. At the last instant, Luke steps aside and chops off the bike's control vanes with one mighty slash. The scout's bike begins to pitch and roll, then slams directly into a tree in a giant ball of fire.

Duwayne Dunham: "George is a big, big believer in time spent in preparation and preproduction. What it costs for a year and a half in preproduction is worth the money because you're able to follow the evolution of the effects and how they might affect the story in the editorial stages and also on the set with the actors. To cut the special effects scenes, *Star Wars* used temp footage from old war movies and used storyboards; *Empire* primarily used storyboards and some moving storyboards; on *Jedi* we used animatics. In the bike chase scene, for instance, we had a miniature forest and miniature bikes with Leia and Luke dolls on them, and we shot the scene on video. Each one of the storyboards was shot and cut together like a movie, using sound effects, voices, etc. . . . Of course, coat hangers were used to move the bikes, but these videos would basically tell us how long the scene needed to be. The visual effects guys could actually predict exactly the length of each shot and never go beyond that, which saved a lot of money. When Richard Marquand started shooting in London, he had the entire bike chase sequence cut together on video, which was quite helpful."

EXT. SCOUT CAMPSITE—FOREST

Han, Chewie, and the droids, along with the rest of the squad, wait anxiously in the clearing. Artoo's radar screen sticks out of his domed head and revolves, scanning the forest. He beeps.

THREEPIO: Oh, General Solo, somebody's coming.

Han, Chewie, and the rest of the squad raise their weapons.

THREEPIO: Oh!

Luke runs out of the foliage.

HAN: Luke! Where's Leia?

LUKE: *(concerned)* What? She didn't come back?

HAN: I thought she was with you.

LUKE: We got separated.

Luke and Han exchange a silent, grim look.

LUKE: Hey, we better go look for her.

Han signals to a Rebel officer.

HAN: Take the squad ahead. We'll meet at the shield generator at oh three hundred.

LUKE: Come on, Artoo. We'll need your scanners.

Luke, Chewie, Han, and the droids move off in one direction as the squad proceeds in another.

THREEPIO: Don't worry, Master Luke. We know what to do.

They move off into the woods.

THREEPIO: *(to Artoo)* And you said it was pretty here. Ugh!

EXT. FOREST CLEARING—LEIA'S CRASH SITE

A strange little furry creature with huge black eyes come slowly into view. The creature is an Ewok by the name of Wicket. He seems somewhat puzzled and prods Leia with a spear. The stubby ball of fuzz jumps back and prods her again.

George Lucas: "The Wookiee planet that I created for *Star Wars* was eventually turned into the Ewok planet in *Jedi*. I basically cut the Wookiees in half and called them Ewoks! I didn't make Endor a Wookiee planet because Chewbacca was sophisticated technologically and I wanted the characters involved in the battle to be primitive. That's why I used Ewoks instead."

Nilo Rodis-Jamero: "I did a lot of designs for the Ewoks. My vision for them was very different from the way they are in the film because I never really saw them as partaking in the battle at the end. So I gave them feet and little arms that would help them hop from tree to tree."

Joe Johnston: "I did a lot of work on the Ewoks; we all did. Once the direction of the design was established, I started doing weapons and different fur patterns so that we could distinguish the characters. If you look at cattle, you'll notice that they all look different, their coats have different patterns. We were concentrating on giving the Ewoks different headdresses; some of them had armor, some of them had ritual kinds of beads, distinctive fur coloring, etc. . . . As it turned out, I think there were really two Ewoks we needed to recognize, but it was an interesting design experience to basically take these teddy bears and come up with six or eight different ones."

LEIA: Cut it out!

Leia sits up and stares at the three-foot-high Ewok. She tries to figure out where she is and what has happened. Her clothes are torn; she's bruised and disheveled.
The Ewok holds his four-foot-long spear in a defensive position. Leia stands up, and the Ewok backs away.

LEIA: I'm not gonna hurt you.

Leia looks around at the dense forest, then sits down with a sigh on a fallen log.

LEIA: Well, looks like I'm stuck here. Trouble is, I don't know where here is. Maybe you can help me.

She looks over at the watchful little Ewok and pats the log beside her.

LEIA: Come on, sit down.

Wicket holds his spear up warily and growls at her like a puppy.

LEIA: I promise I won't hurt you. Now come here.

Leia pats the log again, causing more growls and squeaks from the little bear creature.

LEIA: All right. You want something to eat?

She takes a scrap of food out of her pocket and offers it to him. Wicket takes a step backward, then cocks his head and moves cautiously toward Leia, chattering in his squeaky Ewok language.

LEIA: That's right. Come on. Hmmm?

Sniffing the food cautiously, the Ewok comes forward toward Leia and sits on the log beside her. She takes off her helmet, and the little creature jumps back, startled again. He runs along the log, pointing his spear at her and chattering a blue streak. Leia holds out the helmet to him.

LEIA: Look, it's a hat. It's not gonna hurt you. Look.

Reassured, Wicket lowers his spear and climbs back on the log, coming to investigate the helmet.

LEIA: You're a jittery little thing, aren't you?

Suddenly Wicket's ears perk up, and he begins to sniff the air. He looks around warily, whispering some Ewokese warning to Leia.

LEIA: What is it?

Suddenly a laserbolt comes out of the foliage and explodes on the log next to Leia. Leia and Wicket both roll backward off the log, hiding behind it. Leia holds her own laser gun ready.
Another shot, and still no sight of anyone in the forest. Wicket disappears

underneath the log. Suddenly a large Imperial scout is standing over her with his
weapon pointed at her head. He reaches out his hand for her weapon.

SCOUT #1: Freeze! Come on, get up!

A second scout emerges from the foliage in front of the log.

SCOUT #1: Go get your ride and take her back to base.

SCOUT #2: Yes, sir.

The second scout starts toward his bike as Wicket, crouched under the log, extends his spear and hits the first scout on the leg. The scout jumps, lets out an exclamation, and Leia knocks him out. She dives for his laser pistol, and the second scout, now on his bike, takes off. Leia fires away and hits the escaping bike, causing it to crash into the first scout's bike, which flies end over end and explodes. The forest is quiet once more. Wicket pokes his fuzzy head up from behind the log and regards Leia with new respect. He mumbles his awe. Leia hurries over, looking around all the time, and motions the chubby little creature into the dense foliage.

LEIA: Come on, let's get out of here.

As they move into the foliage, Wicket shrieks and tugs at Leia to follow him.

In the rough draft Leia's encounter with the Ewok (spelled Ewak in this draft; they became Ewoks in the revised rough draft) is similar to the way it is in the film. The little creature is named Wicket and is described as a strange little furry creature with huge yellow eyes. He speaks a funny language made up of squeaks and barks. As in the film, Leia is found by troopers and the Ewok helps her knock them out. Wicket then takes Leia to his village. They go through a small cave that opens into a large cavern; along one wall of the cavern a small village has been built under an outcropping of rocks. Leia meets Teebo; Cheipa, the gray-haired chief; and Logray, the medicine man. Logray starts chanting, and this has a hypnotic effect on Leia. The medicine man stands before her; Wicket and Teebo pin her against the ground while Logray inspects her teeth, eyes, and ears. He then hands Leia a bowl of an ugly-looking brew; she tastes it and drinks the whole thing. Everyone cheers, and a celebration begins to welcome Leia as a new member of the tribe.

EXT. DEATH STAR SURFACE

TIE fighters patrol.

INT. EMPEROR'S TOWER—THRONE ROOM

Two red Imperial Guards stand watch at the elevator as the door opens to reveal Vader. Vader enters the eerie, foreboding throne room. It appears to be empty. His footsteps echo as he approaches the throne. He waits, absolutely still. The Emperor sits with his back to the Dark Lord.

EMPEROR: I told you to remain on the command ship.

VADER: A small Rebel force has penetrated the shield and landed on Endor.

EMPEROR: *(no surprise)* Yes, I know.

VADER: *(after a beat)* My son is with them.

EMPEROR: *(very cool)* Are you sure?

VADER: I have felt him, my master.

EMPEROR: Strange that I have not. I wonder if your feelings on this matter are clear, Lord Vader.

Vader knows what is being asked.

VADER: They are clear, my master.

EMPEROR: Then you must go to the Sanctuary Moon and wait for him.

VADER: *(skeptical)* He will come to me?

EMPEROR: I have foreseen it. His compassion for you will be his undoing. He will come to you, and then you will bring him before me.

VADER: *(bows)* As you wish.

The Dark Lord strides out of the throne room.

Nilo Rodis-Jamero: "On *Jedi,* one of the most exciting things from a design point of view was the advisers who surround the Emperor. I spent a lot of time trying to figure out what they might look like because I thought it was important that through them you might understand what the Emperor's world is like. Coming from a Catholic background, I sort of made a joke, and that's why they look like bishops. So they wear red, and they have elaborate headgear. This was a challenge because it wasn't in the script, and you see them only briefly in the movie."

EXT. FOREST CLEARING—LEIA'S CRASH SITE

Moving through the heavy foliage near the clearing where we last saw Leia, Luke finds Leia's helmet and picks it up with an expression of concern.

HAN: *(offscreen)* Luke! Luke!

Luke runs with the helmet to where Han has found the charred wreckage of a speeder bike in the grass.

THREEPIO: Oh, Master Luke.

LUKE: There's two more wrecked speeders back there. And I found this.

He tosses the helmet to Han.

THREEPIO: I'm afraid that Artoo's sensors can find no trace of Princess Leia.

HAN: *(gravely)* I hope she's all right.

Chewbacca growls, sniffing the air, then, with a bark, pushes off through the foliage.

HAN: What, Chewie? What, Chewie?

The others rush to keep up with the giant Wookiee.

EXT. FOREST—DENSE FOLIAGE

The group has reached a break in the undergrowth. Chewie walks up to a tall stake planted in the ground. There is a dead animal hanging from it.

HAN: Hey, I don't get it.

The rest of the group joins the Wookiee around the stake.

HAN: *(continuing)* Nah. It's just a dead animal, Chewie.

Chewie can't resist. He reaches toward the meat.

LUKE: Chewie, wa-wait! Don't!

Too late. The Wookiee has already pulled the animal from the stake. Sprooing! The group finds itself hanging in an Ewok net, suspended high above the clearing. Chewie howls his regret. Their bodies are a jumble in the net.

HAN: Nice work. Great, Chewie! Great! Always thinking with your stomach.

LUKE: Will you take it easy. Let's just figure out a way to get out of this thing. *(trying to free an arm)* Han, can you reach my lightsaber?

HAN: Yeah, sure.

Meanwhile, Artoo is at the bottommost point in the net. He extends his cutting appendage and begins slicing at the net. The net continues to spin.

THREEPIO: Artoo, I'm not sure that's such a good idea. It's a very long dro-o-p.

Artoo has cut through, and the entire group tumbles out of the net, crashing to the ground. As they regain their senses and sit up, they realize they are surrounded by dozens of Ewoks, each brandishing a long spear.

HAN: Wait . . . ? Hey! Point that thing someplace else.

Han pushes the spear wielded by Teebo out of his face, and a second Ewok warrior comes up to argue with Teebo. The spear returns to Han's face.

HAN: Hey!

Han grabs the spear angrily and starts to go for his laser pistol.

LUKE: Han, don't. It'll be all right.

The Ewoks swarm through them and confiscate their weapons. Luke gives them his lightsaber.

LUKE: Chewie, give 'em your crossbow.

Chewie growls at the furry critters. Threepio gets free of the net and sits up, rattled.

THREEPIO: Oh, my head. Oh, my goodness!

When the Ewoks see Threepio, they let out a gasp and chatter among themselves. The Ewoks begin to chant at Threepio and bow down before him. Chewie lets out a puzzled bark. Han and Luke regard the bowed creatures in wonder. Threepio speaks to them in their native tongue.

LUKE: Do you understand anything they're saying?

THREEPIO: Oh, yes, Master Luke! Remember that I am fluent in over six million forms of communication.

HAN: What are you telling them?

THREEPIO: Hello, I think . . . I could be mistaken. They're using a very primitive dialect. But I do believe they think I am some sort of god.

The others think that's very funny.

HAN: Well, why don't you use your divine influence and get us out of this?

THREEPIO: I beg your pardon, General Solo, but that just wouldn't be proper.

HAN: Proper!?

THREEPIO: It's against my programming to impersonate a deity.

Han moves toward Threepio threateningly.

HAN: Why, you . . .

The Ewoks move in to protect their god, and Han is surrounded by a menacing circle of spears, all aimed at him. He holds up his hands placatingly.

HAN: My mistake. He's an old friend of mine.

EXT. FOREST

A procession of Ewoks winds through the ever-darkening forest. Their prisoners— Han, Luke, Chewie, and Artoo—are tied to long poles.

Each pole is carried on the shoulders of several Ewoks.

EXT. FOREST WALKWAY—MOON FOREST

Behind the captives Threepio is carried on a litter, like a king, by the remaining creatures.

The procession moves along a shaky, narrow, wooden walkway high in the giant trees. It stops at the end of the walkway, which drops off into nothingness. On the other side of the abyss is a village of mud huts and rickety walkways attached to the giant trees. The lead Ewok takes hold of a long vine and swings across to the village square; the other Ewoks follow suit.

EXT. EWOK VILLAGE SQUARE

The procession winds its way into the village square. The group stops before the largest hut.

Han, Luke, Chewie, and Artoo are still bound to their poles. Hans is placed on a spit above what looks like a barbecue pit. Threepio's litter/throne is gently placed near the pit. He watches with rapt fascination. Han, Luke, and Chewie are less fascinated. Chewie growls his concern.

HAN: I have a really bad feeling about this.

Lawrence Kasdan: "The line 'I have a really bad feeling about this' sums up the idea that everything is there before it happens; the characters get a vibration that something is going to happen. If you get in a situation and say, 'I have a bad feeling about this,' very often it turns out to be bad. It certainly has been true in my own life . . . I thought it was a very funny line when I first saw *Star Wars*; that was one of the things that impressed me in the first film."

Suddenly all activity stops as Logray, the tribal medicine man, comes out of the big hut. He goes to Threepio, whose throne has been placed on an elevated platform. He is holding Luke's lightsaber.

Logray speaks to Threepio and the assemblage of fuzzy Ewoks, pointing to the prisoners.

HAN: What did he say?

THREEPIO: I'm rather embarrassed, General Solo, but it appears you are to be the main course at a banquet in my honor.

The Ewoks begin filling the pit under Han with firewood.

The drums start beating, and all the furryheads turn to the large hut. Leia emerges, wearing an animal-skin dress. She sees what's happening at the same moment the prisoners see her.

LUKE: Leia?

HAN: Leia!

As she moves toward them, the Ewoks block her way with raised spears.

LEIA: Oh!

THREEPIO: Your Royal Highness.

Leia looks around at the assembled Ewoks and sighs.

LEIA: But these are my friends. Threepio, tell them they must be set free.

Threepio talks to Logray, who listens and shakes his head negatively. The medicine man gestures toward the prisoners and barks some orders. Several Ewoks jump up and pile more wood on the barbecue with vigor.

HAN: Somehow, I got the feeling that didn't help us very much.

LUKE: Threepio, tell them if they don't do as you wish, you'll become angry and use your magic.

THREEPIO: But Master Luke, what magic? I couldn't possibly—

LUKE: Just tell them.

Threepio speaks to the Ewoks. The Ewoks are disturbed. Logray calls Threepio's bluff.

THREEPIO: You see, Master Luke, they didn't believe me. Just as I said they wouldn't.

Luke closes his eyes and begins to concentrate.

Now the litter/throne, with Threepio sitting upon it, rises from the ground. At first Threepio doesn't notice and keeps talking.

THREEPIO: What-wha-what's happening! Oh, dear! Oh!

The Ewoks fall back in terror from the floating throne. Now Threepio begins to spin as though he were on a revolving stool, calling out in total panic at his situation.

THREEPIO: Put me down! He-e-elp. Somebody help! Master Luke! Artoo! Somebody, somebody, help! Master Luke, Artoo, Artoo, quickly! Do something, somebody! Oh! Ohhh!

Logray yells orders to the cowering Ewoks. They rush up and release the bound prisoners. Artoo crashes to the ground. When the Ewoks set him upright, the little droid is fighting mad. Artoo beeps a blue streak at the nearest Ewok and begins pursuing him, finally getting close enough to zap him with an electric charge. The Ewok jumps two feet in the air and runs away, screaming. Han enfolds Leia in an embrace. Luke slowly lowers Threepio and the throne to the ground.

THREEPIO: Oh, oh, oh, oh! Thank goodness.

LUKE: Thanks Threepio.

THREEPIO: *(still shaken)* I . . . never knew I had it in me.

In the rough draft the *Falcon* has landed on the moon to search for Leia, but the ship has been spotted by Captain Naffer aboard the Imperial Super Star Destroyer, and he reports the matter to Vader. At the forest landing site Luke and his friends fall into a trap; Han, Chewie, and the robots manage to escape. Luke is pursued by a walker and hides inside a giant tree. Ben's image appears, and he tells Luke that now is the time for him to either fight or join his father. Luke comes out of hiding and surrenders. In the meantime, as in the movie, Han and the robots get trapped in an Ewok net because of Chewie. Artoo frees them, and the group is suddenly surrounded by the little furry creatures; when Threepio rises, the Ewoks gasp, thinking he is some kind of god. The Ewoks bring their prisoners back to the village. The little creatures are planning to cook Solo and Chewie, and Threepio tells Artoo to try to scare them. He fires blue streaks at Teebo and chases him around the village. They're eventually rescued by Leia and brought in before the council. Threepio tells of their adventures and their mission, and the Ewoks agree to let them go. Artoo, Threepio, and Wicket go back to the *Falcon* to send a signal to the Rebel fleet, while Teebo, Han, and Leia decide to get the weapons ready.

In the revised rough draft and as in the previous script, the *Falcon* comes out of hyperspace and lands directly on the moon of Had Abbadon, only in this version Luke is not with the group (remember, in this draft he was taken prisoner on Tatooine). In order to save Han and Chewie from being killed by the Ewoks, Threepio raises his hands and shouts at the Ewoks in their squealing language. Threepio barks at them, and they immediately untie Chewie and Han. They follow the tribe inside the chief's hut and are reunited with Leia. As in the previous draft, Threepio recounts their adventures to the tribe, and the Ewoks agree to help Han and his friends fight the Imperial troops.

EXT. FOREST WALKWAY
The sounds of a council can be heard.

EXT. CHIEF'S HUT

Younger Ewoks cram the doorway.

INT. CHIEF'S HUT—COUNCIL OF ELDERS

A glowing fire dances in the center of the spartan, low-ceilinged room, creating a kaleidoscope of shadows on the walls. Along one side a group of ten Ewok elders flanks a larger gray-haired Ewok, Chief Chirpa, who sits on his throne. The Rebels sit along the walls of the hut, with Threepio between the two groups and Wicket and Teebo off to one side.

Threepio is in the midst of a long, animated speech in the Ewoks' squeaky native tongue. The Ewoks listen carefully and occasionally murmur comments to each other.

Threepio points several times at the Rebel group and pantomimes a short history of the Galactic Civil War, mimicking the explosion and rocket sounds, imitating Imperial walkers. Throughout the long account certain familiar names are distinguishable in English: Princess Leia, Artoo, Darth Vader, Death Star, Jedi, Obi-Wan Kenobi. Artoo begins beeping excitedly at Threepio.

THREEPIO: Yes, Artoo, I was just coming to that.

Threepio continues with the Millennium Falcon, Cloud City, Vader, Han Solo, *carbonite, the Sarlacc, bringing the history up to the present time.*

At the end of it the chief, Logray, and the elders confer, then nod in agreement.

HAN: What's going on?

LEIA: I don't know.

Luke has been sharing the joy with smiling visage, but now something passes like a dark cloud through his consciousness. The others do not notice.

Logray makes a pronouncement.

The drums begin to sound, and the Ewoks gesticulate wildly.

THREEPIO: Wonderful! We are now a part of the tribe.

Several of the little teddy bears run up and hug the Rebels.

HAN: Just what I always wanted.

Luke wanders outside into the moonlight. Leia notices and follows.

Chewbacca is being enthusiastically embraced by an Ewok, while Wicket clings to Han's leg.

HAN: *(chuckles)* Well, short help is better than no help at all, Chewie. *(to Wicket)* Thank you.

THREEPIO: He says the scouts are going to show us the quickest way to the shield generator.

HAN: Good. How far is it? Ask him. We need some fresh supplies, too. And try to get our weapons back.

Han pulls Threepio back as he keeps trying to translate.

HAN: *(continuing)* And hurry up, will ya? I haven't got all day.

EXT. EWOK VILLAGE

The walkway is deserted now. The windows of the little huts glow and flicker from the fires inside. The sounds of the forest fill the soft night air. Luke has wandered away from the chief's hut and stands staring up at the Death Star. Leia finds him like that.

LEIA: Luke, what's wrong?

Luke turns and looks at her a long moment.

LUKE: Leia . . . do you remember your mother? Your real mother?

LEIA: Just a little bit. She died when I was very young.

LUKE: What do you remember?

LEIA: Just . . . images, really. Feelings.

LUKE: Tell me.

LEIA: *(a little surprised at his insistence)* She was very beautiful. Kind but . . . *(looks up)* sad. Why are you asking me this?

He is looking away.

LUKE: I have no memory of my mother. I never knew her.

LEIA: Luke, tell me. What's troubling you?

LUKE: Vader is here . . . now, on this moon.

LEIA: *(alarmed)* How do you know?

LUKE: I felt his presence. He's come for me. He can feel when I'm near. That's why I have to go. *(facing her)* As long as I stay, I'm endangering the group and our mission here. I have to face him.

Leia is confused.

LEIA: Why?

LUKE: He's my father.

LEIA: Your father?!

LUKE: There's more. It wont be easy for you to hear it, but you must. If I don't make it back, you're the only hope for the Alliance.

Leia is very disturbed by this.

LEIA: Luke, don't talk that way. You have a power I . . . I don't understand and could never have.

LUKE: You're wrong, Leia. You have that power, too. In time you'll learn to use it as I have. The Force is strong in my family. My father has it . . . I have it . . . and my sister has it.

Leia stares into his eyes. What she sees frightens her. But she doesn't draw away. She begins to understand.

LUKE: Yes. It's you, Leia.

LEIA: I know. Somehow . . . I've always known.

LUKE: Then you know why I have to face him.

LEIA: No! Luke, run away, far away. If he can feel your presence, then leave this place. I wish I could go with you.

LUKE: No, you don't. You've always been strong.

LEIA: But why must you confront him?

LUKE: Because . . . there is good in him. I've felt it. He won't turn me over to the Emperor. I can save him. I can turn him back to the good side. I have to try.

They hold each other and look at each other, brother and sister.

During story meetings Leia's character was judged as being too hard, and it was suggested that she become emotional when Luke reveals to her that she's his sister. Maybe she starts crying and tells him they should run away and hide from all this. In the second draft the scene was played to be a lot more dramatic, with Luke leaving Leia in tears. The bit with Han Solo showing up after Luke leaves to meet Vader was added in the revised second draft.

George Lucas: "The man Leia called Father was obviously not her father. He is part of the group that ends up having to fight Darth Vader in the film that will be out in 2003 [laughs]. The part that I never really developed is the death of Luke and Leia's mother. I had a backstory for her in earlier drafts, but it basically didn't survive. When I got to *Jedi*, I wanted one of the kids to have some kind of memory of her because she will be a key figure in the new episodes I'm writing. But I really debated on whether or not Leia should remember her."

Leia holds back her tears as Luke slowly lets her go and moves away. He disappears onto the walkway that leads out of the village. Leia, bathed in moonlight, watches him go as Han comes out of the chief's hut and comes over to her.

HAN: Hey, what's goin' on?

LEIA: Nothing—I just want to be alone for a little while.

HAN: *(angry)* Nothing? Come on, tell me. What's goin' on?

She looks up at him, struggling to control herself.

LEIA: I . . . I can't tell you.

HAN: *(loses his temper)* Could you tell Luke? Is that who you could tell?

LEIA: I . . .

HAN: Ahhh . . .

He starts to walk away, exasperated, then stops and walks back to her.

HAN: I'm sorry.

LEIA: Hold me.

Han gathers her tightly in his protective embrace.

EXT. FOREST—IMPERIAL LANDING PLATFORM

An Imperial shuttle floats down from the Death Star and lands gracefully on the huge platform.

Now an Imperial walker approaches the platform from the darkness of the forest. The whole outpost—platform, walkers, military—looks particularly offensive in the midst of this verdant beauty.

EXT. IMPERIAL LANDING PLATFORM—LOWER DECK

Darth Vader walks down the ramp of the shuttle onto the platform. Coming out of an elevator, he appears on a ramp on a lower level. He walks toward another ramp exit and is met by three troopers and a commander with Luke, in binders, at their center. The young Jedi gazes at Vader with complete calm.

COMMANDER: This is a Rebel that surrendered to us. Although he denies it, I believe there may be more of them, and I request permission to conduct a further search of the area.

Vader looks at Luke, turns away, and faces the commander.

COMMANDER: He was armed only with this.

The commander places Luke's lightsaber in Vader's hands.

VADER: Good work, Commander. Leave us. Conduct your search and bring his companions to me.

COMMANDER: Yes, my lord.

The officer and troops withdraw. Vader and Luke are left alone on the ramp.

VADER: The Emperor has been expecting you.

LUKE: I know, Father.

VADER: So you have accepted the truth.

LUKE: I've accepted the truth that you were once Anakin Skywalker, my father.

VADER: *(turning to face him)* That name no longer has any meaning for me.

LUKE: It is the name of your true self. You've only forgotten. I know there is good in you. The Emperor hasn't driven it from you fully. That was why you couldn't destroy me. That's why you won't bring me to your Emperor now.

Vader looks down from Luke to the lightsaber in his own black-gloved hand. He seems to ponder Luke's words.

Vader ignites the lightsaber and holds it to examine its humming, brilliant blade.

VADER: I see you have constructed a new lightsaber. Your skills are complete. *(extinguishing the lightsaber)* Indeed, you are powerful, as the Emperor has foreseen.

LUKE: Come with me.

VADER: Obi-Wan once thought as you do. You don't know the power of the dark side. I must obey my master.

LUKE: I will not turn . . . and you'll be forced to kill me.

VADER: If that is your destiny . . .

LUKE: Search your feelings, Father. You can't do this. I feel the conflict within you. Let go of your hate.

VADER: It is too late for me, Son. *(signaling to some distant stormtroopers)* The Emperor will show you the true nature of the Force. He is your master now.

Vader and Luke stand staring at one another for a long moment.

LUKE: Then my father is truly dead.

In the rough draft, after Luke surrenders, Veers receives orders to take him to Vader's Star Destroyer. The shuttle's captain tells Veers that Luke must be taken to the Emperor on Had Abbadon instead, but Veers refuses to obey. The shuttle captain makes contact with Grand Moff Jerjerrod.

Aboard the Star Destroyer Luke is confronted by Vader, who asks him one more time to join him. Luke says that he is now strong with the Force and that Vader's powers no longer affect him. Vader replies that his powers will never destroy the Emperor. Suddenly Jerjerrod walks in, furious at Vader for disobeying his orders to bring Luke to the Emperor; Vader grabs the Grand Moff by the throat and kills him.

In the revised rough draft Vader kills the Grand Moff after he finds out that Luke has been captured and taken to the Emperor.

EXT. ENDOR—RIDGE OVERLOOKING SHIELD GENERATOR

Han, Leia, Chewbacca, the droids, Wicket, and another Ewok scout, Paploo, hide on a ridge overlooking the massive Imperial shield generator.

At the base of the generator is an Imperial landing platform. Leia studies the installation.

LEIA: The main entrance to the control bunker's on the far side of that landing platform. This isn't going to be easy.

HAN: Hey, don't worry. Chewie and me got into a lot of places more heavily guarded than this.

Wicket and Paploo are chattering away in the Ewok language. They speak to Threepio.

LEIA: What's he saying?

THREEPIO: He says there's a secret entrance on the other side of the ridge.

EXT. SPACE—REBEL FLEET

The vast fleet hangs in space. A giant Rebel star cruiser is up at the front, but now the Millennium Falcon *roars up to a spot ahead of it, tiny in comparison.*

INT. *MILLENNIUM FALCON*—COCKPIT

Lando is in the pilot's seat.

LANDO: Admiral, we're in position. All fighters accounted for.

INT. REBEL STAR CRUISER—BRIDGE

ACKBAR: Proceed with the countdown. All groups assume attack coordinates.

INT. *MILLENNIUM FALCON*—COCKPIT

Lando's alien copilot, Nien Nunb, takes some getting used to in the familiar environs of the Falcon's *cockpit. Lando turns to his weird copilot.*

LANDO: Don't worry, my friend's down there. He'll have that shield down on time . . .

The copilot flips some switches and grunts an alien comment.

LANDO: *[to himself]* . . . or this'll be the shortest offensive of all time.

INT. REBEL STAR CRUISER—BRIDGE

ACKBAR: All craft, prepare to jump into hyperspace on my mark.

INT. *MILLENNIUM FALCON*—COCKPIT

LANDO: All right. Stand by.

He pulls a lever, and the stars outside begin to streak.

EXT. SPACE—REBEL FLEET

We are treated to an awesome sight: first the Millennium Falcon, *then Ackbar's star cruiser, then, in large segments, the huge fleet roars into hyperspace.*

INT. ACKBAR'S STAR CRUISER—BRIDGE

The stars streak by Ackbar on his bridge.

EXT. SPACE—REBEL FLEET

The remainder of the Rebel fleet roars into hyperspace. And disappears.

EXT. ENDOR—RIDGE OVERLOOKING CONTROL BUNKER

Han, Leia, Chewie, the droids, and their two Ewok guides, Wicket and Paploo, have reunited with the Rebel strike squad. The entire group is spread through the thick undergrowth. Beneath them is the bunker that leads into the generator. Four Imperial scouts, their speeder bikes parked nearby, keep watch over the bunker entrance. Paploo chatters away to Han in the Ewok language.

HAN: Back door, huh? Good idea.

Wicket and Paploo continue their Ewok conversation.

HAN: *(continuing)* It's only a few guards. This shouldn't be too much trouble.

LEIA: Well, it only takes one to sound the alarm.

HAN: *(with a self-confident grin)* Then we'll do it real quiet-like.

Paploo has scampered into the underbrush. Threepio asks Wicket where Paploo went and is given a short reply.

THREEPIO: Oh! Oh, my. Uh, Princess Leia!

Leia quiets him.

THREEPIO: I'm afraid our furry companion has gone and done something rather rash.

Chewie barks. Han, Leia, and company watch in distress.

LEIA: Oh, no.

EXT. THE BUNKER ENTRANCE

Paploo has slipped out of the undergrowth near where the Imperial scouts are lounging.

HAN: *(sighs)* There goes our surprise attack.

Paploo silently swings his furry ball of a body onto one of the scouts' speeder bikes and begins flipping switches at random. Suddenly the bike's engine fires up with a tremendous roar.

EXT. RIDGE

Han, Leia, and company watch in distress.

SCOUT: Look! Over there! Stop him!

The Imperial scouts race toward Paploo just as his speeder bike goes into motion. Paploo hangs on by his paws and shoots away into the forest.

Three of the Imperial scouts jump on their rocket bikes and speed away in pursuit. The fourth watches them go.

EXT. RIDGE

Han, Leia, and Chewie exchange delighted looks.

HAN: Not bad for a little furball. There's only one left. *(to Wicket)* You stay here. We'll take care of this.

Threepio moves to stand next to Wicket and Artoo.

THREEPIO: I have decided that we shall stay here.

EXT. FOREST

Paploo sails through the trees, more lucky than in control. It's scary, but he loves it. When the Imperial scouts pull within sight behind him and begin firing laser-bolts, he decides he's had enough. As he rounds a tree, out of their sight, Paploo grabs a vine and swings up into the trees. A moment later the scouts tear under him in pursuit of the still-flying unoccupied bike.

EXT. BUNKER

Han sneaks up behind the remaining Imperial scout, taps him on the shoulder, and lets the scout chase him behind the bunker into the arms of the waiting Rebel strike team.

INT. BUNKER

The group enters the bunker silently.

In the rough draft Leia, Han, Chewie, and Wicket arrive at the first gun emplacement. They find out from the Rebel Captain Jode that the other gun has been captured; destroying the communications disk will be no help if they can't knock out the shield generator. Han decides to attack the troopers and leaves with Chewie.

Meanwhile, the droids and Teebo arrive at the *Falcon*, which is heavily guarded. As in the film, the Ewok creates a diversion by jumping on one of the rocket bikes. Artoo and Threepio sneak in and send the signal to Lando. On the way out they're caught by another trooper, and Artoo plows into him; both droids and Teebo escape.

EXT. SPACE—DEATH STAR

The half-completed Death Star hangs in space over the Moon of Endor.

INT. DEATH STAR—EMPEROR'S THRONE ROOM

The elevator opens. Vader and Luke enter the room alone. They walk across the dark space to stand before the throne, father and son, side by side beneath the gaze of the Emperor. Vader bows to his master.

EMPEROR: Welcome, young Skywalker. I have been expecting you.

Luke peers at the hooded figure defiantly. The Emperor smiles, then looks down at Luke's binders.

EMPEROR: You no longer need those.

The Emperor motions ever so slightly with his finger, and Luke's binders fall away, clattering noisily to the floor. Luke looks down at his own hands, free now to reach out and grab the Emperor's neck. He does nothing.

EMPEROR: Guards, leave us.

The red-cloaked guards turn and disappear behind the elevator.

EMPEROR: *(to Luke)* I'm looking forward to completing your training. In time you will call me master.

LUKE: You're gravely mistaken. You won't convert me as you did my father.

The Emperor gets down from his throne and walks up very close to Luke. The Emperor looks into his eyes, and for the first time Luke can perceive the evil visage within the hood.

EMPEROR: Oh, no, my young Jedi. You will find that it is you who are mistaken . . . about a great many things.

VADER: His lightsaber.

Vader extends a gloved hand toward the Emperor, revealing Luke's lightsaber. The Emperor takes it.

EMPEROR: Ah, yes, a Jedi's weapon. Much like your father's. By now you must know your father can never be turned from the dark side. So will it be with you.

LUKE: You're wrong. Soon I'll be dead . . . and you with me.

The Emperor laughs.

EMPEROR: Perhaps you refer to the imminent attack of your Rebel fleet.

Luke looks down momentarily.

EMPEROR: Yes . . . I assure you we are quite safe from your friends here.

LUKE: Your overconfidence is your weakness.

Vader looks at Luke.

EMPEROR: Your faith in your friends is yours.

VADER: It is pointless to resist, my son.

The Emperor has returned to his throne and now turns to face Luke.

EMPEROR: *(angry)* Everything that has transpired has done so according to my design. Your friends *(indicates Endor)* up there on the Sanctuary Moon . . .

Luke reacts.

EMPEROR: *(continuing)* . . . are walking into a trap. As is your Rebel fleet! It was I who allowed the Alliance to know the location of the shield generator. It is quite safe from your pitiful little band. An entire legion of my best troops awaits them.

Luke's look darts from the Emperor to the sword in the Emperor's hand.

EMPEROR: Oh . . . I'm afraid the deflector shield will be quite operational when your friends arrive.

Ralph McQuarrie: "The Emperor was going to be in a cave surrounded by lava. The throne room was down in the lower levels of what turns out to be the Empire's headquarters planet. I imagined it to be dark and spooky with enormous buildings and a metal surface and, down below, huge avenues like on Wall Street in Manhattan. George stated that he wanted a planet that was a city with endless built-up areas. In my mind it was built a thousand years ago, layer after layer. The Emperor's office would be at the bottom of it, so far down that you would have lava."

George Lucas: "In the end it didn't seem necessary to show the home planet of the Empire. It seemed more important that we focus on the major target of what we were going after in the movie. So to show Vader and the Emperor in an area that didn't relate to the story didn't seem necessary. Of course, I had a million different names for the home planet of the Empire, but Coruscant came out of publishing."

INT. BUNKER—MAIN CONTROL ROOM

Han, Leia, Chewie, and the Rebel strike team storm through a door and enter the main control room, taking all of the personnel prisoner.

HAN: All right! Up! Move! Come on! Quickly! Quickly! Chewie!

The Rebel troops herd the generator controllers away from their panels. Leia glances at one of the screens on the control panel.

LEIA: Han! Hurry! The fleet will be here any moment.

HAN: Charges! Come on, come on!

EXT. BUNKER

Several more controllers and stormtroopers run into the bunker, leaving guards at the door. Threepio watches nervously in the bushes.

THREEPIO: Oh, my! They'll be captured!

Wicket chatters in the Ewok language and then takes off full steam into the forest.

THREEPIO: Wa-ait! Wait, come back! Artoo, stay with me.

George Lucas: "There are a lot of different activities going on simultaneously in that particular sequence. And to edit this sequence was one of the toughest things to do because it's hard to storyboard it out and to figure out exactly how everything fits together. It's very difficult when you have different actions happening at the same time and you're trying to make it one cohesive idea, and to make it that one thing leads to another, even though the three different sets of action [the battle on Endor, the battle in space, and Luke's confrontation with Vader and the Emperor] seem very separate. One character has to do one thing

INT. BUNKER.

IMPERIAL OFFICER: Freeze!

Han looks up from setting charges as an Imperial officer enters. He deals with him, but he and Leia spin to find dozens of Imperial weapons trained on them and their cohorts.

COMMANDER: You Rebel scum.

A poised force of Imperial troops surrounds them. Even more pour into the room, roughly disarming the Rebel contingent. Han, Leia and Chewie exchange looks. They're helpless.

INT. *MILLENNIUM FALCON—* COCKPIT

Lando operates the controls to come out of hyperspace.

EXT. SPACE—ENDOR, DEATH STAR, REBEL FLEET

in order to trigger the next thing to happen, even though they're physically not connected. Steven Spielberg is very good with this kind of sequence. He really knows how to storyboard something and shoot exactly what he needs and then put it all together. I'm not able to work that way; I try to cover things, and I try to figure out how to cut it all together later. I'm a little more organic in the way I approach things."

The Rebel fleet comes out of hyperspace with an awesome roar. The **Millennium Falcon** *and several Rebel fighters are at the front as the space armada bears down on its target, the Death Star and its Sanctuary Moon.*

INT. REBEL STAR CRUISER—BRIDGE

Ackbar surveys his Rebel fleet from the bridge.

INT. *MILLENNIUM FALCON—*COCKPIT

Lando flips switches, checks his screen, and speaks into the radio.

LANDO: All wings report in.

INT. WEDGE'S X-FIGHTER—COCKPIT

WEDGE: Red Leader standing by.

INT. GRAY LEADER'S X-FIGHTER—COCKPIT

GRAY LEADER: Gray Leader standing by.

INT. GREEN LEADER'S X-FIGHTER—COCKPIT

GREEN LEADER: Green leader standing by.

INT. WEDGE'S X-FIGHTER—COCKPIT

WEDGE: Lock S-foils in attack positions.

EXT. SPACE—REBEL FLEET

The Rebel fleet converges on the Death Star.

INT. REBEL STAR CRUISER

From the bridge of the Rebel headquarters frigate, Admiral Ackbar watches the fighters massing outside his viewscreen.

ACKBAR: May the Force be with us.

INT. *MILLENNIUM FALCON—*COCKPIT

Lando looks worriedly at his alien copilot, Nien Nunb, who points to the control panel and talks to Lando.

LANDO: We've got to be able to get some kind of a reading on that shield, up or down. Well, how could they be jamming us if they don't know . . . we're coming?

Lando shoots a concerned look out at the approaching Death Star as the implications of what he's just said sink in. He hits a switch on his comlink.

LANDO: Break off the attack! The shield is still up.

INT. WEDGE'S X-FIGHTER—COCKPIT

WEDGE: I get no reading. Are you sure?

LANDO: *(voiceover)* Pull up!

IINT. *MILLENNIUM FALCON*—COCKPIT

LANDO: All craft pull up!

EXT. SPACE—DEATH STAR SHIELD

The Falcon and the fighters of Red Squad veer off desperately to avoid the unseen wall.

INT. REBEL STAR CRUISER—BRIDGE

Alarms are screaming and lights flashing as the huge ship changes course abruptly. Other ships in the fleet shoot by outside as the armada tries to halt its forward momentum.

ACKBAR: Take evasive action! Green Group, stick close to holding sector MV-Seven.

EXT. SPACE—DEATH STAR SHIELD

The Rebel fleet takes evasive action.

INT. REBEL STAR CRUISER—BRIDGE

A Mon Calamari controller turns away from his screen and calls out to Ackbar, quite excited.

CONTROLLER: Admiral, we have enemy ships in sector forty-seven.

The admiral turns to the controller.

ACKBAR: It's a trap.

EXT. SPACE—REBEL FLEET

The Millennium Falcon flies into the Imperial trap.

INT. *MILLENNIUM FALCON*—COCKPIT

LANDO: *(over comlink)* Fighters coming in.

EXT. SPACE

The Millennium Falcon and several squads of Rebel fighters head into an armada of TIE fighters. The sky explodes as a fierce dogfight ensues in and around the giant Rebel cruisers.

INT. REBEL COCKPIT

REBEL PILOT: There's too many of them!

EXT. SPACE

The Millennium Falcon flies through the dogfight.

INT. *MILLENNIUM FALCON*—COCKPIT

LANDO: Accelerate to attack speed! Draw their fire away from the cruisers.

INT. WEDGE'S X-FIGHTER—COCKPIT

WEDGE: Copy, Gold Leader.

EXT. SPACE—REBEL CRUISER

The battle continues around the giant cruisers.

INT. DEATH STAR—EMPEROR'S THRONE ROOM

Through the round window behind the Emperor's throne can be seen the distant flashes of the space battle in progress.

EMPEROR: Come, boy. See for yourself.

The Emperor is sitting on his throne. Luke moves to look through a small section of the window. Vader also moves forward.

EMPEROR: From here you will witness the final destruction of the Alliance and the end of your insignificant Rebellion.

Luke is in torment. He glances at his lightsaber sitting on the armrest of the throne. The Emperor watches him and smiles, touches his lightsaber.

EMPEROR: You want this, don't you? The hate is swelling in you now. Take your Jedi weapon. Use it. I am unarmed. Strike me down with it. Give in to your anger. With each passing moment you make yourself more my servant.

Vader watches Luke in his agony.

LUKE: No!

EMPEROR: It is unavoidable. It is your destiny. You, like your father, are now mine!

In the rough draft Leia and the Rebel Captain Jode have blown the communications dish on Had Abbadon. When the explosion occurs, an alarm goes off aboard Vader's Imperial Star Destroyer. Admiral Piett tells Vader that all communications have been cut off but that their radar has detected a large fleet coming out of hyperspace. Vader orders all available ships to protect the two Death Stars and to send Veers more reinforcements on the Green Moon while he is taking Skywalker to the Emperor. The battle begins both in space and in the forest. Vader and Luke are on their way to the throne room on Had Abbadon, when suddenly Ben appears in their path. Vader pulls out his lasersword; Ben explains that he has come to save him, that the Emperor wants to destroy him. If Vader becomes one with the dark side of the Force, he will lose all identity. If he turns to the good side, he will pass through the Netherworld and Ben will rescue him before he becomes one with the Force. But

Vader won't listen and tells Luke to move along. Ben disappears. Vader takes Luke to the Imperial throne room; he ignites his lasersword and orders Luke to kneel before his Emperor. Luke refuses, and the Emperor tells him that while he may succeed in destroying his father, he won't succeed with him.

In the revised rough draft Luke and a guard enter the vast throne room. On the far side of the room a long, wide flight of stairs leads to a throne. The Emperor asks Luke to approach; young Skywalker tells the Emperor that he cannot turn him to the dark side as he did to his father. The Emperor says that he didn't turn him, he did it himself, and Luke will do the same. Luke replies that he'll never turn to the dark side, and the Emperor orders his guards to take him "to the tombs." Later Luke lies unconscious on a small island in the middle of a lake of lava. A hot wind blows across his face and wakes him. He suddenly becomes aware of a presence behind him; he looks back and sees Ben in the flesh. Ben explains that he's come back to help Luke destroy the Emperor and his father. Yoda appears; while Ben will be at his side, Yoda also will be able to help from the Netherworld.

George Lucas: "Even though at some point Yoda and Ben interfered, I eventually decided that they couldn't connect physically with what Luke was doing. I felt that one of the major issues in the third film is that Luke is finally on his own and has to fight Vader and the Emperor by himself. If you get a sense that Yoda or Ben is there to help him or to somehow influence him, it diminishes the power of the scene."

EXT. FOREST—GENERATOR BUNKER

Han, Leia, Chewie, and the rest of the strike team are led out of the bunker by their captors. The surrounding area, deserted before, is now crowded with two-legged Imperial walkers and hundreds of Imperial troops. The situation looks hopeless.

STORMTROOPER: All right, move it! I said move it! Go on!

George Lucas: "Dealing with the droids is sometimes easier than dealing with the human characters because in a sense, they're more functional. They can actually do things. The fact that Threepio can speak

From the undergrowth beyond the clearing comes Threepio.

THREEPIO: Hello! I say, over there! Were you looking for me?

BUNKER COMMANDER: Bring those two down here.

STORMTROOPER: Let's go.

Artoo and Threepio are standing near one of the big trees. As six Imperial stormtroopers rush over to take them captive, the two droids duck out of sight behind the tree.

THREEPIO: Well, they're on their way. Artoo, are you sure this was a good idea?

STORMTROOPER: Freeze! Don't move!

THREEPIO: We surrender.

a lot of different languages and Artoo can do mechanical things made it easier for me to incorporate them in the story. But by the time we got to the third film, we had so many different characters that it got a little more difficult to deal with all of them. Juggling with all the different characters and keeping them all in the air without ever dropping them was a challenge."

The stormtroopers come around the tree and find the two droids waiting quietly to be taken. As the Imperial troops move to do that, however, a band of Ewoks drops down from above and overpowers them.

THREEPIO: Ohhh! Stand back, Artoo.

In a nearby tree an Ewok raises a horn to his lips and sounds the Ewok attack call. All hell breaks loose as hundreds of Ewoks throw their fuzzy bodies into the fray against the assembled stormtroopers and their awesome two-legged walkers.

Stormtroopers fire on Ewoks with sophisticated weapons while their furry little adversaries sneak up behind the Imperial troopers and bash them over the head with large clubs.

Ewoks in handmade, primitive hang gliders drop rocks onto the stormtroopers, dive-bombing their deadly adversaries. One is hit in the wing with laser fire and crashes.

A line of Ewoks hangs desperately to a vine that is hooked to a walker's foot. As the walker moves along, the fuzzy creatures are dragged behind.

In the confusion of the battle Han and Leia break away and dive for the cover of the bunker door as explosions erupt around them. Han goes to the bunker door control panel.

LEIA: The code's changed. We need Artoo!

HAN: Here's the terminal.

LEIA: (into comlink) Artoo, where are you? We need you at the bunker right away.

Artoo and Threepio are hiding behind a log as the battle rages around them. Suddenly the stubby little astrodroid lets out a series of whistles and shoots off across the battlefield. Threepio, panicked, runs after him.

THREEPIO: Going? What do you mean, you're going? But—but going where, Artoo? No, wait! Artoo! Oh, this is no time for heroics. Come back!

A group of Ewoks has moved a primitive catapult into position. They fire off a large boulder that hits one of the walkers. The walker turns and heads for the catapult, blasting away with both guns. The Ewoks abandon their weapons and flee in all directions.

EXT. OUTER SPACE

The Falcon and other Rebel fighters are engaged in ferocious combat with Imperial TIE fighters, the battle raging around the cruisers of the Rebel armada.

INT. *MILLENNIUM FALCON*—COCKPIT

Lando is in radio communication with the pilots of the other Rebel squads.

LANDO: Watch yourself, Wedge! Three from above!

INT WEDGE'S X-FIGHTER—COCKPIT

WEDGE: Red Three, Red Two, pull in!

The character of Wedge was added in the battle sequence in the third draft.

INT. RED TWO'S COCKPIT

RED TWO: Got it!

EXT. SPACE

The dogfight between Rebel X-wings and Imperial TIE fighters rages.

INT. RED THREE'S COCKPIT

RED THREE: Three of them coming in, twenty degrees!

INT. WEDGE'S X-FIGHTER—COCKPIT

WEDGE: Cut to the left! I'll take the leader!

EXT. SPACE

Wedge shoots down the TIE fighter.

INT. WEDGE'S X-FIGHTER—COCKPIT

WEDGE: They're heading for the medical frigate.

EXT. SPACE

Lando steers the Falcon through a complete flip as his crew fires at the TIEs with the belly guns.

INT. *MILLENNIUM FALCON*—COCKPIT

NAVIGATOR: Pressure steady.

EXT. SPACE

The copilot Nien Nunb chatters an observation.

INT. *MILLENNIUM FALCON*—COCKPIT

The giant Imperial Star Destroyer waits silently some distance from the battle. The Emperor's huge Super Star Destroyer rests in the middle of the fleet.

LANDO: Only the fighters are attacking . . . I wonder what those Star Destroyers are waiting for.

INT. SUPER STAR DESTROYER

Admiral Piett and two fleet commanders watch the battle at the huge window of the Super Star Destroyer's bridge.

COMMANDER: We're in attack position now, sir.

PIETT: Hold there.

FLEET COMMANDER: We're not going to attack?

PIETT: I have my orders from the Emperor himself. He has something special planned. We only need to keep them from escaping.

INT. EMPEROR'S TOWER—THRONE ROOM

A horrified Luke watches the serial battle fireworks out the window as Rebel ships explode against the protective shield.

EMPEROR: As you can see, my young apprentice, your friends have failed. Now witness the firepower of this fully armed and operational battle station. *(into comlink)* Fire at will, Commander.

Luke, in shock, looks out to the Rebel fleet beyond.

INT. DEATH STAR—CONTROL ROOM

A button is pressed, which switches on a panel of lights. Controllers pull back on several switches. A hooded Imperial soldier reaches overhead and pulls a lever. Commander Jerjerrod stands over them.

JERJERROD: Fire!

INT. DEATH STAR—BLAST CHAMBER

A huge beam of light emanates from a long shaft. Two stormtroopers stand to one side at a control panel.

EXT. DEATH STAR

The giant laserdish on the completed half of the Death Star begins to glow. Then a powerful beam shoots out toward the serial battle.

EXT. SPACE—AIR BATTLE

The air is thick with giant ships. Now an enormous Rebel cruiser is hit by the Death Star beam and is blown to dust.

INT. *MILLENNIUM FALCON*—COCKPIT

The ship is buffeted by the tremendous explosion of the Rebel cruiser. Lando and his copilot are stunned by the sight of the Death Star's firepower.

LANDO: That blast came from the Death Star! That thing's operational! *(into comlink)* Home One, this is Gold Leader.

INT. REBEL STAR CRUISER—BRIDGE

Ackbar stands amid the confusion on the wide bridge and speaks into the comlink.

ACKBAR: We saw it. All craft prepare to retreat.

INT. *MILLENNIUM FALCON*—COCKPIT

LANDO: You won't get another chance at this, Admiral.

INT. REBEL STAR CRUISER—BRIDGE

ACKBAR: We have no choice, General Calrissian. Our cruisers can't repel firepower of that magnitude.

INT. *MILLENNIUM FALCON*—COCKPIT

LANDO: Han will have that shield down. We've got to give him more time.

EXT. FOREST—GENERATOR BUNKER

Meanwhile, the forest battle is raging, too.

THREEPIO: We're coming!

Artoo and Threepio make it to the door as Han and Leia provide cover fire.

HAN: Come on! Come on!

The little droid moves to the terminal and plugs in his computer arm.

THREEPIO: Oh, Artoo, hurry!

A large explosion hits near Artoo, knocking him backward. The stubby astro-droid's head is smoldering. Suddenly there is a loud sprooing, and Han and Leia turn around to see Artoo with his compartment doors open and all of his appendages sticking out; water and smoke spurt out of the nozzles in his body.

THREEPIO: My goodness! Artoo, why did you have to be so brave?

HAN: Well, I suppose I could hot-wire this thing.

Han turns to the terminal.

LEIA: I'll cover you.

A walker lumbers forward, shooting laserblasts at frantic Ewoks running in all directions. Two Ewoks are struck down by laserblasts. One tries to awaken his friend, then realizes he is dead.

Duwayne Dunham: "The battle with the Ewoks in *Jedi* was really designed by George. In other words, many gags were shot, as was the basic idea of the battle, but based on what was shot and how it was shot, George went in and pretty much molded the story, and then he would call the special effects guys at ILM and tell them what he wanted to add to each shot. Quite often he would make some pretty interesting things from outtakes or from the end of a shot. In particular, there is a shot where there's a walker that fires; there's an explosion, an Ewok falls over, and another one comes back to him. As I recall, what really happened was that the actor playing the Ewok fell and the other actor turned around, thinking the shot was over. But when George saw this, he just added an explosion and made it look like the walker shot the Ewok and the other one came back to help him."

EXT. SPACE—DEATH STAR

The Rebel fleet continues to be picked off by the Death Star's deadly beam.

INT. *MILLENNIUM FALCON*—COCKPIT

Lando steers the Falcon *wildly through an obstacle course of floating giants. He's been yelling into the comlink.*

LANDO: *(desperately)* Yes! I said closer! Move as close as you can and engage those Star Destroyers at point-blank range.

INT. REBEL STAR CRUISER—BRIDGE

ACKBAR: At that close range we won't last long against those Star Destroyers.

INT. *MILLENNIUM FALCON*—COCKPIT

LANDO: We'll last longer than we will against that Death Star . . . and we might just take a few of them with us.

EXT. SPACE—IMPERIAL STAR DESTROYER

The Rebel cruisers move very close to the Imperial Star Destroyers and begin to blast away at point-blank range. Tiny fighters race across the giant surfaces against a backdrop of laserfire.

INT. REBEL COCKPIT

REBEL PILOT: She's gonna blow!

EXT. SPACE

The control tower of a Star Destroyer blows up.

INT. REBEL Y-WING—COCKPIT

Y-WING PILOT: I'm hit!

EXT. SPACE—IMPERIAL STAR DESTROYER

The damaged Y-wing plummets toward a Star Destroyer and crashes into it, exploding.

INT. EMPEROR'S TOWER—THRONE ROOM

Out of the window and on the viewscreens the Rebel fleet is being decimated in blinding explosions of light and debris. But in here there is no sound of battle. The Emperor speaks to Luke, and Vader watches him.

EMPEROR: Your fleet is lost. And your friends on the Endor moon will not survive. There is no escape, my young apprentice. The Alliance will die . . . as will your friends.

Luke's eyes are full of rage.

EMPEROR: Good. I can feel your anger. I am defenseless. Take your weapon! Strike me down with all of your hatred and your journey toward the dark side will be complete.

Luke can resist no longer. The lightsaber flies into his hand. He ignites it in an instant and swings at the Emperor. Vader's lightsaber flashes into view, blocking Luke's blow before it can reach the Emperor. The two blades spark at contact.

In the rough draft Ben's image appears in the Emperor's throne room; he tells the Emperor that he overestimates his abilities. Yoda also appears, and suddenly the Emperor starts panicking. He orders Vader to destroy his son. The saber by the throne flies into Luke's hands, and the fight begins with Vader and Luke jumping from one rock to another over a bubbling pool of lava.

In the revised rough draft, on Had Abbadon, Vader goes to meet the Emperor (remember, in this draft Luke has been taken prisoner by the Emperor); two guards try to stop him at the door to the throne room. Both guards are stopped in their tracks, drop their weapons, and grab their throats, gasping for air. Vader marches into the throne room, asking the Emperor where Luke is. The Emperor raises his hand, and Vader starts choking; the Emperor tells him that the boy is his to train and that Vader's place is with his fleet. Vader asks for forgiveness and leaves.

Later, after the Emperor has found out that the Rebel fleet has jumped to hyperspace and is on its way for the attack, he takes an elevator down to the tomb's dungeon, where Luke is kept prisoner. Vader follows him. Luke and Ben (remember, in this draft Ben has come back in the flesh to help Luke) feel the presence of the Emperor and Vader approaching; Ben is worried that the two of them could destroy Luke. The Emperor walks in and tells Ben that the boy is his. The image of Yoda appears, threatening him. Vader approaches and tells the Emperor that it's too late to turn the boy to the dark side; Luke and Ben must be destroyed. Luke reaches out, and Vader's lasersword leaps out of his belt into the young Jedi's hands. The Emperor pulls a sword out of his sleeve and throws it to Vader, telling him to destroy Luke; the fight begins.

EXT. FOREST

The battle rages on.

Chewie swings on a vine to the roof of one of the walkers. Two Ewoks cling to him. They land with a thud on the top of the lurching machine.

One of the Ewoks peeks through the window.

WALKER PILOT #1: Look!

WALKER PILOT #2: Get him off of there!

The walker pilot opens the hatch to see what's going on. He is yanked out and tossed overboard before he can scream. The two Ewoks jump into the cockpit and knock the second pilot unconscious. As the mighty machine careens out of control, outside Chewie is almost knocked overboard; he sticks his head into the hatch with a series of angry barks. The Ewoks are too busy and frightened to listen to the Wookiee's complaint. Chewie slips inside the walker.

Chewbacca's walker moves through the forest, destroying another Imperial walker and firing laserblasts at unsuspecting stormtroopers. The Ewoks shout and cheer as the giant machine helps turn the tide of the battle in their favor.

A speeder bike chases Ewoks through the underbrush. As the scout rounds a tree, he is knocked off his bike by a vine tied between two trees.

As a walker moves in, Ewoks cut vines restraining two huge logs, which swing down and smash the walker's head flat.

A walker marches through the undergrowth, blasting Ewoks as it goes. An Ewok warrior gives the signal, and a pile of logs is cut loose. The logs tumble under the walker's feet, causing it to slip and slide until it finally topples over with a great crash.

A scout bike races past and is lassoed with a heavy vine. The other end of the vine is tied to a tree, and the bike swings around in ever-tightening circles until it runs out of rope and crashes into the tree with a huge explosion.

EXT. FOREST—GENERATOR BUNKER

Han works furiously at the control panel as he attempts to hot-wire the door. Leia is covering him.

HAN: I think I got it. I got it!

As the connection is made, with loud squeaks, a second door slides across in front of the first.

Han frowns and turns back to the wires again. Leia suddenly cries out in pain, her shoulder hit by a laserblast.

THREEPIO: Oh, Princess Leia, are you all right?

HAN: Let's see.

LEIA: It's not bad.

STORMTROOPER: *(offscreen)* Freeze!

They freeze.

THREEPIO: Oh, dear.

STORMTROOPER: Don't move!

Leia holds her laser gun ready behind Han, out of view of the two stormtroopers moving toward them. Han and Leia's eyes lock; the moment seems suspended in time.

HAN: I love you.

Another shared look between them as she smiles up at Han.

LEIA: I know.

Lawrence Kasdan: " 'I love you,' 'I know' was very popular in *The Empire Strikes Back*, so when we got to this scene in *Jedi*, we thought it would be fun to use it again."

STORMTROOPER: Hands up! Stand up!

Han turns slowly, revealing the gun in Leia's hand. She disposes of the stormtroopers in a flash. As Han turns back to Leia, he looks up to see a giant walker approach and stand before him, its deadly weapons aimed right at him.

HAN: *(to Leia)* Stay back.

The hatch on top of the walker

Joe Johnson: "Well, the big thing that didn't end up in *The Empire Strikes Back* was the two-legged walker, but it did end up in *Jedi*. You get a brief glance of it in *Empire*, but there was a shot, a much nicer shot, a POV from one of the opens, and Chewie sticks his head out and barks triumphantly.

HAN: Chewie! Get down here! She's wounded! No, wait . . . I got an idea.

INT. EMPEROR'S TOWER—THRONE ROOM

Luke and Vader are engaged in a man-to-man duel of lightsabers even more vicious than the battle on Bespin. But the young Jedi has grown stronger in the interim, and now the advantage shifts to him. Vader is forced back, losing his balance, and is knocked down the stairs. Luke stands at the top of the stairs, ready to attack.

EMPEROR: *(laughing)* Good. Use your aggressive feelings, boy! Let the hate flow through you.

Luke looks momentarily back at the Emperor, then back to Vader, and realizes he is using the dark side. He turns off his lightsaber and relaxes, driving the hate from his being.

VADER: Obi-Wan has taught you well.

LUKE: I will not fight you, Father.

Vader walks back up the stairs to Luke.

VADER: You are unwise to lower your defenses.

Vader attacks, forcing Luke onto the defensive. The young Jedi leaps in an amazing reverse flip up to the safety of the catwalk overhead. Vader stands below him.

LUKE: Your thoughts betray you, Father. I feel the good in you . . . the conflict.

VADER: There is no conflict.

LUKE: You couldn't bring yourself to kill me before, and I don't believe you'll destroy me now.

VADER: You underestimate the power of the dark side. If you will not fight, then you will meet your destiny.

snowspeeders; the speeder is attacking the walker and passes right over its head. Unfortunately at the very end; we were under a deadline and were literally up all night shooting this scene. Someone didn't tighten up the backing of the painted sky, and no one noticed it. The next day in dailies, you could see the background slip, and it slipped about eight inches halfway through the shot . . . It just fell, which completely ruined the shot.

"But the two-legged walker was never in the script; George had not asked for it. It was just something that I thought: Hey, wouldn't it be neat to have a little scout walker, like a two-legged thing? I imagined it to be a vehicle that would provide support for the four-legged ones, something that's quicker and more lightly armed. I built the prototype from model kits just as a desk display, and then the animators took that and cut it apart and attached the pieces to an armature. It happened almost overnight, and it didn't quite make it into *Empire* in the way that it was intended to, but we savedit and used it extensively in *Jedi.*"

Vader throws the lasersword, and it cuts through the supports holding the catwalk, then returns to Vader's hand. Luke tumbles to the ground in a shower of sparks and rolls out of sight under the Emperor's platform. Vader moves to find him.

EMPEROR: *(laughs)* Good. Good.

EXT. SPACE—AIR BATTLE

The two armadas, like their seabound ancestors, blast away at each other in individual point-blank confrontations. The Falcon *and several fighters attack one of the larger Imperial ships.*

INT. *MILLENNIUM FALCON*—COCKPIT

LANDO: "Watch out. Squad at point oh-six.

INT. REBEL COCKPIT

REBEL PILOT: I'm on it, Gold Leader.

INT. WEDGE'S X-FIGHTER—COCKPIT

WEDGE: Good shot, Red Two.

EXT. SPACE

The dogfight rages.

INT. *MILLENNIUM FALCON*—COCKPIT

LANDO: Now . . . come on, Han, old buddy. Don't let me down.

EXT. FOREST—GENERATOR BUNKER

Chewie's walker stands in front of the door to the bunker.

INT. BUNKER CONTROL ROOM

Controllers watch the main viewscreen, on which a vague figure of an Imperial walker pilot can be seen. There is a great deal of static and interference.

HAN/PILOT: *(voice-over)* It's over, . Commander. The Rebels have been routed. They're fleeing into the woods. We need reinforcements to continue the pursuit.

The controllers are delighted.

Duwayne Dunham: "Once the sequences for the battle were shot, they took on a whole different kind of life. For the space battle segments we used a lot of leader with grease pencil markings that indicated that after the special effects were done, we would have a ship or a laserblast. We also used a few video-type shots, which were eventually replaced with the real shots."

Joe Johnson: "There were a lot of different spaceships in the Rebel fleet that had been designed but that we didn't use because there wasn't enough time to build them. Creating new ships comes down to designing something you've never seen before. We've all seen spaceships in different movies, books, and TV shows. What haven't we seen yet? It's always a challenge. It has to do with taking the character of the ship and taking the character who is using it and trying to let the design tell a little bit of the story. Like Darth Vader's Star Destroyer. It's all about him; it's menacing-looking, it's long and lean, it looks evil. The X-wings look like they're basi-

CONTROL ROOM COMMANDER:
Send three squads to help. Open the back door.

SECOND COMMANDER: Sir.

EXT. FOREST—GENERATOR BUNKER

As the door to the bunker opens and the Imperial troops rush out, they're surprised to find themselves surrounded by Rebels, their weapons pointed at them. Ewoks holding bows and arrows appear on the roof of the bunker.

INT. BUNKER

Han, Chewie, and several troops have rushed into the control room and plant explosive charges on the control panels.

HAN: Throw me another charge.

INT. EMPEROR'S TOWER— THRONE ROOM

Vader stalks the low-ceilinged area on the level below the throne, searching for Luke in the semidarkness, his lightsaber held ready.

VADER: You cannot hide forever, Luke.

LUKE: I will not fight you.

VADER: Give yourself to the dark side. It is the only way you can save your friends.

Luke shuts his eyes tightly, in anguish.

VADER: Yes, your thoughts betray you. Your feelings for them are strong. Especially for . . .

Vader stops and senses something.

VADER: Sister! So . . . you have a twin sister. Your feelings have now betrayed her, too. Obi-Wan was wise to hide her from me. Now his failure is complete. If you will not turn to the dark side, then perhaps she will.

Luke ignites his lightsaber and screams in anger.

LUKE: No!

He rushes at his father with a frenzy we have not seen before. Sparks fly as Luke and Vader fight in the cramped area.

Luke's hatred forces Vader to retreat out of the low area and across a bridge overlooking a vast elevator shaft. Each stroke of Luke's sword drives his father further toward defeat.

The Dark Lord is knocked to his knees, and as he raises his sword to block another onslaught, Luke slashes Vader's right hand off at the wrist, causing metal and electronic parts to fly from the mechanical stump. Vader's sword clatters uselessly away over the edge of the platform and into the bottomless shaft below.

cally hot rods. The TIE fighters look frightening, especially the interceptors we used in *Jedi*. They not only look fast and deadly, they were intended to look scary."

The basic idea for the battle on Endor was shaped in the rough draft and pretty much follows the way it was finally designed for the film. However, one interesting moment never made it into the movie; Han throws a cable from the walker to the great metal door of the bunker, and in his attempt to rip it off, he tears half of the walker instead.

Luke moves over Vader and holds the blade of his sword to the Dark Lord's throat. The Emperor watches with uncontrollable, pleased agitation.

EMPEROR: Good! Your hate has made you powerful. Now, fulfill your destiny and take your father's place at my side!

Luke looks at his father's mechanical hand, then to his own mechanical, black-gloved hand, and realizes how much he is becoming like his father. He makes the decision for which he has spent a lifetime in preparation. Luke switches off his lightsaber.

LUKE: Never!

Luke casts his lightsaber away.

LUKE: I'll never turn to the dark side. You've failed, Your Highness. I am a Jedi, like my father before me.

The Emperor's glee turns to rage.

EMPEROR: So be it . . . Jedi.

In the rough draft, during the fight Luke cuts off Vader's artificial arm. The Emperor tells Vader that he is old and weak; if he had destroyed Luke, he would have been given half the Empire to rule. Now the boy himself will have that honor. Vader begs his son to kill him, but Luke says that he fights only in self-defense; he switches off his weapon and throws it to his father. The Emperor orders Vader to kill Luke.

In the revised rough draft Ben and the Emperor watch Luke fight against Vader. Ben tells the Emperor that Luke is stronger than he imagines and has many allies. A crashing blow by Luke causes Vader to lose his balance, and he falls onto one of the small rock islands, his sword hand landing in the molten lava. Vader expects Luke to strike him; the Emperor tells him to kill Vader, but Luke says he will not turn to the dark side.

EXT. FOREST—GENERATOR BUNKER

Han and Rebel fighters run out of the bunker and race across the clearing.

HAN: Move! Move! Move!

The bunker explodes, followed by a spectacular display as the huge shield-generator radar dish explodes along with the bunker.

INT. REBEL STAR CRUISER—BRIDGE

Ackbar, sitting in his control chair, speaks into the radio.

ACKBAR: The shield is down! Commence attack on the Death Star's main reactor.

INT. *MILLENNIUM FALCON*—COCKPIT

LANDO: We're on our way. Red Group, Gold Group, all fighters follow me. *(laughs)* Told you they'd do it!

EXT. SPACE—DEATH STAR SURFACE

The Falcon, followed by several smaller Rebel fighters, heads toward the unfinished superstructure of the Death Star.

INT. EMPEROR'S TOWER—THRONE ROOM

Luke stands still as the Emperor faces him at the bottom of the stairs.

EMPEROR: If you will not be turned, you will be destroyed.

The Emperor raises his arms toward Luke. Blinding bolts of energy, evil lightning, shoot from the Emperor's hands at Luke with such speed and power, the young Jedi shrinks before them, his knees buckling.

The wounded Vader struggles to his feet and moves to stand at his master's side.

EMPEROR: Young fool . . . only now, at the end, do you understand.

Luke is almost unconscious beneath the continuing assault of the Emperor's lightning. He clutches a canister to keep from falling into the bottomless shaft as the bolts tear through him.

EMPEROR: Your feeble skills are no match for the power of the dark side. You have paid the price of your lack of vision.

Luke writhes on the floor in unbearable pain, reaching weakly up toward where Vader stands watching.

LUKE: *(groans)* Father, please. Help me.

Again Vader stands, watching Luke. He looks at his master, the Emperor, then back to Luke on the floor.

EMPEROR: Now, young Skywalker . . . you will die.

Although it would not have seemed possible, the outpouring of bolts from the Emperor's fingers actually increases in intensity, the sound screaming through the room. Luke's body writhes in pain.

Vader grabs the Emperor from behind, fighting for control of the robed figure despite the Dark Lord's weakened body and gravely weakened arm. The Emperor struggles in his embrace, his bolt-shooting hands now lifted high, away from Luke. Now the white lightning arcs back to strike at Vader. He stumbles with his load as the sparks rain off his helmet and flow down over his black cape. He holds his evil master high over his head and walks to the edge of the abyss at the central core of the throne room. With one final burst of his once-awesome strength, Darth Vader hurls the Emperor's body into the bottomless shaft.

The Emperor's body spins helplessly into the void, arcing as it falls into the abyss.

Finally, when the body is far down the shaft, it explodes, creating a rush of air through the room. Vader has collapsed beside the bottomless hole. Luke crawls to his father's side and pulls him away from the edge of the abyss to safety. Both the young Jedi and the giant warrior are too weak to move.

In the rough draft, as in the film, Vader can't bring himself to destroy Luke. The Emperor raises his hands, causing lightning bolts to strike Luke. Luke raises his hands in defense, and the bolts are deflected by an invisible shield. Whenever a bolt hits, the images of Ben and Yoda appear momentarily at the point of impact. The bolts become more intense, and Luke drops to his knees under the pressure. Suddenly the Emperor feels a disturbance; he turns and sees Vader coming at him. Vader grabs the Emperor, and they both fall into a lake of lava.

In the revised rough draft the Emperor raises his hands, causing lightning to strike Ben. Luke leaps in front of him and raises his hands, and the bolts are deflected by an invisible shield. Wherever a bolt hits, the image of Yoda appears momentarily. The bolts become more intense; Ben is knocked unconscious, and Luke drops to his knees. As in the previous draft, Vader grabs the Emperor, and they both fall into the lake of lava. Ben and Luke realize that Vader has turned to the good side.

During story meetings Lawrence Kasdan suggested that in order to give an emotional twist to the story, Luke should die and his sister should take over at the end. George Lucas was opposed to this idea, arguing how upset he was as a child when a hero was killed.

George Lucas: "It would really have put an unfortunate twist on everything if we had killed off one of the main characters. Luke needed to live, and we needed to have Leia and Han together at the end. The fact that the boy gets the girl — or the girl gets the boy — in the end was a key factor and was as important as Luke overcoming his demons. At the same time, I realized that I could kill off Luke if I wanted to, and I tried to play that up as much as I could. It was conceivable that Luke could die or turn to the dark side, and if he did, then it would be up to Leia to redeem everybody."

Another dark idea that Lawrence Kasdan had for the ending was to have Luke put on Vader's mask and say that he's now going to destroy the Rebel fleet and rule the universe. It was discussed that in his confrontation with the Emperor, Luke could pretend that he'd been turned to the dark side. The Emperor would then take him to the controls and tell him to destroy the Rebel fleet; instead, Luke would aim at the Emperor's home planet of Had Abbadon and destroy it.

EXT./INT. SPACE BATTLE—FIGHTERS AND DEATH STAR

Rebel fighters accompany the Falcon *across the surface of the Death Star to the unfinished portion, where they dive into the superstructure of the giant battle station, followed by TIE fighters.*

WEDGE: I'm going in.

LANDO: Here goes nothing.

The X-wing leads the chase through the ever-narrowing shaft, followed by the Falcon *and four other fighters, plus TIE fighters who continually fire at the Rebels.*

Lights reflect off the pilots' faces as they race through the dark shaft.

LANDO: Now lock on to the strongest power source. It should be the power generator.

WEDGE: Form up. And stay alert. We could run out of space real fast.

The fighters and the Falcon *race through the tunnel, still pursued by the TIE fighters. One of the X-wings is hit from behind and explodes.*

LANDO: Split up and head back to the surface. And see if you can get a few of those TIE fighters to follow you.

PILOT: Copy, Gold Leader.

The Rebel ships peel off, pursued by four of the TIEs, while Lando and Wedge continue through the main tunnel. It narrows, and the Falcon *scrapes the side dangerously. Two other TIE fighters continue to chase them.*

LANDO: That was too close.

Nien Nunb agrees.

INT. REBEL STAR CRUISER—BRIDGE

The battle between the Rebel and Imperial fleets rages on.

ACKBAR: We've got to give those fighters more time. Concentrate all fire on that Super Star Destroyer.

EXT. SPACE

Rebel craft fire at the giant Super Star Destroyer.

INT. VADER'S STAR DESTROYER—BRIDGE

CONTROLLER: Sir, we've lost our bridge deflector shield.

Admiral Piett and a commander stand at the window. They look concerned.

PIETT: Intensify the forward batteries. I don't want anything to get through.

EXT. SPACE

Outside the window a damaged Rebel fighter is out of control and heading directly toward the bridge.

INT. VADER'S STAR DESTROYER—BRIDGE

PIETT: Intensify forward firepower!

INT. REBEL FIGHTER COCKPIT

The Rebel pilot screams.

INT. VADER'S STAR DESTROYER—BRIDGE

COMMANDER: Too late!

The Rebel ship hits the Star Destroyer, causing a huge explosion.

EXT. SPACE

The giant battleship loses control.

INT. REBEL STAR CRUISER

There is excitement on the bridge as the battle rages on all sides. They cheer as the giant Star Destroyer is destroyed.

EXT. SPACE—SURFACE OF DEATH STAR

The giant Star Destroyer crashes into the Death Star and explodes.

INT. DEATH STAR—MAIN DOCKING BAY

Chaos. For the first time the Death Star is rocked by explosions as the Rebel fleet, no longer backed against a wall, zooms over, unloading a heavy barrage. Imperial troops run in all directions, confused and desperate to escape.

In the midst of this uproar Luke is trying to carry the enormous dead weight of his father's weakening body toward an Imperial shuttle. Finally, Luke collapses from the strain. The explosions grow louder as Vader draws him closer.

VADER: Luke, help me take this mask off.

LUKE: But you'll die.

VADER: Nothing can stop that now. Just for once let me look on you with my own eyes.

Slowly, hesitantly, Luke removes the mask from his father's face. There beneath the scars is an elderly man. His eyes do not focus. But the dying man smiles at the sight before him.

ANAKIN: *(very weak)* Now . . . go, my son. Leave me.

LUKE: No. You're coming with me. I'll not leave you here. I've got to save you.

ANAKIN: You already have, Luke. You were right. You were right about me. Tell your sister . . . you were right.

LUKE: Father . . . I won't leave you.

Darth Vader, Anakin Skywalker . . . Luke's father, dies.

Luke taking off his father's helmet became a real issue during story meetings. One problem was that by taking the helmet off, Luke might seem to be killing his father, who can't breathe without the helmet. It was suggested that Luke take the helmet off after his father dies. At the same time George Lucas explained that Vader wants to see his son in a human way, without any machinery, and also suggested that Vader's voice should change once the helmet has been taken off to a much weaker version of the same thing, something much older-sounding. Luke's father should be in his sixties, about ten years younger than Ben. He should be burned with scars on his face and have no hair. He should be a continuation of what we saw of him in *The Empire Strikes Back*. He should be sad-looking, not repulsive. Maybe one of his eyes could be completely white with no pupil and the other could be sort of clouded over. Lawrence Kasdan suggested that he might have a light gray beard to give him a little normality.

In the second draft Anakin is described as an elderly man with a scarred face and a white beard. In the third draft the description is a bit more gruesome, suggesting that Vader is a horrible mutant, hardly recognizable as human.

George Lucas: "I didn't have a very specific idea about what Vader might look like underneath the mask. I knew that he had been in a lot of battles, and at one point I thought that he had had a confrontation with Ben and Ben had sent him into a volcano. But he was all but dead, and basically he was manufactured back together even though there was very little left of him. So he is kind of this three-quarter mechanical man and one-quarter human, and the suit he wears is like a walking iron lung. By the time we got to the third film, we were able to articulate what Vader looked like underneath the mask, but until then I just knew that he was pretty messed up simply because he could barely breathe or speak."

EXT. DEATH STAR

A lone X-wing is just in front of the Millennium Falcon *on its swerving bomb run through the immense superstructure of the half-built Death Star. They are pursued by TIE fighters.*

INT. WEDGE'S X-FIGHTER—COCKPIT

WEDGE: There it is!

EXT. DEATH STAR

The Rebels home in on the main reactor shaft. It is awesome.

INT. *FALCON* COCKPIT

LANDO: All right, Wedge. Go for the power regulator on the north tower.

INT. WEDGE'S X-FIGHTER—COCKPIT

WEDGE: Copy, Gold Leader. I'm already on my way out.

EXT. DEATH STAR

The X-wing heads for the top of the huge reactor and fires several proton torpedoes at the power regulator, causing a series of small explosions.

The Falcon *heads for the main reactor, and Lando fires the missiles, which shoot out of the* Falcon *with a powerful roar and hit directly at the center of the main reactor.*

INT. *FALCON* COCKPIT

Lando winces at the dangerously close explosion.

EXT. DEATH STAR

He maneuvers the Falcon out of the winding superstructure just ahead of the continuing chain of explosions.

Nilo Rodis-Jamero: "I had just come back from Hong Kong, and I was really impressed at how crowded that place was; everything is squeezed in. And so my first take on the running around in the inside of the Death Star was unbelievably crowded. If you look at my storyboards on this sequence, there are even a lot of references in Chinese that say 'subway'! But this whole sequence was made in collaboration with Joe, Ralph, and the model makers."

INT. REBEL STAR CRUISER

Ackbar leans on the railing of the bridge, watching the large screen showing the Death Star in the main briefing room.

ACKBAR: Move the fleet away from the Death Star.

EXT/INT. DEATH STAR—IMPERIAL SHUTTLE

An Imperial shuttle, with Luke at the controls, rockets out of the main docking bay as that entire section of the Death Star is blown away.

INT. WEDGE'S X-FIGHTER—COCKPIT

Wedge is relieved to escape the Death Star.

EXT/INT. DEATH STAR—*FALCON* COCKPIT

Finally, just as it looks as if the Falcon will not make it, Lando expertly pilots the craft out of the exploding superstructure and whizzes toward the Sanctuary Moon, only a moment before the Death Star supernovas into oblivion.

INT. *MILLENNIUM FALCON*—COCKPIT

Lando and Nien Nunb laugh and cheer in relief.

EXT. SPACE

The Death Star supernovas into oblivion behind the Falcon.

EXT. ENDOR FOREST

Han and Leia, Chewie, the droids, the Rebel troops, and the Ewoks all look to the sky as the Death Star reveals itself in a final flash of self-destruction. They all cheer.

THREEPIO: They did it!

Han looks down from the sky to Leia, a look of concern on his face. Leia continues to look at the sky as though listening for a silent voice.

HAN: I'm sure Luke wasn't on that thing when it blew.

LEIA: He wasn't. I can feel it.

HAN: You love him, don't you?

Leia smiles, puzzled.

LEIA: Yes.

HAN: All right. I understand. Fine. When he comes back, I won't get in the way.

She realizes his misunderstanding.

LEIA: Oh. No, it's not like that at all. He's my brother.

Han is stunned by this news. She smiles, and they embrace.

EXT. ENDOR FOREST—NIGHT

Luke sets a torch to the logs stacked under the funeral pyre where his father's body lies, again dressed in the black mask and helmet. He stands, watching sadly, as the flames leap higher to consume Darth Vader—Anakin Skywalker.

In the sky above, fireworks explode and Rebel fighters zoom above the forest.

Duwayne Dunham: "Vader burning at the end was not there originally. This was added at the last minute. I remember that we said, 'What happened to Vader? Did Luke leave him on the Death Star?' So the scene was shot up at Skywalker Ranch, and we used the same music from *Star Wars* in the scene where Luke is staring at the two suns on Tatooine."

George Lucas: "The way I work is that I cut the movie together, I look at it and figure out what I'm missing. At that point, it's more about how the movie flows together rather than how the script flows together. I'm acknowledging more and more that a script and a movie are two different things."

EXT. EWOK VILLAGE SQUARE—NIGHT

A huge bonfire is the centerpiece of a wild celebration. Rebels and Ewoks rejoice in the warm glow of firelight: drums beating, singing, dancing, and laughing in the communal language of victory and liberation.

Lando runs in and is enthusiastically hugged by Han and Chewie. Then, finally, Luke arrives, and the friends rush to greet and embrace him.

They stand close, this hardy group, taking comfort in each other's touch, together to the end.

Rebels and Ewoks join together in dancing and celebration. The original group of adventurers watches from the sidelines. Only Luke seems

From the Special Edition:

Luke sets a torch to the logs stacked under a funeral pyre where his father's armor lies; black mask, helmet, and cape. He stands watching sadly as the flames leap higher to consume what's left of Vader.

In the sky above, fireworks explode and Rebel fighters zoom above the forest.

EXT. CLOUD CITY—SUNSET

Fireworks explode above the city as searchlights pan the sky. A twin-pod cloud car zooms in above the festivities.

EXT. TATOOINE—DAY

A skyhopper weaves around buildings as confetti falls over the city, awash in celebration.

distracted, alone in their midst, his thoughts elsewhere.

He looks off to the side and sees three shimmering, smiling figures at the edge of the shadows: Ben Kenobi, Yoda, and Anakin Skywalker.

FADE OUT

END CREDITS OVER STAR FIELD

THE END

EXT. CORUSCANT PLAZA—NIGHT

Confetti falls on the city as hundreds of citizens celebrate. An airspeeder flies overhead. Fireworks explode in the full-moon sky.

In the rough draft Luke tells Leia that she is his sister during the celebration. Han and Leia leave Luke alone; suddenly Ben appears in real flesh and blood and is soon followed by an old man, the good Skywalker. Yoda watches them all celebrate.

In the revised rough draft, after Luke tells Leia and Han that he is Leia's brother, the couple leave him alone with Ben. Yoda suddenly appears as flesh and blood. His stay in the Netherworld has been resolved since Vader has turned to the good side. Yoda also has been able to prevent Vader from becoming one with the Force. Luke's father appears, and they all join the celebration, except for Yoda, who watches them all from the side and lets out a great sigh.

In the second and revised second drafts only the shimmering images of Yoda and Ben appear at the end of the film. The story concludes with Luke looking pensive, "his thoughts elsewhere, perhaps with the shimmering images of Ben and Yoda, or perhaps with someone else, somewhere else."

George Lucas: "I wanted Anakin, Ben, and Yoda together again at the end of the film. That was the whole point because the first three films that I'm currently writing are about them."

George Lucas: "At the very end of the film we've added several shots to show that the whole universe, not just the Ewoks, is celebrating the victory. Now the three movies are much closer to the way I wanted them originally, but I wasn't able to do it at the time I made the films because of the lack of resources. Now the films are more the way I intended them to be."

ABOUT THE AUTHOR

Born in France but now a California resident, Laurent Bouzereau is the author of *The De Palma Cut*, *The Alfred Hitchcock Quote Book*, *The Cutting Room Floor*, and *Ultra Violent Movies*. He produced audio commentaries for special edition laserdiscs of Brian De Palma's *Carrie* and Alfred Hitchcock's *Blackmail* and *Vertigo* and made new subtitle adaptations for eight films by the French director François Truffaut. He also wrote, directed, and produced recent documentaries on the making of Steven Spielberg's *Jaws*, *1941*, and *E.T. the Extra-Terrestrial* and Brian De Palma's *Scarface*. He is currently producing documentaries on Steven Spielberg's *Close Encounters of the Third Kind* and *The Lost World: Jurassic Park*.